T0272517

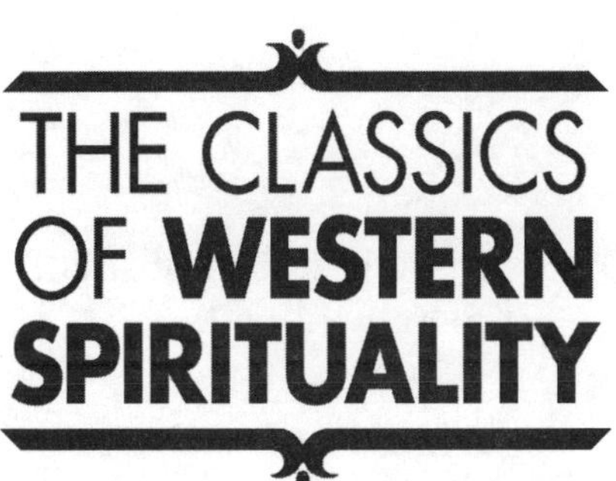
THE CLASSICS
OF WESTERN
SPIRITUALITY

THE CLASSICS OF WESTERN SPIRITUALITY
A Library of the Great Spiritual Masters

The Venerable Bede

On the Song of Songs and Selected Writings

TRANSLATED, EDITED, AND INTRODUCED BY
ARTHUR HOLDER

PREFACE BY
BENEDICTA WARD

PAULIST PRESS
NEW YORK • MAHWAH, NJ

Cover Art: Detail from a stained-glass window designed by Charles Eamer Kempe (ca. 1900); in the Church of St. John the Evangelist, Iffley Road, Oxford, England. Photograph by Lawrence Lew, OP. Used with permission of the photographer.

Cover and caseside design by Cynthia Dunne, www.bluefarmdesign.com
Book design by Sharyn Banks

Library of Congress Cataloging-in-Publication Data

Bede, the Venerable, Saint, 673–735.
[De cantica canticorum. English. Selections.]
On the Song of Songs and selected writings / The venerable Bede ; translated, edited, and introduced by Arthur Holder ; preface byBenedicta Ward.
p. cm. — (The Classics of Western Spirituality)
Includes bibliographical references and index.
ISBN 978-0-8091-4700-7 (alk. paper); ISBN 978-0-8091-0591-5 (alk. paper)
1. Bible. O.T. Song of Solomon—Commentaries—Early works to 1800. 2. England—Church history—449–1066—Early works to 1800. 3. Bible. N.T. Gospels—Sermons—Early works to 1800. I. Holder, Arthur G. II. Bede, the Venerable, Saint, 673–735. Historia ecclesiastica gentis Anglorum. English. Selections. III. Bede, the Venerable, Saint, 673–735. Homilia evangelii. English. Selections. IV. Title.
BS1485.53.B4313 2011
223′.9077—dc22

2010040561

Published by Paulist Press
997 Macarthur Boulevard
Mahwah, New Jersey 07430

www.paulistpress.com

Printed and bound in the
United States of America

CONTENTS

Contributors to This Volume

Editor of This Volume

ARTHUR HOLDER is Dean, Vice President for Academic Affairs, and the John Dillenberger Professor of Christian Spirituality in the Graduate Theological Union in Berkeley, California. He was educated at Duke University (AB magna cum laude and PhD) and the General Theological Seminary (MDiv). A priest of the Episcopal Church, he served parishes in the Diocese of Western North Carolina before moving to Berkeley, where he was on the faculty of the Church Divinity School of the Pacific for sixteen years. He is the translator of *Bede: On the Tabernacle* (1994), co-translator (with W. Trent Foley) of *Bede: A Biblical Miscellany* (1999), and editor of both *The Blackwell Companion to Christian Spirituality* (2005) and *Christian Spirituality: The Classics* (2010). He was co-chair of the Christian Spirituality Group in the American Academy of Religion for 2003–8 and President of the Society for the Study of Christian Spirituality for 2009.

Author of the Preface

BENEDICTA WARD is the Reader in the History of Christian Spirituality in the University of Oxford. She teaches spirituality and church history for the Faculty of Theology and is a supernumerary Fellow both of Harris Manchester College and of St. Stephen's House. She has written seven books on early monasticism and six on the Middle Ages, including *The Venerable Bede* (1990) and *High King of Heaven: Aspects of Early English Spirituality* (1999). She is a member of the Anglican monastic community of the Sisters of the Love of God.

FOREWORD

When the Venerable Bede began his work as a teacher and scholar in the early eighth century, the English people in his homeland of Northumbria had been Christian for fewer than one hundred years. With Christianity had come Latin literacy and the rich heritage of Mediterranean art, music, architecture, and thought. But the roots of this new religious culture did not yet go very deep into Bede's native soil. Unlike the ancient fathers of the church he so admired and sought to emulate, Bede had not received a classical secular education, nor was Latin his native tongue. His school curriculum was monastic in character, and his Latin was primarily the language of the Western church rather than that of Virgil and Cicero. In these frontier conditions there was some urgency to his scholarly task. Many of the English clergy had only a rudimentary knowledge of the Bible and other liturgical texts, and within living memory the Northumbrian church had been seriously divided over such basic issues as the date of Easter and the proper form of monastic tonsure. The leaders of a church that was barely out of its infancy needed to be trained in sound doctrine and inspired to provide preaching and pastoral care for people scattered about the countryside in the villages and on the farms. Remarkably, their teacher Bede turned out to be the most learned theologian of his day, the most renowned church historian since Eusebius in the fourth century, and one of the most influential shapers of early medieval Christian spirituality.

The texts translated in this volume are selections taken from three different works and represent only a small portion of the many volumes that Bede wrote. Consonant with his emphasis on the chronology of salvation history, the volume begins with an Old Testament commentary, moves next to homilies on the New Testament, and finally concludes with the history of the Christian church in Bede's own land. *On the Song of Songs* is one of the earliest complete Latin Christian commentaries on the Old Testament book that Bede called "most difficult to understand," which he interpreted in accordance with ancient tradition as a dramatic dialogue depicting the love relationship between Christ and the church. The *Homilies on the Gospels* are sermons on the gospel texts appointed to be read on certain Sundays and feast days in the liturgical year; here Bede shows himself to be an effective preacher and monastic theologian. Finally, the *Ecclesiastical History of the English People* tells how the coming of his own Anglo-Saxon people to Britain and their conversion to Christianity was but another chapter in the long history of humankind's salvation as ordained by Divine Providence. The selections from that work translated here describe the two great Christian missionary efforts (one Roman, one Celtic) to Bede's native Northumbria, along with his portraits of some great early Celtic and Anglo-Saxon saints (Oswald, Aidan, Hild, Cædmon, and Cuthbert) and a vivid account of the otherworldly journey of a man named Dryhthelm.

Preface

The term "spirituality," made popular by series of volumes such as the present one, is not something that, in its modern meaning, would have been comprehensible to the English monk, the Venerable Bede (673–735), since, like "mysticism," "spirituality" has come to refer only to inner and personal experience, as opposed to theology, doctrine, and liturgy. However, "spirituality" in an older sense of prayer that is part of the invisible objective world revealed through the scriptures in Jesus Christ permeated all Bede wrote. It is entirely appropriate, therefore, that in the selection from Bede's works translated here, priority is given to his commentaries on the scriptures, especially to his exploration of the meaning of the Song of Songs, where attention to doctrine as inner and present reality is overwhelmingly obvious. In his *Ecclesiastical History of the English People* and in the *Life of St. Cuthbert*, Bede pursued the same intention of seeing events and people within the scope of divinity. He was not concerned with historical theology but with theological history. His writings were all a continuation of the central tradition of the early church in interpreting every word of the scriptures and every moment of life as part of the good news of Jesus Christ.

An Anglo-Saxon by birth, from the age of seven Bede lived, wrote, and taught in the new twin monasteries of Wearmouth and Jarrow, leaving his cell only three times for brief local visits connected with his writing, but surrounded by a library of over two hundred volumes, culled for his use from Rome and Gaul by his abbots, Benedict Biscop and Ceolfrith. Bede not only had books, but he read them as well, and he did his utmost to share what they contained: "It was always," he wrote, "my delight to learn, or to teach, or to write" (*Ecclesiastical History* 5.24).

Bede saw himself as living far from the Mediterranean world of the early church in time and in space: "[We] who live at the very end of the world and of the age" (*On the Song of Songs* 3, on Sg 4:16). But he had access to the whole Christian tradition through its literature, above all the scriptures and the commentaries of the fathers of the church upon the sacred page. He determined to follow in the footsteps of the fathers and, like them, to convey the truth about God in Christ to his own race of the newly converted Anglo-Saxons. He was aware of his responsibility to bring alive through his work the central tradition of Christianity and make it available to his own people, claiming them as a new tribe for the new Israel of the church. All his writing was for the service of these new Christians, whether in his commentaries on scripture, the history of their conversion, the lives of their saints, or the books of grammar, natural history, and the reckoning of time that would enable them to enter, through reading, writing, and calculation, into the wide expanses of this new life.

There is an eternal sense about all Bede wrote, and though it can be used to illuminate the practical history of his own times, it is this inner spiritual meaning that is paramount for understanding all his works. Bede was chiefly concerned with God and with the contact of the present age to him. He did not write speculative theology or analyze directly the higher reaches of prayer. He marveled at the visions of heaven and hell told him from such as Dryhthelm or Fursa, and he recorded them with care but did not dwell on them as mystical experiences; rather, they were manifestations of the dimensions of eternity that surround the life of this world and at times break through for the consolation and encouragement of those *in hac lacrymarum ualle* ("in this vale of tears"). In his three versions of the life of St. Cuthbert, the bishop-monk-solitary of Lindisfarne, he noted Cuthbert's likeness to Christ, especially in his sufferings and death, rather than commenting in detail on his way of prayer. Always practical and immediate, Bede had little to say about the high reaches of personal prayer; he was more concerned with charity toward others as a way to God than with "spiritual experiences." Only in his homily on St. John the Evangelist did he write explicitly about contemplation, and then it was within the tradition of the fathers in which contemplation was seen not as something separate from the conduct of daily life or as passivity opposed to action and thought, but as a discipleship in which action both preceded contemplation as a preparation for it and flowed from it as a result. In his sermon on St. John he gives a firm statement of the classic approach to prayer in this way:

> Mystically speaking we can take these things which were predicted by the Lord to Peter and John, and which later took place, as designating the two ways of life in the Church which are carried out in the present, namely the active and the contemplative. Of these, the active is the way of living common to [all] the people of God. Very few ascend to the contemplative, and these more sublime ones [do so] after [achieving] perfection in good deeds. *(Homilies on the Gospels* 1.9)

When Bede commented on the book of the Bible that has formed the major source for Christian mysticism from the third century onward, this sober understanding of Christian living predominated. It was neither to explore the ultimate mysteries of God, nor to shine in the brilliant exposition of mystical doctrine in order to gain academic or clerical approval that Bede wrote on the Song of Songs. It was for the practical use of readers in the present day, in order that they should know more deeply the love of God in Christ here and now. In Bede's view—and in this he was in accord with all his predecessors, both Christian and Jewish—the text of the Song of Songs cannot be understood merely by its critical analysis as a book of the Old Testament. Bede was not trying to see what the text meant in its original context. He did not begin with the text of the Song of Songs and try to decide the meaning it had for the writer. He began rather with the matter of salvation and its application for the reader now. With this as his basis, he assumed that every word of scripture, of which the Song of Songs forms a part, was a gateway into deeper mysteries. So he brought all his knowledge of the world and of past literature as well as of the Bible to bear on each word and phrase in order to explore not its past and superficial meaning but its inner and present application.

Three aspects of Bede's spirituality are apparent. First of all, his understanding of reality was, first and last, biblical. The Bible is for Bede one text in which every word relates the reader to God in Christ. In this he had the highest authority in the story of the words of Christ to the disciples on the road to Emmaus after the resurrection (Lk 24:25–27): "Ought not Christ to have suffered these things and to enter into his glory? And beginning at Moses and all the prophets, he expounded unto them in all the scriptures the things concerning himself." Since the text of the Bible was known by heart, each exegete had a mental concordance of scripture in his head from each word of which he constantly drew enlightenment. Second, Bede, like the fathers, saw each part of scripture as the word of God, and therefore all parts could illuminate the rest. Obscure texts like the Canticle of Habakkuk were therefore seen as entirely usable by Christian readers. As Origen had said, "Every wonderful letter written in the oracles of God has its effects. There is not one jot or one tittle written in scripture which, for those who know how to use the power of the scriptures, does not effect its proper work" (Homily 39 on Jeremiah). Third, Bede read scripture in the patristic tradition where the words were a gateway to understanding more about the nature of Christ or more about discipleship or both. The fathers essentially deconstructed the text of scripture and therefore freed it for contemporary use. This was not a quirky personal approach; all Bede understood he tested by the whole of revelation, taking texts from all parts of scripture to illuminate the one he was reading. To quote Claudius of Turin: "Blessed are the eyes which see divine Spirit through the letters' veil."

This concern with what was inward did not mean any neglect of the outward form of words. Bede followed with keen interest the literal and grammatical meaning of his texts even though he explored them not for their superficial sense in itself but for the inner significance of each detail. Always concerned with the grammatical meaning of words, he was equally alert to the physical appearance of everything mentioned. In his earliest commentary, on the Book of Revelation, he spent time on the nature of each of the jewels of the heavenly city; here in the Song of Songs he examined the nature of the various spices mentioned. His keen curiosity reveled in every word and its meaning. But he did not look at jewels with an eye to their market value or carbon composition; the spices were not explored for their growth value or medicinal use. Likewise, what he turned on the detailed physical descriptions in the Song of Songs was no erotic gaze. He was especially careful in this and in other commentaries to use and not to misuse the superficial meaning of the texts. Bede was no naive writer. He was well aware that the new Christians for whom he was writing would readily seize upon what seemed to affirm their own experience and desires, instead of being transformed by the words into new life in Christ. He wanted to make sure that they saw the Song of Songs not according to their own unregenerate experience of human love but as a kind of shorthand notebook leading them to the deeper reality of God and his love. He does not begin with physical lovemaking and use the text to explore that; he begins with the concept of divine love that is God in Christ redeeming the world to himself, and the transfiguration of human desire toward him. This can be seen, for example, in his commentary on "His cheeks are like beds of spices planted by perfumers; his lips are lilies dripping finest myrrh" (Sg 5:13). Bede did not begin with "lips" themselves but with what comes from them, that is, the words the Lord spoke. He wasted no time in puzzling about whether cheeks actually look like beds of spices; he showed how their inner meaning is to be found through, not in, the image. "Cheeks" he sees as the index of character shown in the face, and he refers to Ecclesiastes 8:1 ("a man's wisdom maketh his face to shine") and relates that to 1 Corinthians 1:24 ("Christ the power of God and the wisdom of God"). The "lovely cheeks" are then seen as a register of the emotions of Christ, and for this he refers to Luke 10:21 for his exaltation; John 11:15 for his grief; John 11:33–35 for his tears; Isaiah 11:3 for his mercy; and Isaiah 53:7 for his silence in death. The "bed of spices" he saw as an orderly display offering charm and fragrance to all who need and want it, but it was not mentioned or examined for horticultural reasons; it signified God made man, the one Mediator, whose teaching is sweet to the hearers. And this Bede supported by a reference to 1 Timothy 2:5. The perfumers and gardeners of Song 5:13 he saw as making sense when seen to refer to the prophets and apostles who organized the words of Christ in writing for all to enjoy. Similarly, when he expounded the verse "Your teeth are like a flock of sheep that have come up from washing" (Sg 6:6), this was not treated by an examination of a highly surprising visual image. Bede is not interested in whether teeth look like sheep—which they obviously do not—but that reaction to the teeth that utter the word of God can be compared to the reaction to the beauty of newly washed sheep; that is, there is wonder in both cases at whiteness and sharpness. What concerns the reader of the Song of Songs is that here the purity of life and alertness of mind required of preachers are underlined. So it was not so much that each word would lead the reader to see the beauty of Christ and his message but that the Spirit of God would illuminate the true meaning of every word and, in the process of absorbing the words, the reader would become more ready to be changed by him.

It is in this ethos of approaching the texts from within the revelation of Christ to the reader that Bede's commentary on the Song of Songs and the other texts represented here can best be understood. They are essentially texts for a living tradition today, and it is appropriate that they should be made available, in Dr. Holder's translation, to a wider audience than Latin readers. This communication by translation is something that would have been welcomed by Bede himself. At the end of his life he wrote to Egbert of York regretting the fact that few Anglo-Saxons would make the effort to learn to read Latin; they preferred Anglo-Saxon and had indeed invented a written language for it when introduced by the missionaries to writing. Highly as he himself prized the Latin texts, Bede, like Alfred the Great three centuries later, thought it better to make the content of the gospel available to all rather than insist in vain on Latin scholarship for the few: "The unlearned, that is to say, those who only know their own language, must learn to say them [the Creed and the Lord's Prayer] in their own tongue.... Thus the whole community of believers may learn of what their faith consists and how they ought in the strength of that belief, to arm and defend themselves against the assaults of evil spirits" (*Letter to Egbert* 5). Bede wrote in order to present inner truth for the use of all his contemporaries, and the selection offered here has the same theme of a focus beyond this world, leading to the same end without end:

> Christ is the morning star who promises and reveals to the saints the eternal light of life when the night of this world is past. (Bede, *Exposition of the Apocalypse* 4, on Rv 2:28)

BENEDICTA WARD, SLG

INTRODUCTION

Most of what we know about the life of the Venerable Bede (673–735) comes from the short autobiographical note appended to his literary masterpiece *The Ecclesiastical History of the English People*, which was completed in 731.[1] Born in the kingdom of Northumbria (in northeast England) on lands that would later belong to the twin monasteries of St. Peter's, Wearmouth, and St. Paul's, Jarrow, Bede tells us that he came to Wearmouth at the age of seven as a child oblate presented to the monastery by his family. Soon thereafter he apparently moved seven miles away to Jarrow, where he spent the remainder of his life. His early monastic training came from Benedict Biscop (the founding abbot of the monastery) and Benedict's successor, Ceolfrith. At the age of nineteen he was ordained a deacon by John of Beverley, the saintly bishop of Hexham, and eleven years later, at the canonical age of thirty, he became a priest at the hands of the same bishop. His daily routine was given over to the fulfillment of a religious vocation that he described as follows:

> I have spent all my life in this monastery, applying myself entirely to the study of the scriptures; and, amid the observance of the discipline of the Rule and the daily task of singing in the church, it has always been my delight to learn or to teach or to write....From the time I became a priest until the fifty-ninth year of my life I have made it my business, for my own benefit and that of my brothers, to make brief extracts from the works of the venerable fathers on the holy scriptures, or to add notes of my own to clarify their sense and interpretation.[2]

Three crucial aspects of Bede's identity are clear from this short note: he was a Northumbrian by birth, a monk by profession, and a teacher by vocation.

As a Northumbrian, Bede was heir to the rich Christian traditions of both Ireland and Rome, each of which had sent missionaries to the area.[3] The Roman and Irish traditions were united in all major doctrines, and both owed allegiance to the pope, but they used different systems for calculating the date of Easter, their monks shaved their heads in different forms of tonsure, and their spiritualities had different emphases, with the Roman adherents stressing order, decorum, and global unity, while the Irish proclivity was for austere asceticism and the relative autonomy of local churches.[4] In Bede's view, the decisive (and correct) resolution came at the Synod of Whitby in 664, where King Oswiu cast his lot with the Roman observance.[5] But it is significant that the climax of the fifth and final book in Bede's *Ecclesiastical History* comes in chapter 22 with the conversion to Roman practices of the Irish monks at Iona, which for Bede seems to have represented the coming together of the best of both ecclesiastical worlds. This "double inheritance of Christian Northumbria"[6] provided Bede with an uncommonly rich and diverse tradition of learning and spiritual practice. Perhaps it was his experience as a Northumbrian, and therefore a witness to the value of blended traditions, that enabled him to develop such a compelling vision of the unification of the various tribes of his island homeland, most of whom he taught to think of themselves as one *gens Anglorum* ("people of the English").[7]

In the second place, we can hardly stress too strongly that Bede's outlook was essentially monastic, and that Bede was very much a monk after the model of Benedict of Nursia and Gregory the Great. While it is true that the rule Benedict Biscop commended to his monks was a *regula mixta* containing elements drawn from seventeen different Continental houses, the influence of the *Rule of Benedict* is pervasive, as is evident in Biscop's final charge to his brethren at Wearmouth-Jarrow (recorded by Bede in his *History of the Abbots*) and in Bede's other writings.[8] Certainly much of Bede's time was spent in the monastery church singing psalms in the daily offices, presiding and preaching at Mass, or engaging in private prayer or meditation.[9] Beyond that, as Jean Leclercq has shown, the monastic culture of early medieval Western Europe had a distinctly literary character.[10] The copying, emendation, and grammatical analysis of texts were necessary prerequisites to the *lectio divina* and meditative prayer enjoined by Benedict and other monastic authorities. Thanks to the indefatigable activity of Benedict Biscop and Ceolfrith as procurers of books, Bede had available to him in the library at Wearmouth-Jarrow one of the best collections of manuscripts—biblical, patristic, to some extent even classical—to be found anywhere in the period.[11] He was himself engaged in the production of books; indeed, at times (as he once complained to his bishop, Acca) he was forced to serve as his own dictator, note taker, and scribe.[12] Reading, writing, and study, along with prayer and worship, were key components of Bede's monastic regimen. But his scholarship was always in the service of his primary vocation, which was that of a Christian teacher concerned above all else with the care of souls.

Bede was declared a "doctor of the church" by Pope Leo XIII in 1899, but in a less formal sense he had been one all along. For Bede, the role of *doctor* (Latin for "teacher") was not so much an office as a charism, a gift of the Holy Spirit bestowed for the edification of the faithful. Alan Thacker has observed that throughout his life, but particularly in his later writings, "Bede was quite preoccupied with the role of those whom he variously called the *spirituales magistri* [spiritual masters], the *sancti praedicatores* [holy preachers], the *rectores* [rulers] or *doctores ecclesiae* [teachers of the church]."[13] This class of spiritual elite (whom Bede considered to be in succession to the apostles and prophets) was the principal audience for his writings, and he wrote as one of its members. Bede was a doctor among doctors; it was his vocation to make the riches of biblical and patristic doctrine available to those pastors and teachers who could not, or would not, seek out those treasures for themselves. Virtually all of these pastors and teachers were monastics (both male and female), but we should not think of them as cloistered contemplatives totally withdrawn from the rest of church and society. In Bede's time the minsters (Old English *mynster*, from Latin *monasterium*) were the only congregational institutions providing pastoral care to the Anglo-Saxon populace. As Sarah Foot has observed:

> Active ministry and contemplative devotion thus became inextricably linked in early Anglo-Saxon monasticism; it was only in the tenth century that formal efforts were made to differentiate between religious establishments according to the functions performed by their inmates. Bede envisaged that all those who adopted the religious life would mix devotion with action; he laid considerable stress in his writings on the responsibilities of teachers and preachers toward the laity and on the performance of good works by religious and clerics, whether these took the form of alms-giving and succoring the needy, or were expressed, as by Bede himself, through the work of scholarship and teaching.[14]

Although ordained clergy and vowed religious were the principal audience that Bede addressed in his writings, he was not unconcerned about the instruction of the laity. The *Ecclesiastical History* was dedicated to "the most glorious King Ceolwulf" of Northumbria, with a preface in which Bede was glad to acknowledge that pious king's enthusiasm for both holy scripture and the deeds and words of illustrious men, "especially those of our own people." Common people, too, had important spiritual responsibilities to discharge, as Bede noted in a homily in which he gave an expansive allegorical interpretation of the shepherds (Latin: *pastores*) in Luke 2:18: "It is not only bishops, presbyters, deacons, and even those who govern monasteries, who are to be understood as pastors, but also all the faithful, who keep watch over the little ones of their house, are properly called 'pastors,' insofar as they preside with solicitous watchfulness over their own house."[15] In fact, Bede considered that all the faithful, not only those with leadership responsibilities, were in need of Christian education. In the year before he died, Bede wrote a letter to Bishop Egbert of York in which he made a strong case for church reform and especially for the provision of teachers to instruct the laity in Christian morality and devotional practice.[16] But despite Bede's obvious concern for the religious instruction of the laity, we have no evidence that he was engaged in direct pastoral ministry with those outside the monastic communities at Wearmouth-Jarrow. He was the teachers' teacher and the preachers' preacher. Through his writings he became the scholars' scholar. To his countryman and younger contemporary Boniface, who wrote to Wearmouth-Jarrow from the Continent after Bede's death to ask for copies of his works, he was "the monk Bede, who, we have learned, shone forth among you of late as a lantern of the church, by his scriptural scholarship."[17]

There is no early medieval "life" of Bede, but his pupil Cuthbert wrote an account of his final days.[18] For about two weeks during the Easter season of 735 he suffered from attacks of breathlessness. During that time he chanted psalms and liturgical antiphons, gave instruction to his students, translated a portion of the Gospel of John into English, made excerpts from Isidore's treatise *On the Nature of Things*, recited an Old English poem about the Day of Judgment, offered prayers of thanksgiving, and wept. On May 25, the eve of Ascension Day, Bede distributed a few small gifts (some pepper, napkins, and incense) to his fellow priests and asked them to offer Masses and prayers for his soul. "I have lived a long time," said Bede, "and the righteous Judge has well provided for me all my life long. The time of my departure is at hand, and my soul longs to see Christ my King in his beauty" (Is 33:17). After directing the young scribe Wilberht to write a final sentence, Bede asked to be turned so that as he sat on the floor of his cell he might be facing the place where he used to pray. Singing "Glory be to the Father and to the Son and to the Holy Spirit," and with his head cradled in Wilberht's arm, he breathed his last.

In the days when recognition as a saint depended on a person's feast day being observed in local church calendars rather than on formal declaration by the pope, Bede's sanctity was acclaimed with at least moderate frequency both in England and on the Continent. Although Alcuin does record one healing miracle worked by his relics,[19] Bede's reputation was based primarily on the influence of his writings. Numerous surviving manuscripts and library catalogs from throughout the Middle Ages attest to the popularity of his works, and he was often cited as an authority by church councils, biblical scholars, and theologians. In 836, when the Council of Aachen declared that Solomon's temple was a figural type of the Catholic Church, it appealed to "the exposition of the other holy and distinguished fathers" given by "the venerable and admirable doctor of modern times, Bede the presbyter."[20] Later generations told fanciful tales explaining how he came to be known as "the Venerable," but what seems most likely is that this customary title for a holy priest became attached to his name because that is how he was cited in the ninth-century collection of homilies edited by Paul the Deacon.

BEDE'S WRITINGS AND SOURCES

Following the example of the Frankish historian Gregory of Tours, Bede concluded the autobiographical note at the end of the *Ecclesiastical History* with a list of his literary works, all of which were written in Latin. Significantly, the first twenty works are biblical commentaries, homilies, and aids to the study of scripture, listed in the order of the biblical books with which they deal. His writings on the Old Testament include commentaries on Genesis, 1 Samuel, Ezra/Nehemiah, Proverbs, the Song of Songs, and Tobit, as well as expositions of the Mosaic tabernacle, the Solomonic temple, portions of 1 Kings and 2 Kings, and the canticle in Habakkuk that was sung in the daily office at lauds on Fridays. (This last commentary was addressed to a "sister in Christ," presumably an unidentified nun at a nearby monastery.) On the New Testament, Bede wrote commentaries on Mark, Luke, Acts, the seven Catholic Epistles (James; 1 and 2 Peter; 1, 2, and 3 John; Jude), and Revelation, as well as fifty homilies on the gospel readings for the liturgical year and a collection of excerpts from Augustine's comments on the Pauline epistles. Omitted from the list of exegetical works were a redacted version of Adamnán's treatise *On the Holy Places* and a miscellany of comments on assorted biblical verses known as *On Eight Questions*. In his exegesis Bede's expressed intent was to "follow the footsteps of the fathers," which for him meant primarily, but not exclusively, Ambrose, Augustine, Jerome, and Gregory the Great (whom Bede was the first to name together as the four great doctors of the Latin church).[21] In addition, he made use of the exegesis of Cyprian, Hilary of Poitiers, Isidore of Seville, and Cassiodorus. On occasion he cited Greek patristic authors such as Origen, Basil of Caesarea, Gregory of Nazianzus, and John Chrysostom, some of whose works were known to him in Latin translations. Some moderation of Bede's fondness for allegorical interpretation was probably due to the influence of the later works of Jerome, whose championship of the *Hebraica ueritas* ("Hebrew truth") in translating the Old Testament struck a responsive chord in Bede. But the prevailing influence on Bede's exegesis was Gregory the Great,[22] and since Gregory had learned so much from Origen, we may with some justification consider Bede as a disciple of the great third-century Alexandrian theologian, albeit for the most part indirectly.

Bede's works on grammar, natural history, and chronology were standard school texts throughout medieval Europe. *On the Art of Metrics* is an introduction to the various types of Latin poetry, with an appendix entitled "On Figures and Tropes" that deals with stylistic figures of speech, including the forms of allegory so important in medieval biblical exegesis. *On Orthography* is a handbook of word usage arranged according to the letters of the alphabet, listing forms whose spelling or meaning might cause difficulty to a reader or scribe. In *On the Nature of Things*, Bede drew on Pliny's *Natural History* and the works of Isidore to discuss the phenomena of earth, heaven, and ocean as part of God's created order. The short treatise *On Times* and the much longer revision entitled *On the Reckoning of Times* deal with the chronology of minutes, hours, days, months, years, centuries, and epochs; both treatises conclude with chronicles of significant events in world history.

In the field of hagiography (writings about the saints), Bede produced two lives of Cuthbert of Lindisfarne (one in verse and one in prose) and a history of the abbots of his own monastery at Wearmouth-Jarrow. His inspiration came from the Bible and from classic Christian biographies such as Athanasius's life of the Egyptian monk Antony, Possidius's *Life of Augustine*, and the *Dialogues* of Gregory the Great. Unlike modern biographers, who tend to focus on the distinctive and unique characteristics of their subjects, medieval hagiographers like Bede were primarily concerned to demonstrate how closely the pious lives and courageous deaths of holy men and women conformed to the supreme model of sanctity presented by Jesus Christ himself. Though based on the evidence of historical fact, hagiography was always intended to edify and inspire as well as to instruct. Although miracles abound in

Bede's lives of Cuthbert, there are none at all in the *History of the Abbots*, where it is the size of the two monastic houses at Wearmouth and Jarrow, the extent of their lands, and the magnificence of their buildings and libraries that serve as signs of the abbots' sanctity.

Bede wrote several hymns and other poetic works, including a long poem entitled "On Judgment Day," of which there is a tenth-century paraphrase in Old English. Some of the hymns are still sung in translation; the Episcopal Church's *Hymnal 1982*, for example, contains those for Ascension Day and the Nativity of St. John the Baptist. The poetry has been little studied in comparison with the historical works, or even with the biblical commentaries, in large measure due to the difficulty of its style. As Michael Lapidge has observed, "The simplicity of his diction masks metaphorical structures of unusual sophistication. But in spite of its apparently simple diction, Bede's poetry is not easy. It requires to be read painstakingly; its metaphors and biblical allusions need to be carefully unraveled."[23]

If Bede's poetry has been seldom read and little studied in recent times, the case is quite different with *The Ecclesiastical History of the English People*. This work, widely acknowledged as Bede's greatest and most enduring achievement, comprises elements of hagiography set within the context of a larger historical narrative. Like the fourth-century *Ecclesiastical History* by Eusebius of Caesarea that was its model, Bede's work tells the story of the church as it was established and increased by God's providential hand. Unlike Eusebius, however, Bede focuses on the history of a single nation; in this, he was following the example of Gregory of Tours in his *History of the Franks*. As Bede explained in the preface addressed to King Ceolwulf, his purpose was primarily didactic: "Should history tell of good men and their good estate, the thoughtful listener is spurred on to imitate the good; should it record the evil ends of wicked men, no less effectually the devout and earnest listener or reader is kindled to eschew what is harmful and perverse, and himself with greater care pursue those things which he has learned to be good and pleasing in the sight of God."[24] Bede went on to explain that he had diligently collated information from a variety of sources, including the writings of earlier historians, archival materials from Canterbury and Rome, reports from numerous correspondents in other parts of the country, the testimony of eyewitnesses, and the hearsay evidence of common report. The five books of the *Ecclesiastical History* take the story from Julius Caesar's invasion of Britain up through a survey of the peaceful and prosperous state of the English church in 731. Noting, however, that a great many Northumbrians of all classes had recently abandoned the art of war for monastic life, Bede issues an ominous warning: "What the result will be, a later generation will discover."[25]

The cause of this anxiety about the rising tide of monasteries is revealed in Bede's last surviving work, the long letter written on November 7, 734, to a former pupil named Egbert, who had become bishop of York. Writing from his sickbed because he was too weak to travel, Bede angrily denounced members of the nobility for founding "false monasteries" on their lands in order to avoid military service. Bede calls on Egbert to abolish those false monasteries, reform the morals of the clergy, instruct the laity in their religious beliefs and duties, and establish new dioceses so that there will be enough bishops to provide pastoral care throughout the north of England. This letter, which combines passionate conviction with pragmatic advice, is clear evidence that Bede was fully engaged with the most controversial issues of church and society in his day. Whereas earlier generations of scholars tended to see Bede as either a holy recluse or an academic of the "ivory tower" variety, more recent appraisals recognize Bede's call for reform of the Northumbrian church as a persistent—even dominant—theme that runs throughout his exegetical, historical, and hagiographical works.[26]

BEDE'S SPIRITUAL TEACHINGS

Although he had an orderly mind, Bede was not a systematic theologian. He had no desire for doctrinal innovation, and he was seldom directly engaged in polemical theological debate. His passion was for application, not speculation. As Henry Mayr-Harting has said, "Bede's greatest strength was in this sphere where doctrine and the practical life of the Christian met."[27] Since he produced no treatise devoted to a single topic such as prayer or Christology, we find his spiritual teachings embedded in his biblical commentaries, homilies, and verbal portraits of the saints. The best way to identify those teachings, then, is simply to read as much of Bede's voluminous corpus of writings as possible, noting the recurrent images and themes. The brief overview of Bede's spiritual teachings that follows focuses primarily on the three works from which selections were made for translation in this volume, but the themes identified here are to be found consistently throughout his writings.[28]

Scripture and Its Interpretation

From his patristic authorities (especially John Cassian), Bede took the doctrine of the fourfold sense of scripture that he expounds in several different places. In his commentary on the Song of Songs he explains how scripture is like a honeycomb that drips "the sweetness of spiritual understanding" when squeezed by the interpreter:

> As only one example, the psalmist says: *Praise the Lord, O Jerusalem!* (Ps 147:12). According to the letter, this surely exhorts the citizens of that city in which God's temple was found to sing praises to him; but according to allegory, Jerusalem is the Church of Christ spread throughout the whole world; again, according to tropology (that is, to the moral sense), every holy soul is rightly called "Jerusalem"; again, according to anagogy (that is, to the meaning that leads to higher things), Jerusalem is the dwelling-place of the heavenly homeland which comprises holy angels and human beings.[29]

In practice, Bede was usually content to interpret each verse at only two levels, the literal or historical, and the higher level that he called mystical, spiritual, allegorical, or typological (*typicus*). (The Song of Songs was a notable exception for him in that it contained "nothing carnal or according to the letter," which is to say that it referred to no actual human sexual relationship and thus had only a spiritual meaning.[30]) In moving from the literal to the spiritual sense, Bede made use of all the exegetical techniques familiar to him from his reading of patristic authors: etymologies, number symbolism, analogies from the natural qualities of plants and animals, the linking of one biblical verse to another by a chain of concordance, and situating the text at hand within the grand narrative of salvation history.[31]

The underlying principle was always one of correspondence, in which the Old Testament histories foreshadowed the story of Christ and the disciples in the New Testament, and the people and events of both testaments provided later generations of Christians with both moral instruction and spiritual insight. All of this Bede would have learned not only from his reading of the fathers but also from the typological way that scripture was incorporated into the daily round of liturgical services, and even from the walls of the monastery church at Jarrow, where Benedict Biscop had installed pictures of matching Old and New Testament scenes, such as Isaac carrying the wood on which he was to be sacrificed paired with Christ carrying his cross.[32] Scripture was not just a repository of true words about God. Bede believed that in the pages of the Bible, God the master teacher was speaking to the church, and directly to the heart of the individual believer.

Whereas modern-day readers may be perplexed by repetitions or apparent discrepancies in the biblical text, for Bede these anomalies were simply invitations to deeper meditation. "Variously and in many ways are the same mysteries of Christ and the church repeated, but the repetitions always add something new that either serves to augment the same mysteries or pleases the souls of the hearers the more through its very novelty."[33] Nor did he hesitate to provide more than one edifying interpretation of a particular verse; a rather extreme example is the treatment of Song 2:4, for which Bede provides seven different explanations of what it might mean for Christ to "set charity in order" in the life of the church.[34] Although Bede does not quote Gregory the Great's famous dictum that holy scripture is a river both shallow and deep, in which a lamb may wade and an elephant can swim,[35] he would certainly have agreed that the Bible provides both a safe haven for the simplest believer and an expansive space full of wonders for the learned to explore.

Christ the Wisdom of God

Bede's theology was thoroughly trinitarian and completely orthodox, in keeping with the creeds and the Augustinian tradition he had inherited. His own piety, however, seems to have been thoroughly Christocentric in character. Nearly all the personal prayers recorded in his writings are addressed directly to Jesus, with many heartfelt ejaculations of supplication and praise. The most famous example is the eloquent prayer that concludes the *Ecclesiastical History*: "And I pray you, good Jesus, that as you have graciously granted that I should drink the words that bring knowledge of you, so also kindly grant that I may come at length to you, the fount of all wisdom, and appear before your face forever." As we have seen, Cuthbert's letter on the death of Bede tells how the dying monk prayed to see "Christ my King in his beauty," which accords well with the frequent allusions to Isaiah 33:17 in Bede's own writings. Such fervent devotion to Christ was a well-known feature of Anglo-Saxon spirituality, as evidenced by the Old English poem *The Dream of the Rood* and the depictions of Christ in majesty on standing crosses at Bewcastle and Ruthwell, as well as in manuscripts such as the Codex Amiatinus from Wearmouth-Jarrow.[36] For Bede, the only path to the vision of God was through intimate communion with the incarnate Lord: "Let us hope that through those sacraments of his humanity with which we have been imbued, we will be able to attain to the contemplation of the glory of his divinity."[37]

This Christocentric piety inspired Bede to include in his commentaries and homilies many hymn-like passages in celebration of the wonderful mysteries of the incarnation and redemption. These paeans of praise often take the form of quasi-creedal recitations of the Lord's actions during the course of ministry, as in this passage from the fourth book of the Song commentary:

> And surely it pertains to the frailty of his humanity that *a child is born to us* (Is 9:6), but to the power of his divinity that he is born of a virgin and that his birth is proclaimed by angelic voices and celebrated with mysteries (Lk 2:1–20); to the power of his divinity that a star shows the wise men where he is to be worshiped (Mt 2:1–12), to the

> frailty of his humanity that he is driven out of his homeland by the plots of a deceitful king (Mt 2:13–5); to the frailty of his humanity that he can be led out and tempted by the devil (Mt 4:1), to the power of his divinity that after conquering the devil and driving him away, he is worthy of being ministered to by angels (Mt 4:11); to the fragility of his humanity that he asks a Samaritan woman for water (Jn 4:7), to the power of his divinity that he is said to be able to provide from himself a fountain of living water (Jn 4:14); to the frailty of his humanity that he grows weary along the road (Jn 4:6), to the power of his divinity that he promises eternal rest to those who follow him (Mt 11:28); to the frailty of his humanity that he sleeps in a boat (Mt 8:24), to the power of his divinity that when awakened he exercises command over the wind and the sea (Mt 8:27); to the frailty of his humanity that he is crucified and dies (Mt 27:33–50), to the power of his divinity that at his death the foundations of heaven begin to tremble, as do also those of earth (Mt 27:45, 51); to the frailty of his humanity that he is anointed with spices and buried (Mk 15:46—16:1), to the power of his divinity that he arose and ascends into heaven. (Lk 24:5, 51)[38]

Following Paul, Bede identified Christ as "the Power and Wisdom of God" (1 Cor 1:24), which enabled him to make free use of feminine imagery associating Christ with the Old Testament figure of Lady Wisdom.[39] At the beginning of the Song commentary, Bede explains that in Song 1:2 ("For your breasts are better than wine") it is the synagogue speaking to Christ the bridegroom. This allusion to the Savior's "breasts" is a clear indication that the Song is to be interpreted figuratively rather than literally, says Bede, but this is really not so surprising since there are several other biblical passages in which Christ is said to possess female body parts.[40] When he comes to another reference to breasts in Song 4:10, Bede writes of Christ as a nursing mother in terms that place him in a line of tradition leading from patristic authors such as Clement of Alexandria, Ambrose, and Augustine through to Anselm, the Cistercians, and Julian of Norwich:[41]

> Although he was the bread of angels, he willed to hide his divinity by taking flesh in order to nourish human faintheartedness and make it fit for that same heavenly bread. For since an infant is not able to eat bread very well, the mother in a certain manner makes the very bread she eats into flesh and feeds the infant from that bread through the lowliness of breasts and the taste of milk. *In the beginning was the Word, and the Word was with God, and the Word was God* (Jn 1:1); this is the eternal food that refreshes angels because they are satisfied with the sight of his glory. And *the Word became flesh and dwelt among us* (Jn 1:14), so that in this way the Wisdom of God who consoles us as a mother may refresh us from that very same bread and lead us through the sacraments of the incarnation to the knowledge and vision of divine splendor.[42]

It is difficult to trace any direct influence that Bede's teaching about "Mother Jesus" may have had on later writers. Nevertheless, his unapologetic and enthusiastic use of feminine imagery in reference to Christ stands as testimony to the widespread acceptance of this usage within the mainstream medieval Catholic tradition.[43]

The Church in History

If Christ can be understood in feminine terms as a mother to the faithful, so can the church be imaged as a woman "on account of her fecundity in good works, and because she never ceases to bear spiritual children for God."[44] Most often it was the physical acts of childbearing and nursing that provided Bede with metaphors for the church's care, but in commenting on the Canaanite woman's supplication of Jesus on behalf of her sick daughter (Mt 15:21–28), Bede said that any Christian soul deceived by evil spirits is a "daughter" for whom Mother Church must importune the Lord, "so that when she cannot cure her by admonishing, entreating, and chiding her from without, he may do so by inspiring her from within."[45] The capable woman in Proverbs 31 is also identified as a type of the church in Bede's commentary on that book,[46] as was the bride in his commentary on the Song of Songs.

Both in his biblical exegesis and in his historical works, Bede was always fully conscious of the historical character of the church on earth. Following Augustine, Gregory, and Isidore, he divided world history into six ages: (1) from creation to the flood, (2) from the flood to Abraham, (3) from Abraham to David, (4) from David to the exile, (5) from the exile to the birth of Christ, and (6) from the incarnation until the Day of Judgment. The sixth age was further divided into three successive periods: that of the earliest Jewish church in Jerusalem, that of the expanding Gentile church, and finally the time when the remnant of Israel will be converted in fulfillment of the prophecy of St. Paul.[47]

Bede's attitude toward Israel and the Jews was complex and ambivalent.[48] On the one hand, the Old Testament synagogue was the "ancient church" of God's faithful people living in expectation of the coming of Christ, celebrating sacraments and keeping laws that prefigured the New Testament dispensation. On the other hand, the "unbelieving Jews" had rejected Jesus and persecuted the infant church. There were no actual Jews in Anglo-Saxon England in Bede's time, but he appears to have transferred much of the conventional anti-Jewish invective onto the British, whom he perceived as the religious and political antagonists of the English, even though they had been Christians long before the English arrived on their shores.[49] For readers today, Bede's derisive comments about both the Jews and the British he saw as heirs to Jewish legalism and obstinacy are the most unappealing aspects of his writings.

When Bede considered the formation of the Christian church in the time of the New Testament, it was a matter of crucial importance for him that both Jews and Gentiles were included among its members. In a rather curious piece of exegesis, he interpreted the joining of the bride's thighs in Song 7:1 as "the union of the two peoples (namely, Jews and Gentiles) from which the one church universal is perfected in unity of faith and is made fruitful with spiritual offspring so that she increases unto the end of the age."[50] Similarly, the two Old Testament houses of worship represented the two peoples who would come to a common faith in that the tabernacle of Moses was fashioned by Jews alone, while proselytes and foreign workers assisted in the building of Solomon's temple.[51] This blending of two peoples into one body was indicative for Bede of the unity in diversity that is fundamental to Christian community. We find an apparent reflection of that multicultural ideal in the opening chapter of the *Ecclesiastical History*, where the five languages spoken in Britain in Bede's time (English, British, Irish, Pictish, and Latin) are compared to the five books of the Pentateuch because they all express the same divine truth.

Another aspect of the early church that repeatedly attracted Bede's attention was its renunciation of private ownership, which he interpreted as biblical warrant for contemporary monastic practice. In the *Ecclesiastical History* he quoted Acts 4:32 ("all things were common to them") in praising the communities established by Augustine at Canterbury (1.26), by Aidan at Lindisfarne (4.25), and by Hild at Whitby (4.23) for imitating the example of the "primitive church." When he came to comment on Song 8:7 ("If one were to give up all the wealth of one's house for love"), Bede could simply say that this verse did not need any verbal explanation since its truth was manifest in the living example of the Lord himself and the early believers "when for the love of truth they were seen to give up everything they possessed in this world and seemed to themselves to have lost nothing, if only they may receive true goods in heaven."[52]

Although Bede celebrated the church as the body of Christ and the fellowship of saints, he realized that in its earthly manifestation it is far from perfection and often ill at ease, suffering as it does from corruption and division within and from persecution without. In his earlier commentaries (such as those on the Apocalypse, Acts, the Catholic Epistles, the Song of Songs, and Proverbs), Bede was particularly concerned with the refutation of heretics and schismatics. In his later commentaries and in the letter to Egbert of 734, his calls for reform focused on the moral purity of the clergy and troublesome conditions in the Anglo-Saxon church such as the proliferation of false monasteries and the bishops' failure to provide adequately for the pastoral care of the flock.[53] Despite his realistic assessment of all these problems, Bede remained confident that with the help of divine assistance the church would ultimately prevail:

> She is not vanquished by strangers because she conquers the rage of persecuting unbelievers by suffering for the crown of martyrdom; she is not corrupted by false believers because she both refutes the dogmas of heretics by believing rightly and avoids the depraved example of certain catholics by living soberly and justly and godly (Ti 2:12); she is not blinded by the smoke of her own lust because she is inwardly ablaze only with the ardor of the Lord's charity.[54]

Pastors and Teachers

Having noted Bede's penchant for maternal imagery to describe both Christ and the church, we should also observe that he applied many of the same feminine images to pastors and teachers. This is especially remarkable since it runs counter to Caroline Walker Bynum's claim that what distinguished twelfth-century Cistercian writers like Bernard of Clairvaux and Aelred of Rievaulx from earlier authors who referred to God or Christ as mother was that patristic writers "do not connect Jesus' mothering with the mothering of earthly men."[55] Bede is clearly an exception, as is evident in his comments about "holy teachers" that directly follow the passage about Christ as nursing mother cited above:

> And *the Word became flesh and dwelt among us* (Jn 1:14), so that in this way the Wisdom of God who consoles us as a mother may refresh us from that very same bread and lead us through the sacraments of the incarnation to the knowledge and vision of divine splendor. But holy teachers also take the bread with which they are fed in a sublime manner and convert it into milk with which they nourish little children, so that the more exalted their contemplation of eternal joys in God, the more humbly are they at the same time taking pity on their neighbors' weakness.[56]

Familiarity with biblical interpretations of this sort will help readers of the *Ecclesiastical History* appreciate such passages as Aidan's speech to his fellow monks on Iona in which he advocates a missionary strategy that begins with "the milk of simpler teaching" (3.5), or the tribute in praise of Hild that "all who knew her called 'Mother'" (3.25). By carrying out their ministries of evangelization, education, and pastoral care, these church leaders were imitating Christ and sharing in his maternal nurturance of God's people.

Bede admonished the clergy and other church leaders to exercise all the virtues appropriate to their high office. He put particular emphasis on discretion ("the mother of all virtues"), diligence in prayer, zeal for learning, industry in preaching, compassion for the weak, compunction for sin, sexual continence, abstinence in food and drink, and above all else, humility. Whatever the clergy proclaim to others, they must first put into practice in their own lives. As Bede wrote in praise of Cuthbert: "And, what is the greatest help in teachers, he first showed in his own behavior whatever he was teaching them to do."[57] This pastoral ideal reflects the strong influence of Gregory the Great as conveyed to Bede not only in the *Book of Pastoral Rule* but also in that pope's biblical commentaries and the *Dialogues* relating the lives and miracles of the Italian saints.

Progress and Stages in the Christian Life

Bede was fond of quoting Gregory the Great to the effect that "no one suddenly becomes the highest, but it is necessary for us to move gradually from the lesser things to the more perfect."[58] He saw the Christian life as a lifelong journey and an arduous ascent toward God.[59] Although all Christians are making the same journey "from virtue to virtue" (Ps 84:7), there is a diversity of graces. Some will excel in mortification of the flesh, some in prayer, some in good works, but all are seeking the same heavenly life.[60] Of course this does not mean that anyone can ignore the other virtues completely, as though continence could be pursued without humility, or mercy without restraint in speech, or prayer without love for the neighbor; all are necessary in order for the Christian's battle armor to be complete.[61] Sometimes Bede focused his attention on individual Christian souls making progress over time by "moving as though by certain stages toward realms above."[62] But at other times he pictured the entire church in heaven and on earth as at a given moment, arranged in hierarchical ranks from the catechumens at the lowest level to the perfect souls who are like the angels in the contemplation of God. Thus both dynamic progress and static stages have a place in Bede's conception of the Christian life. These two ways of considering the spiritual journey led Bede to identify different groupings among the faithful. For example, he said that the church has honey and milk under her tongue (Sg 4:11) when she discerns what to preach to beginners who can digest only milk, what to the proficient, and what to the perfect, who are ready for the honey of heavenly wisdom.[63] This triadic grouping implies a fluidity of progress since the perfect presumably started as beginners and moved through proficiency on their way to the highest state, and the beginners might be encouraged to do the same. But when commenting on the "army drawn up in battle array" in Song 6:3, he invoked a more static triad of rulers (*rectores*, "pastors"), married persons, and the continent (monastics), which he saw as having been prefigured in Ezekiel 14:14 by Noah, Job, and Daniel, respectively.[64] Here the possibility for movement from one grade to another is necessarily limited, since the married could never become ordained clergy or take monastic vows. Bede hoped that all Christians would make progress, but he assumed that some would make considerably more progress than others.

However many twists and turns the Christian soul may make on its spiritual journey, eventually there should be a shift in motivation from fear to love, from strict obedience to the intimate delight of friendship with God. "But as long as someone keeps the divine commandments because of a weakness in the soul (whether a consciousness of sin or a servile fear), that person necessarily puts God in the position of being the Lord, more than the Father or a friend."[65] A good example of someone who made the shift successfully is the monk Adamnán of Coldingham, whose confessor assigned him to fast five days a week as a temporary penance for a specific sin. When the confessor was suddenly called away to Ireland and died there before he could return to remit the penance, Adamnán continued the strict regimen for the rest of his life. "What he had once begun out of fear of God because he felt remorse for his sins," says Bede, "he now continued unweariedly out of divine love because he delighted in its rewards."[66]

Action and Contemplation

Bede's teachings about action and contemplation as the "two spiritual lives of this age" were in continuity with the tradition he had received from Augustine, John Cassian, and Gregory the Great.[67] Like them, he affirmed that contemplation is the higher calling but nevertheless expressed a preference for the "mixed life" as being most appropriate for Christians living this side of heaven. For Christians living in this present age, and especially for pastors, the ideal pattern is oscillation back and forth between contemplative prayer and active ministry, since evangelistic zeal inspires one to love God and that love for God is in turn the best motivation for teaching others.[68]

Bede's conception of the contemplative life for those still on earth focused primarily on liturgical and ascetical practices ("psalms, fasts, prayers, alms, and the other more peaceful activities of this temporal life"), while his primary example of the active life was "the sweaty toil of preaching."[69] Although he certainly believed that both were necessary, he seems to have been most worried that the Anglo-Saxon clergy and monastics of his day would become so engrossed in their pursuit of the delights of contemplation that they would neglect their duty to preach and teach. The joys of contemplation cannot be acquired by the exercise of a person's will or desire, but only as a gift that God bestows upon the chosen few. And even for those fortunate souls, the sweetness of inner contemplation is "brief and rare on account of the heaviness of minds still detained by the burden of the flesh."[70]

Bede never tried to analyze or even describe what contemplation is like from the standpoint of the one who receives it as a gift. Unlike Gregory the Great in this regard, he showed little interest in the psychological aspects of mystical experience.[71] The closest he comes to a positive description of contemplation is when, after speaking of those who are refreshed by reading scripture, he goes on to mention those few who receive "the gift of having a pure mind's gaze lifted up to heaven so that while still in the present time they might have a not inconsiderable foretaste of the sweetness of the life to come."[72] In a very similar passage in a homily, Bede speaks of those who gain a foretaste of heavenly bliss "by contemplating it sublimely in mental ecstasy [*excessu mentis*]," and in his commentary on the canticle of Habakkuk he defines that term as representing a state "when agitated and rendered speechless by a sudden astonishing occurrence, one is left cut off from one's mental faculties."[73] But more often, Bede speaks rather of unfulfilled desires for intimate communion with a divine lover who remains elusive: "The beloved sometimes goes away and turns aside from the bride when although we ask to be inflamed with love of him until there is an effusion of tears, to fulfill the duty of prayer with fixed and unwavering intent, and to transfer all our attention from carnal desires to those that are eternal, he does not always consent to the things for which we wish to pray."[74] Such unfulfilled longing is in part a result of human sin, but it is also a consequence of the incomprehensible nature of God, whose essence cannot be known even by the spiritual senses of the faithful.[75] However much the church may beg to see the Lord in all his glory, time and again he will exhort her "to employ a discerning reckoning of times so that she will not seek on the road the reward that is reserved for her in the homeland, but will remember that for a while she must walk by faith until she is able to come to sight."[76]

Prayer and Worship

Although Bede never wrote a treatise specifically on prayer, it was a subject to which he devoted much attention in his writings. He did not provide much in the way of instruction in methods of prayer, beyond recommending the traditional monastic practices of reciting the psalms with their antiphons, saying the Lord's Prayer with frequent genuflections, meditating on readings from scripture, and participating in the liturgical rounds of the daily office and Mass. He did compile a little book of prayers for use in private devotion, but it consisted wholly of verses selected from each of the 150 psalms.[77] He seems to have assumed that his readers knew *what* to pray; his concern was to teach them *when* and *how* to pray. As a model of perseverance in prayer, Bede pointed to the Canaanite woman who did not desist from her earnest petitions even when the Lord not only delayed healing her daughter but also rebuked her as a Gentile "dog" unworthy of receiving bread intended for the children of Israel (Mt 15:21–28). If the church would only follow that woman's good example, Bede thought, the Lord would eventually turn to her in mercy. But it is not enough to pray frequently; one must pray with proper attention: "For there are those who, when they enter the church, prolong their psalmody or prayer with many words but because the attention of their heart is directed elsewhere they do not reflect upon what they are saying. They are indeed praying with their mouth, but they are depriving their mind of every fruit of prayer because it is wandering outside; they think that their prayer will be heard by God, although those who utter it are not listening to it themselves."[78] Borrowing a phrase from John Cassian, Bede sometimes spoke of the desired kind of prayer as "pure prayer." But as Scott DeGregorio has observed, Bede's use of the term differed from that of his fifth-century monastic predecessor. For Cassian, pure prayer meant prayer without words or images, but for Bede it was not a higher stage beyond vocal prayer but simply "focusing the mind and heart and making them capable of such focus by purifying them through righteous action."[79]

Like many readers of Paul's admonition to "pray without ceasing" (1 Thes 5:17), Bede wondered how to put that good advice into practice when life requires all human beings to eat, sleep, and work in order to survive. Some early Christian teachers had recommended the constant recitation of short phrases from the psalms or the name of Jesus in order to keep the mind fixed on God throughout the day. In his letter to Proba, Augustine had said that Christians fulfill Paul's injunction through their constant desire for eternal bliss.[80] But Bede's preferred approach was to say that all good works are a form of prayer, so that "the righteous pray without ceasing in that the righteous do the things that are just without ceasing, and never cease from prayer unless they fall into sin."[81] So it was that once Cuthbert had become a bishop at Lindisfarne, he considered his exhortation of the weaker brothers as the equivalent of prayer.[82]

In the *Ecclesiastical History* and in his lives of the saints, Bede recorded many extraordinary acts of devotional asceticism of the sort that had come to the Northumbrian church by way of the Irish missionaries. In his commentaries and homilies, however, Bede did not encourage his readers to undertake such heroic acts. He was more inclined to counsel regular participation in corporate acts of worship as the best way to ensure a prayerful life. He had a strong devotion to the eucharist both in the celebration of the Mass and as viaticum for the dying. He drew moral and spiritual reflections from elements of the baptismal ritual, the creeds, the canticles of the daily office, the use of candles and incense in church, the seasons of the liturgical year, and the feast days of the saints. All of these Bede naturally assumed to be part of the nourishment provided by the church for the journey of faith. A story told about Bede after his death may be apocryphal, but it perfectly captures this aspect of his spirituality. Writing to the monks at Wearmouth-Jarrow about their late colleague and patron, Alcuin remembered that Bede had believed that angels visited the monastery church at the canonical hours of prayer, saying, "What if they do not find me there among the brothers? Will they not have to say, 'Where is Bede?'"[83]

Saints, Miracles, and Relics

Most of Bede's historical and hagiographical works celebrate the saints of Anglo-Saxon England not only as examples of moral virtue but also as workers of spectacular miracles, both in life and in death. (As we have previously noted, the exception is the history of the abbots of his own monastery at Wearmouth-Jarrow, which does not include any miracle stories.) These works frequently mention healings and clairvoyant prophecies on the part of missionaries as important factors in the conversion of individuals and nations to the Christian faith. The sanctity and ecclesiastical advancement of future bishops and abbesses is predicted in their parents' dreams, their playmates' comments, and their mentors' prognostications. At the saints' commands storms are calmed at sea, raging fires turn away from inhabited buildings, springs of water appear from rocky soil, and wild animals serve humans by bringing them food or providing bodily comfort. Sudden and dramatic cures occur regularly, as in the Bible, when the saints heal the sick, raise the dead, and cast out evil spirits. Miracles are attested at the tombs of saints like Æthelthryth and Cuthbert, often through contact with a cloth or a small amount of water that has come into contact with the saint's uncorrupted flesh or a fragment of a bone.[84] Even splinters from the wooden cross that King Oswald erected on the battlefield were capable of producing cures.[85] When the nobleman Imma was captured by an enemy after battle and held as a prisoner, his shackles repeatedly fell from his limbs just at the time that his brother the priest, believing him to have perished, was offering Masses for the preservation of his soul.[86]

As sources for his information about such miracles Bede often cited the testimony of eyewitnesses, some of whom he had interviewed personally. There is no doubt, then, that Bede shared the common early medieval belief in the miracles worked by contemporary saints and their physical relics. These miracles, to which he usually gave the biblical name of "signs," were for him a central part of God's providential plan of salvation.[87] He did agree with Augustine and Gregory the Great when they taught that miracles were both less frequent and less spectacular in modern times than they had been in biblical days. Quoting Gregory, Bede explained that the church had needed more miracles at the beginning when its faith was young and tender, just as a new plant must be watered more extensively until its roots are established.[88] But he did not hesitate to affirm with confidence that wonderful miracles continued "even to this day" to demonstrate the power of the gospel in the lives of the saints.

Considering how often Bede's histories and saints' lives record the miraculous deeds of the English saints, it is surprising that his biblical commentaries and homilies pay virtually no attention to modern-day miracles. Those exegetical works frequently deal with miracles, to be sure, but they are the miracles of the Old Testament prophets and of the Lord and his apostles. He usually interpreted those biblical miracles allegorically as being symbolic of spiritual transformation, as in his comment on Mark 8:22: "All the maladies cured by the Lord are signs of spiritual maladies to which the soul draws near through sin to eternal death...so in the gradual healing of this blind man by the Lord is designated the illumination of the hearts of those who are foolish and wandering far from the way of truth."[89] When "the saints" are mentioned as a group, it is often difficult to tell whether Bede is referring specifically to the heroes of the faith, such as the martyrs and holy confessors, or more generally (in Pauline fashion) to the whole community of saints. When he does invoke specific saints by name, it is usually to hold them up as examples of moral behavior, faithful witness, or contemplative practice. But the saints are not only good examples, for Bede also frequently recommended that Christians solicit the intercessory prayers of the saints, which are effective in securing both earthly benefits and heavenly rewards.

Heaven and Hell

When Bede interpreted the mandrakes that are mentioned in Song 7:13, he remembered that Ambrose had noted that this plant possessed sleep-inducing properties that made it useful for treating insomnia. Spiritually, said Bede, the worst insomnia is suffered by the soul who cannot attain eternal rest because she is encumbered by vices and the cares of this world. This sick soul must be brought as a patient to the holy teachers who will act as physicians by putting her into a painless sleep under the anesthesia of spiritual mandrakes. "Then she will recall to mind the eternal punishment of Gehenna's fire which will perpetually torment the souls that neglect their own health, and she will remember the glory of the heavenly homeland in which the souls of the just will be raised to reign with Christ forever."[90] When the pleasures of the world have been surgically removed, the soul can wake up from her deathlike sleep and go on her way rejoicing.

The salutary effect of meditating on hell's torments and heaven's delights that Bede's exegesis draws forth from the unlikely figure of the mandrakes comes to narrative expression in two famous otherworldly journeys recounted in the *Ecclesiastical History*. The story of the Irish monk Fursa (3.19), which Bede derived from a life of that saint, tells how during a serious illness he was twice taken from his body at night and escorted by angels to the other world, first to heaven and then to hell. The other story (5.12) is that of the devout married householder Dryhthelm, who was also taken ill and, according to Bede, actually died one evening and returned to life the next morning. He too went on a visionary journey, escorted by a man wearing bright robes. In his vision Dryhthelm saw a four-part otherworld: a temporary purgatory where sinners who had repented just before death face alternating torments of bitter cold and blazing heat, eternal hell for the reprobate, a flowery meadow of paradise for those who died after having done good works but before reaching perfection, and the heavenly kingdom for those who were already perfect at the time of death.[91] Upon his return to life, Dryhthelm lived austerely as a monk and solitary at Melrose, where he provided a good example even for such distinguished visitors as King Aldfrith, who came repeatedly to listen to his tale. As with all Bede's ruminations on heaven and hell, the final lesson to be learned is that now is the time to repent so that, at the last, one can "see Christ my King in his beauty."

INTRODUCTION TO THE TRANSLATED TEXTS

On the Song of Songs

Bede's commentary on the Song of Songs stands in a long line of Christian allegorical interpretations that take the bride and bridegroom in the Song as figural types of Christ and the church.[92] Inspired by Ephesians 5:21–33 and by Jewish traditions that applied the Song to the love relationship between God and Israel, Greek Christian exegetes such as Hippolytus and Origen had established the fundamental lines of interpretation as early as the third century. Origen's commentary and homilies on the Song, which were partially preserved in Latin translations by Rufinus and Jerome, had great influence on Western patristic commentators such as Ambrose and Apponius in the fourth century and Gregory the Great in the late sixth century. But of these, only Apponius produced a complete verse-by-verse commentary on the Song that has been preserved, so Bede's commentary is the second-oldest complete Latin commentary that has come down to us today.

As the single most important source for the twelfth-century *Ordinary Gloss* on the Song, Bede's work was a rich resource for the hundreds of commentaries produced by monastic and scholastic authors alike throughout the Middle Ages. His interpretation is distinguished by his keen interest in applying the verses of the Song to the history of the church, beginning with the synagogue in the time of the Old Testament.[93] Although he sometimes identifies the bride as "holy church, or every elect soul," his emphasis is on the corporate rather than the individual—or perhaps it would be more accurate to say that he writes of individual souls primarily as members of the body of Christ.

Having established at the beginning of his commentary that the Song of Songs is a dialogical "song of love" between Christ the bridegroom and the church as bride, Bede interpreted each biblical verse in a way that would draw the reader more deeply into that divine conversation. He was not interested in the verse's meaning in the mind of its human author (presumably Solomon) or in the context of its original audience, but rather in the application of the verse to the Christian church in his own day. For example, he noted that the opening words of Song 5:2 ("The voice of my beloved who is knocking") are realized in the lives of believers "when the Lord arouses us to make progress in virtues and when he reminds us to seek after the joys of the kingdom that is promised."[94] Then he observed that as believers we may be said to open the door for the Lord in three different ways: (1) by opening our hearts more widely to receive his love, (2) by unlocking the hearts of our neighbors through preaching, or (3) by cheerfully accepting death. But since the bride in the Song has already opened her heart to Christ and already expressed her desire to die and be united fully with him, it is clear (said Bede) that the Lord's intention in this particular verse was to inspire our renewed dedication to the preaching ministry of the church.

Thus Bede's commentary on the Song of Songs was directed toward the spiritual edification of Christian believers, especially those who exercised leadership as pastors and teachers. Twenty-first-century readers of this commentary may find it easier to appreciate Bede's exegesis if they think of it as a form of pastoral theology—not in the narrow sense of the theology of pastoral care (although that is certainly included), but in the wider sense of a theology that describes and informs the ministry of those persons who are charged with the cure of souls. The question he asked was always both practical and quite specific: "In the pages of holy scripture, what is the Lord saying to us today?" The fact that this commentary is preserved in over sixty extant manuscripts is an indication that Bede's pastoral theology spoke with authoritative wisdom to generations of readers throughout the Middle Ages.

Although the date of Bede's commentary on the Song of Songs has long been considered uncertain, there is good reason to believe that it was composed prior to 716. The fourth book of Bede's *Commentary on First Samuel*, which we know to have been written shortly after Abbot Ceolfrith's departure from Wearmouth-Jarrow for Rome on June 4, 716, contains shorter versions of two complex interpretations of the Song of Songs that appear in the Song commentary. The implication, then, is that the Song commentary was written first, which means that it was probably the earliest of Bede's works on the Old Testament.[95]

In a lengthy prologue to the commentary (not translated in this volume), Bede cautions his readers against the interpretation of that book by Julian of Eclanum, a fifth-century Italian bishop who had defended the teachings of Pelagius against Augustine of Hippo. Calling Julian a "snake in the grass," Bede acknowledges the eloquence of Julian's treatise *On Love* (no longer extant) and admits that it contains some useful passages. However, Bede warns his readers that in exalting the human capacity for love and the possibility of sexual desire untainted by lust, Julian was actually denying the need for God's grace. Although the commentary itself only refutes Julian explicitly in one instance, there are numerous anti-Pelagian passages in which Bede affirms that the believer can do nothing apart from divine assistance.[96]

Bede's prologue concludes with an admission that the Song of Songs is a "book that is very difficult to understand" and the characteristic declaration that in his exposition he will be "following the footsteps of the fathers." Finally, he offers an apology for his frequent citation of information about natural history from authors such as Pliny and Isidore:

> I urge the reader not to think it irrelevant if in this work I propose to explain more fully about the nature of the many trees or aromatic herbs that are contained in this text, in accordance with what I have learned in the books of the ancients. For I have done this not out of a desire to seem presumptuous, but mindful of the ignorance that

> befalls me and my people as a result of having been born and bred far outside the world, that is on an island in the ocean, so that we cannot know about things that go on in the first parts of the world (I mean places like Arabia and India, Judea and Egypt), except through the writings of those who have lived there.

Between the prologue and the beginning of the commentary proper, Bede provided a set of thirty-eight *capitula* (chapter headings), which in this translation are inserted into the text at the appropriate places. Next there is a complete text of the Song of Songs in the Vulgate version, arranged as a dialogue with the speakers identified as the synagogue, the Church, and Christ the bridegroom. After the five books of commentary, Bede added another book containing fifty-three excerpts from the writings of Gregory the Great in which the pope had interpreted the Song, with the comments arranged in the order of the biblical verses. Since there are no excerpts from Gregory's own commentary on the Song, we can safely assume that it was not in Bede's library.

Although Bede mentions him by name only twice, the most important source for this commentary was the fourth-century author Apponius, whose own massive commentary had described the Song as a wedding song chanted by the Holy Spirit at the marriage of Christ and the church.[97] In Apponius, Bede found an exposition of the Song as the progressive narrative of salvation history; moreover, since Apponius made considerable use of Origen's work on the Song (without naming him explicitly), Bede was put in indirect contact with the great third-century Alexandrian expositor of that book. Bede seldom adopted Apponius's interpretations in a straightforward manner, and there are no direct quotations besides the two explicit references. A close comparison of the two commentaries shows, however, that Bede was constantly engaging with the earlier writer's ideas and occasionally borrowing some of his vocabulary.

The translation here, which is the first to be published in any modern language, is from the critical edition prepared by David Hurst for the Corpus Christianorum Series Latina (vol. 119B) in 1983. Particular thanks are due to George Hardin Brown, Scott

DeGregorio, Bede Kierney, and Benedicta Ward, all of whom read drafts of the translation and suggested corrections, improvements, and additional source identifications. They are, of course, not responsible for any errors that may remain.

Homilies on the Gospels

Bede's fifty homilies on the gospels, arranged in two books, include homilies for the two great liturgical cycles of Advent/Christmas/Epiphany and Lent/Easter/Pentecost, for several saints' days, and two homilies for the anniversary of the dedication of a church. There is debate as to whether or not Bede ever preached these homilies aloud in the monastic church at Wearmouth-Jarrow; in any case, in their current form they are clearly highly polished products of literary art.[98] The standard pattern for each homily is a reference to "the gospel reading we have just heard" and an examination of what classical rhetoricians called the "circumstances" of a historical event (who, what, when, where, and why), followed by a verse-by-verse exposition of the text that leads to a hortatory conclusion in which the preacher invites the listeners to apply the gospel lessons to their own lives, and a final doxology.[99] Allegorical interpretations of biblical names, places, objects, and events yield spiritual insights with universal applicability; there are very few topical references. Bede's interest as a preacher is in the great themes of pride and humility, sin and grace, promise and fulfillment, the certainty of judgment, and the hope of heaven in the life to come. Bede's homilies provided nearly one-fourth of the readings found in the ninth-century homiliary of Paul the Deacon, which was read at the night office in monasteries throughout the Middle Ages and beyond.

The three homilies translated here as examples of Bede's New Testament exegesis treat the finding of Jesus in the Temple at the age of twelve (after Epiphany), the healing of the Canaanite woman's daughter (Lent), and the dedication of a church (with an exposition of the description of Solomon's temple in 1 Kings). The translation is from the critical edition by David Hurst in Corpus Christianorum Series Latina (vol. 122) that was published in 1965. An excellent English translation of all fifty homilies can be found in the two volumes of *Bede the Venerable: Homilies on the Gospels*, translated by Lawrence T. Martin and David Hurst, published by Cistercian Publications in 1991.

Ecclesiastical History of the English People

Although his contemporaries and generations throughout the Middle Ages knew Bede as an exegete, computist, grammarian, and homiletician as well as a historian, in the modern era it has been the *Ecclesiastical History* for which he has been most highly regarded. This work remains the principal written source for any history of Anglo-Saxon England up through its completion in 731, and Bede is justly renowned as the "father of English history." *The Ecclesiastical History of the English People* is certainly a national history of the early English people in that it recounts their arrival in Britain, the establishment of their kingdoms, their internecine tribal warfare, and the beginnings of their vernacular poetry in written form. But the work is most definitely an *ecclesiastical* history in that Bede's primary focus throughout is on the formation of the English as a divinely favored (even "chosen") Christian people whose history is in many ways a recapitulation of the biblical story of Israel. Moreover, the purpose of this historical account was to further the ongoing conversion of the English people and their rulers by teaching them to see behind the course of human events to the deeper meaning of God's providential plan.

There have been many English translations of the *Ecclesiastical History*, beginning with the ninth-century version commissioned by Alfred the Great. The selections translated here include Bede's account of the conversion of his native Northumbria in response to the evangelistic efforts of missionaries from Canterbury and Iona, his hagiographical portraits of some famous Celtic and Anglo-Saxon saints (Oswald, Aidan, Hild, Cædmon, and Cuthbert), and the visionary narrative of Dryhthelm's otherworldly journey, which played so large a role in the development of medieval understandings of purgatory and the afterlife.

The two most reliable modern translations are by Leo Sherley-Price as revised by R. E. Latham in the Penguin Classics series (London: Penguin Books, 1955; latest revision 1990) and by

Bertram Colgrave for the Oxford Medieval Texts edition of 1969, corrected and reprinted with new notes in The World's Classics series, edited by Judith McClure and Roger Collins (Oxford: Oxford University Press, 1994). If justification is needed for another translation of the selections given here, it may be found in this translation's rather more literal approach to Bede's theological vocabulary and imagery. Both Sherley-Price and Colgrave, as historians translating mainly for the purpose of historical study, occasionally turn to paraphrase in order to explain terms and phrases that are no longer familiar in a secular context. For readers interested in Bede's spirituality, however, there is considerable value in preserving his rich biblical allusions and technical ecclesiastical vocabulary intact. The translation here is from Charles Plummer's edition found in *Venerabilis Baedae opera historica* (Oxford: Clarendon Press, 1896). This edition differs only very slightly from that of R. A. B. Mynors in the Oxford Medieval Texts edition, and it has the advantage of being in the public domain and thus readily available for free on the Internet. In addition, Plummer's introduction and notes, which are still of value even if occasionally outdated in matters of detail, deal much more thoroughly with Bede's theology and spirituality.

ABBREVIATIONS

CCSL	Corpus Christianorum Series Latina
CSEL	Corpus Scriptorum Ecclesiasticorum Latinorum
LCL	Loeb Classical Library
Lindsay	*Isidori Hispalensis episcopi Etymologiarum sive originum libri XX*, ed. W. M. Lindsay, 2 vols. (Oxford: Clarendon Press, 1911), no pagination.
PL	Patrologia Latina
SC	Sources Chrétiennes

Part One

ON THE SONG OF SONGS

On the Song of Songs
Book 1

Whoever desires to read the Song of Songs, in which that wisest of kings, Solomon, describes the mysteries of Christ and the church (that is, of the Eternal King and his city) under the figure of a bridegroom and a bride, should remember first of all that the whole congregation of the elect in general is called "the church," and yet now, for the sake of distinction, that portion of the faithful which preceded the time of the Lord's incarnation is particularly named "the synagogue" and that which followed it "the church."[1] For surely the ancient scripture is accustomed to designate the faithful people of that time with both terms. Now the name that is "synagogue" in Greek means "gathering together" [*congregatio*] in Latin, and "ecclesia" means "calling together" [*conuocatio*]—with which name it seemed more fitting for the faithful of this time to be called because of their greater comprehension of spiritual knowledge. For it is appropriate for those who know how to hear and discern to be called together, but even stones or any other insensible things can be gathered together. Now these two portions of the righteous are sharers in one and the same faith and love of Christ, although they have different sacraments in accordance with their times, as the apostle Peter testifies when he says: *Why are you putting God to the test by placing on the necks of the disciples a yoke that neither we nor our ancestors have been able to bear? On the contrary, we believe that we will be saved through the grace of the Lord Jesus, just as they will* (Acts 15:10–11).

---

1. The synagogue desires for the Lord to come in the flesh and runs with devoted love to meet his coming.

For just as we hope and also believe that we will be saved by the Lord's incarnation, passion, and resurrection, which have already been accomplished, so also did that former part of the church, which expected the same incarnation, passion, and resurrection of the Lord and Redeemer as things yet to come, believe that she was going to be saved through the grace of him whose coming she so earnestly desired. Therefore, it is her voice that resounds at the very beginning in a song of love to him, after the holy prophets have both shown her the way to live and foretold the coming of him who, *as a bridegroom coming forth from his wedding chamber* (Ps 19:5; Vulg. 18:6), would endow the whole world with the grace of a new blessing. Going beyond the voices of the heralds, she began to desire rather the presence of her King and Savior himself, saying:

Let him kiss me with the kiss of his mouth (Sg 1:1), which is to say openly, "I entreat that he would not always appoint angels and prophets to teach me; now at last, let the one who has been promised for so long come himself and instruct me with the light of his own presence, and comfort me by speaking to me with his own mouth, as if he were bestowing a kiss. But let him also patiently receive the touch of my mouth—that is, let him not disdain to listen to me and to educate me when I inquire about the way of salvation." Truly, this desire for him was evidently fulfilled at that time when, as we read in the gospel, after Jesus had sat down *his disciples came to him and* he opened *his mouth, saying: "Blessed are the poor in spirit, for theirs is the kingdom of heaven"* (Mt 5:1–3). For he who at that time opened his mouth and proclaimed to the world the unheard-of joys of the heavenly kingdom was the one who had so often opened the mouths of the prophets, through whom he announced his coming to the world. Now as soon as the synagogue who longs for the Lord to come has said to the prophets who are predicting him: **Let him kiss me with the kiss of his mouth** (that is, "Let him impart to me the gifts of his teaching"), she suddenly turns to him for whom her desire has been burning and adds,

For your breasts are better than wine (Sg 1:2; Vulg. 1:1), as if she were to say openly: "The reason that I long for you to come and renew me with your kisses is that the sweetness of your presence incomparably surpasses all those gifts that you have sent through the heralds of your coming." For she speaks of the fermentation of knowledge of the law as "wine," but by "breasts" she means the first principles of evangelical faith, concerning which Paul says: *I fed you with milk, not solid food* (1 Cor 3:2); and again: *For I decided to know nothing among you except Jesus Christ and him crucified* (1 Cor 2:2). Therefore, the breasts of the Bridegroom are better than wine because all those whom the first principles of the New Testament regenerate *by water and the Spirit* (Jn 3:5) they afterward render fit for entrance into heavenly life, whereas prolonged observance of the law was never able to do this even among those who were so aroused by the taste of supernal sweetness that they could truthfully say: *And your chalice which inebriates, how excellent it is!* (Ps 23:5; Old Latin 22:5), as the Apostle confirms when he says: *For the law brought nothing to perfection* (Heb 7:19). Now if the breasts of Christ (that is, the first beginnings of faith in the Lord) are better than the wine of the law, how much more does the wine of Christ (that is, the perfection of evangelical doctrine) surpass all the ceremonies of the law? If the sacraments of his incarnation lead to life, how much does the knowledge of his divinity glorify? How much the vision of it? For the Bridegroom himself signifies that he has not only milk but also wine when he says in what follows: **I drink wine with my milk** (Sg 5:1). In the gospel he mystically signifies how much his own wine excels the wine of the law when the old wine was running out at the wedding feast that typified the church, and from water he made new wine that was truly quite deserving of greater praise (Jn 2:1–10). And justly does she refer to the "breasts" of the Bridegroom, which is a part of the female body, in order that at the very beginning of the Song she might clearly show that she is speaking figuratively, just as in the Apocalypse (which is itself also a typological book[2]) when John says of him: *I saw in the midst of the seven lampstands one like the Son of Man, clothed with a long robe*, he adds, *and girded with a golden sash across the paps* (Rv 1:12–13). But even the Bridegroom himself (that is, our Lord) does not shrink from applying to himself a figure of the feminine sex, when through Isaiah he says: *Shall I who make others to bear [children] not bear [children] myself? says the Lord; shall I, who give the power of generation to others, be barren*? (Is 66:9) And again: *As a mother caresses [her child], so will I comfort you* (Is 66:13). And in the gospel, to the unbelieving city: *How often would I have gathered your children together, as a hen gathers her chicks under her wings, and you would not!* (Mt 23:37).[3]

The glowing ardor of the best ointments (Sg 1:3; Vulg. 1:2). The best ointments are the gifts of the Holy Spirit with which the breasts of Christ are glowing, because the holy teachers—namely, the ministers of evangelical milk—excel in love of virtues through the anointing of the Spirit. And surely the ointments with which the prophets and priests were visibly anointed in the law were good, but the best ointments are those with which the apostles and the successors of the apostles are invisibly anointed, concerning whom Paul says: *And it is God who has anointed us and has also sealed us and given the pledge of the Spirit in our hearts* (2 Cor 1:21–22); and the apostle John: *And as for you, let the anointing that you received from him abide in you, and you do not need anyone to teach you; but as his anointing teaches you about all things*, and so forth (1 Jn 2:27). Again, they are glowing with the best ointments when they pour forth far and wide the report of their good work or preaching, as they themselves say: *Now thanks be to God, who in Christ Jesus always makes us to triumph, and through us manifests in every place the aroma that comes from knowing him* (2 Cor 2:14). Now she explains why his breasts are glowing with the best ointments when she adds:

Your name is oil poured out (Sg 1:3; Vulg. 1:2). For we should not marvel if the members of that ointment give off an odor, since he himself took his name from oil, as he was evidently called "Christ," that is "anointed"—doubtless with that anointing of which Peter says: *How God anointed him with the Holy Spirit and with power* (Acts 10:38). Surely the Holy Spirit is accustomed to be understood by the name "oil," as the prophet bears witness when he says in praise of the same Bridegroom: *God, your God, has anointed you with the oil of gladness beyond your companions* (Ps 45:7; Vulg. 44:8). Therefore, his name is oil that is not just dripping but even poured out, because, as his own forerunner [John the Baptizer] says of him: *God gives the Spirit without measure, for the Father loves the Son and has given all things into his hand* (Jn 3:34–35). And not without cause can we consider those among his elect, upon whom he has most bountifully lavished the gifts of his Spirit, to have had oil poured out upon them, just as that grace which was previously kept hidden among the Jewish people alone has now flooded the ends of the whole world in broad daylight, thus fulfilling the prophecy that says: *I will pour out my Spirit upon all flesh* (Acts 2:17; cf. Jl 2:28). The apostle Peter explains this when he says: *Being therefore exalted by the right hand of God, and having received from the Father the promise of the Holy Spirit, he has poured out this gift that you see and hear* (Acts 2:33).[4] Therefore his name is oil poured out, because it is rightly named after what it is, that is, the one who is full of the Holy Spirit is rightly named after what he does, which is to anoint the hearts of the elect with the gift of that same Spirit.

Therefore the young maidens have loved you (Sg 1:3; Vulg. 1:2). Those she calls "young maidens" are the souls reborn in Christ who have cast off the uncleanness of the old self.[5] The more they cling to the love of their Creator, the more they know that it is only by his grace that they receive the remission of sins and the gifts of the Spirit by which they make progress in virtue. Hence they openly profess and say: *The love of God* (namely, the source of all virtues) *has been poured into our hearts through the Holy Spirit that has been given to us* (Rom 5:5). Now we should not doubt that the saints of old who loved the Lord with perfect charity and also the bands of their pious companions can mystically be called "young maidens," who by faith in the truth scorned the examples of the ancient sinner and ran after the rewards of new life with undoubting hope. Hence one of them who was already certain of future blessings speaks of his own soul, saying: *Your youth is renewed like the eagle's* (Ps 103:5; Vulg. 102:5). But even more aptly do these things apply to the heirs of the New Testament, who are properly said to be begotten by God through the washing of grace as children of adoption. The more they love him, the more of his gifts do they obtain, so that as soon as their flesh has been dissolved, if they have lived rightly, they mount up to the joys of the heavenly kingdom.

---

2. The early church laments that she has been darkened by persecution from unbelieving Jews and, trembling, calls upon the assistance of her beloved Redeemer.

Draw me, we will run after you (Sg 1:4; Vulg. 1:3). Thus far it has been the voice of the synagogue (that is, of that people who with devout faith preceded the incarnation of the Savior) who in the beginning of the Song responds to the prophets who had been predicting him for a long time: **Let him kiss me with the kiss of his mouth**—that is, "Let him appear himself and, speaking mouth to mouth (Nm 12:8), let him confer upon me examples of living and gifts." In the short verses that follow thereafter, she signified what manner of gifts of his these might be, and how much they ought to be loved by chaste souls. Here she is joined by the voice of the church, that is, of those who have come to faith after the time of his incarnation. Earlier, [the synagogue] prayed that the Lord might come and give her the kiss of peace; now [the church], knowing that he has already come in the flesh and then returned to heaven, no longer implores him to come down to her in the same way, but desires rather that she might follow him to heaven. But because she sees that she cannot do this by herself, rightly does she implore the aid of him to whom she wishes to come. **Draw me**, she says, **we will run after you**, as if she should say openly, "We were indeed desiring to run in your ways, to follow in the footsteps of your works which you marked out while you were living on the earth, to come to you as you are ruling in heaven; but because without you we can do nothing (Jn 15:5), we pray that you will deign to give us your hand, that you will help us with your support as we run toward you; for the only way we are able either to run rightly or to finish the course is if we run with you as our guide and helper." Hence the Apostle who properly boasts, saying: *I have fought the good fight, I have finished the course, I have kept the faith* (2 Tm 4:7), clearly teaches in another place whether he can direct his own way by himself and come to the Lord who draws him, saying: *But I worked harder than any of them—though it was not I, but the grace of God that is with me* (1 Cor 15:10). And when it is said in the singular number, **Draw me**, it is properly added, **we will run**, because the church of Christ is one throughout the world, but it also consists of many faithful souls, which are in this passage called "young maidens" on account of the vitality of their new way of life.

The King has brought me into his chambers (Sg 1:4; Vulg. 1:3). The chambers of the eternal King are the inner joys of the heavenly homeland into which holy church has now been brought through faith and will in the future be brought more fully in reality. Now the bride is speaking to the young maidens—that is, the church of Christ is saying to the faithful souls that are its own members recently reborn in Christ: "The reason that I am praying to the Bridegroom that he might help us with his hand lest we should grow faint as we are running after him is that I have already had a foretaste of the sweetness of the heavenly kingdom, I have already tasted and have seen that the Lord is sweet (Ps 34:8; Vulg. 33:9), I have already become acquainted with the good things which he has revealed to have been prepared for me in heaven." Soon afterward, turning to him who has revealed these things to her, she hastens to give thanks to her King and Lord for his benefits, saying:

We will exult and rejoice in you, remembering your breasts more than wine (Sg 1:4; Vulg. 1:3), which is to say openly, "We will by no means extol ourselves for the gifts we have received, but in everything that we enjoy we exult, or rather, we always will exult and rejoice in your mercy, remembering in every respect how much you have deigned to restore us with kindness, how you have deigned to temper the austerity of the law with the grace of evangelical faith."

The righteous love you (Sg 1:4; Vulg. 1:3). "The reason that we will exult and rejoice not in ourselves but in you, remembering your gifts, is that all those who are righteous in heart have learned that you are to be loved before all things and above all things, and that they could never become righteous if they put any love before you, from whom alone they have every good thing they possess." And we should consider what she says further above: **The young maidens love you**, but now she says, **The righteous love you**. [These two verses] should be put together, because she spoke of no other youthfulness than uprightness of heart, since those who have put off the impurity of the old self have put on *the new self which is created according to God in justice and holiness and truth.* (Eph 4:22–24) Again, **the righteous love you** because none can truly love the Lord unless they are righteous. For whoever will violate the rectitude of justice, whether by an action or a word or even a thought that is improper, in vain do they think that they love the Creator whose admonitions they despise. *For the love of God is this, that we keep his commandments*, as John the Evangelist bears witness (1 Jn 5:3).

But after holy church has been led into Christ's chambers through the knowledge and hope of celestial blessings, after she has learned to love him with a righteous heart and to rejoice and exult in his grace alone, it remains to be shown what struggles she endures for the sake of that same love of him, and what afflictions she bears for the sake of acquiring the blessings which she has tasted. There follows:

I am black but beautiful, O daughters of Jerusalem (Sg 1:5; Vulg. 1:4). She is undoubtedly "black" with respect to the misfortune of her afflictions, but "beautiful" in the comeliness of her virtues; or, rather, in the sight of the Judge who sees within she is all the more beautiful the more often she is harassed and, as it were, disfigured by the afflictions of fools. Now she calls the souls to whom she is speaking "daughters of Jerusalem" because they have been initiated into the heavenly mysteries and are longing for their dwelling place in the heavenly homeland. For in order to console them in their tribulations the holy mother says, **I am black but beautiful, O daughters of Jerusalem**, as if she were saying openly, "I do indeed appear exceedingly vile in the eyes of my persecutors, but before God I am shining brightly with a glorious confession of the truth, for which reason you ought to be less sorrowful amid the labors of this exile in which you remember that you are citizens of a heavenly homeland, and in which you hasten through the adversities of a collapsing world toward the vision of eternal peace."

Like the tents of Cedar, like the curtains of Solomon (Sg 1:5; Vulg. 1:4). Cedar was the son of Ishmael, of whom it was said: *His hand will be against everyone, and everyone's hand against him* (Gn 16:12). The truth of this prediction concerning him is proved by the fact that the nation of the Saracens who are descended from him is today hated by everyone,[6] and it is also affirmed by the psalmist besieged by vexations when he says: *I have dwelt with the inhabitants of Cedar; my soul has long been a sojourner. With those who hate peace I am peaceable* (Ps 120:5–6; Vulg. 119:5–7). For we do not read that David endured any animosity from the Ishmaelites, but wishing to exaggerate the evils he was suffering from Saul or from his other adversaries, he complained that he was being harassed by the degradations of that nation that never took the trouble to be at peace with anyone at all. And contrary to them is Solomon, who was peaceable both in his name and in his life. Accordingly, as scripture bears witness: *All the kings of the earth desired to see the face of Solomon, that they might hear the wisdom that God had put into his heart* (2 Chr 9:23). Therefore she says, **I am black but beautiful, like the tents of Cedar, like the curtains of Solomon**, in such a way as to distinguish between being black like the tents of Cedar, and being beautiful like the curtains of Solomon. For just as holy church is quite often rendered dark by the torments of unbelievers, as if she were the whole world's common enemy, in fulfillment of the word that the Lord speaks to her: *And you will be hated by all because of my name* (Mt 10:22), just so is she always fair in the sight of her Redeemer as if she were truly worthy, whom the King of peace himself deigns to look after. And we should note that Cedar, who by his very name already signifies "darkness,"[7] designates either evil persons or unclean spirits, just as Solomon also, who is understood as being "peaceable" even by the mystery of his name, indicates him of whom it was written: *His authority shall be multiplied, and there shall be no end of peace upon the throne of David, and upon his kingdom* (Is 9:7). And when the church is said to be black like the tents of Cedar, this is asserted not as if it were really so, but according to the opinion of those fools who imagine that she furnishes in herself a dwelling place for vices or for evil spirits, but when she is called beautiful like the curtains of Solomon, this is asserted as if it really is the case, because just as Solomon was accustomed to make tents for himself out of the skins of dead animals, in the same way the Lord gathers the church together to himself from those souls who have learned to renounce carnal desires. Therefore he said to all: *If any want to come after me, let them deny themselves and take up their cross and follow me* (Mt 16:24); and the Apostle says: *Put to death your earthly members* (Col 3:5). Certain persons who read this verse as "I am black and beautiful" say that in her carnal and false members[8] the church is black like the tents of Cedar, but in those who are spiritual she is beautiful like the curtains of Solomon.[9] But if we attend to what is written concerning the Lord: *We have seen him, and he had no form nor comeliness* (Is 53:2), which was not said concerning his sin (for he had no sin at all), but of his suffering, surely it is obvious that the church also is said to be black not on account of sins or the defects of sinners, but on account of her own trials and sufferings, with which she is continuously vexed.

Do not think to consider me, for I am swarthy because the sun has discolored me (Sg 1:6; Vulg. 1:5), which is to say openly, "O daughters of Jerusalem (that is, souls devoted to God), do not think that I who am despised should be admired by people, because the fiery trials that I do not hesitate to endure for the sake of my internal beauty have rendered me dark on the outside; nevertheless, heavenly grace has granted that I should be lovely on the inside." This is similar to that [saying] of the apostle Peter: *Dearly beloved, do not think to marvel at the fiery heat which has come upon you to test you, as though some unusual thing were happening to you, but rejoice that you are sharing Christ's sufferings* (1 Pt 4:12–13). And surely the Lord himself is at times signified by the word "sun," as it is said of his ascension: *The sun arose, and the moon stood still in its order* (Hab 3:10–11; Old Latin 3:11), and at times his elect, as he himself says, *The righteous will shine like the sun in the kingdom of their Father* (Mt 13:43). But in this place the heat of tribulations is more fittingly represented by the word "sun," in accordance with what he himself says concerning the seeds sown on rocky ground: *But when the sun rose they were scorched, and because they had no root they withered away* (Mt 13:6), which he afterward explains in this way: *And when tribulation and persecution arise on account of the word, that person is immediately tempted into evil* (Mt 13:21), clearly declaring that tribulation and persecution are represented by the word "sun." Therefore, just as those who remain quietly in the house often have fairer limbs, but the members of those who are employed in the vineyard or garden or in any other kind of outdoor work are very frequently darkened by the sun, so also the more earnestly holy church prepares herself for spiritual combat, the more hotly inflamed are the assaults that the ancient enemy resolves to mount against her. And as often as *sinners are praised in the desires of their soul and evildoers are blessed* (Ps 10:3; Old Latin 9:24), just as frequently are they reproached by the righteous in the virtues of their own soul, and those who do right are reviled, as Paul testifies when he says: *We are reviled, and we bless; we suffer persecution, and we bear it; we are blasphemed, and we entreat* (1 Cor 4:12–13). But he teaches that the faithful ought to disregard the darkening caused by this blasphemy, or rather they ought to rejoice in it on account of what the Lord came forth saying: *Blessed are you when people revile you and persecute you and speak all that is evil against you* (Mt 5:11), and so forth. Since holy church has testified that she is indeed comely on the inside with respect to her faith and virtues, but made swarthy on the outside by persecutions, it then remains for her to show from whom she will suffer the fury of the first persecution. There follows:

My mother's children have fought against me and made me keeper of the vineyards; my own vineyard I have not kept (Sg 1:6; Vulg. 1:5). This is the voice of the early church, which endured wars of tribulations from the very same synagogue from which she took her fleshly origin, as the Acts of the Apostles very thoroughly teaches. The first thing we should note in this verse is that the bride of Christ justly declared herself to have been discolored by the sun, as she was accustomed to work outdoors cultivating or keeping her own vineyard. Now there was in Jerusalem one vineyard of Christ, namely the early church, which was consecrated by the coming of the Holy Spirit on the day of Pentecost (that is, on the fiftieth day after the Lord's resurrection; Acts 2:1–4). At that time the apostles themselves were her keepers. And afterward, when persecution arose in the times of the blessed martyr Stephen and *all except the apostles were scattered throughout the regions of Judea and Samaria* (Acts 8:1), it came to pass that there were more vineyards (that is, there were churches of Christ in more places) because those who were scattered here and there were preaching the word. Surely it was through the action of Divine Providence that the very scattering of the Jerusalem church was the occasion for the founding of more churches. For this reason it is appropriate that while our [Latin] codices say that they "were scattered," in the Greek[10] it says *diesparesan* (that is, "they were disseminated") *throughout the regions of Judea and Samaria*, and a little later, *Those who had been disseminated went about preaching the word of God* (Acts 8:4), because the persecutors were intending to drive the church out of Judea, but unwittingly they were spreading the seedbed of the word more widely, and by persecuting one church in Jerusalem they were unwittingly causing many churches to come into existence in other places. Therefore, after it had been said that the early church would be dark with afflictions because the children of her mother (that is, of the parricidal synagogue) were going to fight against her with hatred, it immediately went on to tell how much she was going to profit from the attacks of those same afflictions, adding in the persona of those to whom the office of preaching was entrusted: **They made me keeper of the vineyards; my own vineyard I have not kept**, as if it were to say openly, "The harshness of the persecutors was beneficial and useful for me in that I became the keeper of many more vineyards (namely, churches of Christ) after their tempest scattered the original vineyard (that is, the church that I at first undertook to plant and to keep in Jerusalem)." Now, the statement that she had not kept the vineyard must be understood as referring not to her disposition, but to the place. For surely there was a considerable portion of the church that withdrew from Jerusalem at that time which nevertheless retained the full integrity of the faith in a heart firmly fixed, or even took up the office of preaching with a devoted voice, as we have already indicated. Certain ones suppose that what is said, **They made me keeper of the vineyards; my own vineyard I have not kept**, should be interpreted in such a way that the church of Christ is signified by the name "vineyard," and the various decrees of the law and the assorted traditions of the Pharisees are understood by the term "vineyards," and they say that those who put the church in the vineyards are those believers who were compelling her to maintain the ceremonies of circumcision and the carnal law. Among these was that man who says, *By punishing them often in all the synagogues I compelled them to blaspheme; and since I was so thoroughly enraged against them, I persecuted them even as far as foreign cities* (Act 26:11), and for that reason she did not keep her own vineyard when many of the faithful were scattered from Jerusalem like shoots of the heavenly vine; however, their root could never be torn out from that place. But the elect need to invoke the Redeemer's help all the more earnestly when their faith is tested by greater hostility from the wicked. Therefore, as soon as holy church has lamented that her mother's children have risen up against her, as soon as her own vine has been shaken by their assault, it is right for her to turn to the Lord with an anxious heart and invoke the memory of his promise: *In the world you have distress, but have confidence; I have overcome the world* (Jn 16:33). She says:

Show me, you whom my soul loves, where you pasture [your flock], where you lie down at midday (Sg 1:7; Vulg. 1:6). Now, it is appropriate for her to call him whose assistance she entreats "the one my soul loves," because the graver the danger from which she desires to be delivered, the more does she love him through whom she knows that she will be delivered. Similar to this is that saying of the psalmist: *I love you, O Lord, my strength* (Ps 18:1; Vulg. 17:2), which is to say openly, "The reason that I do not cease to love you with my whole heart is that I perceive that I can have no strength apart from your grace." She also signifies that he is a shepherd when she says: **where you pasture [your flock], where you lie down at midday**, in accordance with what he himself testifies in the gospel: *I am the good shepherd, and I know my own and my own know me* (Jn 10:14). He pastures his sheep and lies down among them at midday, because he refreshes the hearts of his faithful ones with the memory of his heavenly kindness lest they wither away on the inside from the heat of trials, and it has been his custom to abide graciously among them. For on this account the psalmist says: *The Lord pastures me, and I lack nothing; in the place of pasture, there he has brought me* (Ps 23:1–2; Vulg. 22:1–2); hence John says: *Those who abide in charity abide in God, and God in them* (1 Jn 4:16). Therefore, since *many false prophets* (Mt 24:11) arise in the world saying: *Look! Here is the Christ! Look there!* (Mt 24:23), it is always necessary for the church of Christ to discern through careful examination who they are in whose profession and work he can be found, and to entreat him with pious cries that he might deign to show himself, saying: **Show me, you whom my soul loves, where you pasture [your flock], where you lie down at midday**.

Lest I begin to wander after the flocks of your companions (Sg 1:7; Vulg. 1:6), as if she were to say openly, "Since persecution brings me a multitude of adversaries after the fashion of the noonday heat, I beseech you to declare to me, O my Redeemer and Protector, where I might find those who have been refreshed with the grace of your presence, or which ones among all the dogmas are in harmony with the truth of your gospel, so that I might not run into the assemblies of those who have long been separated from you and have chanced to stray from your protection, where I would be without your guidance and thus could by no means walk in the way of truth." For even heretics cannot incongruously be called his "companions," inasmuch as they carry around his name or creed or sacraments.[11] And did the bride of Christ not do these things when the false apostles (namely, his companions) came from Antioch and proclaimed, *Unless you are circumcised according to the law of Moses, you cannot be saved* (Acts 15:1)? For after she had been wearied by no little heat of dissension and questioning she at last sent Paul and Barnabas to the apostles and elders in Jerusalem to discern with greater certainty what the truth of the gospel might be, and when the debate was concluded it was determined that the Lord Christ was the shepherd who dwelt among those being instructed by James, Cephas, John, and the other apostles, and that his church should be kept in his sheepfold, free from the flocks of the companions (that is, from the crowds of heretics). And has the bride of Christ not also done these things often in subsequent times? For when her mother's children fought against her (that is, when heresies grew up to oppose her from within), she was soon diligently gathering councils of the fathers together in order to inquire what the truth of the faith might be.

---

3. Chiding the fearful church, the Lord reminds her that she has been given grace against all assaults of her enemies.

But since this same bride (that is, the church of Christ), when she had sought the help of his presence in the midst of tribulations, had gone on to say in the persona of the fainthearted, **Lest I begin to wander after the flocks of your companions**, he at once responded to her anxiety with kindly rebuke like that saying in the gospel: *You of little faith, why did you doubt*? (Mt 14:31). For there follows:

If you do not know yourself, O fairest among women, go forth and follow the tracks of the flocks (Sg 1:8; Vulg. 1:7). He asks, "How can you talk as if I could on any account forsake you in the time of trial, and how can you complain that you have been blackened by too much heat as if from the noonday sun while you were keeping our vineyard? Through the washing of regeneration I have previously made you the fairest among women (that is, among the synagogues of other doctrines), but I have arranged for your beauty to be restored through the great ordeal of tribulation. But if by chance you neither know these things, nor remember that no one *is crowned without contending according to the rules* (2 Tm 2:5), then **go forth** from my company **and follow the tracks of the flocks** (that is, imitate the erratic deeds of those who go astray), although I myself have resolved that you are truly the keeper of my one flock, for which there is *one sheepfold and one shepherd*" (Jn 10:16).

And pasture your kids beside the shepherd's tents (Sg 1:8; Vulg. 1:7); that is, "Feed the lost disciples who have abandoned the words that are given by the one Shepherd through the council of prudent teachers and followed after the doctrines of foolish teachers, for surely I have commanded you that if you love me (Jn 21:15), you will indeed pasture my sheep (that is, the souls who serve me in simplicity and innocence) with the word of salvation, and it is my will that you should attend to this duty with so much care that you would prefer to suffer every misfortune and even to undergo the anguish of death rather than to leave off feeding them. How can you not know that you have been betrothed to me under the condition that you are to pasture your kids (that is, those who have associated with erring teachers) rather than to wait on the wanton and proud, who are rightly called both 'kids' and 'your kids,' namely those who are to be positioned on the left hand at the judgment (Mt 25:33), but they are yours since they have not been instructed according to the rule of my commandments but rather according to your errors (that is, the ones in which you were held fast before you were united with me)." Now the Lord is not saying these things by way of commanding but rather by way of threatening and insinuating what would happen to those who separate themselves from the unity of ecclesiastical peace because they cannot bear the misfortunes of trials, as in the gospel when he says, *Either make the tree good, and its fruit good; or make the tree bad and its fruit bad* (Mt 12:33), he is not commanding us to do evil, but he is teaching what reward awaits those who do evil. But since the Lord does not want holy church to be ignorant of her true self, but that she should readily desire to learn what gifts she has received from him and what she ought to suffer and to do for the sake of his love, he consequently indicates what her status is when he goes on to say:

I have compared you, my friend, to my company of horsemen among Pharaoh's chariots (Sg 1:9; Vulg. 1:8.) Surely his "company of horsemen" is what he calls the host of the children of Israel whom he freed from slavery in Egypt. Leading them through the Red Sea into the desert, he eventually brought them into the land promised to them as an inheritance. The chariots of Pharaoh, who was pursuing them because he wanted to drag them back into servitude, he caused to sink into the same sea. Now he calls them a "company of horsemen" from then on, because just as a charioteer is accustomed to preside over a company of horsemen, the Lord himself then ruled over that same people in such a way as to take charge of it, and guided it in such a way as to lead it along the way of salvation. Clearly the one being compared to this company of horsemen is his church, which he made his friend through the water of regeneration, for he has taught her that when persecutors threaten she should always have faith in his help, just as that former people was certainly terrified and very fearful when Pharaoh's chariots came upon them but was saved at that time by heavenly protection. For it happened then that a fiery pillar gave light for the people of God but thickest darkness covered the Egyptian hordes so that all through the night they were unable to come near to one another, and this constantly happens also in the night of this world when Divine Providence uses meticulous discernment to separate the righteous from the reprobate, illuminating the righteous with his grace and leaving the reprobate in blindness as they deserve. But since it also happened that when they came to the Red Sea the children of Israel were delivered by the parting of the waves, but the waters returned upon the Egyptians and they were drowned along with their horses and chariots, is it not evident that the very stream of death that will come upon all mortal beings carries away the wicked to destruction while for the pious it opens up the way to salvation? And as for all the rest of the things that we read as having happened to that same company of God's horsemen (that is, to the Israelite people) in the time of the Egyptian persecution, the more diligently they are examined, the more clearly are they found to have anticipated in figure the holy universal church of which this people was a portion. And since this verse teaches how the Lord protects the church in the midst of misfortunes, it remains to be shown how much the church herself preserves the love of the same Lord and Protector when misfortunes occur. There is added:

Your cheeks are beautiful as a turtledove's (Sg 1:10; Vulg. 1:9). It is said that it is the nature of the turtledove that if it is deprived of the companionship of its mate it will never be joined to another.[12] This is appropriately applied to the chastity of the church, for even though death has deprived her of the Lord who is her Bridegroom, nevertheless she can by no means accept the company of strangers, since she holds so dear the remembrance of the one whom she knows to have been resurrected from the dead and to reign now in heaven, and she is content with only the love of him to whom she longs to come one day. For this reason she is accustomed to declare in words she learned from an eminent teacher: *For neither death, nor life, nor angels, nor principalities, nor things present, nor things to come, nor power, nor height, nor depth, nor any other creature, shall be able to separate us from the love of God which is in Christ Jesus our Lord* (Rom 8:38–39). This is what holy church says when she is fearful that perhaps she might turn aside from the way of truth by wandering after the examples of the foolish: **Lest I begin to wander after the flocks of your companions**. Therefore, since the seat of decorum is in the cheeks, Truth himself rightly says to her in reply: **Your cheeks are beautiful as a turtledove's**, which is to say: "I have adorned you with such virtue of wholesome modesty that neither the desire for transitory things nor the noisy dogmas of the foolish ever seduce you into drawing back from the chastity you have promised to me in good faith." Now he shows how very important it is to keep this sobriety, by adding:

Your neck as jewels; we will make you necklaces of gold, inlaid with silver (Sg 1:10–11; Vulg. 1:9–10). Surely it is through the neck that we both take in food to nourish the body and bring forth words with which we declare the secrets of our hearts to our neighbors. For this reason the role of the church's teachers is rightly represented by the neck, since they both instruct the unlearned with an edifying word and in the process of that same instruction convey the food of salvation to the members of the holy church entrusted to them. Clearly, this neck is rightly compared to jewels. Now jewels are ornaments that customarily dangle from the necks of virgins. However, all the ornaments of married women are also frequently represented by the word "jewels," because the constancy of spiritual teachers is protected and at the same time adorned with the insignia of heavenly virtues, inasmuch as they show forth in deeds what they teach in words. The necklaces [*murenulae*] are also ornaments for a virgin's neck, namely, little chains woven with golden bands and sometimes embroidered as well with additional silver bands that, as this verse indicates, take the name of a kind of serpent because they bear a close resemblance to a striped eel [*murenae*].[13] Now these aptly signify the weaving together of the divine scriptures through which the loveliness of holy church increases when every single one of the faithful strives to shine with virtues by observing the words and deeds of the fathers more and more. For the gold from which he says that the necklaces are to be made is the splendor of the spiritual sense, and the silver with which he states they are inlaid is understood as the luster of heavenly eloquence. Now what he promises in the plural, **we will make you**, is said with reference to those through whom sacred scripture has been ministered to us by the agency and cooperation of God's Spirit, of whom there have been very many from the time in which Solomon foretold these things until that which is to come. Therefore, he encircles the bride's neck with gold necklaces inlaid with silver because he has prepared divine diadems for the church by inspiring those whom he has placed in authority with responsibility for teaching his faithful, and he encircles her neck with necklaces fashioned by the craftsman's art when every faithful soul continually looks toward the holy scriptures in all that she says or does, or perhaps I should say in everything that she lives and hopes, and diligently directs both her mind and her words according to their pattern, and thus this little verse is joined to the one above, for the reason that holy church's cheeks are beautiful as a turtledove's (that is, that her modesty remains inviolate) is because frequent meditation on divine scripture does not allow her to err.

In this place the old translation[14] reads thus: **We will make you likenesses of gold with embellishments of silver while the king is at his table**. In this verse the splendor of the heavenly homeland is doubtless expressed by the word "gold." To us in this life holy scripture reveals the likenesses of this splendor, and not the incorruptible splendor itself, because as the Apostle says, *Now we see* *through a mirror and in obscurity* (that is, in likenesses), *but then face to face* (1 Cor 13:1). Accordingly, Moses himself, to whom (as we read in Exodus) *God spoke face to face as one speaks to a friend* (Ex 33:11), since he realized that he had not seen God's glory itself, prayed saying: *If then I have found favor in your sight, show me your way, that I may know you* (Ex 33:13), and again he says: *Show me your glory* (Ex 33:18); for the Lord showed himself also when he said to him in reply: *You cannot see my face, for no one shall see me and live* (Ex 33:20). Therefore, the vision of the divine countenance is denied to us only as long as we are in this mortal life, but what is denied [now] has been promised to our hearts in the world to come. Now in the present [age] the likeness of his face and of his everlasting beauty has not only been shown to the fathers when the Lord appeared in the company of angels, but even today it is being shown to us who read what the fathers have written, when we endeavor to remember the things they said about the glory of the heavenly homeland and continually long to see them. Now these likenesses are made with embellishments of silver because the heavenly mysteries are revealed to us with the splendor of spiritual sayings. And because we need the likeness of these sorts of consolation and help only while we are in this life and not in the life to come, it is aptly added, **while the king is at his table** (that is, while Christ is in his secret place and has not yet appeared to us *in the glory of his Father* to repay *everyone according to his work*) (Mt 16:27); for then, as Isaiah says: *The eyes* of the saints *will see the king in his beauty* (Is 33:17);[15] hence the Apostle also says: *Your life is hidden with Christ in God; when Christ who is your life appears, then you also will appear with him in glory* (Col 3:3–4). Now Christ the King was at table (that is, in his hidden place) not only prior to the incarnation and after his ascension into heaven, but also during that time in which he appeared in flesh and was visible to the world, for at that time he did not show either the glorification of his assumed humanity or the eternal glory of his divinity to the faithful who accompanied him constantly while he was in flesh, which he has promised, however, to all the elect as faith's reward in the life to come. But our version [i.e., the Vulgate], which was taken directly from the Hebrew original, joins the last part of this little verse that is under discussion here, in which it says **while the king is at his table**, to the verse which follows.

4. Comforted by the Lord's words, the church calls to mind his manner of life in the flesh, his passion, and his resurrection.

Surely the church, having received such gifts or promises from her Creator, continually responded and further declared the devotion with which she would undertake these works, saying: **While the king was on his dining couch, my nard gave forth its fragrance** (Sg 1:12; Vulg. 1:11). Now "the king's dining couch" is what she calls the time of his incarnation, during which he deigned to be humbled for our sake and to be brought down himself so that we might be raised up. Clearly, on this dining couch he has willed both to refresh his church with life-giving food and to be refreshed himself with her good deeds. For this reason he says: *I am the living bread that came from heaven; whoever eats of this bread will live forever* (Jn 6:51); and again to the disciples, concerning the people who believe in him, he says: *I have food to eat that you do not know about* (Jn 4:32). And the fragrance of nard represents the ardor of right action. **While the king was on his dining couch**, she says, **my nard gave forth its fragrance**, because when the Son of God had appeared in flesh the church increased in its fervor for heavenly virtues—not that she had no spiritual persons devoted to God before his incarnation, but because she subjected herself without any hesitation to the more rigorous practice of virtues at the time when she learned that access to the heavenly kingdom is open to all who live rightly, as soon as the bonds of flesh are dissolved. Now we should note that the figure in this little verse was also fulfilled according to the letter in the deeds of Mary Magdalene, who contained a type of the church when she anointed the Lord's head and feet with an ointment of nard as he was reclining at supper (Mt 26:6–7; Mk 14:3; Lk 7:37–38), *and the house was filled with the odor of the ointment* (Jn 12:3), as the holy gospels bear witness. In one of them it is also indicated what kind of nard that was, for it is said: *A woman came with an alabaster jar of ointment of nard of very precious spikes* (Mk 14:3), evidently because its *tips extend themselves into ears and therefore they fill up the spikes and leaves with a double portion of nard* oil.[16] The naturalists write that it is the chief among ointments, hence it was deservedly used in anointing the body of the Lord; and, as they say, *it is a shrub planted with a root that is heavy and thick, but* *short, and black and brittle although succulent; smelling like the cypress, with a bitter flavor and a leaf that is small and thick. Now there are* many kinds of it, but it is *the Indian variety* that is more precious *than all other herbs.*

My beloved is to me a bundle of myrrh that shall lie between my breasts (Sg 1:13; Vulg. 1:12). And we read that this was fulfilled according to the letter for the sake of our salvation when, after his passion was complete and his body had been taken down from the cross, *Nicodemus came bringing a mixture of myrrh and aloes, [weighing] about a hundred pounds*, and they took his *body and wrapped it in linen cloths with the spices* (Jn 19:39–40; Vulg. 38–39). The church's beloved, therefore, became a bundle of myrrh when the Lord was covered with myrrh and aloes and enfolded in linen cloths; clearly he lies between the bride's breasts when the church in her inmost heart meditates unceasingly on the death of her Redeemer. For who does not know that the heart is located between the breasts? And the bundle of myrrh will lie between the bride's breasts whenever any soul dedicated to God attentively remembers that apostolic saying that *those who belong to Jesus Christ have crucified their flesh with its vices and desires* (Gal 5:24) and is eager (as far as she is able) to imitate his death, by which she knows herself to have been redeemed. But because after the death of our Mediator and Savior there soon follows the glory of resurrection, the bride rightly adds:

My beloved is to me a grape-cluster from Cyprus in the vineyards of Engaddi (Sg 1:14; Vulg. 1:13). Surely the meaning of this little verse according to the surface of the letter is this: "Just as the island of Cyprus produces grape-clusters that are larger than those from other lands, and just as those that grow in the Judean city that is called Engaddi are nobler than those from other vineyards, inasmuch as the liquid that comes from them is not wine but balsam,[17] that much dearer to me is my beloved than all those to whom I am joined in love, so that no creature can separate me from his affection." But typologically, in the same way that myrrh on account of its bitterness signifies the sorrow of the Lord's passion, in which he took both myrrh and wine to drink from the soldiers and was anointed with myrrh by the disciples when they laid him in the tomb, just so, as we have already said, it is not unseemly for a grape-cluster to indicate the joy of his resurrection. For *wine gladdens the human heart* (Ps 104:15; Vulg. 103:15). Therefore the Lord, who had been a bundle of myrrh in his passion, became a grape-cluster of Cyprus at the resurrection. Accordingly, he lies between the bride's breasts because he has turned into a grape-cluster of the vineyard, which is the reason that holy church never puts the memory of the Lord's death away from her heart, since the one who died for her trespasses also rose from death for her justification (Rom 4:25) and gave her an example of being raised after the anguish of death, so that she might follow in his footsteps. It is also appropriately mentioned that he is in the vineyards of Engaddi, for, as we have already said, in the vineyards of Engaddi there is produced balsam, which is customarily mixed with olive oil and consecrated by the bishop to make chrism so that with the imposition of priestly hands all the faithful may be signed with this anointing through which the Holy Spirit is received, and with which the altar of the Lord is anointed when it is dedicated, and the other things that are to be sanctified.[18] For this reason the divine gifts are very rightly represented by the vineyards of Engaddi. And the Bridegroom is in the vineyards of Engaddi both because the Lord himself was filled with the Holy Spirit when he appeared in the flesh, and because he bestows the gifts of his Spirit on believers. Now the balsam trees are referred to as "vines" because they are lifted up in the manner of vines, which support themselves without assistance, *more similar to the grape than to the myrtle*, distinguished by *permanent foliage; standing less than two cubits in height, with a seed that is most like the grape in taste, reddish in color; with branches thicker than those of the myrtle.* At a certain time of year they exude balsam, but farmers also cut into their boughs using sharpened stones or bones as knives (for the touch of iron does damage) so that a lovely sap with a pleasing odor flows out from these incisions in falling drops and is *collected by being caught in a little horn with tufts of wool.*[19] This [sap] is often called *opobalsam* because it flows out of the hollow of a horn, for in Greek a hollow is referred to as an *ope*,[20] *and the larger vein of each of these trees is pierced three times every summer: first for the sake of the drops, second for the seed, third for the small amount of bark on its wood.*[21] All of these things, if carefully considered, correspond most aptly to our Redeemer, who was humble but full of grace and virtue when he appeared in the flesh and *was wounded for our iniquities* (Is 53:5) and from whose wounds poured forth the sacraments of our life and salvation (Jn 19:34). For this reason also the one who is the power and wisdom of God (1 Cor 1:24) says in Ecclesiasticus: *And my fragrance is like the purest balsam* (Sir 24:15; Vulg. 24:21). Very marvelous indeed is the order of the words: first, the bride says that her nard gave its fragrance to the king while he was reclining at table; then she compared him to a bundle of myrrh; third, she calls him a grape-cluster of Cyprus; and lastly she relates that he is in the vineyards of Engaddi. First, too, while the Lord was lying down at supper, the devout woman anointed him with nard; then, when he had been crucified, buried, and anointed with myrrh, the disciples wrapped him in linen cloths; and after these things he soon returned in the joy of the resurrection to distribute spiritual gifts to the faithful. Nor should we neglect to mention that Engaddi is interpreted as "fountain of the kid";[22] this name obviously indicates the bath of sacred baptism into which we descended while we were yet sinners deserving to be on the left hand, but have now ascended cleansed from the filthiness of sinners and reckoned among the number of the sheep (Mt 25:31–33). And it is well that when she has signified the joy of the Lord's resurrection by saying, **My beloved is to me a grape-cluster from Cyprus**, she immediately added, **in the vineyards of Engaddi** (that is, in the fonts of the kid), which is to say openly: "in the spiritual gifts that are conferred on the faithful at the time of baptism."

---

5. The Lord praises her whom he has comforted. Responding to him with a twofold praise, she desires to enjoy a little peace with him in this present life.

Thus far, the church has been receiving from her Redeemer gifts that she invokes as tokens of love. Then he responds to her by way of reward: **Behold, you are beautiful, my friend; behold, you are beautiful; your eyes are those of doves** (Sg 1:15; Vulg. 1:14). "Behold, you are beautiful in the pure works with which you live *soberly and justly and piously in this world* (Ti 2:12); behold, you are beautiful in the simplicity of heart with which you apply yourself to good deeds for the purpose of eternity alone, awaiting *the* *blessed hope and coming of the glory of the great God* (Ti 2:13). Your eyes are those of doves, the eyes of your heart are simple and pure and utterly free from all duplicity of deceiving or pretending; behold, they are greatly blessed because such [eyes] as these will see God" (Mt 5:8). Again: "Your eyes are as those of doves because your spiritual senses are endowed with understanding"; for since the Holy Spirit descended upon the Lord in the form of a dove (Mt 3:16), rightly are the spiritual senses and gifts signified by the terms "doves" or "those of doves." Again, Christ's friend has the eyes of a dove because every soul that truly loves him inwardly is not like a bird of prey aroused by any craving for external things, nor does she contemplate any harm that she might inflict upon living things; for they say that the dove is gentle by nature and contemplates everything that happens with a heart that is simple, meek, and humble (Mt 11:29). Now, when she hears that a twofold beauty (namely, of both work and purpose) has been brought together in her by the Lord, she then responds in a devout voice:

Behold, you are beautiful, my love, and comely (Sg 1:16; Vulg. 1:15), as if she should say openly: "Surely whatever I possess of beauty, simplicity, and spiritual grace I have doubtless received through your generosity, by which I have come to possess both the remission of sins and the ability to do good. But you are truly beautiful and comely beyond compare, you who are God, begotten of the Father before all worlds, and when the time for my redemption arrived you were conceived and born of the Holy Spirit and the Virgin Mary,[23] not only free from every stain of sin but also full of grace and truth (Jn 1:14), and you came into the world and lived in the world, and to all those who partake of your grace you have even granted that they might also [share in] the virtues of your beauty. Therefore you are beautiful and comely, that is, admirable both in the eternity of your divine nature and in the dignity of the humanity that you assumed." Since the splendor of this beauty is accustomed to be known more clearly by hearts that are more serenely undisturbed by external activity, in accordance with that [saying] of the psalmist: *Be still, and know that I am God* (Ps 46:10; Vulg. 45:11), she rightly adds:

Our couch is full of flowers (Sg 1:16; Vulg. 1:15). For at times holy church takes her rest with the Lord her Bridegroom on a couch, as it were, and at times she stands with him in battle against enemies. Surely she stands in battle when very violent assaults of trials rise up and she faithfully engages in combat against the ungodly to the point of shedding her blood, but she takes her rest on a couch when the peace of untroubled times smiles on her and she is obedient to him, and when she keeps her mind's eye quietly focused on contemplating the glory of his majesty. For this reason the same couch is properly said to be full of flowers, because any of the saints who may enjoy times of tranquility then have leisure to devote themselves even more to readings, holy fasts, prayers, and other spiritual delights while they are resting from the labors of their tribulations. Then they lift themselves up higher to contemplate heavenly things, when they receive a calm period of time without disturbances from outside. Now the church's couch is rightly understood as being full of flowers, not only because of the works of purity through which any of the elect attain the fruit of eternal life, but also because of the progeny of the faithful that the church herself is accustomed to produce by water and the Spirit (Jn 3:5) to be fragrant before God with the flower of faith. *With the Lord working with her and confirming the message* (Mk 16:20), she devotes herself all the more zealously to this activity when through his generosity she has received a time that is peaceful and undisturbed by persecution from her enemies. And throughout the entire text of this book we should note that the bride always desires to tarry with her beloved in the house, whether on the couch or in some other interior place, which is more appropriate for the female sex, but the Bridegroom himself, as befits the male, is calling his friend rather to work either in the vineyards or in the gardens or in some other outdoor place. Doubtless this is because holy church desires, if possible, always to serve the Lord in the tranquility of worldly peace, and to produce and educate celestial progeny for him, but he arranges for her to be vexed with tribulations at present so that being purified she may attain to eternal joys, lest, if all temporal prosperity should come to her, she would sigh less for the celestial homeland because she had been seduced by dwelling in her present exile. And so the bride of Christ, desiring to live a quiet life in that place, consequently indicates the sorts of houses in which she wishes to receive him, saying:

The beams of our houses are of cedar, our paneled ceilings of cypress wood (Sg 1:17; Vulg. 1:16). Surely what she calls her houses are the various assemblies of the faithful throughout the world from all of which the universal church herself is comprised. Now the beams and paneled ceilings represent the diverse orders of the faithful within the same houses of the church; for surely both of them are accustomed to be placed on high, but beams are a means of support while the paneled ceilings serve more as decoration than as support. Therefore, let the beams signify the holy preachers by whose word and example the edifice of the same church is held together so that it is able to stand firm, who by the solidity of their teaching keep out the tempests of heretical influence lest they should bring her down; let the paneled ceilings be compared to Christ's simpler servants, who are more adept at adorning the church with their distinctive virtues than at defending her with words of teaching and protecting her against the fury of perverse doctrines. Now the paneled ceilings rest upon the beams to which they are attached, because those in the holy church who desire to shine with virtues on high must adhere with all their mind to the words and examples of the most eminent fathers, by which they are raised up from the vanity of earthly things. And these beams are properly said to be of cedar, and the paneled ceilings of cypress wood, because it is well known that both of these trees are of an utterly incorruptible nature, extraordinarily tall, with a distinctive aroma,[24] which aptly agrees with those who are able to say with the Apostle: *We are the good aroma of Christ to God* (2 Cor 2:15), and: *Our conversation is in heaven* (Phil 3:20), and: *Who will separate us from the love of Christ? Tribulation* and other things? (Rom 8:35). But since the aroma of the cedar is sometimes used to drive away serpents, according to that [saying] of the poet:

Learn how to kindle fragrant cedar in the stables
and expel noxious serpents with the smell of galbanum,[25]

it is suitable to apply this to the smell of the same support for the paneled ceilings, that is, to the doctors who ward off the poisonous doctrines of heretics with the power of the heavenly word and drive them away before they seduce the simple. Also, its *resin*, which *is called cedar-pitch, is so very useful for preserving books that when smeared with it they neither suffer from worms nor decay with time.*[26] Who does not see how much this agrees with the same holy preachers who through their spiritual understanding produced the holy scripture, which cannot ever be corrupted by the cunning of heretics or consumed by the age of a world that is falling into ruin, so that *until heaven and earth pass away, not one iota, not one stroke*, should pass *from the law until all is accomplished* (Mt 5:18)? When the Lord said this concerning the law, how much more did he intend for it to be understood concerning the gospel? Cypress, inasmuch as it is employed in curing diseases of the body and also because it does not shed the loveliness of its foliage in the onslaught of winds, represents the constancy and efficacy of those who, like paneled ceilings, adorn holy church with the higher ornaments of virtues. Therefore the bride (that is, holy church or every elect soul) marvels at the beauty of her beloved, praises the softness and purity of the flowering couch, and proclaims the interior loveliness that decorously shelters the beloved in her houses, but because in the circumstances of the present time labor is much more appropriate than rest, and in this life the elect should perform godly deeds with Christ's assistance rather than enjoy quiet repose with Christ, rightly does he call his beloved bride forth from her repose to the exercise of labors and to participation in the things that are to be endured from the wicked.

---

6. Recalling the joy of the Virgin Mother, the Lord also describes with due praise the virtue of charity in his bride.

[The Lord] goes on to say: **I am a flower of the field and a lily of the valleys; as a lily among thorns, so is my friend among daughters** (Sg 2:1–2). "You do indeed enjoy blooming in repose with secret virtues, O friend, but remember that I am the flower of virtues, from whom alone all the fruits of the Spirit proceed and in whom alone you are able to have flowery rest. Now I am a flower of the field because I want the charm of my fragrance to be known throughout the whole wide world, which I am by no means able to fill unless you occasionally interrupt the repose that you enjoy and prepare yourself to exercise the office of preaching. And I am a lily of the valleys rather than of the mountains, because I am doubtless accustomed to show and reveal either the brightness of my glorified humanity or the splendor of eternal deity to those who humbly submit themselves to accept the authority of my faith and love, who seek to follow my will rather than their own, who although they enjoy contemplating me interiorly in repose nevertheless do not refuse to go forth to the labor of preaching in accordance with my command; for I myself have allowed you to share in my brightness, so that you may be compared to a lily, namely, by appearing luminous in the perfection of your deeds and exquisite in the splendor of your pure heart. But in order that you may not by chance wish to possess the security of repose in this life, know that at present it is necessary for you to live among the reprobate and to endure daily the barbs of the wicked, but you should be expecting a rest in the future alone with the elect. For **as a lily among thorns, so is my friend among daughters**, because not only do you have to suffer evil things from those who are strangers to you in every way, both in thought and in profession, but very often you are also sharply goaded by the shamelessness of those same souls that you rejoiced to have accepted among the number of your daughters through the font of rebirth and through faith and the reception of the heavenly sacraments."[27]

Certainly it is possible to understand what he says, **I am a flower of the field**, as referring to his birth from an undefiled virgin, and it is possible to understand what he adds, **and a lily of the valleys**, as referring to the humility of his parents. For he appeared as a flower not of the garden or the farm but of the field, since he took flesh from the Virgin Mother's chaste flesh, which knew no sin and was very full of virtue, of whom Isaiah said: *A rod shall come forth from the root of Jesse, and a flower shall arise from his root* (Is 11:1), and he put himself forth as a lily among the valleys because from above he chose humble and poor parents for himself, from whom he was born God and human. For this reason the psalmist also says: *And the valleys shall abound with grain* (Ps 65:13; Vulg. 64:14), for he is grain because he nourishes us with the bread of life, and he is a lily because he has divinity in human form as though it were the splendor of gold in dazzling white. And pleasingly, in the lily the whiteness first reveals itself little by little on the outside, and then there appears the lovely golden color that was concealed within, because when the Lord was born into the world those who saw him at first supposed him to be a sublime human being, but as time went on they realized that he was true God; but all the elect also stretch out toward the contemplation of his divine brightness by receiving the sacraments of his humanity. Therefore, when the church, wearied with adversities, had said to the Lord: **Behold, you are beautiful, my love, and comely; our couch is full of flowers**, and the other things that follow, doubtless desiring to devote herself to the contemplation of his beauty and comeliness in times of serenity and to bring forth flowers for him, whether of good works or of faithful souls, he responds: **I am a flower of the field and a lily of the valleys; as a lily among thorns, so is my love among daughters**, as if he were to say openly, "Remember that although I was able to be born from a virgin and although before the ages I am God, at the end of the ages I humbly appeared in the world as a human being, always showed myself in the company of the humble and the poor in spirit, and walked in the paths of humility even unto death. You also must cease to desire the security of repose for yourself in this world, since you begin to shine whiter and softer, rather like a lily among thorns, if you quite willingly show the sweetness of your comeliness although you are afflicted with prickles, even those of your own kind."

---

7. Having been brought into the knowledge of heavenly mysteries, the church longs to be refreshed and to rest under the protection of her Redeemer.

Now when the church has been praised by the Lord because she has kept the purity of her faith unspoiled among the barbs of the faithless and has shone more gloriously among the terrors of the wicked, she immediately reciprocates in reply by exalting him with great praise, and because the Holy One is especially prominent among the faithful deeds of good people, she declares: **As an apple tree**, she says, **among the trees of the woods, so is my beloved among sons** (Sg 2:3). Now this is what the psalmist says: *For who in the skies shall be compared to the Lord, or who among the children of God shall be like unto God*? (Ps 89:6; Vulg. 88:7). Therefore, as an apple tree that is pleasing in its appearance, smell, and taste is accustomed to excel among the trees of the woods, so is the God-man justly deemed superior to all the saints who are pure human beings, and so does his power surpass the merit of those who are children of God by grace, since he is a son by nature. For this reason John says: *And we have seen his glory, the glory as of the only begotten from the Father, full of grace and truth* (Jn 1:14); for this reason the apostle Paul [says]: *And Moses indeed was faithful in all his house as a servant, for a testimony of those things which were to be spoken, but Christ as the son in his own house* (Heb 3:5–6). Therefore let the cypress shine and the cedar lift itself up in height; let the other trees of the woods show forth the wonders of their comeliness, odor, and strength; the apple tree distinguishes itself above them all because in addition to its fragrance and appearance it has a sweet flavor and the ability to give nourishment. Let all the righteous shine with their virtues; the one born from a virgin excels them all because he serves us with the provisions of eternal life. For this reason it is properly added:

I sat down under his shadow, which I desired, and his fruit was sweet in my throat (Sg 2:3), as if it were to be said openly, "Therefore I judge that my love is to be preferred above all others, because I understand that the only relief I have found from the heat of tribulations is in the shelter of his kindness, for which I am constantly burning with desire, because I perceive the sweetest fruit of his gifts, by which I am confident of being forever refreshed." Now holy church desired to catch her breath a little under her Maker's shadow when she was complaining that she had been blackened too much by the sun of persecutions because her mother's children were fighting against her, and when she was crying out in an anxious voice imploring him to come to her aid: **Show me, you whom my soul loves, where you pasture [your flock], where you lie down at midday;** when, not only wearied by the tedium of afflictions but enticed by the memory of his beauty and comeliness, she was saying, **Our couch is full of flowers;** and she showed that her desire had been fulfilled when she says: **I sat down under his shadow, which I desired, and his fruit was sweet in my throat**. We should also note that she declared above that the beams of their houses were of cedar and the paneled ceilings of cypress wood, and yet she did not say that their shelter was sufficient or that she was content to contemplate their sublimity and beauty, but she was earnestly seeking the tree of life alone, that she might rest in its shadow and be refreshed by its fruit, because even though all the saints can offer us sublime examples of their virtues, and show the way to heaven by their preaching, and carry our suffrages to the Lord through their intercessions, nevertheless it is not to any of them but only to our beloved Savior that we must say: *But the children of human beings will put their trust under the shelter of your wings; they will be inebriated with the abundance of your house* (Ps 36:7–8; Vulg. 35:8–9). For this reason it is rightly said that **as an apple tree among the trees of the woods, so is my beloved among sons**. For the Son is justly preferred to all the children of God, because as a shady tree he shelters us from the heat of a persecuting world, and as an unfading apple tree he refreshes us with heavenly sweetness. Subsequently, she shows that this refreshment is as effective as it is sweet, when she says:

The king brought me into the wine cellar, he set charity in order in me[28] (Sg 2:4). "As soon," she says, "as he has touched the throat of my heart with the sweetness of his grace, I feel that I have been renewed in spirit and transported from delighting in things below to heavenly pleasures, as if I have been brought into a wine cellar and refreshed with the fresh fragrance as well as the taste of wine; for this reason the one who has given me such gifts has rightly directed me to love him in return with unquenchable charity." Now typologically, because the grace of the Holy Spirit is accustomed to be designated by the word "wine," as the Lord bears witness when he says that new wine is to be put into new wineskins (Mt 9:17)—that is, that the fire of the gifts of the Spirit is to be poured into clean hearts—the church should be understood as being the wine cellar in whose unity alone the Holy Spirit is accustomed to be given and received. Therefore the beloved brings his friend into the wine cellar because the Lord has built the church by bringing it together from throughout the whole world into one house for himself, which he has consecrated with the gift of his own Spirit. Because by his own working this building stands upon the strong foundation of charity, after she has said that she has been brought into the wine cellar she rightly adds: **He set charity in order in me**. Now she said, **He set charity in order in me;** that is, he graciously granted that my charity should be ordered so that they love the Lord their God with all their heart, all their soul, and all their strength, and their neighbor as themselves (Mk 12:30–31), and even bear lovingly with their enemy as well (Mt 5:44). Referring to anyone who fails to preserve the order of this charity, whether by ignorance or neglect, the Orderer and Giver of charity says: *Whoever loves father or mother more than me is not worthy of me; and whoever loves son or daughter more than me is not worthy of me* (Mt 10:37). However, the ordering of charity can also be rightly understood as arranging it for the sake of making something firm, because things that are randomly laid out are weak, but things that are laid out in an orderly manner remain steady, so that it is aptly said that the Lord ordered charity in the church because he is known to strengthen it with appropriate augmentations in the hearts of her faithful. Now one can understand that which is said, **He ordered charity in me**, as if it were being said: "He loved me with an ordered charity; that is, he indeed joined all my members (that is, all the elect) together with kindly charity, but (as is fitting) he embraces those who are more distinguished with greater affection, because it is said: For *when he had loved his own who were in the world, he loved them to the end*" (Jn 13:1). Therefore he loved them all, but nevertheless a more tender love is suggested for one in particular when it is said: *That disciple whom Jesus loved* (Jn 21:7). He loves some of those in the church more than others because of the difference in their merits. Again, **He ordered charity in me;** that is: "He loved me first and by loving me allowed me to learn to love him in return." For this reason he says: *You have not chosen me, but I have chosen you* (Jn 15:16); for this reason the apostle John says: *This is charity, not that we loved God but that he loved us and sent his Son to be the propitiation for our sins* (1 Jn 4:10). Again, the Lord ordered charity in the church because the same charity with which he chose her from before the ages he has shown to some of those making progress by degrees over the course of time, for as the Apostle bears witness: *God has commended his charity to us in that while we were yet sinners Christ died for the impious* (Rom 5:8); and in continuing manifestation of this same charity John says: *See what charity the Father has given us, that we should be called children of God; and that is what we are* (1 Jn 3:1). Again, the Lord himself says of that same perfect charity than which nothing can be greater and which can never be diminished (1 Cor 13:8–13): *Now those who love me will be loved by my Father, and I will love them* (Jn 14:21), and the rest. For he says in the present tense: *Now those who love me*, which they cannot do unless he comes to love them first and by the grace of his Spirit incites them to love him. When he then goes on to say in the future tense, *They will be loved by my Father and I will love them and reveal myself to them*, what does it mean except that those who are being loved by God even now, so that they are able to love by believing, will then be loved to such an extent that they love more fully by seeing him, and when his face is revealed they will love him more truly with all their strength, inasmuch as they endure nothing from things below that might deter them from this love? Therefore the Lord orders charity in the church, either because he loves her, or because he arouses her to keep her love for him and for the neighbor in the prescribed manner. And in the next verse he teaches how far above the love of things below this charity elevates the mind that it has completely absorbed, when it is said:

Prop me up with flowers, encompass me with apples; for I am faint with love (Sg 2:5). Surely the soul that truly tastes her Maker's charity ordered in her is faint with love because when he arouses her to seek the light of eternity she doubtless grows weary from this love of that which is temporal, so that the colder she becomes in her zeal for a world that is passing away, the more ardently does she rise up to contemplate the joys of an eternal kingdom.[29] But let us consider the bed into which the soul that burns with this sort of love desires to sink down when she is weary. **Prop me up with flowers**, she says, **encompass me with apples; for I am faint with love**. The tender beginnings of the virtues are designated by flowers and their perfection by apples. Therefore, the soul fainting with love entreats the daughters of Jerusalem (that is, the souls that have preceded her in longing for heaven), asking them to support her beginnings with their good examples and repeatedly call them to her mind, whether they are just beginning to travel the path of virtues, or on the way, or at the end, so that by considering the particularly pleasant fragrance of their flowers and apples, as it were, she might recline more gently and sweetly in the affection of her Maker. This can also be understood as referring to the works of the saints that we keep in mind, and to the deeds or sayings that we gather as if from the meadows and groves of the writings of the fathers who preceded us.[30]

His left hand is under my head, and his right hand will embrace me (Sg 2:6). In Christ's left hand she signifies his temporal gifts, and in his right hand the blessedness of eternal life.[31] For this reason it is written elsewhere of the one who is the power of God and the wisdom of God (1 Cor 1:24): *Length of days is in his right hand*, and *in his left hand riches and honor* (Prv 3:16). Therefore holy church shows (or the soul completely intent upon the love of her Redeemer shows) what kind of rest it could be that she was seeking so greatly in this life, and how in the exile of this pilgrimage she desires to recline with her beloved on that couch flowering with virtues. **His left hand**, she says, **is under my head, and his right hand will embrace me**. Now the ruling part of her mind she calls her "head," and the beloved puts his left hand under his bride's head when the Lord bolsters the hearts of the faithful with the ability to know him while they are still sojourning in this life, when he raises them up through participation in his sacraments, when he gives them the pledge of his Spirit, and when he supplies them with the consolation of the sacred scriptures. But his right hand will embrace her because after this life he promises her the eternal kingdom of life in heaven. And it is properly said that the left hand supports the head and the right hand will embrace her, because we do indeed receive temporal favors to assist us on this pilgrimage, but in heaven we shall see rewards without end. Moreover, the bride, who above was seeking to be propped up with flowers and encompassed with apples because she was faint with love, now testifies rightly that she has the beloved's hand under her head, since although all those who love their Creator rejoice in the flowers of virtue, though they take pleasure in the progress of the neighbors with whom they come to see his face, though they delight to remember the examples of the ancient saints by which they are inspired to love God and the neighbor more ardently, nevertheless, the one hope of those who desire true rest is to be upheld by the hand of their Creator. And surely the left hand is first so that through it they might merit to attain the right hand's embrace; for his right hand will not embrace anyone whom his left hand has not first lifted up to be caressed, that is, no one will see his splendor on high in the future who has not been lifted up in the present by reclining faithfully on the mystery of his humility. And Paul, who taught that he was a faithful servant of this bride when he said: *For I have espoused you to one husband, to present you as a chaste virgin to Christ* (2 Cor 11:2), was he not anxious for the Bridegroom's left hand to be placed under her head so that he might bring her to the embrace of the right? For he says: *I decided to know nothing among you except Jesus Christ, and him crucified* (1 Cor 2:2); again he exhorts her to strive for the embrace of his right hand when he says: *Seek the things that are above, where Christ is, seated at the right hand of God* (Col 3:1), and: *When Christ who is your life is revealed, then you also will be revealed with him in glory* (Col 3:4). Therefore she says, **His left hand is under my head, and his right hand will embrace me**, as if she were to say openly: "The temporal things given to me by my Lord and Savior do indeed help me by enabling me to rest a bit from the lusts and confusions of the world, but I take greater pleasure in the promise of those eternal things with which I shall be rewarded forever."

8. He adjures believers not to disturb the peace of the church.

But the Lord's subsequent response shows how very lovely to him is the sleep of his bride (that is, of the church or of any elect soul), when it is said: **I adjure you, O daughters of Jerusalem, by the wild goats and the stags of the fields: do not arouse or awaken the beloved until she wishes** (Sg 2:7). Calling them "daughters of Jerusalem," the Bridegroom adjures the souls burning with desire for the heavenly homeland not to arouse the bride while she is resting in his love, or to presume to disturb her with human distractions while she is sleeping comfortably. For any troublesome person who hinders the mind of the elect while they are devoutly speaking to God in prayer or meditating on the divine commandments or promises in sacred texts is surely rousing the bride of Christ from blessed slumber before she wishes. For she wishes to awaken when she has been refreshed by this happiest of slumbers, because she has learned when it is proper to devote herself to divine services, and when it is appropriate to return again in order to take care of the necessities due to human weakness.

Therefore, whoever is not afraid to hinder any of the faithful while they are intent upon heavenly pursuits is actually doing harm to the virtues that person supposed them to have in abundance. For this reason the Bridegroom properly adjures the daughters of Jerusalem not to do this by the wild goats and the stags of the field, for surely wild goats and stags, which are clean animals hostile to poisons, represent the works of the spiritual virtues, which are as capable of defying the venomous tricks of the ancient enemy, or rather even destroying and eliminating them, as they are preeminent in purity. And when he speaks of wild goats and stags, he pleasingly adds "of the fields" so that he might clearly show that the virtues spring up and are nourished in the simplicity of pure minds flourishing with sincere faith. And so the Bridegroom adjures the daughters of Jerusalem by the wild goats and the stags of the fields that they must not arouse or awaken the beloved until she wishes, as if he were saying openly, "I call all the faithful to witness, and by each of those virtues that they desire to nourish in their own hearts I adjure them not to despise the pious pursuits of their brothers and sisters, and not to hinder them by intruding upon them indiscriminately, but rather let all rejoice in their neighbors' progress as in their own, in such a way that they are as afraid of inflicting a loss of spiritual profit upon the brothers and sisters as upon themselves, since one certainly diminishes one's own virtues if one disdains to preserve the virtues of neighbors or even to assist them as far as one is able." Willingly receiving the Bridegroom's admonition, the bride responds without delay:

The voice of my beloved! (Sg 2:8). It is understood: "This is [the voice] I have heard adjuring the daughters of Jerusalem that while I am resting in his embrace they are not to stir me up until I wish." For it is very necessary for the soul filled with God to rejoice when in the midst of the world's misfortunes she has been allowed to receive his consoling voice, whether through the gift of secret inspiration or through hearing and meditating on the sacred scriptures; for although we are not yet permitted to gaze upon the face of our beloved, much has already been given to us in that we are refreshed from time to time by the sweetness of his words in the holy scriptures, and much is given to those who are allowed the even greater gift of having a pure mind's gaze lifted up to heaven so that while still in the present time they might have a not inconsiderable foretaste of the sweetness of the life to come. For this reason, after the joyful bride has said, **The voice of my beloved!** since she still desires to see that same beloved presently but is not yet able to do so, she adds:

Look, he comes, leaping upon the mountains, bounding over the hills (Sg 2:8). Surely the ones she calls "mountains" and "hills" are those who in the singular purity of their minds transcend holy church's common life as if it were the flowery surface of the fields, and the more they free themselves from desiring things below, the more capable they become of contemplating things above. Isaiah was speaking of such as these when he described the coming in flesh of the *Mediator between God and humankind* (1 Tm 2:5): *And in the last days the mountain of the house of the Lord shall be prepared as the highest of the mountains, and it shall be lifted up above the hills* (Is 2:2). For he is rightly called that mountain which is the highest of the mountains and lifted up above the hills (that is, higher than the highest among humankind), since in the last days he has surely appeared as a human being among humans, although as God he existed with the Father before the ages. Now when the beloved comes he is said to leap upon these mountains and bound over those hills because the Lord is accustomed to illumine the hearts of the sublime with the abundant grace of his visitation. And he is pleasingly said not to stay upon these hills but to leap or bound over them, because the sweetness of inner contemplation is as lofty on account of the apprehension of heavenly things as it is brief and rare on account of the heaviness of minds still detained by the burden of the flesh. For *the corruptible body weighs down the soul, and the earthly dwelling presses down the mind that ponders many things* (Wis 9:15). We should not think it contrary to this verse that in the gospel the beloved himself makes promises to his bride, saying: *Lo, I am with you always, to the end of the world* (Mt 28:20); and again: *Those who love me will keep my word, and my Father will love them, and we will come to them and make our home with them* (Jn 14:23). For surely he always abides with all the saints through his faith and love and through the help of his grace, but whenever he wishes he may choose to appear in a more excellent way to a few who are more sublime. For it is for those few who are compared to both mountains and hills on account of their loftiness of heart to say: *For if we are out of our mind it is for God; if we are sober, it is for you* (2 Cor 5:13); but to all the faithful it is said that *God abides in those who confess that Jesus is the Son of God, and they abide in God* (1 Jn 4:15). It is for the faithful heart of the whole church to hear that *God is charity, and those who abide in charity abide in God, and God in them* (1 Jn 4:16), but only the perfect can say: *For we did not follow cleverly devised fables when we made known to you the power of our Lord Jesus Christ, but we had been beholders of his greatness* (2 Pt 1:16). A clear example of this beholding is added when it is said:

My beloved is like a wild goat or a young deer (Sg 2:9). And indeed all those who are accustomed to investigate the nature of these beasts find much about them that corresponds very closely to the church's beloved, that is, to the Lord and Savior. But in this text we should give particular attention to the fact that they delight to live on the mountaintops and to leap very nimbly, for which reason we see them less frequently than cattle or asses or other beasts of that kind, which we can use as often as we please once they have been tamed.[32] Aptly, this is often compared to the height of heavenly contemplation, which is not subject to the will of the human beholder but to the grace of God, who appears whenever he chooses. I am confident that when Isaiah (a distinguished mountain, to be sure) saw the Lord himself sitting on a throne high and lifted up, and when he saw the heavenly multitude praising him in one accord (Is 6:1–3), it was not at the time of his own choosing but when the Lord willed it. And when Paul (himself a mountain looking far down upon earthly things, and *at the summit touching the sky*[33]) was caught up into Paradise and was caught up to the third heaven and heard secret words that humans are not permitted to speak (2 Cor 12:2–4), it was not at the time he himself arranged but when God pleased. Surely it agrees with both the humility and the reality of the humanity assumed by the Lord that he is compared not to a deer but to a wild goat and a young deer, which are smaller beasts, since he appeared among human beings not only as a human, but as a humble human. He became a young deer because he took true material flesh from the flesh of his ancestors before him; for *he was made from the seed of David according to the flesh* (Rom 1:3); and David himself [says]: *As the deer longs for fountains of water,* *so longs my soul for you, O God* (Ps 42:1; Vulg. 41:2); and again: *He made my feet like those of a deer* (Ps 18:33; Vulg. 17:34). But it is doubtless to those who share his life that he also speaks of other deer: *The voice of the Lord prepares the deer* (Ps 29:9; Vulg. 28:9); for surely he prepares the deer when he ministers gifts of virtues to the faithful, because it is not by their own power but by divine largess that they direct their mind's path to higher things, that they drink continuously from the fountain of life, that with their spiritual sense of smell they drive the serpents of heretical discourse out of the deceivers' hiding places and trample them underfoot, that they ruminate on the word of life, and that in everything they do they keep their steps safely within the bounds of discretion. Therefore the voice of the Lord prepares the deer because his grace gathers the saints together into the citadel of virtues. The beloved of the bride (that is, of the church or of every faithful soul) was justly born as the offspring of these deer, because from the forefathers came *Christ according to the flesh, who is over all, God who is blessed forever* (Rom 9:5). And seeing that the sublimity of the contemplative life has been expressed in these verses, what still remains to be shown is the perfection of the active life that is common to the whole church. There follows:

See, he stands behind our wall, looking through the windows, watching through the lattices (Sg 2:9). At one time the beloved remains near the bride, but at another time he appears leaping upon the high mountains, because our Lord and Savior shows himself to those who are more perfect when he wills to be seen for a while, even *through a mirror and in obscurity* (1 Cor 13:12), but to all the elect he always displays the invisible grace of his presence. Therefore it is properly said of the display of his presence: **See, he stands behind our wall**, because he doubtless abides with us (or, I should rather say, he abides in us) in such a way that he is invisible to us, as John attests when he says: *No one has ever seen God; if we love one another, God abides in us, and his charity is perfected in us* (1 Jn 4:12). Now the wall that shuts us off from the sight of him is the work of that mortality that we acquired by sinning. In our first parent we were made in such a way that if we had never consented to sin then all of us who are elect would always have perceived the light of divine contemplation tirelessly and with no effort, but now only a very few of the more perfect are able to see it when through the utmost effort their hearts are purified in faith. But in this wall the divine mercy makes windows and lattices through which he watches us, because when our minds were weighed down, as it were, with the blindness of this world he disclosed the grace of his knowledge to us, and he frequently refreshes us with the light of his secret inspiration.

---

9. Appearing in the flesh, the Lord rouses the church to preaching since the long winter of infidelity is over, and with portents of what is to happen he commands her to apprehend and refute the foul crafts of heretics.

And since the blessed Creator most of all desires for the sight of this inspiration to call us from the love of temporal things so that we may attain the joys of heavenly peace, it is rightly added: **And my beloved says to me: Arise, make haste, my friend, my dove, my fair one, and come** (Sg 2:10). *Everything has its season, and in their times all things pass under heaven.* (Eccl 3:1) Thus the bride of Christ (namely, the church or every elect soul) has a time to rest, and another time to arise and go to work. Accordingly, above he adjured the daughters of Jerusalem not to arouse or awaken her until she wished, and now he commands her instead to arise and come to him in haste. He is no longer willing to come to her on a couch flowering, as it were, with heavenly pursuits, but (as the following canticles indicate) he is commanding her rather to go out with him to tend the vineyards and to drive the hostile animals away from them. In order to excite and inflame her zeal, he adds that the warmth of spring promotes active labor once the winter winds are gone, and that the arrival of the birds of spring and their song makes country places more pleasant than palaces, while the growth of flowers offers farmers the hope of fruit to come.

But since we have already drawn a few things together from the surface of the letter, let us now turn to write of the meanings that can be extracted from the allegory. It was described above under the figure of wild goats and young deer how the Lord discloses the profundities of heavenly secrets in the contemplation of things above, and under the figure of his standing behind our wall and watching through the windows and lattices it was described how even though he remains invisible he frequently illumines the whole church out of regard for its life-giving compunction. It is now left to be shown how he incites her to the office of preaching or to the practice of good works. **Arise**, he says, **make haste, my friend, my dove, my fair one, and come**. "Arise from that bed which is so very agreeable to you, in which you delight to devote yourself to psalms and prayers and other pursuits of life; make haste and come in order to apply yourself also to your neighbor's welfare through the practice of zealous preaching." For whenever we perform works of virtue for his sake, it is as though we are making haste with so many steps to the Lord, who is calling us.

For now the winter is past, the rain is over and gone, the flowers appear on the earth (Sg 2:11–12). This is what the Apostle says: *The night is passed, and the day is drawing near; let us then lay aside the works of darkness and put on the armor of light* (Rom 13:12). For the shadows of night, as well as the harshness of winter and rains, represent the tempest of infidelity that covered the whole world until the time of the Lord's incarnation; but when the Sun of righteousness dawned upon the world to disperse and drive away the wintry infidelity and falsehood of former times, flowers appeared on the earth because from that time the beginnings of the infant church were evident in the faithful and pious devotion of the saints.

The time of pruning is come (Sg 2:12), namely, of that which the Lord mentions in the gospel, when after he has said that he is the true vine and his Father is the vine-dresser, he immediately goes on to say: *Every branch in me that bears no fruit he takes away, and every one that bears fruit he will purge to make it bear more fruit* (Jn 15:2). The function of pruning is also rightly understood in accordance with what the Apostle says: *Stripping yourselves of the old self with its deeds, clothe yourselves with the new* (Col 3:9–10); which he explains elsewhere when he says: *So then, putting away every falsehood, let every one of you speak the truth to your neighbor* (Eph 4:25); and again: *Thieves must not steal anymore; rather let them labor, working with their hands that which is good* (Eph 4:28).

The voice of the turtledove is heard in our land (Sg 2:12). The voice of the preacher is heard in the land that already began to be ours as soon as it received the word of faith. It is also spoken of in the psalm for the first day after the Sabbath[34] (that is, for the Lord's resurrection, which took place on the first day after the Sabbath): *The land is the Lord's, and the fullness thereof* (Ps 24:1; Vulg. 23:1). Since its sound signifies the end of winter and the coming of spring, the voice of the turtledove is suitable for those who know how to say that *the darkness is passing away and the true light is already shining* (1 Jn 2:8). And since it humbly expresses itself in song with a resounding sigh, the voice of the turtledove corresponds to those who as resident aliens remember the homeland promised to them and are accustomed to say: *But we ourselves, who have the firstfruits of the Spirit, sigh within ourselves while we wait for adoption as children and the redemption of our body* (Rom 8:23), who also cry out to those who hear them: *Lament and mourn and weep; let your laughter be turned into sorrow and your joy into lamentation* (Jas 4:9). This bird, because it is a lover of chastity that always tarries on the heights of the mountains and in the tops of the trees, imitates the life of those who declare to themselves and to their own that *it is good for a man not to touch a woman* (1 Cor 7:1), and that *our conversation is in heaven* (Phil 3:20); for anything that avoids human dwellings and conversation and prefers to live in woods and wildernesses holds forth a type of those whose minds are separated from the world even though their bodies are in the world, and who long to see rather the things that are above.

The fig tree has put forth its green figs (Sg 2:13). Green figs are the ones that are early and immature and inedible, which fall to the ground if they are shaken even lightly. And the fig tree put forth its green figs at the sound of the turtledove when the apostles who were preaching in Judea and the synagogue put forth many who had a zeal for God but not according to knowledge (Rom 10:2), who preferred to hold to the imperfect and, as it were, still immature observance of the letter of the law rather than to receive the sweetness of spiritual understanding that it contains.

Apponius expounded this verse as meaning that the fig tree put forth its green figs when the synagogue produced apostles who were begotten from her to serve believers with the sweetest food of doctrine.[35]

But regardless of whether the synagogue put forth apostles who preached the gospel or those who still strove to prefer the ceremonies of the law to the gospel, what followed then was faith and salvation for the whole world. Therefore it is rightly added:

The vines blossom and give forth their fragrance (Sg 2:13). Surely the blossoming of the vines represents the beginnings of the churches that were propagated from the one in Jerusalem, which was the first to be planted, and their fragrance represents the fame of those [churches] that spread far and wide. For what is more pleasant than the fragrance of a vine in blossom? For the juice extracted from their blossoms makes a kind of drink conducive to both health and enjoyment. Who does not readily see that it is comparable to the fame of good work? Therefore the example of vines that produce *wine to gladden the human heart* (Ps 104:15; Vulg. 103:15) is suited both to the churches of the faithful in general and particularly to those among the elect who bear in themselves the fruit of joy and spiritual delight in accordance with that [saying] of the Apostle: *This is our glory, the testimony of our conscience* (2 Cor 1:12); and as the psalmist says: *All the glory of the king's daughter is within* (Ps 45:13; Vulg. 44:14).

St. Jerome expounds these verses in this way: *The voice of the turtledove is heard in our land. The turtledove, a bird most chaste that always lives in high places, is a type of the Savior;* and a little later, *and as soon as turtledove calls to turtledove, the fig tree put forth its green figs, that is, they lopped off the precepts of the old law, and the vines blossoming from the gospel gave forth* their *fragrance.*[36]

On the Song of Songs
Book 2

Arise, my friend, my bride, and come, my dove, into the clefts of the rock, into the hollows of the wall (Sg 2:13–14). If, according to the Apostle's exposition, *the rock was Christ* (1 Cor 10:4), what are the clefts of the rock except the wounds that Christ endured for our salvation? Surely the dove settles down and builds her nest in these clefts when each gentle soul or the whole church considers the Lord's passion as the only hope for her salvation, and when in the sacrament of his death she believes herself to be protected from the snares of the ancient enemy as from the preying of a hawk, and by means of the same [sacrament] is also engaged in producing offspring for [the Lord], whether in the form of spiritual children or of virtues. For this reason, when Jeremiah is recalling heretics under the guise of Moab to the unity of the church's faith, he says: *Leave the cities and live on the rock, O inhabitants of Moab! Be like the dove that builds its nest on the highest mouth of a cleft* (Jer 48:28). Now a wall for the protection of vineyards is customarily constructed out of stones, for which reason it is said in the song of Isaiah:[1] *My beloved had a vineyard on a hill in a fertile place, and I surrounded it with a wall* (Is 5:1–2, Old Latin); therefore [the wall] signifies the guard of celestial powers with which the Lord surrounds his vineyard the church so that it may not be ravaged by unclean spirits invading as though they were fierce beasts. For on this account the psalmist says: *The angel of the Lord encamps around those who fear him, and shall deliver them* (Ps 34:7; Vulg. 33:8); and concerning angels the Apostle says: *Are they not all ministering spirits, sent to serve for the sake of those who are to receive the inheritance of salvation?* (Heb 1:14). In this wall, then, Christ's bride and friend finds refuge like a dove in a hollow, so long as holy church knows that she is being defended by the angelic host against the deceptions of the devil. And so the Lord exhorts the same church, as he exhorts every soul devoted to him, to the exercise of conscientious and productive labor, and he says: **Arise, make haste, my friend, my dove, my fair one, and come, for now the winter is past** (Sg 2:10–11), and the rest until he says, **Arise, my friend, my bride, and come, my dove, into the clefts of the rock, into the hollows of the wall**, as if he were to say openly, "When the storm of heathen life has been banished by heavenly kindness, when the flowers of wholesome conduct have already come forth on the earth, when the unjust have begun to be separated from the just, and vices from virtues by the sickle of learned discretion in the manner of a heavenly vine being separated for drinking[2] by zealous vinedressers, when the herald of salvation has already resounded far and wide in the world, when the world itself has been converted to knowledge of the truth and the most agreeable report of new life has been spread throughout the nations, I entreat you, O faithful soul, O company of faithful souls that I love so much, to whom I have brought tokens of my friendship, whom I have considered worthy of being united to me as a bride, to whom I have imparted simplicity of mind through the infusion of my dove-like Spirit, for the sake of whose health and life I have endured wounds and death, to whom I have granted the help of heavenly protection against invisible enemies, I entreat you, I say, do not allow the effects of such gifts as those you possess to grow slack in idle loafing, but hasten rather to prepare yourself with industry and zeal for the battle that is necessary for the sake of eternal rest."

Show me your face; let me hear your voice (Sg 2:14). "You who desire to hide yourself in the concealment of secret repose like a dove in the clefts of a rock or in the hollows of a wall, I beseech you to come forth into the public place of action, show your faith by works (Jas 2:18), and reveal your interior beauty as an example for others on the outside as well. For as the one who sees the innermost places of the heart, I judge that your face is being shown to me at the time when I determine that your activity in service of your neighbors is shown to be *without spot or wrinkle or anything of that kind* (Eph 5:27); for as long as anyone does it to one of the least of these, one does it to me (Mt 25:40–45). And let me hear your voice, namely the voice of praise or preaching; that is, the one that either praises me in psalms and hymns and spiritual songs (Col 3:16) or through its preaching calls upon the neighbors' mouths and minds to praise me." Therefore, the bride shows her face to the Lord in those works that she performs directly in his sight, and she shows her voice to him in the things that she says profitably before him. Again, we should attentively consider what he says: "**Show me your face**," he says, "your own (that is, holy and immaçulate), not that of another; for surely I made it literally so by washing it clean in water, and through the anointing of the Holy Spirit I made it perfectly so by signing upon you the light of my countenance (Ps 4:6; Vulg. 4:7). And let me hear your voice (that is, the one that I taught you to use on the day of your testimony, the one with which you promised me to preserve your chastity), not that of another." Again: "Show me your face, let me hear your voice; remember to show your face to me and not to others, to let your voice be heard by me and not by others." That is, "Take care to do good works and speak holy words for the sake of my love, and not for any other reason." For those whose good deeds or words are expended for the sake of human favors show the beauty of their faces or the sweetness of their voices to strangers, rather than to the Creator. But also, according to the letter, women who are at pains to deceive fools by embellishing their bodily appearance and making their words softer than oil (Ps 55:21; Vulg. 54:22) are transgressors against this commandment of the Lord, and on that account they remain excluded as undeserving of that praise with which the Lord glorifies his bride when he adds:

For your voice is sweet, and your face is comely (Sg 2:14). Sweet indeed to the Lord is the voice of that soul for whom he knows it to be sweet either to proclaim the words of the Lord to her neighbor or to resound herself with praises to the Lord with the prophet: *How sweet are your words to my throat, more than honey to my mouth* (Ps 119:103; Vulg. 118:103). And the face that appears comely to the Lord is the one that is eager to show herself worthy to see his own face, who is accustomed to say to him from the depths of her heart: *My face has sought you; your face, Lord, will I seek; do not turn your face away from me* (Ps 27:8–9; Vulg. 26:8–9). But concern for our cleanliness is not enough unless we are also able to correct as far as possible those who go astray, and unless we are careful to defend weaker ones against their snares.

Catch us the little foxes that ruin the vines, for our vine is in blossom (Sg 2:15). Surely the foxes that ruin the vines are the heretics and schismatics who try as much as possible to tear up the blossoming vines of Christ (that is, the immature minds of the faithful) with the tooth of false doctrine. Would that we had never known them! Therefore, Christ commanded his bride, with her attendants whom he is accustomed to call "daughters to Jerusalem" (that is, with the preachers eminent in holy humility), to catch the little foxes (that is, she should strive with conscientious labor to capture and subdue the subtleties of the deceitful as soon as they begin), since as time goes by and they grow larger it will be all the more difficult to keep them from injuring his spiritual vines, the longer the time that they have been feeding upon them. And pleasingly did he first say "vines" in the plural, and then put it in the singular, **for our vine is in blossom;** for he refers to many vines as being one vine, in the same way that he desires the many churches throughout the world to be one church in him. Surely he said that the vines are in blossom in order to show that communities of the elect are multiplying far and wide. And after he had advised her to catch the foxes, it was appropriate that he should then use the term "vine" in the singular, in order to teach that heretics must be thoroughly hunted down and driven out, lest the church's faith, which ought to be one, should be divided and torn to pieces by their molestation. Now the nature of foxes aptly agrees with the manners and words of heretics, for they are exceedingly devious animals, to be sure, that hide themselves in ditches or caves and when they come out they *never* run *along straight paths but in twisting circles.*[3] It is easy for anyone to understand how these things correspond with the deceptions and deceits of heretics. Nor should we neglect to mention that when he is speaking to the daughters of the church he does not say, "Catch for yourselves," or "your vine is in blossom," but he says: **Catch us the little foxes that ruin the vines, for our vine is in blossom**, so that on this account he may more fully arouse all those who are able to subdue or correct the wickedness of heretics or bad catholics, by indicating that in doing this they are serving him, and by showing that he himself rewards the conscientious labors of those who guard the vineyard that is his own.

---

10. Being well-disposed toward the Lord's commands, the church very frequently prays for him to come to her aid through the grace of secret inspiration.

Thus it is for good reason that his friend and bride then responds to this sort of affection from him with a dove-like simplicity of heart: **My beloved is mine and I am his; he feeds among the lilies** (Sg 2:16). The meaning of this reply is as vast as its expression is brief. For one can rightly understand it as: **My beloved is mine and I am his**, meaning that "We are joined to one another in true and sincere love"; and also as: "**My beloved is mine**, since he has given me such words of his divine exhortation, consolation, and promise, **and I am his**, since in my conduct I always offer a face that is clean, and in my speech, a voice that is pure and graceful." But since pronouns have a great deal of force, it can also very properly be understood as follows. The church (that is, the whole company of the elect) says: "**My beloved is mine**, and there is no one else for me," and again: "**My beloved is mine**, and he belongs to no other"; this you understand as meaning that he shows the perpetual favor of his love, and she gives fruit in return. "**And I am his**, in that I desire no other; I who am his, not belonging to some other crowd of people"; this you understand as being always closely joined [to him] in complete devotion to humility and obedience. Now aptly congruent with all these meanings is that which follows, **he feeds among the lilies;** that is, he is accustomed to take pleasure in the fairest and sweetest fragrance of my virtues, he delights in the most agreeable crop of churches blooming throughout the world. For it is the case that the holy church universal is sometimes designated by the name "lilies" in the plural, and sometimes by that of one lily. For he says **as a lily among thorns, so is my love among daughters** (Sg 2:2), just as the same church, which is never anything but one, is represented by a plurality of vines when he says, **the vines blossom** (Sg 2:13), and also by a vine in the singular when he added, **for our vine is in blossom** (Sg 2:15). For it is said in the singular that *the multitude of believers* is *of one heart and* *soul* (Acts 4:32), and on the other hand it is most aptly announced in the plural that the same faithful unity of heart and soul is not held only by a few, but by the multitude of believers. Now we should note as well in this place that lilies, which are used to heal limbs scorched by fire,[4] also correspond to the deeds of the saints, for if the flames of vices happen to overtake the hearts of the faithful to burn them, [the saints] immediately apply the healing relief of neighborly love to them, and so that they will not be consumed by the fire of lust or luxury or pride or wrath or the heat of other evil deeds, [the saints] diligently care for them by supplying the cooling relief of their own consolation and exhortation. Some interpret the Lord's feeding "among the lilies" to mean "among the fairest choirs of virgins,"[5] and rightly so, because they are both radiant on the outside with the chastity of their flesh, and distinguished on the inside by the unblemished splendor of their heart. Again, the Lord feeds among the lilies (that is, among the most pleasing virtues or companies of the saints) for the very same reason that he is born among them, because he who is the *Mediator between God and humankind* (1 Tm 2:5) has willed to become one nature with his church; whence the same church is also accustomed to be called his body (1 Cor 12:27), and *he is the head of the body, the church* (Col 1:18). He is born among the lilies when the number of the faithful in the church is increased through the font of rebirth, and he feeds among the lilies when the faithful who are truly his members make progress in the love of things above by means of the most illustrious examples of the faithful who have gone before. And we should note that here the beloved is said to feed himself, while above the bride said that he was feeding others: **Show me, you whom my soul loves, where you pasture [your flock], where you lie down at midday** (Sg 1:7; Vulg. 1:6). Surely he is fed in us, because we are his body and limbs from his limb; he feeds us, because he is our head, concerning whom every one of us rightly boasts when we say: *Now my head is lifted up above my enemies* (Ps 27:6; Vulg. 27:6), which you understand as meaning that we too will soon be lifted up and gathered together into our head. And since this feeding of the Lord that takes place in the progress of the saints extends until the end of this age, when they will surely attain that vision of him beyond which they will have no further progress to make, it is rightly added:

Until the day breathes and the shadows retire (Sg 2:17), that is, until the dawning of the eternal light of the age to come and the departure of the retiring shadows of this present life of ignorance and error, in which we faithful grope for a while in darkness, even though we have the lamp of God's word. For not long after that day desired by all nations begins to breathe (that is, to show itself), the Lord who has been feeding among the lilies (that is, among the assemblies of the saints) will then refresh them in turn with the vision of his eternal glory. *I shall be satisfied*, it says, *when your glory appears* (Ps 17:15; Vulg. 16:15); and *Blessed are you who are hungry now, for you will be satisfied* (Lk 6:21). This comparison of the present life with the shadows of night and the life to come with the day is not contrary to the Apostle's saying in which he testifies concerning this life that we now lead, saying: *The night is passed, and the day has drawn near* (Rom 13:12); for, to speak briefly, this present life of the faithful in which they lay aside *the works of darkness* and put on *the armor of light* (Rom 13:12) is day in comparison with [the life] of the unfaithful, who know nothing of the true light and love it not, but it is still darkest night in comparison with [the life] of future blessedness, in which the true light is contemplated without end. But because holy church acknowledges two spiritual lives in this age—one active, the other contemplative—it happens that divine scripture is accustomed to speak sometimes of one, sometimes of the other, and sometimes of both at once. Thus, further above it makes mention of the contemplative [life] when it says of the Lord: **Look, he comes, leaping upon the mountains, bounding over the hills. My beloved is like a wild goat or a young deer** (Sg 2:8–9), and then it begins to speak of the active [life]: **See, he stands behind our wall** (Sg 2:9) and the rest until it says: **Catch us the little foxes that ruin the vines, for our vine is in blossom** (Sg 2:15). All of these things are properly distributed so as to arouse us for the duty of good work. Later, it added concerning both [lives] at the same time: **My beloved is mine and I am his; he feeds among the lilies until the day breathes and the shadows retire** (Sg 2:16–17). Thus the beloved feeds among the lilies in both lives, because the Lord is delighted and refreshed in his members both exteriorly, in the pure deeds of his elect, and interiorly, in their sweet contemplation of things eternal. And this [continues] until the day of true light breathes, for at that time we will no longer labor in good works, nor, since we are to be made perfect suddenly and in an instant, will we contemplate heavenly things *through a mirror and in obscurity* (1 Cor 13:12), but for eternity the whole church at once will see the King of heaven in his beauty (Is 33:17). Since every foretaste of this vision, however small, gives no small delight to the bride of Christ, it is aptly added:

Turn, my beloved, be like a wild goat or a young deer on the mountains of Bether (Sg 2:17). "You have awakened me," she says, "and called me forth to cultivate the vineyards (that is, to instruct the company of the faithful and increase their number); you have commanded me to drive away the loathsome subtleties of those who are like little foxes attacking those vineyards; you have wanted me to show you my face and let you hear my voice when you promise to show me how to know you in part, even though I do not yet see your face clearly, and when you speak to me as if through windows and lattices. I entreat you, then, to turn from instructing all in general in order to enlighten the hearts of the perfect to a higher degree, and just as the sight of a wild goat or a young deer in the mountains is rare indeed but brings delight to those who gaze upon it, let some traces of your greatness be present in the loftiest minds. I pray that you will allow some who are still on the way to see, even if only from afar, the sweetness of immortal life that you promise to give as a reward to all your members." Now when it says **on the mountains of Bether**, the name "mountains" also corresponds to the minds of those who have learned to open the eyes of the heart for the contemplation of heavenly things. For "Bether" is interpreted as "house arising" or "house of night-watches,"[6] and it is right that those whose souls rise up more eagerly than others in their desire for heavenly things, and who keep watch more zealously in order to comprehend them, should understand the heavenly secrets to a higher degree than the rest. But if it is read, as some codices have it, "upon the mountains of Bethel" (that is, God's house), there is absolutely nothing to dispute about. For it is surely evident that the hearts of the just are rightly called "mountains of God's house," doubtless to distinguish them from the mountains of Samaria and Esau and others of that sort (that is, those of heretics and of all the proud). In another version we see written a Latin name for this: "upon the mountains of nectars and spices." This too corresponds to the minds of the saints, which are not dried up with superfluous thoughts but are like aromatic trees always supplied with the wholesome nectars of inner sweetness and charity, which nectars and spices this book very often signifies under the name of "tower of myrrh" and "aloes" and other things of that sort.

---

11. The church of the Gentiles relates how she in turn came to faith in Christ. Rejoicing in her prayers, he commands the faithful not to disturb her repose.

But since lovers of the truth come not only from among the Jews but also from the Gentiles, and one church of the faithful is gathered together from the two peoples, it remains for this song of love to relate specifically that after Judea's calling and sweetest colloquy with her Redeemer, the Gentiles also will in their turn come to the knowledge of their salvation to such a degree that once it is acquired they will hold fast to it with love. Thus there follows the voice of the church chosen from among the Gentiles:

Upon my bed at night I sought him whom my soul has loved; I sought him but found him not; I will rise and go about the city, through the streets and squares; I will seek him whom my soul has loved; I have sought him and found him not (Sg 3:1–2). "For a long while," she says, "I have with great diligence sought the Lord whom my soul now loves completely; I loved him even then, though I did not yet know him, inasmuch as I loved the principles of wisdom, truth, and divine worship. But since I sought him on my bed (that is, while still subject to the enticements of my flesh), since I sought him by night (that is, in the darkness of profound ignorance, for there was no angel or prophet or any reliable teacher at all to show me the light of divine knowledge), I was by no means able to find him whom I sought. For when I ascertained that in reality I would never acquire the truth that I was seeking by my own ingenuity, I proposed in my soul to rise up from the bed of carnal desires, prepare for the hard work of life-giving investigation, go about on the lands and on the sea, undertake instruction both publicly and privately from all those whom I might hear to be wiser, and inquire diligently if I might find any true wisdom and any certainty anywhere that would lead to eternal blessedness. But although with a great deal of effort I traveled through the world discerning the words of those who are wise, I could learn nothing certain or reliable about the way of truth." Now these [words] of the Gentiles testify that they longed to know God, desiring him but not yet knowing him. In their searching after truth and wisdom, the schools of the philosophers[7] traversed many lands and produced as many books, as that scripture testifies that says: *Now the Athenians and all the foreigners living there would spend their time in nothing but telling or hearing something new* (Acts 17:21). The Apostle's statement testifies to this when he says while arguing in the same court of the Athenians: *As I went about and looked at your idols, I found also an altar on which was written "To an unknown god." What therefore you worship in ignorance, this I proclaim to you. The God who made the world and everything that is in it, since this one is Lord of heaven and earth he does not dwell in temples made by hand* (Acts 17:23–24). Also testifying to this is the devotion of Cornelius the centurion, who learned to seek knowledge from God through divine worship, prayers, and alms (Acts 10:2). Again, testifying to this is the Ethiopian who came from the ends of the earth to the temple of the Lord to appeal to one whom he did not know how to worship, and who burned with so much love of the truth of which he was ignorant that while he was sitting in his chariot he was applying himself to reading those things that common report frequently considered to be divine (Acts 8:27–28); but the Lord, who saw how long this person had been persistent in searching for the truth, finally deigned to reveal himself to the seeker at last, and the one who had inspired him to seek granted that he might find, in accordance with what he himself had already promised long ago, saying through the prophet: *When the poor and needy seek water, and there is none, and their tongue is parched with thirst, I the Lord will hear them, I the God of Israel will not forsake them. I will open rivers on the sloping mountains and fountains in the midst of the plains* (Is 41:17–18). These fountains are doubtless those of which the thirsting psalmist spoke: *As the deer longs for fountains of water, so longs my soul for you, O God* (Ps 42:1; Vulg. 41:2), and these rivers are those which [the Lord] himself promised to the faithful, saying: *As scripture says, "From the belly of the one who believes in me shall flow rivers of living water*" (Jn 7:38; cf. Is 44:2–3, Zech 14:8). And for this reason there is rightly added:

The sentinels who guard the city found me: "Have you seen him whom my soul has loved?" (Sg 3:3). Surely the sentinels who guard the city are the heralds of truth, who are always vigilant with dutiful attention to guard the holy church that is spread throughout the entire world, and who persevere in preaching the word, lest she be corrupted by faithless persons. These, then, are the ones who found the Gentiles attentive to the search for truth and showed them what they were seeking: Philip, who disclosed the light of the gospel to the eunuch and taught him to understand the words of the prophet that he was reading (Acts 8:29–35); Peter, who imbued Cornelius and his household with the heavenly grace that he so greatly desired (Acts 10); Paul, who made God known among the Athenians who were worshiping him in ignorance (Acts 17:16–31); and all those who have revealed the presence of the Creator to those who have been seeking and desiring it for so long. For the Gentiles who were going to be transformed by Christ's gift into his bride said as if to the sentinels of the city: **"Have you seen him whom my soul has loved**?" when they willingly undertook to listen to the teachers who were coming to them and eagerly sought to discern whether the way that they were preaching was true.

Scarcely had I passed them by, when I found him whom my soul has loved (Sg 3:4). Whoever wishes to enjoy the doctrine of truth ought not to approach it hastily and carelessly, for one who desires to find her beloved needs to pass very skillfully by those who preach in his name and consort familiarly with their assemblies, so that she may thereby deserve to attain to the knowledge of him that they preach nearer by; for we also say that we have "passed by" a book that we have read through to the end. For this same reason the angel said to Daniel about the mysteries he had seen: *Many shall be passing by, and knowledge shall be multiplied* (Dan 12:4). Therefore it says: **Scarcely had I passed them by, when I found him whom my soul has loved**. For the seeker of truth should pass by the sentinels—which is, as we have said, to associate with the assemblies of faithful teachers, to unite with them, and to pass through their sayings and writings by frequent meditation. This happens just a little while after one finds the beloved whom one has been seeking, which accords with the voice of Paul and Isaiah: *The Lord will make the word shortened on the earth* (Rom 9:28; cf. Is 10:23). Of course, he himself says: *The one who believes and is baptized will be saved* (Mk 16:16), and concerning him the Apostle says: *But what does it say? "The word is near, in your mouth" (that is, the word of faith that we preach); because if you confess with your mouth that Jesus is Lord and believe that God raised him from the dead, you will be saved* (Rom 10:8–9; cf. Dt 30:14).

I held him and will not let him go until I bring him into my mother's house, and into the chamber of her that gave birth to me (Sg 3:4). "Having taken so long to find the one I was seeking," she says, "I held him all the more earnestly once he was found. I declare openly that I will never let him go, but I intend always to persevere and advance so greatly in loving him that I will endeavor to recall also the synagogue, through whom I heard the word and received the ministry of rebirth, to faith in his name." For it is certain that at the end of the age Judea will accept the faith that she now fights against faithlessly, which surely cannot take place except through the teaching and ministry of those from among the Gentiles who are found faithful. For the Apostle plainly says: *A partial blindness has come upon Israel, until the fullness of the Gentiles has come in. And so all Israel will be saved* (Rom 11:25–26). However, when the church says, **I held him and will not let him go until I bring him into my mother's house, and into the chamber of her that gave birth to me**, we should not understand this as though she will let Christ go after she furnishes the people of the synagogue with the ability to believe in his name, but rather as though it means that she loves him with such affection and desires the things that belong to him with such great diligence that she intends to make the kindred people subject to him also, in accordance with that [saying] of the psalmist: *Our eyes look to the Lord our God, until he has mercy upon us* (Ps 123:2; Vulg. 122:2). For there is no reason to lift one's eyes to God in order to beg for mercy when one has already returned them to oneself after having received that same mercy, except that the greatest proof of having received mercy is for someone's eyes to be always intent upon God, and for that person to be contemplating his glory without end. Now we should note that according to the letter the sequence [of events] in this chapter was also fulfilled in Mary Magdalene, who contains a type of the church. For when the Lord, whom she had loved with her whole mind while he was alive, was taken away from her sight by death and the grave, she was in fact so possessed by love of him that she sought him on his bed in order that the memory of him might not grow faint in her breast when his members were laid to rest (Mk 16:1–6; Jn 20:11–18). She sought him for the two nights during which he was resting in the grave, but she did not find him because the time had not yet come for him to rise again. Early in the morning she got up and came to the tomb with spices, seeking him eagerly, but it happened that she did not immediately find him whom she was seeking, for some of those angels who protect the church found her first. She asked them about the Lord, and when she heard that he had arisen, she was able to see him at last. She held him and would not let him go farther, realizing that he had truly conquered death. But she also hastened to bring him into her mother's house, because in the congregation of disciples who had preceded her in Christ and aroused her to devotion by their examples, she proclaimed that he had risen from the dead. There follows:

I adjure you, O daughters of Jerusalem, by the wild goats and the stags of the fields: do not arouse or awaken the beloved until she wishes (Sg 3:5). If we remember the verses above, we will not read these as meaning that the bride went peacefully to sleep, but rather that springing out of bed she was able with a great deal of laborious seeking to find her beloved. And why does that same beloved now adjure the daughters of Jerusalem not to arouse or awaken her, unless perhaps it is as if the soul has fallen into a most happy sleep because she has learned how to be at rest in the divine love? For just as someone who is sleeping closes the eyes of the body against exterior things and quite frequently opens the eyes of the heart in a vision of things that are secret, so doubtless in like manner does the mind devoted to heavenly love separate itself from concern about visible things in order to stay awake more perfectly and unrestrictedly for the contemplation of things invisible. Nor should we marvel that love, which turns the mind's attention away from a craving for visible things and toward those invisible things that it ought to desire, should be compared to sleep, since it is also compared to death itself when this same song says: **Love is**

strong as death (Sg 8:6), for just as death kills the body, so also does the inner life of charity cut it off from exterior pleasures. For this reason the daughters of Jerusalem (that is, all the souls of the faithful who already long for the fellowship of the citizens of heaven) are rightly adjured not to arouse the beloved (that is, not to distract the mind devoted to God from its attention to heavenly desires through relentless interruption). This can also be rightly understood with reference to the whole church, for to disturb her peace is contrary to the will of Christ.

Since we have already discussed these things above at length, let it suffice for us to treat them rather briefly now. This much, at least, the reader will remember: that the reason this verse is repeated in the song of love is so that the Lord might indicate that he was no less concerned for the church gathered from the Gentiles than for that gathered from the Jews, but was equally desirous that each of them should be at peace, since in both of them there was brought together his one household and family, most beloved and holy. At one time [the Christians in] Judea actually believed that they alone were loved by God, and that the word of salvation had been entrusted only to them and not to the uncircumcised Gentiles as well. Luke bears witness to this when he says: *Now the apostles and the believers who were in Judea heard that the Gentiles had also accepted the word of God. So when Peter had gone up to Jerusalem, those who were of the circumcision disputed with him, saying, "Why did you go in to uncircumcised men and eat with them?"* (Acts 11:1–3); and in another place: *Now on the following Sabbath almost the whole city gathered to hear the word of God. But when the Jews saw the crowds, they were filled with jealousy; and they contradicted the words that Paul was speaking* (Acts 13:44–45). Thus it is also right for us to understand the fact that he adjures the daughters of Jerusalem not to arouse the beloved as meaning that he commands those from among the Jews who were the predecessors in faith that they should not disturb or contradict the salvation of those from the circumcision who come to faith together with them. And when it says, **until she wishes**, this can be understood as meaning that the church of the Gentiles would voluntarily subject herself to vigils and labors for the Lord's sake.

12. The synagogue marvels at the church's faith, which is unexpectedly devoted to the mortification of the flesh and the virtue of prayer.

Wherefore the voice of the same daughters of Jerusalem adds in admiration that the grace of the Holy Spirit has been poured out among the nations: **Who is she that comes up through the wilderness, like a column of smoke from aromatic spices**? (Sg 3:6). "Who is she," they say, "who deserves such praise and wonder? She has not been purified by the mystery of circumcision, nor has she yet been washed in the font of rebirth, but even so she has already been perfumed with the grace of the Holy Spirit; already she speaks in tongues and magnifies God! (Acts 10:45–46). We never recall this having happened among our nation, from which came the fathers who received the covenant of circumcision, and us who received the washing of baptism." **She that comes up through the wilderness**. She ascends from base desires to the heights of virtue, lifting her eyes to the eternal mountains (Ps 121:1; Vulg. 120:1)—or rather, lifting them up and longing to attain to him who dwells in heaven (Ps 123:1; Vulg. 122:1). Now she comes through the wilderness; that is, through the midst of those nations that were not fertile enough to produce the fruits of virtue, to whom came no prophet from God's people, no patriarch, no angel to instruct them in the worship that leads to a better life. Her faith, therefore, is all the more wonderful in that she so very recently came to know and accept it unequivocally, in accordance with what the Lord himself testifies in praise of her, saying: *I know where you are living, where Satan's throne is. Yet you are holding fast to my name, and you have not denied faith in me* (Rv 2:13). Now this was said as an example of the Israelite people who were freed from the darkness of servitude in Egypt and came up by way of the wilderness to the land of promise. For this reason the wilderness can also be rightly understood in a positive sense, as representing that way of life which is separated from the charms of the world in order to be completely devoted to the study of God's law and the observation of the heavenly precepts; which so hungers and thirsts for justice (Mt 5:6) that it feeds only on the manna of the heavenly word (Dt 8:3) and drinks only from the fountain that flows out of the spiritual rock (1 Cor 10:4), to whom she eagerly and ardently sings: *My soul thirsts for you in so many ways, and my flesh also: in the wilderness, and where there is no road, and where there is no water* (Ps 63:1; Vulg. 62:2–3). Therefore the church comes up through the wilderness so that she may come into the kingdom that is promised. But the manner of her coming up is also shown, when there is added:

Like a column of smoke from aromatic spices (Sg 3:6). Smoke is known to come from fire, naturally seeking higher places as it is being consumed, and gradually disappearing from human sight. The church goes up in this same fashion when, enkindled by the fire of the Holy Spirit with love of her Creator, she strives with every kind of virtue to reach out for heavenly things and does not cease from what she has begun until, having been drawn away from human things, she is carried off to the invisible joys of life in heaven. And just as it is possible for smoke to divide so that part of it is being produced while at the same time part of it has already been produced and is hastening to realms above, so also, until the end of the age, the church is always being born anew in some of its members through the grace of the Holy Spirit, and in others who were earlier born in God it is always being gathered together unto heaven. Rightly is she compared not simply to smoke that can be diffused in any sort of way, but to a column of smoke, in order to signify both the unity of her faith and her direct ascent to realms above. On the other hand, concerning God's enemies who raise themselves up not in consideration of heavenly desire but only in the arrogance of pride, it is said that as soon as *they are honored and exalted, they vanish; like smoke they vanish away* (Ps 37:20; Vulg. 36:20). And as the lust of the world burns and smokes in the mind of the wicked, so on the contrary does the glowing ardor of virtues burn and smoke in the heart of the good. Therefore, after it said, **like a column of smoke**, rightly did it add:

From aromatic spices of myrrh and frankincense, and all the powders of the perfumer (Sg 3:6). Surely myrrh, which is used to embalm corpses—as the sacred and holy arrangement of things in the Lord's sepulcher certainly shows—points to the continence of the flesh; frankincense, which is customarily burned before God in prayers, expresses the virtue of prayer, as the psalmist also testifies by praying: *Let my prayer*, he says, *be set forth as incense in* *your sight* (Ps 141:2; Vulg. 140:2); "all the powders of the perfumer" represent all the works of virtue, and the reason that they are compared not to whole perfumes but to those that have been reduced to powder is so that we might be admonished to discern with unfailing attention the good things that we do, and to examine them as though with the sieve of careful discernment to make sure that nothing improper remains in them.[8] Now we should note that in referring to aromatic spices it rightly names myrrh first, and then frankincense and all the powders of the perfumer, in accordance with that order in which the Lord also puts them when he says in the gospel: *Let your loins be girt and your lamps burning* (Lk 12:35), which is to say in other words: *Turn from evil and do good* (Ps 34:14; Vulg. 33:15); mortify the desires of the flesh and in your heart offer prayers that are acceptable to God. Therefore the beloved heavenly bride comes up through the wilderness like a column of smoke from aromatic spices of myrrh and frankincense and all the powders of the perfumer because holy church or every perfect soul rises up by daily advancing to greater heights of virtue when she is induced by the flame of charity to render unto the Creator the sweetest ardor of continence and prayer, and indeed of all the fruits of the Spirit. However, it can also rightly be understood that Christ's beloved comes up like a column of smoke from aromatic spices of myrrh and frankincense and all the powders of the perfumer because his one and only church is constituted out of many faithful individuals who blossom with diverse virtues. Some are more like myrrh, earnestly mortifying the desires of the flesh after the example of him who said: *I punish my body and subject it to servitude* (1 Cor 9:27); some are like a form of frankincense, devoting themselves to particularly frequent prayers; still others exert themselves in offering to God the fruits of good works; nevertheless, all are inflamed by the one fire of the Spirit, and like a single column of smoke they seek the heights of a common heavenly life with completely undivided zeal and devotion. The careful reader should not think it antithetical but rather understand it as altogether fitting that the very same beloved is said both to be sleeping and to come up through the wilderness; for she is shown to sleep when the daughters of Jerusalem are adjured not to stir her up, and the daughters of Jerusalem themselves testify in concert that she is coming up, when they continually reply: **Who is she that comes up through the wilderness**? For surely she sleeps and comes up at one and the same time when the soul avoids external cares and carnal desires as much as she can, and also advances through good deeds and thoughts to attain to the vision of her Creator.

---

13. She replies that she has come up to delight in the bed and in the palanquin of the King of peace (that is, in the repose and inner refreshment of souls), and especially in the King's beauty. She calls upon those who are admiring her to perceive his splendor also.

After it says that she comes up through the wilderness, it also indicates whence she comes up, or the reason why she has come up, when it is added in the voice of the very church that is coming up: **Look, it is the bed of Solomon! Surrounding it are sixty strong men of the strongest of Israel** (Sg 3:7), and the rest up until it says: **The ascent of purple; the middle parts he covered with charity for the daughters of Jerusalem** (Sg 3:10). Her ascent is to the bed or the dish of Solomon (that is, of the King of peace,[9] namely, our Lord and Savior)—the bed upon which she rests in eternal peace, and the dish from which she is refreshed without end at the banquets of life. Now the middle parts of his dish to which she ascends are covered with charity in order to encourage her ascending, for although the ascent to it is purple (that is, very bloody from battle), nevertheless the sweetness of charity that it is seen to contain invites the daughters of Jerusalem (that is, the souls of a pious disposition) to ascend to it often. Thus the bed of Solomon is the glory of heavenly blessedness in which the King of peace himself rests forever with his saints. The King's own beloved (that is, the church) daily travels toward this bed through the wilderness of this world; in part she has already arrived, inasmuch as she has sent her faithful ahead toward future rewards, but she will arrive completely when at the end of the age the Creator and King of his heavenly city will gather his elect together from the four winds (Mt 24:31) and, as it is said elsewhere, he will gird himself and have them recline at table, and he will come and serve them (Lk 12:37). But also in this life there is a bed of Solomon in the saints' peaceful way of life, which is hidden away from worldly anxieties, for their struggles with vices have already been suppressed or put to sleep so that their life imitates the felicity of eternal peace. For this reason the prophet says: *And his abode was established in peace, and his dwelling in Sion* (Ps 76:2; Vulg. 75:3)—that is, in the sublime contemplation of blessings to come;[10] and the apostle Peter says: *If you are reproached in the name of Christ, you are blessed, because the Spirit of glory and of God is resting upon you* (1 Pt 4:14).

Now it is aptly consistent with both of these beds that it is said that **surrounding the bed of Solomon are sixty strong men of the strongest of Israel**, because the holy preachers guard the church's present quiet and peace against the attacks of heretics, and with fixed attention the more perfect contemplate the internal rest of the celestial homeland. Therefore it is properly said that strong men surround that bed of the King, and it is properly added a second time **of the strongest of Israel**, since Israel is interpreted as "the man who sees God,"[11] and those who either watch over the present peace of the church through their preaching or look upon her in heaven through contemplation must take care to stay awake, stand firm in the faith, act bravely, be strengthened (1 Cor 16:13), and thus render themselves worthy of the divine vision. **Of the strongest of Israel**, it says, because all those who travel toward the joys of the divine vision are rightly considered as being named Israel. But the strongest among them, as it says, are surely those who are raised up to heaven by the gift of contemplation, or else those who duly undertake to carry out the ministry of preaching. And these are aptly designated by the number sixty, because such as these doubtless expect the denarius of eternal reward for the completion of their good work. For since in six days God completed the preparation of the world and on the seventh rested from his works (Gn 2:1–2), the number seven rightly suggests the day of completed action, for the sake of which one hopes for eternal rest. And anyone who knows how those who labor in Christ's vineyard will receive a denarius for their wages (Mt 20:2) also knows that the rewards for good works are represented by the number ten.

All holding swords, and most expert in warfare (Sg 3:8). They are holding those swords of which the Apostle says: *Take the helmet of salvation and the sword of the Spirit, which is the word of God* (Eph 6:17), and they are most expert in that warfare concerning which the same [Apostle] admonishes, saying: *Put on the armor of God, so that you may be able to stand against the wiles of the devil. For our struggle is not against flesh and blood, but against rulers and powers,* and so on (Eph 6:11–12). And rightly are they most expert, because those who are stationed on earth and confined in the flesh are greatly in need of skill in waging war as they struggle *against the spiritual forces of evil in the heavenly places* (Eph 6:12), and they are greatly in need of skill (or rather, of God's grace) when the frailty of the flesh fights against the [fallen] archangel well versed in warfare for so many thousands of years.

Each of them with his sword upon his thigh because of nighttime terrors (Sg 3:8). Procreation is customarily represented by the thigh of the flesh; wherefore it is written: *And all the souls of those who came out of Jacob's thigh were seventy [in number]* (Exod 1:5). And the soldiers of Christ have swords upon their thighs when they restrain the impulse of carnal desires with the rigor of the spiritual word, and they do this because of nighttime terrors (that is, lest they be overthrown by the snares of the ancient tempter if he should find them careless and unarmed, and lest having been conquered they defile the true Solomon's bed, which they are supposed to be guarding).[12] This can be taken to refer equally to both of those we have called beds of the eternal King (that is, to the present peace of the church and to that which is to come). For the holy teachers are fearful that the condition of the present church might be violated by the darkness of heretics, and those who habitually open their mind's eye to the contemplation of future joys are fearful that the night of demonic disturbance might obscure for them the light of divine revelation. Now if the strongest men of Israel, in whom there is no guile (Jn 1:47) and who are most expert in warfare, if they have their swords upon their thighs because of nighttime terrors, what must I and those like me do? How much more should we serve the Lord in fear, we who are both less expert in spiritual combat and less able to carry out the things we have learned? Our only recourse is to hold fast to him, to put our hope in him who cannot be vanquished, to seek his protection by frequently saying with the prophet: *The Lord is my light and my salvation; whom shall I fear?* (Ps 27:1; Vulg. 26:1). He is our light because he teaches us to wage war, and our salvation because he makes us brave and unconquerable in war; for if we persist in praying, perhaps we too may deserve to hear with that same prophet: *His truth shall surround you as a shield; you shall not be afraid of the nighttime terror* (Ps 91:4–5; Vulg. 90:5).

Some interpret the strong men who surround the bed of Solomon as referring to the angels who contend against the powers of the air for the sake of the peace of holy church.[13] What seems to have slipped their minds is that it says: **Each of them with his sword upon his thigh**. For how do those who have no fleshly nature restrain or cut off the attraction of the flesh with the sword of continence, since they have nothing to resist?

Therefore the church coming from the Gentiles says: **Look, it is the bed of Solomon! Surrounding it are sixty strong men of the strongest of Israel**, and the rest [that follows], as if she were to say plainly: "Why are you amazed, O daughters of Jerusalem (that is, the believers from the Jewish people) that I am coming up through the wilderness as though sweetly perfumed with the oils of virtue? See how peaceable is the King to whose company I am hurrying; his intimate bed of rest that I am hastening to reach is protected from the snares of the wicked and accessible only to the good. But if it pleases you to hear it, I will also describe the multitude of his riches."

King Solomon made himself a palanquin from the wood of Lebanon (Sg 3:9). A palanquin, then, is something that either bears the bodies of those who are sitting or reclining at a banquet, or is used to carry someone about from place to place in order to save time. Holy church is rightly compared to one of these because she both lifts believers up to the feast of eternal blessedness and is herself carried about throughout the whole world by the ministry of her preachers. Now the Lord made himself this palanquin from the wood of Lebanon because he built the church out of souls strong both in mind and in constancy. Surely the wood of Lebanon is greatly renowned for its height, its appearance, and its incorruptible nature.[14]

He made its pillars of silver (Sg 3:10). [Scripture] says: *James, Cephas, and John, who were acknowledged to be pillars* (Gal 2:9). Doubtless he made these pillars of silver because he trained the holy teachers to strengthen the church's faith and to raise her up with the brightness of the heavenly word.

The pillow of gold (Sg 3:10). He made a pillow for the palanquin when he promised the faithful the hope of perpetual rest. He says: *Take my yoke upon you, and learn from me; for I am gentle and humble in heart, and you will find rest for your souls* (Mt 11:29). And he made this pillow of gold because he has prepared for us the divine vision of himself in an eternal rest that is gleaming with glory. For this reason, then, it is said: *Now those who love me will be loved by my Father, and I will love them and reveal myself to them* (Jn 14:21).

The ascent of purple (Sg 3:10). Genuine purple dye is made from the blood of shellfish.[15] Therefore the ascent to Solomon's palanquin is purple because our King and Lord *loved us and washed us in his blood to take away our sins* (Rv 1:5). And nothing but purple is found in the ascent to this palanquin because no one comes into the church without being imbued in the sacraments of the Lord's passion. For this reason he himself says: *Unless you eat the flesh of the Son of Man and drink his blood, you have no life in you. Those who eat my flesh and drink my blood have eternal life, and I will raise them up on the last day* (Jn 6:53–54).

The middle parts he covered with charity for the daughters of Jerusalem (Sg 3:10), evidently with that very charity with which he suffered for our sake; for *no one has greater charity than this, to lay down one's life for one's friends* (Jn 15:13); and as the Apostle says: *But God commends his charity to us in that while we still were sinners Christ died for the ungodly* (Rom 5:8). So he covered the middle parts of his church with this [charity] in the fashion of a coverlet upon which faithful souls may rest in comfort, in that he completely filled her on the inside with the love of heavenly things. And this is what it adds: **for the daughters of Jerusalem**, that is, for the souls burning with desire for heavenly things. For the more God commends his greater charity to us by suffering for our sake, the more he enkindles us to love him in return and to suffer for his sake. The purple ascent can also be understood as referring particularly to those who shed their blood for Christ's sake. Rightly are they said to have ascended to the golden pillow by way of the purple ascent, because they have reached the splendor of perpetual rest by way of the labor of intense tribulation. Aptly suitable to them is what follows: **The middle parts he covered with charity**. For surely the reason that they are ready to shed their blood for the King of heaven is that he himself has inflamed the middle parts of his palanquin (that is, of their hearts) with his own charity. Hence it is appropriate that when the Apostle was describing the purple ascent of [Christ's] palanquin, saying: *But we also glory in tribulations, knowing that tribulation produces patience, and patience trial,* he was careful immediately to add something concerning the golden pillow by saying: *and trial hope, and hope does not confound us,* and finally he concluded with reference to the charity with which the middle parts have been covered: *because God's charity has been poured into our hearts* (Rom 5:3–5). Therefore the church of the Gentiles replies to the amazed daughters of Jerusalem who praise her as she ascends to heaven like a column of smoke from aromatic spices. She explains that she is coming up because the bed of the peaceable King to which she hastens is protected from the attacks of the wicked, and because, even though the ascent to it is steep, she hopes to be refreshed upon his palanquin, which has a pillow shining like gold and middle parts covered with charity. For this reason, she runs in haste to make her ascent, knowing that *those who abide in love abide in God, and God in them* (1 Jn 4:16). Having said these things in a marvelous and pleasing order, after having already expounded the King's gifts to her, she begins to proclaim also his own appearance and his apparel, and she invites everyone to see it. After she herself has been called, she endeavors to call others also to take up the duty of evangelizing when she subsequently adds:

Come, O daughters of Sion, and look at King Solomon (Sg 3:11). Now the daughters of Sion are the same as the daughters of Jerusalem (that is, souls longing for the joys of a heavenly homeland). For Sion is said to mean "watchtower" or "watcher," and Jerusalem "vision of peace";[16] both of these names are appropriate for the residents of that heavenly city in which they both enjoy perpetual peace and always contemplate their Creator's face. **Come**, therefore, **O daughters of Sion, and look at King Solomon**: "Come away from the stormy life of the world so that you can see the King of peace; in thought and deed, come out of the midst of Babylon if you wish to have a place in the heavenly Jerusalem, in accordance with the same true Solomon's command, which says: *Go out from her midst, my people, so that you do not take part in her transgressions*" (Rv 18:4). For this reason also, desiring to separate us from worldly society and to call us forth to heavenly joys, he was willing to suffer outside the city walls for us, as the Apostle also explains very pleasingly and very fully, saying: *Jesus suffered outside the gate in order to sanctify the people by his own blood. Let us then go out to him outside the camp and bear his reproach, for here we have no lasting city, but we are seeking one that is to come* (Heb 13:12–14). And because we confess that our Lord Jesus Christ is not only the true Son of God but also the true Son of Man—eternally begotten as Son of God before the ages, but made Son of Man at the appointed time at the end of the ages—after it is said: **O daughters of Sion, look at King Solomon**, rightly is it immediately added:

In the diadem with which his mother crowned him (Sg 3:11). This is to say openly: "Look at the Lord in his humanity, which he took from the Virgin Mother and placed at the right hand of the Father's majesty." Surely his mother crowned him with a diadem when the blessed and undefiled Virgin conceived by the Holy Spirit and from her own flesh supplied him with the material for the most holy flesh in which he appeared in the world and dwelt among us (Jn 1:14), in which he died so that he might destroy the kingdom of death (Heb 2:14), in which he rose so that he might restore life to us, and which by ascending to heaven he lifted up to the glory of an eternal kingdom. Therefore the daughters of Sion who look at King Solomon in the beauty of his nature also marvel in astonishment at the diadem with which his mother crowned him, because so long as the elect believe and confess that the glory of the Son of God is equal to that of the Father and of the Holy Spirit, they also acknowledge that the human nature he assumed, in which he conquered death's dominion, has been glorified forever—not, to be sure, by the power of its own substance, but through the operation of the Word that assumed it (that is, the only Son of God). Marveling greatly at the vision of his diadem, one of the noblest daughters of Sion who had already come out from the land of earthly concupiscence said: *But we see Jesus, who for a little while was made less than the angels, crowned with glory and honor because of the suffering of death* (Heb 2:9).

On the day of his betrothal and on the day of his heart's gladness (Sg 3:11). At the time of his incarnation he came forth from the Virgin's womb like a bridegroom from his chamber (Ps 19:5;

Vulg. 18:6) to join the church to himself. This was the day of his heart's gladness, because he rejoiced that through his incarnation Providence was going to bring the world to the knowledge and vision of eternal divinity. For this reason it is written of the time when many multitudes were coming to believe in him: *At that hour he exulted in the Holy Spirit and said, "I praise you, Father, Lord of heaven and earth, because you have hidden these things from the wise and prudent and have revealed them to children"* (Lk 10:21). For this reason the Redeemer, who through his own blood brought the human race back to heaven, speaks to the citizens of heaven, saying: *Rejoice with me, for I have found my sheep that was lost* (Lk 15:6). Therefore, since the daughters of Jerusalem were marveling earlier at the coming of the bride, saying, **Who is she that comes up through the wilderness**? and so forth, it is appropriate for her to respond by praising the bed, praising the palanquin of the Bridegroom, and finally praising the Bridegroom himself to whose embrace she was hastening, and to be mindful of the bride's humanity that he took up into God, which the ministry of the pure Mother brought forth when the time came for [the bride's] betrothal, so that she might with justice show that she thirsts after the glory of seeing his divinity, for the sake of which [glory] God himself had taken on the condition of human nature. Then she who had so thoroughly given herself over to the praises of her Redeemer is moved by maternal concern to invite her attendants the daughters of Sion to praise him also, and in return she herself receives from her Bridegroom and Redeemer the praise she deserves.

---

14. Delighting in the church's faith, the Lord commends all her members (that is, each individual person among the faithful) with the praise that is particularly appropriate, and he predicts that the rage of persecutors will turn to regard her for whom he bore the wounds of the cross out of love.

In [the Lord's] voice there is added: **How beautiful you are, my friend, how beautiful** (Sg 4:1). Having said that the church is beautiful, he repeats [the word] "beautiful" because he sees that she is praiseworthy both in action and in proclamation, namely, in the action by which she comes up to him through the wilderness like a column of smoke from aromatic spices, and in the proclamation through which she urges her neighbors to come up and commune with him also, when she says: **Come, O daughters of Sion, and look at King Solomon** (Sg 3:11). And rightly does action come first and proclamation afterward, in accordance with his own example concerning which it is written: *The things that Jesus began to do and to teach* (Acts 1:1).

Your eyes are those of doves apart from that which is concealed within (Sg 4:1). "Excellent and honorable are your faculties for perceiving spiritual things in contemplation; through them you have merited to see and know both my gifts, which you have just expounded, and my diadem, which you have proclaimed." For since (as we have already mentioned) the Holy Spirit appeared in the form of a dove (Mt 3:16), spiritual grace is rightly signified by the name of that [bird]. **Apart from that which is concealed within.** "Apart from the invisible reward in heaven, which you are not yet able to see during your pilgrimage on earth." For the beauty of this glory is greater than that of which she has been accounted worthy at the present time, and when he praises the simplicity of her eyes (that is, her knowledge of things hidden), he pleasingly calls her his friend, in accordance with that [saying] of the Lord's: *I will not call you servants any longer, because the servant does not know what his master is doing; but I have called you friends, because I have made known to you everything that I have heard from my Father* (Jn 15:15).[17]

Your hair is like flocks of goats that come up from Mount Galaad (Sg 4:1). If the eyes of the bride are rightly understood as the acuteness of the spiritual senses, it is not inappropriate to take the hair as referring to the countless numbers of common thoughts that in the saints are unfailingly attentive to heavenly things, even if they are sometimes occupied with the management of things temporal. For it is written that *Paul had decided to sail past Ephesus, so that he might not have to spend time in Asia; for he was making haste, if it were possible for him, to keep the day of Pentecost in Jerusalem* (Acts 20:16). In this place he was, to be sure, occupied with thoughts of this sort in reference to an earthly journey, but he was undertaking that earthly journey for the purpose of a heavenly reward. The same thing must also be understood of the art of tentmaking, which he was exercising with Aquila and Priscilla (Acts 18:1–3), for the thoughts with which they were practicing [that trade] were indeed temporal, but they were drawn to practice it in consideration of things eternal, so that they were in fact supporting the ministry of the gospel through this earthly labor. For this reason the same hairs of the bride are aptly compared to flocks of goats that come up from Mount Galaad. For these are clean animals, accustomed to climbing steep slopes covered with rocks or trees in order to seek pasture, since (as we have said) the thoughts of the elect, although concerned with earthly things, are nevertheless intent upon the things of heaven, and even when they must concern themselves with maintaining the flesh, they direct the mind's attention rather to the soul's welfare and celestial refreshment. But the eyes of the bride can also be understood as holy church's preachers, through whom she beholds the secrets of heavenly mysteries that the common crowd of believers cannot. The hairs can be taken as referring to the faithful peoples who, although they are not as expert in watching after and guiding the church's flock, nevertheless adorn it with utmost comeliness through their many acts of obedience. The Lord himself [was speaking] of such as these when, as he was warning the disciples, who were being sent out to preach, that *you will be hated by all because of my name*, he immediately added by way of consoling them: *and not a hair of your head will perish* (Lk 21:17–18), which is to say openly: "Although persecutors rage with hate, they cannot snatch away even the least of these who belong to me, your head." Now hairs of this sort are properly compared to flocks of goats; for sinners are often designated by goats, and when the entire church confesses truly that she is unable to abstain from sin, how much more do those whose station in life is ordinary need to acknowledge that "*in many things we all offend*"? (Jas 3:2). Therefore the faithful have sin, but nevertheless through their daily progress in good works they are proceeding toward that life in which they will be free from every sin. For this reason it is aptly added that these are the goats **that come up from Mount Galaad**. Surely all those who are united with the body of their Redeemer live on the mystical mountain, but goats come up higher from that same mountain (that is, they seek to find pasture at the heart of the mountain itself) when all the humble are so conscious of their sins and frailty that anxiety about their own weakness constantly arouses them to endeavor to raise themselves up to the pastures of heavenly life that they desire to obtain in Christ. Indeed, we read in the Book of Numbers and in Chronicles that Mount Galaad had exceedingly good and rich pastures (Num 32:1; 1 Chr 4:40). This applies especially well to that high and very fruitful mountain concerning which the city that was built on it (that is, holy church herself) is accustomed to say: *The Lord pastures me, and I will lack nothing; he has set me there in a place of pasture* (Ps 23:1; Vulg. 22:1). And this agrees with the very name of the mountain, which means "mound of testimony,"[18] for the Lord is surely a mound of testimony because gathered together and united in him is the multitude of all the saints, namely, of the living stones who are, as the Apostle says, *commended by the testimony of faith* (Heb 11:39). The bride's hairs, then, are compared to flocks of goats that are always striving to ascend higher in order to pasture on this mountain, because the less that either the temporal thoughts of the elect or the church's weaker masses find themselves to be without fault, the more intensely do they seek the help of him by whom they understand themselves to have been delivered.

Your teeth are like a flock of shorn ewes that have come up from the washing (Sg 4:2). Just as the church's weaker folk who are still dedicated to action are designated by hairs, so in the same way the more perfect, those suited for governing the church, are designated by teeth, doubtless because they excel in such great number, interiorly refresh [the church] from the word with such strength, and adorn the church outside with good works, although they do not enter fully into the depths of the mysteries.[19] Is he not rightly called a tooth of the church, the one to whom is said: *Get up, Peter, kill and eat* (Acts 10:13)? "Kill in the wicked what they have been, by teaching them to denounce what they have worshiped and to bring themselves, having been made good through the profession of the true faith, into the unity of your body, which is the church of Christ."[20] And the same teachers were, to be sure, previously signified by the name of "eyes," but they are eyes because they accurately perceive the secrets of spiritual mysteries, while they are teeth because they take hold of the ungodly with the word of truth and by correcting and cleansing them transform them into members of the holy church. They are the church's teeth because they prepare the bread of God's word for those little children who are unable to chew it for themselves. For whenever nursemaids want to persuade infants to give up milk and gradually adjust to bread, they use their teeth to chop up little pieces of bread, and then they put them in a tiny lump into the mouths of the infants for them to suck on along with their milk. Similarly, holy mother church has teachers who like breasts administer the milk of softer doctrine (1 Cor 3:2) to beginners, and she has those (the very same ones) who are well practiced in presenting the bread of the more robust word to those who are further along. But in order for them to make progress gradually, as is right, it is necessary for [the teachers] to encourage them to learn increasingly more profound things in stages, beginning with the more obvious aspects of spiritual secrets, which they discuss in a careful and thorough exposition as though they were giving the faithful things already chewed with the teeth, so that by doing these things over and over again they gradually render them capable of comprehending deeper mysteries. Now these teeth are rightly compared to a flock of shorn ewes that have come up from the washing, because they have been made clean in the baptismal font and also stripped bare through the removal of their riches.[21] And it is true that all of Christ's sheep are cleansed in the washing of life, for *unless one is born again of water and the Spirit*, and so forth (Jn 3:5); but it is the perfect, and especially those entrusted with the responsibility of pasturing his sheep, who give up all their possessions (Lk 14:33). This is what we read as having been done by the apostles, who were the church's first and preeminent teeth, and by a great multitude of those in the early church (Acts 4:32).

All pregnant with twins, and no barren one among them (Sg 4:2). The sheep of Christ bear twin offspring because all those whom the holy teachers bring forth for God by preaching, they instruct in the twofold love (that is, of God and neighbor); they bear twins because they train the disciples whom they teach in the knowledge of faith and right action.[22] **And no barren one among them**: among the sheep there is no supreme pastor who does not bring forth the offspring of good work; among them there are also a great many who rejoice in the offspring of works and of teaching; but those who are taken out of this life as soon as they have been washed in the font of salvation should not be counted as being among the barren. For they have progeny in the faith that they have professed for themselves, or that others have professed on their behalf, and they have the pledge of good works that they would be carrying out in company with Christ's sheep, if only things had been as they expected. It is written of such as these: *Being perfected in a short period, they fulfilled a long time; for their souls were pleasing to God, therefore he hastened to bring them out of the midst of iniquity* (Wis 4:13–14).

Your lips are like a scarlet thread and your speech is sweet (Sg 4:3). The bride's lips are likened to scarlet because the church never ceases to proclaim that she has been redeemed by the price of the Lord's blood, but continually she sings: *But may I never boast of anything except the cross of our Lord Jesus Christ* (Gal 6:14). And we should note that her lips are compared not simply to scarlet, but to a scarlet thread, for a thread is used to tie hairs together. Now if the bride's hairs are taken as referring to the faithful peoples, what is to be understood by the thread that ties them together and suitably arranges them on the head, except the doctrine of truth by which the untutored souls of believers need to be strengthened and carefully attached to the love and worship of their Creator, lest having been delivered from evil they should fall down as a result of worthless deeds and escape from the clasp or costume of the true Head, thereby obstructing his eyes (that is, the ones that ought to be showing them the light of justice) through their unseemly loosening? For just as the good things done by disciples sometimes become an example of virtue for their masters, so does their slothfulness often work to the detriment of the teachers' good deeds. Therefore it says, **Your lips are like a scarlet thread and your speech is sweet**, because the doctrine the church uses to restrain the minds of the weak from wantonness is shaped and colored, as it were, by the memory of the Lord's suffering. For nothing is more effective in keeping pleasure seekers away from carnal desires than for them to hear or reverently recall that the Lord of glory deigned to become incarnate and suffer for their sake. Hence the Lord rightly regards such speech by the church as sweet, since he rejoices greatly when he observes us reciting it to one another and meditating upon it so that we may know that he came down to us from heaven. If we have said that thoughts are represented by hairs and the spiritual senses of the faithful by eyes, this brings the exposition to a proper conclusion, for there is no easier method by which we can curb the endless wandering of superfluous thoughts than for us to rehearse often and constantly bear in mind the memory of the Lord's blood. But also, as often as we carelessly allow harmful thoughts into our mind and then, with a sudden regard for God, mark the sign of the holy cross on our chest and throw off that vile thing we were pondering, it is as though we are tying up our hair with a scarlet thread, because we are using the sign of the cross to bind the inconstant thoughts which, if this saving cord is taken away, completely mar the beauty of the head by waving all about, thereby disturbing the tranquility of the mind and obscuring the sight of the eyes, for they becloud the grace of the spiritual senses with their shameless musing on carnal things.

Like a piece of pomegranate, so are your cheeks beside that which lies hidden within (Sg 4:3). As we have said above,[23] modesty is designated by the cheeks, doubtless because they are subject to turn red whenever we blush with shame. Now it is not inappropriate for the pomegranate, because it is rose colored, to indicate the mystery of the Lord's passion, just as scarlet also does.[24] For it was fitting that the manner of our redemption should be made known by a frequent repetition of figures in the sacred song, in the same way that it is in the other writings of the prophets. Therefore, since holy church is not ashamed of the cross of Christ but even rejoices in insults and sufferings for Christ's sake and is accustomed to carry his cross as her standard, with good cause is she said to have on her face cheeks in the fashion of a pomegranate. Nor is it superfluous that they are compared here not to a whole pomegranate but to a piece of it; for surely in a pomegranate that is split the red part that was evident is seen, and the white part that lay hidden inside is revealed. Therefore, the bride has the redness of a pomegranate in her cheeks when the church confesses the mystery of the Lord's cross in words, and she shows the whiteness of that same split pomegranate when though assailed with afflictions she shows the innocence of a pure heart in deeds, and when she displays the cross of her Redeemer, which contains saving grace within. Again, she shows a crimson color in her cheeks when the first and most prominent of her members (that is, the holy martyrs) shed their blood for Christ, and she adds white to it when in the midst of what they have to suffer, and even when their passion has been completed, they shine brightly with miracles. Nor should we fail to mention that the pomegranate contains a great number of seeds within one outer husk, which is why it is also called the "apple with many seeds," which are indeed invisible while the pomegranate is still whole but seem to increase beyond counting when it is split. Similarly, the more completely that holy church happens to be crushed with adversities, the more clearly does she reveal how many seeds of virtue she comprehends under the covering of one faith. And rightly is there added: **beside that which lies hidden within**; for surely all are able to hear in the church the confession of the saving cross, all are able to behold the church's afflictions, and unbelievers along with believers are able to see and even to marvel at the splendor of the spiritual gifts by which she heals the sick, raises the dead, cleanses lepers, casts out demons, and other things of that sort (Mt 10:8); but she alone knows the extent to which her attention is held by the life which is unseen, or how much she is inflamed with love by the vision of her Creator, and with affection by the growth of her members.

Your neck is like the tower of David, which is built with bulwarks (Sg 4:4). Concerning the neck, we said above that it signifies the holy teachers who are constantly nourishing the church by refreshing her with spiritual food and strengthening her in faith with words of holy exhortation.[25] But it is also the case that the neck connects the body to the head, since it is set in between them, and this aptly suits those by whose ministry the church is joined together with Christ, for they conveyed to her the life-sustaining food that they received from the Lord himself. The Apostle speaks of them when he commends the grace of the gospel: *When it had begun to be declared by the Lord, it was confirmed to us by those who heard him* (Heb 2:3). On this account it is written of him: *And he gave the loaves to the disciples, and the disciples [gave them] to the crowds, and all ate and were filled* (Mt 14:19–20); in the same way that this happened physically, so also does it signify the spiritual deeds of the Lord, for surely it was the bread of heavenly doctrine that he entrusted to the first members of his church (namely, the apostles), which they immediately chewed up for the body of his church, which was placed beneath them, and the ministers of the word who followed them in turn did the same, so that this life-giving food was able to fill the whole world. Surely this neck is rightly said to be like the tower of David. For if David's city is the church of Christ, then the impregnable tower in that city is the constancy of the preachers who were raised up on high to be stronger than the rest of the faithful so that they might defend the structures of the faith and repulse the missiles of the enemy by a mighty hand and a beloved king, which is what the name David signifies.[26] Now the bulwarks with which this tower was built are understood as the fortifications of either the holy scriptures or the divine gifts. For the bride's neck was likened to a tower when the Lord made the church's first teachers invincible against enemies by giving them the grace of the Holy Spirit; he added bulwarks to that tower when *he opened their mind that they might understand the scriptures* (Lk 24:45), and the words of their preaching proved true to the sayings of the fathers who had gone before them; he added bulwarks to the tower when he also bestowed upon them the gifts of the signs they were going to perform so that they might add new works of power to accompany the new divine reality that they were preaching, and more easily bring those whom they were teaching to the salvation of their souls by curing their bodily diseases.[27]

A thousand shields hang from it, all the armor of strong men (Sg 4:4). The thousand shields that hang from the tower of David are the countless garrisons of divine protection by which the holy preachers receive the Lord's help themselves, so that they cannot be conquered by enemies, and by which they also teach their hearers to be sustained against the assault of enemies, whether visible or invisible. **All the armor of strong men** refers to all the instruction, whether in conduct or in heavenly doctrine, through which the same teachers not only escape but also conquer armies of evil spirits when through their preaching they snatch away from those [spirits] a great many of those held ensnared under their dominion, and transform them from vessels of wrath into vessels of mercy (Rom 9:22–23). And when mention is made of spiritual warfare, it is appropriate that the tower of David is set as the example, and not the tower of Solomon, although the name and the character of both of these kings very often contain the figure of the King Eternal. But since David is interpreted as "strong hand or beloved," rightly is the Lord designated by this name here in this place where it is being taught that he wages war against the enemies of the church, in order that she may proceed undaunted into battle, mindful that she is aided by him who cannot be conquered, and in order that she may more vehemently strive to conquer since she knows that it is his beloved face to which she will draw near after the enemy has been conquered.

On the Song of Songs
Book 3

Your two breasts are like two young goats that are twins (Sg 4:5). Variously and in many ways are the same mysteries of Christ and the church repeated, but the repetitions always add something new that either serves to augment the same mysteries or pleases the souls of the hearers the more through its very novelty. Therefore the same teachers who were above designated by the name of "eyes" or "teeth" or "neck" are now expressed by the word "breasts." For they can rightly be called eyes, since they perceive the secrets of mysteries; rightly are they called teeth, since in reproving the ungodly it is as though they are chewing them up and transforming them into tender and humble [members] in the body of the church; rightly are they called a neck, since in preaching eternal joys it is as though they are providing the whole body of the church with the breath of life and preparing the doctrinal food with which she is nourished unto salvation; and they are also quite aptly referred to as breasts, since they supply the milk of the life-giving word to those who are still infants in Christ. Now it is not without purpose that it goes on to specify the number and say **two breasts**, even though no woman is accustomed to have any more or fewer than two breasts. Surely it says two breasts in order to indicate that the children of two peoples (namely, the Jewish and the Gentile) have been nurtured in faith. Accordingly, Paul says: *James, Cephas, and John, who were acknowledged to be pillars, gave to me and Barnabas the right hand of fellowship, that we [should go] to the Gentiles and they to the circumcised* (Gal 2:9), and so forth. And see what Peter, who was sent to the circumcised, says: *Like newborn infants, desire the rational milk without guile, so that by it you may grow unto salvation, if indeed you have tasted that the Lord is sweet* (1 Pt 2:2–3). In saying this he also explains the sacrament of the church's breasts when he asserts that desiring the rational milk is to taste that the Lord is sweet. Again, let us consider whether Paul, who was sent to the uncircumcised, also performed the function of breasts. He says: *And I, brothers and sisters, could not speak to you as spiritual people, but rather as carnal, as infants in Christ; I gave you milk to drink, not solid food* (1 Cor 3:1–2). Now these two breasts are like two young goats that are twins, because they are the offspring of him to whom it is said quite often in this song: **My beloved, be like a wild goat or a young deer** (Sg 2:17). They are like young goats because with the eyes of their most pure heart they discern what things they ought to do, what things they ought to avoid; with a keen mind they perceive that way of virtues on which they ought to advance while turning away from circuitous verbal digressions, and they rejoice to hasten nimbly along the path of good works from the vale of tears to the place that God has determined, so that going from virtue to virtue they may merit to see him in Sion (Ps 84:6–7; Vulg. 83:7–8)—that is, in the contemplation of his eternal dwelling.[1] For surely goats possess both nimbleness of foot and exceedingly great keenness of sight. Therefore their natures are suitably compared with those who are commanded to instruct the unlearned about the rewards of knowledge and virtue. **Like two young goats**, it says, **that are twins**. It is appropriate that they are twins, because all the teachers of both peoples are instructed in one and the same faith and renewed by one and the same sacrament so that they can bring all those whom they teach into the one church of Christ. For this reason Peter says concerning those believers who were from the uncircumcised: *And God, who knows hearts, testified by giving them the Holy Spirit, just as to us; and he has made no distinction between us and them, purifying their hearts by faith* (Acts 15:8–9).

Who pasture among the lilies until the day breathes and the shadows retire (Sg 4:5–6). The holy teachers pasture among the pure and luxuriant flowers of the divine scriptures and, so that the milk of life-giving doctrine with which they feed the infants may not be wanting, they read in the writings of the fathers what they should do and how they ought to teach, and they fill their hearts with vital nectars, as it were, even unto the end of this age. For after the day has breathed—that [day] for which the psalmist was longing when he said: *One day in your courts is better than a thousand* (Ps 84:10; Vulg. 83:11)—it will no longer be the time for teaching or learning, in fulfillment of the prophecy that says: *And none of them shall teach his neighbor, saying, "Know the Lord," for they shall all know me* (Jer 31:34), but when all the darkness of this world has retired and passed far away, the saints *shall shine like the sun in the kingdom of their Father* (Mt 13:43), all receiving rewards in proportion to what they have learned and done and taught.

Now it is pleasing how much it accords with natural science that it speaks of the night's departure as the retiring of shadows, since the darkness of night, as the philosophers say, is nothing else than the earth's shadow; for as the sun circles the earth it is always spreading light around, and with it the day, but it leaves the other side (that is, the one from which it is absent) in the shadow of darkness.[2] And this is that primordial division by which God divided the light from the darkness (Gn 1:4–5). Evidently these shadows begin to lengthen gradually in the east as soon as the sun sets, and the closer the sun comes to setting beneath the earth, the more they increase, stretching out until in the middle of the night, when the sun is positioned beneath the middle of the earth, they reach their zenith and fill the middle of the earth, and then as the sun gradually appears they are gradually shifted toward the west until the coming of dawn, when they retire and fade away. Now the reason that the earth's shadows do not reach the heavens is that the sun, having been created greater than the earth, makes it cast a pointed shadow that comes to an end before it extends to the heavens, and the sun's splendor, which is spread all around every part of the earth, has an unrestricted view of the heavens that it illuminates. Therefore the present life is night,[3] and Christ is the Sun of righteousness (Mal 4:2), whose light is often hidden from us by a large mass of earthly desire so that it cannot be seen, and the more he acts with strict justice and recedes from us, the more we are in darkness; the more he graciously returns, the more we are enlightened. Now we will truly enjoy his light after all the darkness of this present distress and blindness has already retired and been dispersed so that *we will see him as he is* (1 Jn 3:2). Nevertheless, mindful of our salvation in every respect, he has by no means left the night of this life completely in the dark, but as if fixing stars in heaven he has set before us the examples of the saints, by which we have gone forward in good works with feet that do not stumble.

I will go to the mountain of myrrh and to the hill of frankincense (Sg 4:6). In myrrh there is expressed the mortification of the flesh or of the passions for the sake of piety or endurance; in frankincense, the devotion of prayer striving toward heaven. Now the mountain of myrrh and the hill of frankincense are the sublimity of mind of those who both courageously prevail in the wrestling match with the flesh and ardently lift themselves up to the love of heavenly things. The Lord surely comes to this mountain and hill because he will quite often deign to visit and to dwell in the hearts of those who apply themselves to virtues. Hence he says: *I will dwell in them and walk among them* (2 Cor 6:16). Therefore when the Lord praises the church and enumerates the virtues of all her members, he quickly adds: **I will go to the mountain of myrrh and to the hill of frankincense**, which is to say openly: "I will visit them, and by my benevolent manifestation I will graciously glorify those whom I regard as being sublime in virtue of their suffering or of their prayer; I will quite often come and make my home (Jn 14:23) with those whom I judge to be cleansing themselves from defilement of body and spirit and to be making sanctification perfect in the fear of God" (2 Cor 7:1)—not that he intends to forsake her whom he had been praising and go to others, but rather that he determines to add new peoples daily to his same church and to extend her throughout the whole world. Perhaps it is not inappropriate for these things to be understood as being a discourse addressed to the church of the Gentiles concerning the calling of the synagogue, which is to take place at the end [of the age]. For he is responding to her desire further above when she had found him and said: **I held him and will not let him go until I bring him into my mother's house** (Sg 3:4). Indeed, in the preceding verse he taught that the church of the Gentiles would never abandon him, when he says: **Your two breasts are like two young goats that are twins who pasture among the lilies until the day breathes and the shadows retire** (Sg 4:5–6); that is: "There are among you teachers who instruct the two peoples, and they agree together in love that is humble and pure, until the end of the age when the day of eternal retribution will appear." Finally, he clearly indicates that he is going to call the Jews also, when he adds: **I will go to the mountain of myrrh and to the hill of frankincense**—not that he will be able to find her at the height of virtue when he comes, because she had long since departed from faith in him when she gave him a bill of divorce, but rather that by coming to her he was going to render her worthy of his company. For this reason it is then appropriate for him to add concerning the most ample beauty of the church, which is one and the same, whether it is gathered together from Judea or from all the nations throughout the world:

You are altogether beautiful, my friend, and there is no spot in you (Sg 4:7). "Not only are you beautiful in the more distinguished members of the elect, which I have enumerated, but you shine with the comeliness of virtues and are free from the spot of vices even in those who appear small and weak." For *he has blessed all those who fear the Lord, both small and great* (Ps 114:13; Vulg. 113:13); hence John also says in his Apocalypse concerning that same church's heavenly homeland: *There shall not enter into it anything defiled, or that practices abomination or falsehood, but only those who are written in the Lamb's book of life* (Rv 21:27). For these things are said not because it is possible in this life for any one of the saints to be either free from all sins or perfect in virtues—since it is truly written that *there is no righteous person on earth who does good and does not sin* (Eccl 7:20; Vulg. 7:21)—but rather because holy church, insofar as she is the church of Christ, is upright in faith and pure in deed, and if anything unclean or improper touches her, it does not affect her, but she makes every effort to purge it from herself very quickly, as though it were a foreign substance. Similar to this is that [saying] of blessed John: *All who have been born of God do not sin, because his seed abides in them, and they cannot sin because they have been born of God* (1 Jn 3:9); for insofar as the seed of God's grace by which they have been born again abides in the righteous, to that extent they cannot sin, but insofar as they sin, to that extent the grace by which they were born again has forsaken them for a time in order that they may recognize that they have lost that [grace] by which they were living uprightly. After this life, when they are cleansed from every spot and shine brightly with perfect beauty, [that grace] will bring them into that city into which, as has been said, nothing polluted can enter, and then this will truly be fulfilled in the

Bridegroom's friend, in that she now makes a total effort on behalf of virtue so that she may be altogether beautiful and that there may not be any spot in her.

Come from Lebanon, my bride; come from Lebanon; come (Sg 4:8). If we follow the Hebrew etymology, Lebanon is interpreted as radiance; if the Greek, frankincense.[4] Accordingly, in the place above where we read **to the hill of frankincense** (Sg 4:6), some manuscripts have "to the hill of Lebanon." Now anyone can easily see that both names signify industriousness in virtue. The Lord's bride (that is, the church or the holy soul) comes to him not only when she is called forth from the body to receive the reward of eternal recompense, but, even while living in this world, she is advancing to better things through the sacrificial offerings of so many good works, as though with so many steps approaching him who alone is good (Mk 10:18); but after the bonds of the flesh are dissolved, then she will come all the way [to him] when she merits to see his face. Therefore he perceives that the bride is located in Lebanon and admonishes her to come to him, because when the Lord sees the faithful soul radiant with good deeds and offering the incense of pure prayer to him, he is pleased with her devout works and exhorts her to persevere in what she has begun. Whether he does this through the secret admonition of his own inspiration, or through meditation on the divine scriptures, or through the exhortations of the other faithful, or even through the hardships or blessings of passing things, he is surely acting toward her with providential kindness, so that if she is being worn away by the troubles of this present exile she will more ardently desire the homeland of eternal rest, and if she has been chosen to profit from present favors, she will long more dearly for the unfailing joys of the heavenly city. Now he commands the bride to come from Lebanon three times, because he asks for his elect to make progress in good works, in wholesome speech, and in pure thought. Or perhaps he is saying, **Come from Lebanon, my bride; come from Lebanon; come**: "Come by leading the best life you can while living in the body; come when you are released from the body to receive eternal life for your soul; come a third time after you have received the body to see the resurrection's perfect joys." And because many of the elect receive an everlasting reward not only on account of the purity of their own lives but also on account of their correction of others whom they were teaching, there aptly follows:

You will be crowned from the peak of Amana, from the top of Sanir and Hermon, from the dens of lions, from the mountains of leopards (Sg 4:8). Amana, Sanir, and Hermon are mountains of Cilicia and Judea, noted as haunts for lions and leopards, as also for other wild beasts. Clearly, they designate the proud hearts of unbelievers, in which unclean spirits have taken residence. Contrary to them is what the Lord says through the prophet concerning the elect: *Upon whom does my Spirit rest, except upon the one who is humble and gentle and that trembles at my words*? (Is 61:2, Old Latin). Surely lions are demons on account of their pride, as are leopards on account of their cruelty or various malicious habits.[5] Therefore, whenever holy church through her preachers rescues souls of this sort from the power of darkness and converts them to knowledge of the true light, it is as though the same preachers receive the crown of life not only for themselves but also for those whom they have acquired for the Lord, in accordance with that [saying] in Proverbs: *Children's children are the crown of the aged, and the glory of children is their fathers* (Prv 17:6); and the Apostle says of those he was teaching: *What is our glory, or hope, or joy, or crown of glory? Is it not you, in the presence of our Lord Jesus at his coming*? (1 Thes 2:19). And we should note that it does not say: **You will be crowned** from Amana, Sanir, and Hermon, but **from the top of Amana, from the peak of Sanir and Hermon**. Therefore, when the church converts the common rabble to the Lord, she obtains a crown from the sides of the mountains on which beasts have been lurking, because she receives a reward for saving an enemy people; but when she brings those princes of malice, those persecutors of the people, into the way of life, she is doubtless crowned from the peak and the top of the mountains, since the victor's prize increases with the difficulty of the contest. Similar to this is that which is added: **from the dens of lions, from the mountains of leopards**. For the dens of lions and the mountains of leopards are those incited by the more violent fury of evil spirits to inflict injury on Christ's flock, who gain the upper hand by force and deceit; he will recall them with the church to the grace of humility and piety; from them she is crowned, because she will rejoice on account of their eternal salvation. On the contrary, those without virtue who pursue the good with so much guile are quite aptly called dens not of lions but of wolves. For this reason the Lord says of the scribes who deceitfully promise obedience but have no power against the church: *Foxes have holes, and birds of the air have nests; but the Son of Man has nowhere to lay his head* (Lk 9:58; cf. Mt 8:19–20). Surely by the name of "foxes" he was referring to their frivolity and deceit, and by the term "birds" he was referring to their mind's overweening pride.[6] But whenever the church saves these also, she brings it about that the Son of Man takes the rest appropriate to his humility and integrity even there, in the place in which vile spirits were previously making themselves at home with boasting and levity.

You have wounded my heart, my sister, my bride, you have wounded my heart (Sg 4:9). This saying is also easily understood, because by mentioning his wounded heart he wishes to express the great love that he has toward the church, whom he rightly calls his sister and bride. Rightly does he call her "bride" [and "sister"] because he has joined her to himself by a covenant of marriage in heaven, and because he also deigned to be made human and to become her brother by nature. It can also be understood according to that which Isaiah says: *But he was wounded for our iniquities, crushed for our sins* (Is 53:5). Then he explains how it follows that she has indeed caused him to sustain this wound, saying:

By one of your eyes and in one hair of your neck (Sg 4:9). We have said above[7] that by the church's eyes we understand either her spiritual senses or those teachers who are accustomed to perceive and disclose the spiritual things that belong to her, and farther on[8] that we take hairs as referring to the multitude of peoples that, even though they cannot attain to the full height of that word in which the Lord says: *If you wish to be perfect, go, sell what you have, give to the poor, and you will have treasure in heaven; then come, follow me* (Mt 19:21), nevertheless they are traveling toward heaven along the way of good works concerning which he had previously spoken, saying: *If you wish to enter into life, keep the commandments: You shall not murder; You shall not commit adultery; You shall not steal; You shall not bear false witness; Honor father and mother; also, Love your neighbor as yourself* (Mt 19:17–19), but while in that case the eyes are described as plural in number and a multitude of hairs (whether of rulers or hearers) is designated, here, on the other hand, the single eye refers to the unity of teachers or of the spiritual knowledge that they teach, concerning which it is written: *There is one Lord, one faith, one baptism, one God and Father of all* (Eph 4:5–6). Again, what is being praised in the single hair of the neck is the unity of those who are accustomed to cling to their spiritual masters with pious devotion and to cover the neck in the manner of hairs by their reverent obedience; for above it was also evident that the same teachers are indicated by the church's neck.[9] Luke points to the unity of this hair when he says: *The multitude of believers were of one heart and soul; none of them said that anything they possessed was their own, but they held all things in common* (Acts 4:32); and subsequently he indicates what the neck to which that hair was connected was doing, when he says: *And with great power the apostles gave testimony to the resurrection of our Lord* (Acts 4:33). Therefore he says:

You have wounded my heart, my sister, my bride, you have wounded my heart by one of your eyes and in one hair of your neck, as if he were saying openly, "O catholic church, you truly appear beautiful and spotless to me in the whole form of your body, in which you extend far and wide throughout the world, but this above all is the thing that incites me to love you so marvelously, that you demonstrate that you maintain the unity of your faith and love both in your faithful prelates and in their subjects; this is the thing that has prompted me to receive the wound of death so that you may live, that I have been longing to endow you with unity in all your members (that is, in the great and in the small, in the more noble and in the ordinary), that with one like mind among all you may travel toward that life in which there reigns the unity of true peace and glory."

---

15. He describes the sweet fruit of the works of those who preach his doctrine, and the most sweet fragrance of their reputation.

How beautiful are your breasts, my sister, my bride (Sg 4:10). Just as the neck, eyes, and teeth are understood with reference to the church's teachers, so also are the breasts, but with the distinction that he was referring to them by those other names at a time when they were either speaking wisdom among the perfect or refuting their opponents, but when to the weak they become weak so that they might benefit the weak (1 Cor 9:22), then it is not inappropriate to say that they fulfill the function of breasts, because they are imparting the milk of softer doctrine to the mind of infants—that is, to those who are not yet capable of receiving the bread of the more excellent word. For they are teeth when they reprove the restless; they are breasts when they console the faint-hearted and defend the weak. And rightly does he praise and marvel at his sister and bride for the beauty of the breasts, because in the Lord's eyes it is a great work and a wondrous virtue when one who provides the more perfect with profounder secrets of truth does by no means disdain to instruct the weak in the first principles of faith. Rightly does the Lord bear witness that such a soul is for him a sister and a bride, doubtless because he judges her most worthy of being joined to him in love, since he perceives that she has become an imitator of his work; for he also did not shrink from becoming weak for a time so that he might change us from weak to strong, and even to die so that we might live. Although he was the bread of angels, he willed to hide his divinity by taking flesh in order to nourish human faintheartedness and make it fit for that same heavenly bread. For since an infant is not able to eat bread very well, the mother in a certain manner makes the very bread she eats into flesh and feeds the infant from that bread through the lowliness of breasts and the taste of milk.[10] *In the beginning was the Word, and the Word was with God, and the Word was God* (Jn 1:1); this is the eternal food that refreshes angels because they are satisfied with the sight of his glory. And *the Word became flesh and dwelt among us* (Jn 1:14), so that in this way the Wisdom of God, who consoles us as a mother, may refresh us from that very same bread and lead us through the sacraments of the incarnation to the knowledge and vision of divine splendor. But holy teachers also take the bread with which they are fed in a sublime manner and convert it into milk with which they nourish little children, so that the more exalted their contemplation of eternal joys in God, the more humbly are they at the same time taking pity on their neighbors' weakness.

Your breasts are more beautiful than wine (Sg 4:10). At the beginning of this song we have already explained the verse in which it is said: **For your breasts are better than wine** (Sg 1:1), and it was understood that these words indicated that the very first principles of evangelical faith surpassed the virtue of the Mosaic law, since the law made no one perfect (Heb 7:19) inasmuch as it was not able to bring even its most excellent devotees into the kingdom of heavenly life, while the grace of faith leads those who are reborn in the font of baptism (even children and those who die at that young age) to celestial joys. For there are also many texts showing that the ceremonies of the law are compared with wine, but especially the one in which the wine runs out at the church's mystical marriage in order that the Lord might perform the miracle of making far better wine out of water (Jn 2:1–9). There it was made known by means of a type that the literal observance of the law was about to come to an end, and that she who was veiled in the letter would be unveiled by the grace of the gospel and inebriated with spiritual love in the house of a celestial marriage (referring to holy church, whom Christ deigned to consecrate as his bride). Therefore the bride's breasts are more beautiful than wine, because the first principles of evangelical faith surpass the decrees of the law, even those that are shown to have sparkled to no small degree with the taste and sweetness of virtues. But we should note very carefully in these words that above it was the bride who [praised] the breasts of her beloved, but here it is instead the beloved himself who praises the breasts of his bride and sister and testifies that they are to be preferred to wine; for we should not think that this sacred exchange was inserted into the song to no purpose, but rather that through it the unity of Christ and the church is commended more highly. For *he is the head of the body, the church* (Col 1:18), and she is the body that belongs to his head. For this reason the Apostle says: *They shall be two in one flesh; this is a great mystery, and I am speaking of Christ and the church* (Eph 5:31–32). And the reason that the breasts of the Bridegroom and of the bride are praised in a similar way, as if they were the same, is that the teachers of the church are the same as the teachers of Christ—of the church, because they teach her, but of Christ, because they teach as he directs; [hers], because they teach her his precepts; [his], because by teaching her they are calling her forth into fellowship with him. Accordingly, the Apostle who says: *Paul, a servant of Jesus Christ* (Rom 1:1), has also said: *And ourselves your servants* *through Jesus* (2 Cor 4:5), and in another place: *For all things are yours, whether Paul or Apollos or Cephas* (1 Cor 3:21–22).

And the odor of your ointments is above all spices (Sg 4:10). The odor of the church's ointments is the fame of the spiritual gifts of which it is written: *Their sound has gone forth into every land* (Ps 19:4; Vulg. 18:5) and so forth; and when Mary Magdalene as a type of holy church anointed the Lord with nard, it is written: *And the house was filled with the odor of the ointment* (Jn 12:3), in which it is mystically figured that the whole world would be filled with the devoted services of the church, which she would render to her Redeemer. But if the observance of the law is rightly expressed by the name of "wine," so that it might be tested by the higher authority of the gospel, what hinders the sweetest reputation of the saints of that former time from being indicated by the name of "spices"? Therefore it says, **The odor of your ointments is above all spices**, because there is no doubt that the fame of Christian faith, having been spread throughout the world, has expanded much more widely than that of those righteous ones who were among the earlier people; whence this [fame], which waged a public battle before the eyes of the world when it renounced the worship of the gods, also endured public persecution from the world until it was victorious at last. For it is not fitting for the bride of Christ to be compared to things that are base and of little value, whether it be to wine that is consumed in the tasting, or to aromatic spices that are scattered by the wind, although it may indeed be a very modest form of praise for the one who observes the law, if it means that draughts [of wine] or aromatic spices are all things that are able to transcend the senses of the flesh.

Your lips are dripping honeycomb, [my] bride (Sg 4:11). A honeycomb is honey in wax,[11] and honey in wax is the spiritual sense of the divine scriptures in the letter that is rightly called a dripping honeycomb; for a honeycomb drips when it has more honey than its wax chambers can hold, doubtless because the fecundity of the holy scriptures is such that a verse that was written in a short line fills many pages if one squeezes it by careful examination to see how much sweetness of spiritual understanding it contains inside. As only one example, the psalmist says: *Praise the Lord, O Jerusalem!* (Ps 147:12). According to the letter, this surely exhorts the citizens of that city in which God's temple was found to sing praises to him; but according to allegory, Jerusalem is the church of Christ spread throughout the whole world; again, according to tropology (that is, to the moral sense), every holy soul is rightly called "Jerusalem"; again, according to anagogy (that is, to the meaning that leads to higher things), Jerusalem is the dwelling place of the heavenly homeland that comprises holy angels and human beings.[12] Now it aptly agrees with all of these (although in several different ways) that this Jerusalem that is ordered to praise the Lord means "vision of peace"; for a single holy soul cannot sing as many praises to God as can the whole church throughout the world, nor can the praises sung by the universal church while she is on pilgrimage on earth away from the Lord be as perfect as those she sings in the presence of her Lord when she is blessed to reign in heaven; neither can the peace that the saints have while [they live] in hope of seeing God and being delivered from evil be considered equal to the vision of that peace which they have in repose, when having been delivered from every evil they delight in God, who is the highest good. Therefore the honeycomb is not only full of honey but it is also dripping from the lips of the bride when the church's teachers show that it contains the manifold abundance of inner sweetness, whether in the figures of the law, or in the prophetic sayings, or in the mystical words and deeds of the Lord himself, and then prepare from them the sumptuous dishes that are most pleasing to her faithful members (that is, to worthy listeners) and most salutary for their souls. Nor is it contradictory that above the bride's lips are compared to threads and now to a honeycomb, when here she takes delight in satisfying with honeycombs, there she fastens hair by tying it up; the former nourishes within, the latter binds without. For surely the same teachers are both threads in their salutary precepts and a honeycomb in their heavenly promises: threads, when they restrain us from the disarray of carnal desires; a honeycomb, when they promise the gifts of celestial joys to those who are good. Again, they are threads in openly teaching us what we ought to do and what we ought to avoid; they are a honeycomb in disclosing whatever mystery of salvation is contained within types, whether deeds or words.[13]

Honey and milk are under your tongue (Sg 4:11). Milk signifies the instruction given to children; honey, the teaching suitable for the more perfect. The Apostle teaches about milk when he says by way of reproach to some who have fallen away from faith: *And you have become like those who need milk, not solid food* (Heb 5:12). It also teaches about the honey that is wisdom when it says: *As it is not good for a person to eat much honey, so it is that the searcher of majesty shall be overwhelmed with power* (Prv 25:27). Now we are not being forbidden to eat honey, but only to eat much of it, because we are not being kept from searching out God's majesty in every way—particularly since it is sung to him in praise of the righteous: *They shall speak of the magnificence of its majesty and of your holiness* (Ps 145:5; Vulg. 144:5)—but we are rather being called away from probing into those things that exceed our capacity. For this reason it also says elsewhere concerning the lovers of heavenly wisdom: *You have found honey? Eat what is sufficient for you, lest being glutted you vomit it up* (Prv 25:16). Now it is appropriately mentioned that she has honey and milk under her tongue; for she has the word of God under her tongue when she utters it by speaking; she has it under her tongue when in her heart she diligently considers what things ought to be uttered; she has honey and milk under her tongue when she knows rightly how to discern what things must be said to beginners, what things to those making progress, and what things to those who are perfect in the knowledge and love of [God]. And at the appropriate time she dispenses these things through the tongue's ministry, according to the capacity of the hearers.

And the odor of your garments is like the odor of frankincense (Sg 4:11). The church's garments are her works, as John testifies when he tells of her future blessedness, saying: *The marriage of the Lamb has come, and his wife has made herself ready, and it has been granted to her that she should clothe herself with fine linen, bright and pure, for fine linen is the righteousness of the saints* (Rv 19:7–8); and blessed Job: *I put on righteousness, and it clothed me with my judgment, as with a garment and a diadem* (Job 29:14). Now frankincense, as we have often said, indicates the celestial desires of the righteous and the ardor of frequent prayers seeking the heights. Thus the odor of the bride's garments is aptly likened to the odor of frankincense, because all the works that holy church performs for the

Lord are like prayers offered on her behalf. There is no other way in which we can fulfill that apostolic [command] to *pray without ceasing* (1 Thes 5:17), unless everything we do out of devotion serves as a form of devout intercession commending us to our Creator; for neither the Apostle himself nor any of the saints could always have time for prayer in the sense that they never devoted some time to sleep or eating or the other necessities of this life, but the righteous pray without ceasing in that the righteous do the things that are just without ceasing, and never cease from prayer unless they fall into sin. And so the odor of their garments smells like the odor of frankincense because the fame of their good works ascends to divine judgment after the fashion of prayers. Now this little verse is in harmony with the one above that says: **And the odor of your ointments is above all spices;** for there by the name of "ointments" is shown the inpouring of the Holy Spirit by which the hearts of the faithful are illuminated and made ready for spiritual combat, and here by the term "garments" are indicated those deeds of the righteous that are done on the outside. For this reason, and with a pleasing distinction, those works done by human beings are compared to the odor of frankincense, but the odor of the church's ointments is said to surpass all spices, since those gifts that come through divine generosity are beyond all comparison.

Of course it is well known that there is frequent reference to frankincense in this song, and that it has a typological meaning, but I should like to provide a little information about the nature of that spice for the benefit of those unacquainted with it. In Arabia there is a tree whose bark and foliage are, as they say,[14] similar to that of the laurel; the sap it produces, which is like that of the almond tree, is collected twice a year, in the autumn and in the spring. In the very hottest time of the summer, however, incisions are made in the bark of the trees in order to prepare them for the autumnal collection. Out comes a viscous foam, which *thickens into a solid mass, in which place nature demands that after it has been caught on a mat made of palm leaves which sticks fast to the tree it is scraped with an iron tool because* it appears to be *covered in bark.*[15] This frankincense is *most pure and white in color. In the middle of winter, incisions are made in the bark for the second gathering in spring; it is thought that this [gathering], which comes out reddish in color, is not comparable to the first, and that [the sap] from young trees is whiter, but that from older ones is more fragrant. That which hangs down from the roundness of the drop, we call "masculam";* the drop squeezed out *by shaking we call "manna." The region that produces frankincense* is called Sarvia, which *the Greeks say signifies "mystery." Impassable with rocks on all sides and inaccessible from the right-hand side due to the crags of the sea, it juts out with one narrow path of trees. Its length is* a hundred [Roman] miles (or eighty, as others report); *its width half as much. Mountain ranges rise and fall steeply, and on the plain trees spring up of their own accord. It is known to have clay soil, with springs that are far apart and full of lye.* We have reported these things concerning the nature and location of frankincense just as they have been related in the books of the ancient writers.

If one attends diligently to these things, nearly all of them correspond figuratively to the virtues of the saints, especially since the region from which [frankincense] originates is called "mystery." For the fact that the trees spring up of their own accord aptly coincides with those whose highest virtue is not compelled by the edicts of the law but wondrously proceeds from a voluntary offering, as the Lord says: *If you wish to be perfect, go, sell,* and so forth (Mt 19:21). What does it indicate that frankincense pours forth like tears from incisions in the trees, unless it is the compunction of those who are humble in heart, from which springs prayer that is pure and sweetened with tears? That its springs are far apart but full of lye is consistent with those from whose belly, as scripture says (Jn 7:38), flow rivers of living water (that is, gifts of spiritual teaching) that are also suitable for cleansing the minds of their neighbors. For surely lye is most useful both for curing infirmities and for washing away dirt. That the region is fenced about on all sides with a rampart of rocks and crags corresponds to the merits of those of whom the Lord speaks in a parable: *There was a man, a householder, who planted a vineyard and put a fence around it* (Mt 21:33); for surely the Lord planted the church by instructing her in the precepts of life, and he put a fence around her by guarding her on all sides with the shield of his protection, so that she cannot be destroyed by the wicked, whether spirits or human beings.

Now after the Lord praised each member of the church individually, last of all he deliberately commended also the unguents with which she was anointed all over; truly, none is counted among her members, whether small or great, unless it has been consecrated by the infusion of this spiritual unction, for anyone to whom this is wanting does not belong to the body of the church. He also praised her garments (that is, her works of righteousness), because with them her whole body is also adorned; truly, one is not worthy of eternal life in her unless one is clothed with works of righteousness that one has either performed oneself or, in the case of an infant, that others have performed for one and in one's behalf. But since the most excellent Lover thought it tedious to praise his bride's members separately, and thought it unnecessary to liken each one of her features to a single thing of value, he praises all of her at the same time and compares many important aspects at once by adding:

A garden enclosed is my sister, my bride, a garden enclosed, a fountain sealed, and so forth, up to the place where he says: **A fountain of gardens, a well of living waters that flow rushing from Lebanon** (Sg 4:12–15). Now the church is a garden because she brings forth diverse buds of spiritual works, which are subsequently enumerated under the names of various spices; she is a fountain because she is overflowing with saving doctrine, with which she waters the minds of her faithful as if they were seedbeds that she herself had prepared. Thus it is written: *The words of a person's mouth are deep water, and the fountain of wisdom is an overflowing fountain* (Prv 18:4); hence the Apostle also says: *I planted, Apollos watered, but God gave the growth* (1 Cor 3:6)—*I planted* the spices of virtues, as it were, in the Lord's garden; *Apollos watered* as though from the sealed fountain of celestial doctrine; but the Lord aided his own workers, as it were, lest they should labor in vain. Now that garden is enclosed because the church continues steadfast under the fortified protection of her Lord and Redeemer, so that she may never be violated by the malicious intrusion of faithless people or unclean spirits, or hindered from producing celestial fruits as a result of being trampled on from every direction. That fountain is sealed because the word of faith that is defended by the seal of the gospel can never be disturbed by any incursion of those who go astray. For *there is one Lord, one faith, one baptism, one God and Father of all* (Eph 4:5–6). Someone who tries to break that seal of the living fountain does go astray but cannot profane the fountain of life; on the contrary, a wicked person who intrudes into it faces certain death, after the example of the Egyptian army, which was destroyed in the mystical baptism of the Red Sea while the people of God were saved, because [the Egyptians] had presumed to enter into the holy place not believing but persecuting. And since the same holy church that is designated by the name of a garden watered by a sacred fountain was at first located in the little field of Judea but was soon made to extend everywhere throughout the entire world, rightly is it added:

The things you send forth are a paradise of pomegranates with the fruits of the orchard (Sg 4:13). Since the early church that was in Jerusalem produced abundant peoples for God by water and the Spirit, it is properly said that the sacred garden sustained by the watering of the divine fountain has sent forth a paradise not of just any sort of trees but a paradise of pomegranates with the fruits of the orchard. Surely pomegranates, which are red with the color of blood, suggest the triumphs of those in the church who after having been sealed along with others in the washing of the font are also baptized in their own blood, and the fruits of the orchard indicate the works of virtue common to all, or else those who do such works of virtue. Pomegranates, however, which are the first things this garden is said to send forth from itself, can also rightly be taken as referring to the whole company of the baptized, since the regenerating font itself is doubtless consecrated in the mystery of the Lord's passion. For *all of us who have been baptized into Christ Jesus were baptized into his death, for we have been buried with him by baptism into death, so that, just as Christ was raised from the dead by the glory of God, so we too might walk in newness of life* (Rom 6:3–4). Now after the pomegranates follow the fruits of the orchard and of spices worthy of the grace of such a beginning, because after we have come up from the font sprinkled with the precious blood through which we are made God's children, it follows that we must bear the sweet-smelling fruit of the virtues with which the very grace of our regeneration is always adorned and continues to increase.

Cypress with nard, nard and saffron (Sg 4:13–14). *Cypress is a* spice-*tree in Egypt with leaves similar to those of the jujube and a seed like that of the coriander, with a distinct smell. This [seed] is baked in oil and pressed (after which it is called the cypress)*, and from it is prepared an ointment fit for a king; *the finest* is in Egypt, *the second best* in

Ascalon of Judea, the third best on the island of Cyprus. Some *say that this is the tree that in Italy is called the ligustrum.*[16] Now concerning the manna, we read that *it was like coriander seed, white* (Ex 16:31), and since the seed of the cypress is declared to possess the same quality, it rightly designates the very same blessing that comes down from heaven. Now this seed is put in oil and baked when the gift of celestial grace is received by hearts glowing with the grease of charity and thrown into the flames of trials so that the extent and quality of its virtue may be more readily apparent to everyone. Now nard contains a type of the Lord's burial, as is testified by Mary's act of anointing him with that spice just before his passion, just as he himself also explains when he says: *By putting this ointment on my body she has prepared me for burial* (Mt 26:12). And the Lord's garden or fountain sends forth cypress when the church teaches those freed from slavery to seek the grace of heavenly food before all things, to preserve the light and unction of love in their heart, and not to be overcome by the fire of tribulations but rather to treat those things as an opportunity to show the nature and the amount of divine grace that their seed has received. And nard is added to cypress when she very studiously instructs them in the faith of the Lord's passion and at the same time teaches them to imitate it by suffering. Saffron, which has a flower the color of gold, indicates those who shine with the more abundant grace of charity, which surpasses all virtues just as gold does all other metals. *Now*, it says, *faith, hope, and charity abide, these three; and the greatest of these is charity* (1 Cor 13:13). In contrast to this, when Jeremiah is lamenting the ruin of his fellow citizens he says: *Those who fed on saffron have embraced dung* (Lam 4:5); surely those who fed on saffron embrace dung when those who once appeared to be red with the most gracious flowers of charity afterward begin to plunge themselves into the loathsome mire of vices. But saffron is also said to bring soothing relief to the bodily members of those who are weary, which is consistent with the actions of that same supreme virtue that helps souls temper the heat of carnal pleasures and enkindles them to desire the joys of a heavenly homeland.[17] And it is easy to see why nard is said to dispel stiffness and bring warmth to bodily members that have grown cold, since the memory of the Lord's passion drives the benumbing fear of dying away from the hearts of the faithful, inflaming them and making them nimble enough to imitate his death, not only by mortifying their vices but also by laying down their lives for his sake (cf. Jn 15:13).

Cane and cinnamon, with all the trees of Lebanon (Sg 4:14). Cane, which is also called cassia, is counted among the spice-trees. Now it has a *coarse* purple *bark* that is reported to be useful for curing the ailments of many bodily organs. Because of its small size, it is reckoned by some to be among the fragrant herbs.[18] Precisely on account of this small size, it rightly signifies those who are humble in spirit, to whom belongs the kingdom of heaven (Mt 5:3), for as though clothed in purple they are always mindful of the Lord's passion, and it was such as these who were always ready to suffer for the Lord's sake, saying: *Because of you we are being put to death all day long; we are accounted as sheep for the slaughter* (Ps 44:22; Vulg. 43:22). For this is also the virtue that enables us most of all to restrain the impulses stirring within us and to resist lewdness as though it were a bodily affliction, when reflecting upon what God suffered for us we realize we suffer less than we deserve. Cinnamon contains the figure of that same virtue; for this tree is also as *small as a shrub* but with a distinctive potency and odor, and twice as efficacious as cane for use as a medicine.[19] Hence it is appropriate for us to understand that scripture wishes to express growth in humility, inasmuch as it places cinnamon after cane; for what is said to be blackish or ashen in color agrees with the souls of the humble, who are so conscious of their own frailty that they have learned to say to God in their daily prayers: *I will speak to my Lord, though I am but dust and ashes* (Gn 18:27); and again: *I despise myself, and do penance in dust and ashes* (Job 42:6). And the cinnamon tree, which is the color of ashes, is properly placed after purple-colored cane because contempt for our own virtue arises in us through the remembrance of the Lord's wounds. And the *bark* of this [tree], which is of great value, takes the name cinnamon *because it is round and slender like a cane*. For in Greek something without blemish is called "*amomum*."

Cane, it says, **and cinnamon, with all the trees of Lebanon**. Just as cane and cinnamon designate the humble thoughts of the righteous, so also do the trees of Lebanon designate their sublime deeds, doubtless because they are not only like cane and cinnamon in possessing a fragrance and a healing quality, and not only do they display as much glory in their bark, but they are also conspicuous for their immense height and great strength. For this reason they are suitable for use in larger buildings, as is also attested in this same song in which it was said further above: **Our rafters are of cypress wood** (Sg 1:17; Vulg. 1:16); and again: **King Solomon made himself a litter from the wood of Lebanon** (Sg 3:9). Therefore cane and cinnamon come forth in the Lord's garden with all the trees of Lebanon because those in the holy church who are remarkable for their humility and patience are one with those who firmly support the same church by preaching and performing deeds of power in that together they expect the palm of a heavenly reward.

Myrrh and aloes, with all chief ointments (Sg 4:14). Myrrh and aloes represent the continence of the flesh, doubtless because it is characteristic of those spices that bodies anointed with them are less likely to decay, as the texts describing the Lord's burial also bear witness. For in the same way that the corruption of mortal flesh designates the rottenness of riotous living, so does its embalming (understood typologically in a positive sense) aptly designate the virtues of continence and chastity with which our members are restrained from vices. And the chief ointments are those concerning which the Apostle says, *But strive for the greater gifts. And I will show you a still more excellent way. If I speak in the tongues of mortals and of angels, but do not have charity, I become as a noisy brass or a tinkling cymbal* (1 Cor 12:31—13:1), and the other things that the great master of eloquence so marvelously articulated concerning those great virtues, among which charity holds the highest place. It is truly a pleasing combination for myrrh and aloes to be growing in the Lord's garden along with all the chief ointments, because we must restrain the flesh from licentiousness if we are to receive the greater gifts of the Spirit. The converse to this has been said: *Because wisdom will not enter into a malicious soul, or dwell in a body enslaved to sin. For the Holy Spirit of discipline will flee from deceit* (Wis 1:4–5). Now *myrrh* is *a tree in Arabia, up to five cubits in height, similar to the thistle which* the Greeks call *the acanthus; its oil is green and bitter, which is also why it takes the name "myrrh."*[20] All these things aptly correspond to the mortification of the flesh, which seems bitter for a while but is always voluntarily undertaken in hope of a verdant homeland, namely, that one of which Peter says: *He has given us a* *new birth into a living hope through the resurrection of Jesus Christ from the dead, and into an inheritance that is incorruptible, undefiled, and unfading, kept in heaven* (1 Pt 1:3–4). Now [mortification] is compared to the thistle because it temporarily afflicts the body with the pricks of hardships in order to save the soul eternally. And since its freely flowing oil is more precious, while that which is extracted through a cut in the bark is of less value, who does not understand by this that in God's eye it is more virtuous when one strives to punish one's healthy and active body and subject it to servitude (1 Cor 9:27) even when blessed externally with material abundance than when one reluctantly curbs the wantonness of the flesh and forces it to accept the remedy of abstinence only under the pressure of illness or the world's other adversities? However, it should by right also be counted among the great virtues when one bears the chastisements of fatherly correction patiently, humbly, and joyfully, so that through them one may attain to the gifts of the promised inheritance (cf. Heb 12:5–11). Aloes also, if they are very attentively considered, are themselves aptly likened to those who are continent; for it is *a tree with a most sweet and exquisite odor*, for which reason the ancients burned *its wood on their altars in the place of incense*[21] and its sap flows most bitter, but suitable for very many medicines. In like manner, it is harsh indeed to practice continence and the restriction of carnal pleasures, but deservedly renowned for its virtue and most pleasing to the Judge who sees within.

A fountain of gardens, a well of living waters that flow rushing from Lebanon (Sg 4:15). A fountain of gardens springs forth among the other things in the Lord's enclosed garden because from the early church there went forth into the world the heavenly teaching that produced many churches (that is, spiritual gardens) for the Lord. It is properly added concerning this fountain: **a well of living waters.** What is a fountain if not a well? A well is always down deep, but a fountain is always sunk to the depths and can also be on the land's highest mountain. Therefore, one and the same teaching of the church is both a fountain of gardens because it produces spiritual fruits in those whom it instructs, and a well of living waters—a well indeed, because it is not open to everyone nor is it readily visible, but it is, on the contrary, stored up in the hearts of the saints through the revelation of the Holy Spirit. Hence *none of* *the rulers of this age understood* it; *for if they had understood, they would not have crucified the Lord of glory; but*, it says, *God has revealed it to us through his Spirit, for the Spirit searches everything, even the depths of God* (1 Cor 2:8, 10). Now these are living waters because they are the divine and heavenly words that come forth unceasingly from the invisible treasury of divine grace and bring to life all those whom they wash and refresh with water. For waters are said to be "living" when they flow eternally from an underground spring, doubtless in distinction from those that are either collected in cisterns or pools from an abundance of rain showers, or flow in torrents with a great rush for a while after the snows melt but disappear when fair weather returns. Rightly compared with these is the shallow and swollen ostentation of worldly teaching, which often seems to pour forth endless streams running deep with many kinds of eloquence and learning, but as soon as the Sun of righteousness begins to shine with the summer heat of gospel brightness, they all dry up as though they had never been. The Lord himself complains of them when he says through the prophet: *They have forsaken me, the fountain of living water, and dug out cisterns for themselves, cracked cisterns that can hold no water* (Jer 2:13); and Isaiah says: *Behold, the Lord will ascend upon a swift cloud and come to Egypt* (Is 19:1); and a little later: *And the water of the sea will be dry, and the river will be forsaken and dry* (Is 19:5).

A well, it says, **of living waters that flow rushing from Lebanon** (Sg 4:15). **From Lebanon**, it says: from the church that is clear and deep throughout her life (for Lebanon is interpreted as "clarity"[22]) and that pours forth streams of saving wisdom upon her hearers as though they were fields she was covering with it. Thus the Lord says in the gospel: *The one who believes in me, as scripture says, out of that one's belly shall flow rivers of living water*, and the evangelist adds by way of explanation: *Now he said this about the Spirit, which believers in him were to receive* (Jn 7:38–39). For living waters flow from the belly of the believer when holy proclamations flow out of the hearts of the faithful. **That flow**, it says, **rushing from Lebanon**. It rightly added **rushing** so that it might not only designate for us the descent of living waters but might also show the unconquerable force with which they come. For just as no one can hold back rivers that are running down from a high mountain, so it is with the flow of the apostolic word that came forth from a heavenly source and was divinely compelled to run in such a way that no opposing forces could overcome it in a struggle or deflect it from its course before it could supply souls with the water of life-giving teaching; this is the sort of [flow] that is in the psalm: *The rush of the river makes glad the city of God* (Ps 46:4; Vulg. 45:5). It deservedly makes the church glad, not only because she receives from God a river of living waters, but also because that river comes with such a rush of heavenly grace that it cannot be impeded by any obstacle from a contrary force. The well of living waters can also not inappropriately be taken as signifying those who have searched their hearts for every single thing that belongs to earthly thought, and who are constantly striving to dig it up, bring it forth, and cast it away by honest confession, so that in the recesses of their breasts they may duly prepare a pure and humble dwelling place worthy of God and make an opening in themselves for the living waters (that is, for the heavenly gifts) that will cleanse them thoroughly through streams of hidden inspiration. They are following the example of the blessed patriarch Isaac[23] who, although hindered by the Philistines, managed to dig wells for his use and that of his own people. With holy labor he cleaned out [the wells] that they had maliciously tried to cover over, and he continued to dig in the valley until he was able to obtain living water. So it is with us, who must contend with evil spirits that try to disturb the water of wisdom in us—or to shut it off entirely if they can—by filling up our minds with the stones of vices. But with skillful industriousness we catch those trials that they hurl against us and strive to shut them out with frequent prayers and vigils, so that we may have room for the invisible gifts.

---

16. He permits her to be tried by the winds of the tribulation so that his constancy may be demonstrated more fully.

But when the Lord has said that his garden is to be enclosed, to be supplied from a fountain of living waters, and to contain trees fragrant with spices and perfumes, when he has declared that it should be irrigated with waters of wisdom that should come from wells on account of hidden mysteries and should be living [waters] on account of the eternal blessings to which those who drink of them are led, and when he has indicated that they should flow straight along in a steady and unconquerable rush, it remained for him to say that although those adversaries would by no means be denied an opportunity to assail all the things constructed so sturdily and in order, [his garden] would be shown that it cannot be injured in any way by the many terrible things coming from every direction; on the contrary, the more it is assailed by the blasts of adversity, the more fully will the inner sweetness of its fruits be revealed. Hence it is now added in the Lord's own voice:

Arise, north wind, and come, south wind; blow through my garden that its fragrant spices may flow (Sg 4:16). By the north wind and the south wind he is surely indicating the storms of frequent trials with which the church had been buffeted so that she might learn how much spiritual grace she possesses, and how much inner strength. Now if we consider that what distinguishes the north wind from the south wind is that one of them is cold and the other hot,[24] it is not inappropriate to take the north wind as referring to the terrifying harshness of the world, and the south wind as referring to its deceitful charms; for surely the Lord himself shows that his garden is tested by assaults of both kinds, when in the course of explaining the parable of the good seed he says: *And the one that was sown on rocky ground, this is the one who hears the word and immediately receives it with joy; yet such a person has no root, but [endures] only for a while, and when trouble and persecution arise on account of the word, that person is immediately made to stumble. And the one that was sown among thorns, this is the one who hears the word, but the cares of this world and the deceitfulness of riches choke the word, and it remains fruitless* (Mt 13:20–22). Now even though the Lord seems to say in the imperative mood: **Arise, north wind, and come, south wind; blow through my garden that its fragrant spices may flow**, he is not commanding the reprobate to do evil, but simply permitting them to use their free will as they wish, since he has the power to accomplish his own good purposes through their evil deeds, and then at the final judgment to render unto them the torments they deserve for their evils. Accordingly, *the Lord hardened Pharaoh's heart* (Ex 10:20) so that he would afflict [the Lord's] own people, but a short while after he had delivered those who were afflicted, he inflicted eternal punishment upon the one who had afflicted them. And when he spoke to the chief of all his enemies concerning blessed Job: *Behold, he is in your hand* (Job 1:12), and that one went forth and smote him with the heaviest of blows, does it not seem to you that he was saying to the harshest and most turbulent of winds: **Blow through my garden that its fragrant spices may flow**? For fragrant spices flowed from the garden on a blast of wind when that holy man who was buffeted by adversities spread the odor of his marvelous constancy in virtue so very far and wide that the ardor of its unerring sweetness has even permeated to us who live at the very end of the world and of the age. Now when the church hears that she must prove herself amid the blasts of trials, she by no means contradicts what her beloved has foreseen and determined, but lest she should be overcome by adversity or corrupted by prosperity, in all things she seeks the help of the one *who brings out the winds from his storehouses* (Ps 135:7; Vulg. 134:7) and who, as blessed Job says, *gave the winds their weight* (Job 28:25), which is to speak in other words of the one who does not allow us to be tested beyond that which we can endure (1 Cor 10:13).

---

17. Conscious of her own devotion, she prays that he will come to inspect her.

Let my beloved come into his garden, she says, **and eat the fruit of his apples** (Sg 5:1). "Let the Lord come into his church so that he may keep her unstained and always fertile with the fruits of faith. He who has promised that he was going to remain with me until the end of the age (Mt 28:20), let him come and help me all the more graciously when he sees that my enemies are attacking me with greater trials, and let him benevolently grant that he himself may be beloved by me before all things; for I am confident that I will truly be able to say: *I love you, O Lord, my strength* (Ps 18:1; Vulg. 17:2), and: *He delivered me from my strongest enemies, and he set me upon the heights* of the heavenly kingdom" (Ps 18:17, 33; Vulg. 17:18, 34). **And let him eat the fruit of his apples**. And let him freely inspect the works of his saints and receive them with joy, in accordance with what he himself says to his disciples concerning the Samaritans who would believe in him: *I have food to eat that you do* *not know about* (Jn 4:32), which he shows that he had spoken concerning the calling of the Gentiles by going on to say: *My food is to do the will of him who sent me and to complete his work. Lift up your eyes and see the fields that are already white for the harvest, and the reaper is receiving wages and is gathering fruit for eternal life* (Jn 4:34–36). On the other hand, when he was hungry he looked for fruit on the Jewish fig tree and condemned it to be withered forever because he found none; he did this in order to signify figuratively that he was hungering for the salvation of the synagogue but because she refused to bear the fruit of salvation she had been punished in retribution with eternal infidelity. This can be understood as having been spoken particularly by the voice of the church's perfect members, namely, those who remember to serve God with sincere and rapt attention. **Let my beloved come into his garden and eat the fruit of his apples**, as if it were to say openly: "Would that the benevolent Lord would come quickly to give us the wages of our faithful devotion, and just as we have always taken care to love him and to render him that fruit of righteousness that he himself has given us, so let him show us his love's richest recompense by receiving us unto himself." While it is fitting for the saints to say this at every time, how much more fitting is it when they see the present church's condition being shaken by stormy trials?

---

18. Declaring that he has already come to her and savored her pious works, the Lord commands the citizens of heaven to rejoice in her good [deeds] also.

Responding immediately to their desire, he himself testifies in a pleasant voice that he has already done the things they have asked: **I have come into my garden, my sister, my bride** (Sg 5:1). "I have come," he says, "into my garden very often. In fact, I never cease to do this throughout the time of her pilgrimage, but I come to correct those who go astray, and to help those who are weak, and to strengthen the faith of those who doubt, and to feast upon the perfect fruits of those who do well as if upon the sweetest of banquets, and to defend those who struggle against the assaults of the enemy, and to reward those who overcome the enemy by crowning them with an eternal vision of myself."

I gathered my myrrh with my spices (Sg 5:1). Myrrh represents those who have either ended their lives in martyrdom or *crucified* their *flesh with its vices and desires* (Gal 5:24). Spices in general represent all those who are distinguished by the fame of their good works. He gathers his myrrh with his spices when he uses a sort of sickle of death, as it were, to cut his martyrs off from this life, and along with them the rest of the elect who have attained to the maturity of the perfection granted them, and brings them to the inner joys of blessedness in heaven.

I ate honeycomb with my honey, I drank wine with my milk (Sg 5:1). Comparable to honeycomb are those who know how to search out the sweetness of the spiritual senses within the sacred writings and to clarify it for the salvation of their hearers by preaching. Similar to honey are those who long to delight in tasting the delicacies of the word, which are set before them, and to feed on them insatiably. Wine also expresses the robust and excellent preachers of heavenly things; milk expresses the hearers who are still weak; and when the Judge who sees within approves the life that belongs to them all, differing indeed in the diverse modes of their devotion but united in one hope of a heavenly reward, it is as if he is eating honeycomb with honey and drinking wine with milk. Now he not only takes delight in the pious deeds of the elect, but he also invites his faithful to such a communal feast for the soul (that is, to the saints' communal celebration of their good desires) when he immediately adds:

Eat, my friends; drink and be drunk, my dearest ones (Sg 5:1). That is: "You are my friends, because you do what I have commanded you (Jn 15:14), and also my dearest ones, because you embrace me with perfect charity. I entreat you that when your hearts have been filled with the deeds of the saints as though with particular delicacies you will not only take care to recall them to memory but will transform the very memory of them into the fruit of imitation." For this is what it means for us to be drunk after eating honeycomb and honey, and after drinking wine and milk: that we not only rejoice over good people's marvelous virtues, but follow after them and by remembering them shake off the sluggishness of our mind and vigorously rouse it to love things eternal. On the contrary, the prophet says to certain ones: *You eat but are not satisfied; you* *drink but are not drunk* (Hg 1:6). Surely one eats the delicacies of the table of life but is not satisfied, and drinks the cup of salvation but is not drunk, if one has learned the words of the scriptures and has come to know the examples of the righteous, but has neither changed one's earthly life nor corrected one's behavior. One drinks but is not drunk if one hears the commandments of life with rejoicing but remains sluggish and indolent in fulfilling them.

Now if we wish to understand the saying above in which the Lord says, **I ate honeycomb with my honey** and **I drank wine with my milk** (Sg 5:1) as meaning that he has transferred his saints from this world to the heavens and brought them into the company of the citizens on high who are truly his body, it will follow that this admonition of which we are speaking now is to be understood as given to those citizens of heaven. For after he said that he had eaten honeycomb with his honey and drunk wine with his milk (that is, that he had gathered his saints together by adding them to his body in heaven), he immediately turns to face those inhabitants of heaven and says these words to them: **Eat, my friends; drink and be drunk, my dearest ones**, which is to say in other words: *Rejoice with me, for I have found my sheep that was lost* (Lk 15:6). And in a most apt comparison, the ones likened to honeycomb and honey are those who have found favor with the Lord from the foundation of the world, whom he carried away with him when he rose from the dead and brought from the lower regions to the heavenly kingdoms, so that what is being compared to honey is the sweetness of the holy souls whom he has raised up to eternal joys in heaven, and what is being compared to honeycomb is the no lesser happiness of those who merit through him to ascend to the courts of the heavenly city, both in their bodies and in their immortal souls. Concerning the latter, the evangelist clearly testifies that when the Lord died on the cross *the tombs were opened, and many bodies of the saints who had fallen asleep were raised, and after his resurrection they came into the holy city and appeared to many* (Mt 27:52–53). For those who were resurrected from the dead when the Lord arose are also believed to have ascended to heaven at the time of his ascension, since there is no reason that faith should be reduced to the level of the foolishness of certain ones who think that these people afterward returned to the dust and that those to whom they had appeared alive a little while before shut them up like the dead for a second time in the tombs that had previously been thrown open. So the Bridegroom eats honeycomb with his honey when the Lord led to eternal life all those who had served him faithfully from the beginning of this life—some rejoicing in the immortality of the flesh, some still awaiting the rewards of resurrection—and lifted them all up to a common blessedness of ineffable glory among the angelic dwelling places.

Up to this point the Lord has been praising the comeliness and virtues of holy church in a very long discourse beginning from the place where he says: **How beautiful you are, my friend, how beautiful; your eyes are those of doves** (Sg 4:1). This praise was prolonged for so long that she was also being opposed by adversaries who were putting her to the test. As soon as this begins to happen, she calls upon the aid of her Redeemer alone, and he did not disregard her prayers but under the name of "myrrh" and "spices" gathered into the heavenly homeland those who were either being tried by afflictions or adorned with other virtues. But by the name of "honeycomb," "honey," and "milk" he also declared that the church's whole life, which is divided between the teachers and the hearers, was acceptable to him. When these things have been completed, there follows the voice of the church, who longs to cling to the Lord in secret and silent contemplation rather than to incite the hostility and fury of the wicked against herself through the labor of preaching.

---

19. Resting from the tumults of the world, the church is awakened by the Lord's voice to correct those whose hope and love for him have already begun to grow cold.

She says: **I sleep and my heart keeps watch** (Sg 5:2), as if she were to say, "When the winds of persecution ceased for a while, I began to have a little rest in the Lord even in this present life, and while already freely enjoying the repose of this rest, with the whole desire of my heart I do not cease to keep watch for that rest which knows no end. I sleep because by the gift of his grace I enjoy a little tranquility in this life through my worship of him, since I am neither as completely occupied with the labor of preaching as was the early church, nor am I disturbed by as many conflicts with unbelievers as innumerable companies of the infant church had to endure in those first days. And my heart keeps watch because the more I am free from external attacks, the more deeply do I perceive within myself that he is the Lord." Surely holy church says these things in the person of those who desire to serve the Lord in the serenity of this temporal life by psalms, fasts, prayers, alms, and the other more peaceful activities of this temporal life. But since this life is one of labor, not of rest, she soon hears the Lord's voice arousing her and exhorting her to the sweaty toil of preaching so that she will remember that in the time of this exile she has not been denied an inner foretaste of the peace she desires, but neither is she allowed to enjoy it forever in its fullness. For there follows:

The voice of my beloved who is knocking: Open to me, my sister, my friend, my dove, my spotless one (Sg 5:2). The beloved knocks on our door when the Lord arouses us to make progress in virtues and when he reminds us to seek after the joys of the kingdom that is promised, just as we also knock on his door when we ask him to give us progress in virtues and an entry into the kingdom, since we are doubtless mindful of what he has promised when he says: *Knock, and it will be opened for you* (Lk 11:9). But he also declares that he knocks on our door when he says: *Behold! I stand at the door and knock; if anyone hears my voice and opens the door, I will come in to him and dine with him, and he with me* (Rv 3:20). Now there are two ways in which we open to the Lord when he knocks, for it may be that when his love comes into our hearts we open wide to receive with greater fervor that which we have already possessed for some time, or else by preaching either fear of him or his love [for us] we unlock our neighbors' hearts so that they may receive that which they have never yet possessed. And there is a third knocking of the Lord on our door, when through the infirmities that are set before us he reminds us that we are being carried away from this life of which he himself says in the gospel: *And you are like those people who are waiting for their lord to return from the wedding, so that they may open to him as soon as he comes and knocks* (Lk 12:36). Now we open to the Lord in this way as soon as he knocks if we cheerfully accept death and are not afraid to face the judgment of the one whom we remember that we have pleased by our good works and have always honored in accordance with that [saying] of the psalmist: *And the king's honor loves judgment* (Ps 99:4; Vulg. 98:4).

Even so, if we consider it carefully, here in this place the Lord seems to be desiring that opening of the faithful soul that takes place in the instruction of her neighbors. For it is apparent that she had opened her heart to him and that she was longing to be freed from the bonds of the flesh so that she might go to him, for she was able to say: **I sleep and my heart keeps watch**. And it is apparent that the beloved had already come in to her, for she was honoring him under the insignia of so many and such great titles that he could say: **My sister, my friend, my dove, my spotless one**. "'My sister,' because you have been made a co-heir of my kingdom; 'my friend,' because having left the yoke of servitude you have been made privy to my secrets; 'my dove,' because illuminated with the gift of my Spirit; 'my spotless one,' because you have been set apart from the affairs of business and lifted up before the eyes of God." But when he says: **Open to me**, he is undoubtedly asking that the minds of those who were not yet worthy of these titles should be opened to him by the act of preaching, as is also made clear by the following words in which it is said:

For my head is full of dew, and my hair with the drops of the night (Sg 5:2). *The head of Christ is God* (1 Cor 11:3), as the Apostle says, and his collected hairs are the thoughts in the mind of his faithful ones, which are not loosened when they get wet but stay bound together by discipline. Dew and the drops of the night that fall from the sky in the midst of the clouds when it is cold are doubtless minds that are dark and gloomy and always seeking earthly things. It was said of such as these that because iniquity was abounding, the charity of many was growing cold (Mt 24:12). Now the Lord commanded us to love him and to love our neighbor, but when we worship him with less love than we should, and (which is even worse) when many are possessed with no feeling of charity toward him at all, is the head of Christ not full of dew? And whenever the wicked lay hatred instead of love upon the servants of Christ who have collected themselves by keeping watch over their minds and who cling very closely to the love of their Creator, is his hair not being drenched with the drops of the night, and does it not carry the oppressive coldness of gloomy persecution like a heavy weight upon it? Therefore, when this sort of time is threatening, the Lord with good cause rouses the church from the sleep of sweet pursuits that she has been enjoying and commands her to apply herself to preaching the word, and to give warmth and light to the hearts of the wicked by frequent exhortation, and to open to him those that had been closed against him, making it impossible for him to come in and *dwell* in them *through faith* (Eph 3:17), since he prefers for many to attain salvation through her labor rather than for her to be at rest among the few who had been saved, although she deserves praise for her frequent meditation on celestial blessings.

---

20. Pleading to be excused from ministry out of love for rest, she is incited to action by her secret compunction. She makes a beginning, but results do not immediately follow the beginnings. Then she observes the virtues of great teachers and casts off whatever is clinging to her from the lusts of the world.

Now when she has been called forth to the labor of preaching, the church replies to the Lord: **I have taken off my garment; how should I put it on again**? (Sg 5:3). It is as though she were saying openly, "I have forsaken the affairs of things below; why should I take them up again?" For one who is girded for the duty of preaching and who takes on the responsibility of spiritual guidance still needs to keep watch in order to provide those to whom he preaches with eternal things, and to assist them with temporal necessities; therefore, the church is speaking in the person of those who prefer to take care of their own affairs in secret rather than to be occupied with difficult tasks, saying that to have cast off one's garment means that one cannot put it on again. For a garment figuratively indicates the affairs of this world, as the Lord himself testifies when, speaking of his own coming at the last judgment, he says: *And the one in the field must not turn back to get a coat* (Mt 24:18), mystically admonishing that one whose hand and mind are employed in growing spiritual fruits must never go back to pursuing the obligations of this world, once they have been cast aside.

I have washed my feet; how shall I soil them? (Sg 5:3). "As for the thoughts with which I was once accustomed to touch the earth, I have already washed them with the frequent tears of secret compunction, and as far as it was possible for mortals to do, I have made them worthy to enter into heaven, so that I am able to say that *our feet were standing in your courts, O Jerusalem* (Ps 122:2; Vulg. 121:2); that is, although I have not yet merited to enter within the very walls of the heavenly city, nevertheless I have already endeavored to purify my thoughts to such an extent that in the rapt gaze of my heart I have often been mindful of having received no small foretaste of some of the firstfruits of its joys. How, then, can I ever defile them by leaving the height of contemplation to return to the filthiness of the world?" For once someone has undertaken the responsibility for temporal assistance of which we have spoken, it is very difficult for even the most distinguished teacher to avoid being occasionally stirred in some sinful way by arrogance or anger—by anger, if people do not humbly attend to the teacher who is speaking of things divine and heavenly; but by arrogance, if they all listen with humility and the teacher wins great multitudes of believers in the Lord. Anger disturbs the teacher whose discourse is censured; arrogance puffs up the one whose discourse is praised. For this reason James says: *Not many of you should become teachers, my brothers and sisters, since you assume a stricter judgment; for in many things we all offend* (Jas 3:1–2). For this reason also the Lord himself washed the feet of his disciples after they returned from preaching (Jn 13:5), signifying that not even the very greatest preachers can keep the thoughts with which they touch the earth completely free from sin, but nevertheless he is gracious enough to wash it away, no matter what it may be. Therefore the church enjoys the sweet and wholesome pursuits of a quiet life in those who have merited to have experience of such things, and she pleads for them to be excused from the duty of preaching by saying somewhat like Moses: *I beseech you, Lord, send whomever you wish to send* (Ex 4:13). But since the Lord wishes that our love for him should be made known especially in love for our neighbors—for which reason also, when Peter declared for a third time that he loved him, he in like manner responded for a third time: *Feed my sheep* (Jn 21:17)—there is aptly added:

My beloved put forth his hand through the opening and my belly trembled at his touch (Sg 5:4). Surely the beloved puts forth his hand through the opening when through secret compunction the Lord invisibly enkindles us to perform virtuous works. He puts forth his hand to stop us from desiring when he brings us back to the memory of what he has graciously wrought in us—not only that we are human, but also that we belong to him. He puts forth his hand to us when he reminds us of what he did for us when coming from the Father's bosom into our public streets he deigned not only to be incarnate and to live on earth in order to make us both spiritual and heavenly, but also to die in order that we might live forever. Thus our belly has good cause to tremble when he touches us in this way, for whenever we recall his works of mercy our conscience grows fearful, in accordance with that [saying] of the prophet: *I have considered your works and I have grown very fearful* (Hb 3:2; Vulg. 3:1), and we hasten to rise up as far as we are able in order to care for our neighbors' salvation, for which God became incarnate and died. Surely the heart is often designated by the term "belly," for just as food is digested in the belly, so are thoughts processed by careful reconsideration in the heart. So it is for this reason that Jeremiah says: *My belly, my belly is in pain* (Jer 4:19); for what good did it do his hearers if their teacher complained that his belly was in pain? But he was eager to help them by bearing witness against the reprobate whose actions were disturbing his conscience and filling it with inner pain. Now the term "belly" can be taken as referring to the weakness and infirmity of those who either fear to undertake the office of teaching because they think themselves less than worthy, or flee from it because they enjoy the leisure of their repose. And the bride's belly trembles at her beloved's touch when at the incitement of divine compunction the church's weaker members dispel the sluggishness of inactivity and rouse themselves for the exercise of good works and even rise up to take thought for their neighbors by preaching. For this is what follows:

I rose to open to my beloved (Sg 5:5). Surely to open to the Lord here signifies to preach the word of the Lord. For we open to the Lord not only when we receive his coming into our heart through love, but also when by teaching those whose hearts have been closed against the truth we persuade them that they ought to accept it. And it is appropriate for the bride to say that she has arisen to open to the beloved, for it is absolutely necessary that someone who decides to preach the truth must first rise up to put into practice the things that are being taught, lest the one who is preaching to others should become a reprobate (1 Cor 9:27). Consistent with this are the words that follow, in which it is said: **My hands dripped with myrrh; my fingers were full of the finest myrrh** (Sg 5:5). For "hands" are understood as referring to the works that are done through the hands, and "fingers" are understood as referring to the discretion by which the works are directed, since no others of our members are divided into more parts than the fingers, and no others are more suitable for bending. That is why the Lord, when he was about to give judgment concerning the adulteress, first *wrote with his finger on the ground* (Jn 8:6) and then explained the judgment that was being applied, mystically admonishing us that whenever we decide to correct or judge others, in all humility we must first examine our conscience with scrupulous discretion, taking careful consideration lest we too should be put to the test. Now it has often been said that myrrh signifies martyrdom and continence of the flesh. Thus it clearly means that the bride's hands are dripping with myrrh when a holy soul hands herself over to works of continence, and her fingers are full of the finest myrrh when, examining herself with painstaking discretion, she finds that she is living continently solely in view of a heavenly reward. As for those who strive after the glories of human recognition, who (as the Judge himself bears witness) *have received their reward* (Mt 6:2), they doubtless seem to be dripping myrrh from their hands, but they certainly do not have fingers full of the finest myrrh, because even if they hand over not only their goods to the poor, but their bodies to the flames, if they do not have charity, it profits them nothing (1 Cor 13:3). If one wishes to teach another, therefore, one ought to abstain from the charms of the flesh and prepare oneself to suffer for confessing the faith; rightly, then, after [the bride] said, **I rose to open to my beloved**, she immediately added, **My hands dripped with myrrh**, and since the same continence or suffering ought to be undertaken only for the purpose of an eternal reward, she rightly went on to say: **my fingers were full of the finest myrrh**.

Again, the bride's hands are dripping with myrrh when her workers (that is, the holy teachers) subject their bodies to the mortification that brings salvation, and her fingers are full of the finest myrrh when she profits from tribulations to such an extent that her endurance of them is even said to be unconquerable, in accordance with that [saying] of the Apostle: *But we even glory in tribulations, knowing that tribulation produces patience, and patience trial, and trial hope, and hope does not confound us* (Rom 5:3–5).

I opened the bolt of the door to my beloved (Sg 5:6). The bride opens the bolt of her door to the beloved when every elect soul makes the temple of her heart worthy to be visited and inhabited by God, and she opens the bolt of the door to her beloved who is knocking when a sudden inspiration inflames her with desire for celestial things and she endeavors to open wide the bosom of her mind in order to receive a taste of his heavenly sweetness. Above, it was said that the beloved touched her by putting forth his hand through the opening and caused her to tremble with fear when she was inflamed by the ardor of his touch. Now, she desires not just to be touched by his hand through a narrow opening, but rather to throw open the door of her heart so that she may enjoy his most felicitous embrace (that is, to be more fully satisfied by the sweetness of divine illumination, which she has already experienced briefly and to a very small degree). But since the perfect vision of eternal joys is not granted to any of the elect in this life but is reserved for all the righteous in the other life where they will receive their rewards, it is rightly added:

But he had turned and gone away (Sg 5:6). For this is what the psalmist says: *The human being arrives at a high heart, and God shall be exalted* (Ps 63:7–8, Vulg.), for the higher that the human heart purified by faith and prayer raises itself in order to contemplate the glory of the divine vision, the higher is that which it seeks found to be, and the higher does it ascend toward that which is to be acquired only at the time of the recompense that is promised. Similar to this is that [saying] of the Preacher: *I said, "I will be wise," and [Wisdom] departed even farther from me than she had been before* (Eccl 7:23–24; Vulg. 7:24–25). Nor should we fail to mention that she does not simply say, "I opened my door," but rather says, **I opened the bolt of the door to my beloved**. For she had closed the chamber of her heart with a bolt dropped from above to keep a wicked person or robber from entering, in accordance with that [saying] of Solomon: *With all watchfulness keep your heart, for from it life proceeds* (Prv 4:23). She opened to the beloved so that when all the throngs of unclean persons had been driven away she might offer her Maker an open place within herself. Nor should it be thought contrary to this that above we said that the bride opens to the beloved who is cold from the drops of the night and from the dew when the church or the faithful soul enkindles the ignorant or uncaring hearts of her neighbors to praise the Creator, and now we are explaining how she unlocks the bolt of her door to the same beloved by throwing her mind wider open to his entrance through the process of compunction. For both things happen at one and the same moment, since the inner breath that enkindles a person to acquire souls for God is also accustomed to enkindle one to love one's Maker more ardently, and there is certainly no better motivation for someone to teach than the love of God. And whenever one is pleased to open the neighbor's soul by teaching so that it may receive the gifts of divine affection, it is equally necessary for one to renew one's own mind by doing the same, and to open oneself more widely so that divine grace may come in. Accordingly, in the words that follow the bride has clearly come to know how much progress she was making when she endeavored to open the neighbors' hearts, which she had seen to be closed to the Lord, solemnly relating that he for whom she was burning for so long was weighted down by the faithless sluggishness of others as though by dew and drops of the night, for there follows:

My soul melted as he spoke (Sg 5:6). She is saying: "The more sweetly I received the voice and presence of my beloved through the opening of secret compunction, the more sublimely did whatever was cold in me become warm, and whatever was hard begin to melt, to such a degree that nothing was sweet to me unless I was dissolving in tears, and thus with tears and lamentations I am now pleased to seek after the one who has touched me for an instant with his grace, since I was unable to keep him from departing. And the melting of my former hardness and the flooding of my soul in me was increased no small amount because I observed the charity of many growing cold, as he himself lamented (Mt 24:12), and because he was covered with the drops of the night (that is, with the gloomy attacks of the wicked). Since enemies have overthrown his law, for that very reason have I endeavored to love his commandments more and more, beyond gold and topaz" (Ps 119:126–27; Vulg. 118:126–27).

I sought him, and did not find him; I called, and he did not answer me (Sg 5:6). This is the voice of those in the holy church who, having transcended concern for things that are passing away, have been accustomed to advance only toward the highest goods, ever desirous of entering the heavenly homeland. It is quite certain that they cannot always feel the exact same degree of delight as they wish in their desire for things above, for this virtue does not depend upon the will of a mind raised up to heavenly things, but upon the gift of God who raises it up and illuminates it. Therefore, however often a chaste soul desires either to go to the Lord or to acquire a foretaste of future blessedness while still in the flesh, as soon as she obtains that which she demands she must yet say with a sigh that **I sought him, and did not find him; I called, and he did not answer me.** For he is always found by those who seek him rightly, so that he may have compassion, and he always answers those who call upon him rightly, so that he may give thought to their eternal salvation; but he does not always answer or allow himself to be found at once, so that what he promises to those who reach the homeland, this he may give as advance payment to those who are still proceeding on the journey of this exile. Accordingly, every day when we say frequently to the Father on bended knee, "May your kingdom come," we do not doubt that we are being heard, even though we do not immediately receive that for which we ask, but we patiently and cheerfully await the result of our prayer until we attain it at last.

The guardians who go around the city found me; they beat me, they wounded me (Sg 5:7). The guardians who go around the city are the holy teachers to whom the care of the church has been delegated so that by their word and example they may protect her from the assault of false teachers and enkindle more and more her fear and love for her Creator.[25] They surely do go around the city, for in every place throughout the entire world, wherever the holy church is spread, one finds either their bodily presence and their living voice, or their teachings and deeds set down in writing. Finding the bride wearied from searching for the beloved, they beat and wound her, because when they discover a soul that is anxious with love for things above they inflame her all the more with the word of their doctrine, and as long as they detect that anything earthly has remained in her, they crush and wound her as if by striking her they were rendering her insensible to everything that is below. For when the Apostle describes the armor of God he says: *And the sword of the Spirit, which is the word of God* (Eph 6:17). What wonder is it, then, if one touched by this sword is said to be beaten and wounded? Thus the wound from the stroke of this sword is understood as being the one concerning which she says elsewhere: **I have been wounded with love** (Sg 2:5, Old Latin).

They took my cloak from me, those guardians of the walls (Sg 5:7). The same eminent teachers are guardians of the walls when they also endeavor to build up those who stand to govern and defend the church. I believe that Timothy, Titus, and other such workers for truth were the walls of the city of God. And when Paul gave them precepts to encourage them, should he not be understood as a guardian of the walls? Surely he shows himself to be a guardian of the city, which he diligently encircles, when in enumerating his virtuous deeds he says: *And besides those other things, my daily insistence, the care of all the churches* (2 Cor 11:28). Once again, he has shown himself to be a guardian of the walls when he says to Timothy: *But you must be vigilant, labor in all things, do the work of an evangelist, fulfill your ministry* (2 Tm 4:5), and other things of this sort. And to Titus he says: *For this reason I left you in Crete, so that you should put in order the things that are lacking, and should appoint elders in every city, just as I also prescribed for you* (Ti 1:5). Now the guardians of the walls take away the cloak of the bride, who is beaten and wounded when the apostles or the apostolic men carry off the bands of transient things from any soul touched by divine love, so that having been extricated from base concerns she may with unrestricted movement seek the face of her Creator. For surely the cloak designates the same thing that the garment did above, in the place where she says: **I have taken off my garment** (Sg 5:3); that is, it designates involvement in earthly affairs.

---

21. She beseeches the more perfect among her faithful that at the time of their compunction or prayer they too would commend her to the Lord.

I adjure you, O daughters of Jerusalem, if you find my beloved, tell him that I am faint with love (Sg 5:8). The bride is rightly faint with love when, having been beaten and wounded by the sword of the Spirit, she puts off the mantle of carnal desire, for as a holy soul gains strength in God, her fondness for this world becomes more feeble and infirm. Nor should we be surprised that the perfect soul is said to be faint in regard to the things of the world, since the Apostle does not hesitate to speak of those who have completely abandoned the world as being dead: *For you have died, and your life is hidden with Christ in God* (Col 3:3); and concerning himself: *The world has been crucified to me, and I to the world* (Gal 6:14). The daughters of Jerusalem are the citizens of the heavenly homeland, some of whom are still on pilgrimage on earth, and some of whom are already reigning there. But when she says here: **I adjure you, O daughters of Jerusalem, if you find my beloved, tell him that I am faint with love**, she appears to be addressing that part of [the homeland] that remains on earth. Although they do not yet merit to see the Lord perfectly, nevertheless they often find him when they receive him in their hearts through love. Therefore the bride adjures these daughters of Jerusalem that, if they see her beloved, they should tell him that she is faint with love. Surely we are this bride and friend of God himself and of our Lord inasmuch as we cling to him and are made one spirit with him (1 Cor 6:17), and when, enkindled with desire for things eternal and longing for the face of our Creator, which we do not yet see, we come to those servants of his whom we believe to be leading the angelic life on earth and we humbly ask them to commend us to the Lord at the time of their devout prayer and to intercede for us so that we may merit to see his face. In so doing, we assuredly adjure the daughters of Jerusalem to tell God how much we love him, and to invoke heaven's assistance so that we may see his glory, just as they do.

---

22. They, in turn, ask her to tell them about those sweet virtues of his by which they are incited to burn with greater love for him.

Hence the reply given by his daughters of Jerusalem is clearly such as to agree in every respect with the devout conversation of the faithful, for there follows: **Of what sort is your beloved of**

beloved, O fairest of women? Of what sort is your beloved of beloved, that you so adjure us? (Sg 5:9). That is, for one brother or sister to speak openly to another, and one faithful person to another: "I see that you are burning with love for the Redeemer, for you speak about him to me and repeatedly greet me with an exhortation, so that the same love grows in my heart also when I hear of his favors and gifts. Indeed, I began to fear him long ago, as I became conscious of my sins, but now, as my soul grows stronger and I have already become more confident about the forgiveness of sins, it pleases me to hear something about his love. Come, then, I entreat you, and tell me: of what sort is your beloved of beloved? That is, on what account should he be loved rather than feared?" You also have a saying of this sort in the song of Isaiah: *For the vineyard of the Lord of hosts is the house of Israel and the man of Judah his beloved planting* (Is 5:7). Now "beloved of beloved" can be understood as "Son of the Father," just as he is rightly believed and confessed to be "light from light" and "God from God."[26] For just as there is one splendor and one deity of the Father and the Son, so is there also one love, as John bears witness when he says: *And everyone who loves him who begot, loves him who was born from him* (1 Jn 5:1).

---

23. She complies with their requests, reciting the renown of his virtues and powers with the praise that is due. Again, she inquires[27] about the kind of people among whose minds his footsteps are accustomed to be found.

There follows an appropriate response from the bride to those who are inquiring: **My beloved is white and ruddy, chosen from among thousands** (Sg 5:10). He is white because when he appeared in the flesh *he committed no sin, and no deceit was found in his mouth* (1 Pt 2:22), and ruddy because *he washed us from our sins by his blood* (Rv 1:5). And appropriately is he first white, then ruddy, because he first comes into the world innocent of blood and afterward goes out of the world bloody from his passion. He is chosen from among thousands because from the entire human race God took *one Mediator between God and humankind* (1 Tm 2:5) through whom the world is reconciled, and he alone among mortals was worthy to hear from heaven: *This is my beloved Son, with whom I am well pleased* (Mt 3:17); that is, "in whom I have found no fault that offends me, and a full measure of virtue in which I have rejoiced." Hence the Preacher properly says of him: *One man among a thousand I found, but a woman among all these I have not found* (Eccl 7:28; Vulg. 7:29)—implying that he shines with perfect righteousness, for he also declares that this should be understood by these words when he says in the following verse: *This alone I found, that God made human beings right, but they have entangled themselves in endless questions* (Eccl 7:29; Vulg. 7:30).

His head is the finest gold (Sg 5:11). The Apostle says that *the head of the woman is the man, the head of the man is Christ, and the head of Christ is God* (1 Cor 11:3). This head is the finest gold because just as no metal is considered more precious than gold, so does the unique and everlasting goodness of God rightly surpass all the good things that he himself has made.

His hair is like the branches of palm trees, black as a raven (Sg 5:11). The hairs of the beloved's head are the companies of saints, which are attached to God by faithful obedience, and they are deservedly compared to the branches of palm trees, because they await the sweetness of an eternal reward. Hence there is also that [saying] of the psalm writer: *The righteous will flourish like the palm tree* (Ps 92:12; Vulg. 91:13). Rightly are they said to be black as a raven, because they do not hope to be able to possess this sweetness by themselves, but to receive it from him who says: *Just as the branch cannot bear fruit by itself unless it abides in the vine, neither can you unless you abide in me* (Jn 15:4), or perhaps I should say that they do not perceive themselves to be anything by themselves except darkness, as the Apostle teaches: *Once you were darkness, but now you are light in the Lord* (Eph 5:8). Nor is it surprising that before the washing of regeneration we should be compared to the blackness of ravens, when Mistress Truth[28] says to the apostles themselves who are already following after her: *If you then, who are evil, know how to give good gifts to your children* (Lk 11:13). But let us also see whether the Lawgiver perceives in the hair of the Bridegroom something like ravens among the branches of palm trees; for when he looked upon the light of divine glory he immediately acknowledged the darkness of human wickedness and condemned it, saying: *The Ruler,* *the Lord God, merciful and gracious, patient and of great compassion, and true, who keeps mercy for thousands, who takes away iniquity and wickedness and sin, and no one on one's own is innocent before you* (Ex 34:6–7). Therefore the hairs of the Bridegroom (that is, the companies of the righteous) are like the branches of palm trees, black as a raven, because they know that it is through the Ruler's mercy that they travel toward the joys of victory, and not of themselves.

Now this little verse can also be taken as referring to those spirits who eternally cleave to their Creator in the heavenly homeland, for the higher they are when they see the glory of his unchangeable and eternal majesty, the more truly do they consider every created thing as though it were slight and of little value.

Apponius interprets the hairs of the Bridegroom as the virtues of the angels and goes on to say: *But in having spoken of the branches of palm trees it has taught that the aforementioned ministries are never brought down from their power and office but always remain aloft; like the hair of palm trees always maintaining the vigor of verdure, they are lifted up to the heights and are never associated with the weakness of decay.*[29]

Julian[30] speaks of them in this way: *While the form of his locks seems to imitate the splendor of gold, his hair is also signified by another comparison. His hair is like the branches of palm trees, no doubt because they also appear to be curly and golden.* And a little later: *It is as though it were saying, "Multitudes of his saints, both humans and angels, serve God and celebrate the King's honor with continual praise, and though the dignity of their ministries is so conspicuous that they are as eminent as palm trees and shine like gold, they nevertheless understand him whom they serve to such an extent that they derive some basis for their loftiness; otherwise, they would appear dusky and dark in view of their great humility."*

But instead of "the branches of palm trees," another translation simply describes his hair as "fir-like." And since we know that in Greek the fir tree is called the *elate*, it seems that "branches" [*elatas*] here is not Latin but a Greek word referring to the name of a particular tree. This also seems to be shown by Pliny the Younger when he is writing about ointments, for he says: *Moreover, there is a tree, which we call the fir, that is associated with the same ointments; some call it the "elate," while others call it the palm or the spathe.*[31] It is understood that by these words he is referring to the *elatae* as trees that are somewhat similar to the palm or the fir in that they are used in preparing ointments. Therefore our translator called them *elates* of palms (that is, firs of palms) so that we would understand that they are not the common sort of firs used for buildings and boats, but a special kind that is suitable for ointments. This is also appropriately suited to the figures. For the Bridegroom's hair can be compared with trees that produce ointments because when the companies of saints, which are like hairs closely attached to their Creator's head, are filled with the grace of virtues as they zealously serve the Divine Majesty, it is as though they adorn the Bridegroom's head like hairs similar to ointments. Accordingly, Mary Magdalene's great devotion was expressed in a mystery when she was anointing the Lord's head with nard, for she made her hair serve the function of branches of palms, that is, of trees fragrant with spices (Mk 14:3; Jn 12:3).

His eyes are like doves on brooks of water (Sg 5:12). John discloses what should be typologically understood of the Bridegroom's eyes when, after recalling that he had seen a Lamb having seven horns, he immediately added by way of explanation: *which are the seven spirits of God sent out into all the earth* (Rv 5:6). Now what he calls "the seven spirits" are the seven gifts of one and the same Spirit, which Isaiah distinguishes in the well-known list of divine activities (Is 11:2–3), for *the Holy Spirit of discipline will flee from the deceitful* (Wis 1:5). It is pleased, however, to abide with those souls who make themselves transparent and clear like living waters, who do not allow themselves to contain anything that is dirty or dark, or anything unworthy of being approved by people who love the truth or by that very Truth who searches minds and hearts (Ps 7:9; Vulg. 7:10). And it properly says not "on pools of water" but "on brooks of water." For if you want to know whence these waters are derived and where they hasten, it is made known by our Lord himself, who is the Fountain of life from which they spring and from whom the hearts of the elect have acquired whatever purity and lucidity they may possess. He says: *There shall be in him a fountain of water springing up to eternal life* (Jn 4:14). For there are some who appear to possess purity of word or deed but either fail to direct that purity toward the heavenly realms, or only pretend to do so; they are surely comparable not to brooks but to pools of water. And those who make room in themselves for unconcealed filth or for evil spirits are not like clean waters but more like the mires in which pigs are pleased to wallow. Therefore pigs delight in bogs and doves in brooks of water, because unclean spirits find a fitting home for themselves in unclean breasts. But *blessed are the pure in heart, for they will see God* (Mt 5:8), and they will be filled with the light of divine gifts. Because these gifts are freely given to the faithful only as a result of heavenly benevolence, there is aptly added:

They are washed with milk and settle down beside brimming streams (Sg 5:12). The gifts of heavenly largess and kindness are rightly indicated by the term "milk," doubtless because mothers who feed their infant children minister the nourishment of milk to them free of charge for the sake of natural affection. Therefore the doves to which the eyes of the Bridegroom are compared are washed with milk because *by grace you have been saved through faith, and this is not your own doing, for it is the gift of God* (Eph 2:8). Now these doves (that is, the gifts of the Spirit) are said to be washed with milk even though they never possessed any filthiness at all, just as it is said in the psalm: *The words of the Lord are pure words, silver tried by fire, from the earth, purified seven times* (Ps 12:6; Vulg. 11:7), although it is evident that they had never possessed any earthly defilement that needed to be purified by fire. Even so, it is rightly believed that the Father's co-eternal Son was born from the Father, and it is also rightly and truly confessed and believed that there was never a time when he was not born. And you find innumerable other things of this sort in the scriptures.

These doves also settle down beside brimming streams because those spiritual graces are pleased to dwell in all the hearts that overflow with the love of virtue, in order that those who diligently strive for heavenly things with a purity of sincere intent may be illumined by a heightened sense of their presence. But if we want to understand the Lord's eyes as the preachers of his word, we will find that they are like doves on brooks of water. They are like doves because they are innocent (Mt 10:16), and they are on brooks of water because they are enriched with spiritual grace (which is often designated by brooks of water), and because they are vigilant in attending to the holy scriptures, which are themselves also frequently represented by the term "waters." Being thoroughly instructed in those [scriptures], they are able to discern and avoid the devil's snares more easily, since doves settle down on brooks of water not only to drink or bathe or because the place is lovely and clean, but no less because they want to be able to see the shadow of an approaching hawk reflected on the water, so that they can flee away from the enemy when danger threatens.[32] The figural meaning of this characteristic is evident, for we need to keep meditating upon the flow of divine words so that by reading what the saints have done or said our minds may be alerted to the ways in which the ancient enemy tries to conquer us by direct assault or trip us up by tricks of deception. Whenever we perceive his impending snares, we must immediately enter into the clefts of our rock (that is, the security of the Lord's protection, which is our only refuge), and we must strive to defend ourselves with the sign of his passion. But we must also swiftly fly to seek the hollows of the wall; that is, we must ask the saints, both angels and humans, for their continual intercessions on our behalf before the mercy of the kind Creator. This is obviously a necessity for all the faithful, but especially for those who bear not only the burden of responsibility for themselves, but also that of guiding and teaching others. For they are holy church's most reliable and watchful guardians, on whose account she had previously heard from the Lord: **Arise, my friend, my bride, and come, my dove, into the clefts of the rock, into the hollows of the wall** (Sg 2:13–14). Now it is properly said of the same doves (that is, of the spiritual ministers of the word) that **they are washed with milk and settle down beside brimming streams**, so that they might be made known to have been renewed first of all by the washing of baptism, which is not unreasonably expressed by the word "milk," since they are reckoned among those means of grace by which holy church in its infancy was either born or nourished.

Now if we suppose there is a difference between brooks of water and brimming streams, it is possible to take "brooks of water" as a reference to the learning of the Old Testament, whose worshipers truly knew how to say to God: *The children of human beings shall put their trust in the protection of your wings* (Ps 36:7; Vulg. 35:8), lest, that is, they should be snatched away by the snares of the powers of the air as if by the talons of hawks. *They are inebriated with the abundance, and you give them drink from the river of your delight; for with you is the fountain of life* (Ps 36:8–9; Vulg. 35:9–10). "Brimming streams" cannot unsuitably be understood as the perfection of gospel teaching, the fullness of which is such that there can be none greater, at least for those who remain in this life. The evangelist was distinguishing one from the other when he said: *The law was given through Moses; grace and truth came through Jesus Christ* (Jn 1:17). And because the knowledge of both testaments has been granted to the teachers of truth, rightly are **the eyes** of the Lord said to be **like doves on brooks of water, which are washed with milk and settle down beside brimming streams**.

On the Song of Songs
Book 4

His cheeks are like beds of spices planted by perfumers; his lips are lilies, dripping finest myrrh (Sg 5:13). Just as the words that he spoke are represented by the Lord's lips, so in the same way do his cheeks represent both his modest gentleness and the severity of his countenance. For if it can rightly be said of an innocent person that *a person's wisdom shines in that one's countenance* (Eccl 8:1), how much more did the utmost power and wisdom shine in the countenance of that person who is the power of God and the wisdom of God to those who consider him correctly (1 Cor 1:24)? **His cheeks**, it says, **are like beds of spices planted by perfumers**. That is to say: "Even as beds of spices that are arranged decently and in order display for observers the great charm of both their fragrance and their appearance, so did the *Mediator between God and humankind* (1 Tm 2:5), when he appeared in human form, both illumine those who were near with the sweetness of his teaching, and with his reputation draw to himself those who were far off." Now you should understand that the perfumers by whom these beds are arranged are the prophets and apostles, who in absolutely concordant narration set down upon the sacred page not only his words but also his manner of life, [the prophets] telling of the mysteries of his incarnation that were to come, and [the apostles] telling of them as having come to pass. With regard to the loveliness of his cheeks, I believe that we should ascribe it to those occasions when he exulted in the Spirit rejoicing over the faith of the little ones (Lk 10:21), grieved over the hardness of heart of those without faith, rejoiced when he was about to raise Lazarus for the disciples' sake so that they might believe (Jn 11:15), wept and was himself troubled with them when he saw that [Lazarus's] sisters and friends were weeping (Jn 11:33–5), *began to grow sorrowful and be sad* when his passion was drawing near (Mt 26:37), never indulged in laughter or superfluous words, did not judge according to what his eyes saw or reprove according to what his ears heard (Is 11:3), but like a sheep that is led to the slaughter, and like a lamb before the shearer, so he did not open his mouth (Is 53:7).

His lips are lilies dripping finest myrrh: lilies, because they disclose the brightness of the heavenly kingdom; dripping finest myrrh, because they proclaim that one must attain to [this brightness] by despising present delights. It says: *From that time Jesus began to proclaim, "Repent, for the kingdom of heaven has come near"* (Mt 4:17). Likewise, his lips are lilies because he bids us to gleam with the splendor of holiness, and they are dripping finest myrrh because he commands us to preserve [that holiness] by bravely enduring whatever adversity may befall. He provided lilies in his lips when he instructed his hearers to be poor in spirit, mournful, meek, hungering and thirsting for righteousness, merciful, pure in heart, and peaceful (Mt 5:3–9). And when he was promising each of them the reward of eternal blessedness, he also added myrrh to the lilies, because he immediately added: *Blessed are those who suffer persecution for righteousness' sake, for theirs is the kingdom of heaven* (Mt 5:10). Likewise, his lips were gleaming like lilies when he taught that in one and the same person he was both truly God and truly human. Surely the golden-colored interior [of the lilies] is appropriately suited for the truth of the divinity that was in Christ, especially since it is threefold, as though figuring the glory of the Holy Trinity, which is one and undivided; the white exterior, however, suitably represents the purity and sanctity of the humanity he assumed. But the lips themselves were also dripping finest myrrh when he predicted that the humanity that he had assumed was going to suffer fetters, scourgings, spitting, reproaches, and death. Therefore, his lips imitate both the appearance and the fragrance of death when he says: *The Son of Man is to come in the glory of the Father with his angels, and then he will repay everyone for the work that has been done* (Mt 16:27); they drip finest myrrh when he says: *But first he must suffer many things and be rejected by this generation* (Lk 17:25).

His hands are rounded gold, full of hyacinths (Sg 5:14). The hands come in order after the lips; that is, the church praises her Redeemer's works after his words, because by deeds of power he has shown that we ought to believe those things that he taught in words. For this was the reason that when he was teaching on the mountain the crowds were indeed amazed at his teaching (Mt 7:28), but in order that faith might follow amazement, when he was coming down from the mountain he cleansed the supplicant leper simply by the touch of a hand (Mt 8:1–3). This was also the reason that the inhabitants of his own hometown were amazed at the things he did, saying: *Where did he get this wisdom and these deeds of power*? (Mt 13:54); surely they were referring to his lips as "wisdom," and to his hands as "deeds of power." Now his hands are properly said to be rounded, in order to indicate that he had both ready power and unerring knowledge of what must be done. It is well known that turning something round is easier than other crafts, and less prone to error, for anyone who wields a trowel or a knife or an ax or a hammer has to work very hard to avoid going askew, frequently applying the carpenter's square and keeping a watchful eye on the task at hand, but a person who turns something round on a wheel has no need for an external rule but is able to keep the tool straight and complete the work without any assistance.[1] Therefore, the Lord's hands are rounded because he is ready and able to do whatever he wishes, for he speaks and things happen. Accordingly, he said: *Stand up, take up your mat, and walk*, and at once the man who had lain paralyzed for thirty-eight years stood, *took up his mat, and began to walk* (Jn 5:8–9). His hands are rounded because he holds the entire rule of righteousness within himself. Unlike us, he is not so needy that he has to be instructed from the sacred writings lest his work should turn away from what is true. Accordingly, it is said of him: *How does this man know his letters, when he has never been taught*? (Jn 7:15). Now he knew them because he himself was older than the letters and the law; in fact, he was himself the framer and judge of the law.

Rounded gold, it says, **full of hyacinths** (Sg 5:14). It is clear from frequent exposition that gold signifies that excellence of divinity, which surpasses all things. Therefore, his hands are of gold because no faithful person can fail to know that the deeds of power he carried out in human form were effected by divine authority. They are also said to be full of hyacinths, doubtless because they arouse in us the hope and love of heavenly things. For the hyacinth is a precious stone the color of the sky.[2] Evidently the Lord has hyacinths in his rounded hands so that he might use those precious stones to adorn the vessels of election that he is preparing for glory (Rom 9:23); that is, that he might gladden the hearts of his elect with the desire and expectation of heavenly glory. But if we understand "hyacinth" as the tint designated by that name, it will still provide a meaning in accordance with the truth; for hyacinth is a tint the color of purple, with a pleasing fragrance, whence the poet includes it as an example when he enumerates love's treasures: *Its gifts are laurels and sweetly blushing hyacinth*.[3] And the Lord's hands are full of purple flowers, because when he was about to die that we might live, he shed them on the points of the nails through the redness of his own blood. But the old translation[4] instructs us that in this passage we should understand the word "hyacinth" as referring to precious stones rather than to flowers, because it says: *His hands are rounded gold, full of tharsis*. Among the Hebrews *tharsis* is the name of the stone that we call chalcedony.

His belly is of ivory, set with sapphires (Sg 5:14). The belly is the weakest of our members, doubtless both because it lacks the support of bones and because it encompasses within itself the intestines, which are so highly susceptible to dangerous injury. But ivory is the bone of an elephant, which is commonly recognized as a cold-blooded animal of great chastity. For this reason the dragon often attacks the elephant and seeks its death, because he wants to cool his own burning entrails with a drink of its blood.[5] Now the sacred history bears witness to the color of the sapphire when it says: *And they saw the God of Israel; under his feet there was something like a work of sapphire stone, and like the heaven when it is clear* (Ex 24:10). Therefore, the belly of the beloved suggests the frailty of his humanity, through which he became like us in rank. Ivory indicates the splendor of chastity through which, while in the flesh, he remained free from the corruption of the flesh. Sapphires express the sublimity of the heavenly virtues with which he shone while in the flesh.

His belly, it says, **is of ivory, set with sapphires**, as though she were to say openly: "It is true that there is in him a frailty which pertains to his mortal substance, but since it is utterly free from the lewdness of mortality, it instead shines brightly with the marks of his divine works." And she appropriately said that his belly was completely made of ivory, and not completely covered with sapphires but rather set with sapphires, in such a fashion that the sapphires appeared in part, and the ivory in part. His belly was of ivory because the frailty that he had put on was free from all sin, so that it would be found to have no more fervor for anything depraved than would the tusk of a dead elephant, and it was set with sapphires because amid the sufferings of the humanity he assumed he was continually revealing the signs of his eternal divinity. And surely it pertains to the frailty of his humanity that *a child is born to us* (Is 9:6), but to the power of his divinity that he is born of a virgin and that his birth is proclaimed by angelic voices and celebrated with mysteries (Lk 2:1–20); to the power of his divinity that a star shows the wise men where he is to be worshiped (Mt 2:1–12), to the frailty of his humanity that he is driven out of his homeland by the plots of a deceitful king (Mt 2:13–15); to the frailty of his humanity that he can be led out and tempted by the devil (Mt 4:1), to the power of his divinity that after conquering the devil and driving him away, he is worthy of being ministered to by angels (Mt 4:11); to the fragility of his humanity that he asks a Samaritan woman for water (Jn 4:7), to the power of his divinity that he is said to be able to provide from himself a fountain of living water (Jn 4:14); to the frailty of his humanity that he grows weary along the road (Jn 4:6), to the power of his divinity that he promises eternal rest to those who follow him (Mt 11:28); to the frailty of his humanity that he sleeps in a boat (Mt 8:24), to the power of his divinity that when awakened he exercises command over the wind and the sea (Mt 8:27); to the frailty of his humanity that he is crucified and dies (Mt 27:33–50), to the power of his divinity that at his death the foundations of heaven begin to tremble, as do also those of earth (Mt 27:45, 51); to the frailty of his humanity that he is anointed with spices and buried (Mk 15:46—16:1), to the power of his divinity that he arose and ascends into heaven (Lk 24:5, 51). To the frailty of his humanity pertains what Isaiah says: *There is in him no form or beauty for us to see*, and a little after, *and his countenance was as one hidden and despised, and we esteemed him not* (Is 53:2–3). To the power of his divinity pertains what John says: *We have seen his glory, the glory as of the Only-*

begotten from the Father, full of grace and truth (Jn 1:14). Therefore, Christ's belly is of ivory and set with sapphires because his immaculate and undefiled incarnation repeatedly shone forth with the wonders of his divine majesty.

For we should note that scripture says of the color of sapphire that its appearance is like that of *the heaven when it is clear* (Ex 24:10). Now the sublimity of divine majesty is not incongruously represented by the term "clear heaven," as the psalmist attests when in describing the incarnation of our Redeemer he says: *His going out is from the highest heaven, and his course is toward the height thereof* (Ps 19:7; Vulg. 18:7). For this is what he says to the disciples concerning himself: *And you have believed that I came from God; I came from the Father and have come into the world; again, I am leaving the world and going to the Father* (Jn 16:27–28). But the bride herself saw the beauty of a sapphire in her beloved's belly of ivory when in the voice of her first pastor [Peter] she said: *You are the Christ, the Son of the living God* (Mt 16:16), doubtless because in the Son of Man—holy, blameless, undefiled, and separated from sin (Heb 7:26)—she recognized the pristine fullness of his divinity.

His legs are marble columns that are set upon bases of gold (Sg 5:15). This reference to the Lord's "legs" suggests the paths of his incarnation, by which he deigned to come for our salvation. These columns are appropriately compared to marble, because they are both strong and upright. For what is stronger than marble, and what is straighter than a column? And did the psalmist not perceive the firmness of marble in his legs when he said: *And like a bridegroom coming forth from his bridal chamber, he rejoiced like a giant to run his way*, and so on (Ps 19:5; Vulg. 18:6)? And did he not also see the uprightness of columns when on another occasion he said: *The Lord is just in all his ways* (Ps 145:17; Vulg. 144:17)? For it was on this account that his legs were never broken while he was hanging on the cross, even though the governor had given permission (Jn 19:31–33), in the same way that his garments could not be torn (Jn 19:23–24). Surely his tunic remained undefiled so as to signify that nothing will ever violate the unity of the church, which is the garment chosen for himself, having no spot or wrinkle (Eph 5:27). His legs remained intact so that the mystery of his coming in flesh might continue holy and undefiled by the hammer of any wrong teaching. For surely

Pilate is interpreted as "the mouth of the hammerer."[6] But even if an ungodly hammer makes ready to strike through the mouth of a heretic, the marble columns stand, because they are more than strong enough to repel the blow of the one who is striking. And even if unsound teaching speaks unsoundly of the Lord, the truth of the gospel stands, and will prevail. Concerning these columns there is aptly added:

They are set upon bases of gold (Sg 5:15). Surely these bases of gold are the counsels of Divine Providence by which everything that was to be created in the temporal world was determined eternally before the world was made, and in which our Savior's incarnation was predestined along with our salvation in him. The Apostle bears witness to this when he says: *Just as he chose us in him before the foundation of the world, that we might be holy and blameless in his sight in love* (Eph 1:4); and the apostle Peter says that we have been redeemed *with the precious blood of Jesus Christ, like that of a lamb unspotted and undefiled, foreknown indeed before the foundation of the world, but manifested in the last times* (1 Pt 1:19–20). Therefore, the marble columns that are compared to the Lord's legs are set upon bases of gold because all of our Savior's steps—those by which he willed to come down to earth from heaven, and to dwell upon earth, and after the earth to descend to the regions below, and after the regions below to rise up from the grave and return to heaven—are as firm as marble, as upright and heaven-seeking as columns, and as much in accord with the rule of Divine Providence as if they were set upon bases of gold. Of these bases, he himself says: *For I have not spoken on my own, but the Father who sent me has himself given me a commandment about what to say and what to speak;* and if you want to know why these bases are of gold, listen to what follows: *And I know that his commandment is eternal life* (Jn 12:49–50).

His appearance is like Lebanon, choice as the cedars (Sg 5:15). She is saying: "How shall I try to describe each of his features more fully? How shall I briefly impart the sum of them all? In the same way that Mount Lebanon in Phoenicia is remarkable for its renowned height and breadth, so does my Lord surpass all those who have come forth from the earth by right of his more eminent grace, and just as that mountain is forested with noble trees, so does he lift up all the saints with his presence lest they slide away to the depths below, and he keeps them rooted in himself so that they cannot be shaken by the winds of temptation. As every splendor of the forest gives way before the cedar's beauty, strength, height, and fragrance, so is my beloved *the most handsome of the sons of humanity, with grace flowing from* his *lips, for which reason God has blessed* him *forever* (Ps 45:2; Vulg. 44:3), and (as the psalm goes on to describe) so in other ways does he greatly surpass the measure of his companions." And we should note that the same beloved is compared both to Lebanon (which brings forth remarkable trees) and to the cedar (which is one of those trees that Lebanon brings forth), as though he brings forth trees and holds them up, and at one and the same time is brought forth among those trees and is held up by himself. For our Lord Jesus Christ nourishes when through the grace of his divinity he brings forth to life all the elect from the beginning of the world until its end, and he carries himself among humanity because when he chose to make himself human he filled humanity in common with the grace of his Spirit, although he was far higher than the rest. Thus is it said of them: *Now each of us was given grace according to the measure of Christ's gift* (Eph 4:7), but of him: *For God gives the Spirit without measure*, for *the Father loves the Son and has placed all things in his hand* (Jn 3:34–35). Therefore the Lord is as choice as the appearance of the cedar, because he surpasses the entire grove of the holy church in which he was born with a unique and matchless dignity. His appearance is like Lebanon, which produces the cedar along with other excellent trees, because he chose to become human himself along with his elect, just as he created *the tree of life in the midst of Paradise* (Gn 2:9). It is as though an artist were to use the appropriate colors to paint himself in his own place along with the others, or as though some historian (for example, Moses the Lawgiver or John the Evangelist), in the course of relating many memorable things about many people, were to write about himself in his own place. So it is that the dazzling mountain that goes by the name of Lebanon (that is, our Redeemer) brings forth the cedar, which is certainly more excellent than the other trees, along with the innumerable fruit-bearing trees that it brings forth to praise the name of the Lord; that is, he brings them forth along with himself, who not only praises the name of the Lord (Ps 113:1; Vulg. 112:1) but was also blessed himself when he came in the name of the Lord (Ps 118:26; Vulg. 117:26).

His throat is most sweet, and he is altogether desirable (Sg 5:16). If, when it was said above that his lips are brightest lilies, we take the mention of his mouth as referring to his words, how else should we understand his most sweet throat, other than as the flavor within those same words? For many of those who read or hear them are able to speak the words of the Lord, and are quite adept at analyzing the mysteries of the faith, but you will find very few who truly savor this sweet taste in the palate of their hearts. For this reason it is said in praise of the most excellent among the saints: *They shall proclaim the memory of the abundance of your sweetness, and shall rejoice in your justice* (Ps 145:7; Vulg. 144:7). Surely those who rejoice in God's justice are the ones who are wont to taste the abundance of the sweetness of his love within, and to proclaim its memory by preaching to their neighbors; for anyone who has never learned to taste his sweetness must be in fear of the justice of his judgments, rather than rejoicing in them. Accordingly, when Peter proclaims to us the memory of the Lord's most abundant sweetness, which he had already tasted so well, he says: *Long for the reasonable milk without guile, so that by it you may grow into salvation—if indeed you have tasted that the Lord is sweet* (1 Pt 2:2–3).

Likewise, because the living breath comes forth through the throat to the lips so that he is able to speak, just as the Lord's lips are the words that he was speaking, so can we quite easily understand the throat as the inner and hidden character of piety and kindness through which he was able to speak outwardly to us. For Paul says: *The grace of God our Savior has appeared to all humanity, instructing us to renounce impiety and worldly passions, and in this world to live soberly, and justly, and piously, while we wait for the blessed hope and coming of the glory of our great God* (Ti 2:11–13). Now his lips were like lilies at the time when he gave us the hope of the coming of the glory of our great God; his lips dripped most pure myrrh when he instructed us to renounce impiety and worldly passions, and live soberly, and justly, and piously; and his throat is that eternal grace that was contained in this promise and instruction when he willed to appear to us, which is certainly most sweet to us, since apart from it we can have no sweetness at all. Accordingly, the beloved himself shows that his throat conveys sweetness not only in his speaking voice but also in his breath, when appearing to his first disciples (that is, to the members of his bride) *he breathed on them and said: "Receive the Holy Spirit"* (Jn 20:22).

And, it says, **he is altogether desirable** (Sg 5:16). Christ, who is altogether God, is also human (that is, the Word is both soul and flesh), and he is altogether desirable because he is to be apprehended not only in the unchangeable majesty of his eternal divinity, but also in the glorified substance of the humanity he assumed, for the apostle Peter says: *On him the angels desire to look* (1 Pt 1:12). Let me amplify what I am saying: he was altogether desirable even before the glorification of his humanity. He was altogether desirable right from the very beginning of his conception up to the triumph of his passion; desirable to his mother when she said: *Behold the handmaid of the Lord; let it be to me according to your word* (Lk 1:38); desirable to the blessed womb that bore him, and desirable to the breasts that nursed him (Lk 11:27); desirable to the angels who were singing a hymn at the time of his birth (Lk 2:13–14); desirable to the shepherds who were glorifying and praising God when they saw him; desirable to the wise men who came from the East to seek him and, when they merited to find him, worshiped him by offering him gifts (Mt 2:1–11); desirable to old Simeon, who was awaiting the vision of his nativity that had been promised to him, until at the end of his life he took him in his arms, blessed God, and looked upon death with joy (Lk 2:25–32); desirable to Anna the prophetess who, when she saw his birth, was also rendering to the Lord the praises due his name (Lk 2:36–38); desirable to all those who saw him in the temple at the age of twelve, astounding the elders and teachers with heavenly wisdom (Lk 2:41–52); desirable to the disciples when they immediately left behind everything they owned and followed after him when he called (Mt 4:18–22); desirable to them when they said: *Lord, to whom shall we go? You have the words of eternal life* (Jn 6:68); desirable to all the people and the tax collectors who acknowledged the justice of God when they heard his words (Lk 7:29); desirable to Peter on the mountain when he says: *Lord, it is good for us to be here* (Mt 17:4); desirable to the thief on the cross when he prayed: *Lord, remember me when you come into your kingdom* (Lk 23:42). He was desirable not only to those who loved him when they saw him in the flesh, but also to those of whom he says to the disciples: *Many prophets and righteous people longed to see what you see, but did not see it, and to hear what you hear, but did not hear it* (Mt 13:17), and also even to us, for although we were born into the world after his ascension into heaven, we hold in common with the saints before us the promise of his saying: *If I go and prepare a place for you, I will come again and will take you to myself, so that where I am, you may be also* (Jn 14:3).

Such a one is my beloved, and this is my friend, daughters of Jerusalem (Sg 5:16). The more devotedly holy church or any individual soul loves God, the more intimate is her friendship with God. But as long as someone keeps the divine commandments because of a weakness in the soul (whether it be a consciousness of sin or a servile fear), that person necessarily puts God in the position of being the Lord, more than the Father or a friend, and is never able to attain to the perfection of those apostles who merited to hear: *Now I have called you friends, because I have made known to you everything that I have heard from my Father* (Jn 15:15). But on account of his extraordinary faith and love Abraham too *was called the friend of God* (Jas 2:23), and the Lord spoke to Moses *as one speaks to a friend* (Ex 33:11). Having heard about the qualities of the beloved for which they had been seeking, the daughters of Jerusalem go on to add another question:

Where has your beloved gone, O fairest among women? (Sg 6:1; Vulg. 5:17). There is variation in the personages who speak in the song in order to make it more beautiful. The rest of the daughters of Jerusalem represent the same church of Christ that is identified as the bride. She is regarded as being the daughters of Jerusalem or of Sion because she comprises many souls and because she takes her origin from that heavenly city which is the mother of us all (Gal 4:26). But she is called "bride" or "sister" or "friend" or another name of that sort in order to signify that she remains one and undivided, even though she is dispersed far and wide throughout the world. And the variety of personages speaking among themselves concerning the Bridegroom is, as we said above, that pleasing conversation among themselves through which Christ's faithful people stir one another up to love him. The bride admonishes the daughters of Jerusalem that if they find her beloved they should tell him that she languishes for love of him, doubtless because the whole catholic church rejoices together when all the elect pray to the Lord for her condition. The daughters of Jerusalem entreat the bride to tell them about her beloved because the faith of Christ should not be learned or taught except in catholic unity. And, having heard about his appearance, concerning which they were inquiring so earnestly, they go on to ask where he has gone, because it is also within the unity of the holy church that one ought to learn about the kind of heart and the manner of life in which the Lord is most likely to be found. Therefore, when we come together with one another to hold converse about the Lord with pure intent and to be, as it were, so many daughters of Jerusalem, let us all perfectly aspire for heaven, and let us truly profess that we are pilgrims upon earth, and that our homeland is in heaven. And yet, every one of us is rightly said to be speaking with the bride of Christ and seeking a response from her when we make careful provision because we do not wish to say or hear from a brother or sister anything other than what is dictated by the rule of catholic peace.

Now the church is called "fairest among women" because it is obvious that while the churches of Christ throughout the world may be as fair as the spiritual flower of fertile women, fairer still is the whole catholic church, which includes all of them within its own members. For it would be unsuitable for us to take the women in this passage as referring to the synagogues of errant heretics or schismatics, whether Gentiles or Jews. For it cannot be saying that the bride of Christ is the fairest among those women who prove not to have been fair at all, but rather among those women who are the fair churches of Ephesus, Smyrna, Pegamum, Thyatira, Saris, Philadelphia, Laodicea (Rv 2:1—3:22), and innumerable others throughout the world such as are completely dedicated to God, for it is truly right to say that the fairest of these is she in whom all of them are made into one.

It says: **Where has your beloved gone, O fairest among women? Which way has your beloved turned, that we may seek him with you**? (Sg 6:1; Vulg. 5:17). Now the Lord is said to go away and turn aside not as though the Lord ever abandons those whom he has previously acquired and goes off to acquire others, but, since divine power is by its nature able to be present and attentive everywhere, whenever it wishes to go away and turn aside in order to bring others into company with itself, it does so in such a way that it is nevertheless able to keep those whom it had previously gathered to itself in the grace with which they have begun. This accords with what [God] says to Moses: *Gather for me seventy men of the elders of Israel, whom you know to be the elders and teachers of the people, and bring them to the door of the tabernacle of the covenant, and I will take some of your spirit and give it to them* (Nm 11:16–17)—not that he diminished the grace already given to Moses, but that he made them partakers of the same grace that Moses possessed. Analogously, when we ignite a candle from a flame of fire, we set it aflame with light while the flame from which we ignite it remains intact. It is also possible to understand this as meaning that the beloved sometimes goes away and turns aside from the bride, when, although we ask to be inflamed with love of him until there is an effusion of tears, to fulfill the duty of prayer with fixed and unwavering intent, and to transfer all our attention from carnal desires to those that are eternal, he does not always consent to the things for which we wish to pray. Rightly, then, do we ask those whom we believe to have knowledge, and whom we believe to be worthy of such a question, where the Lord has gone and where he has turned, since we eagerly desire the help of those whose virtues and purity of mind provide more abundant proof of the presence of divine grace in themselves, so that, being instructed by their examples and exhortation, we too may merit to increase more and more in yearning for our beloved. And well do they say, **that we may seek him with you**, since every soul that tries to seek Christ apart from the fellowship of holy church is thenceforth rightly classed not among the daughters of Jerusalem but among those of whom the mother of Samuel (who was a type of the church) spoke to the priest of the synagogue when he was despising her: *Do not count your handmaid as one of the daughters of Belial* (1 Sm 1:16).

---

24. She replies that he delights in the pious desires and fruitful works of the saints and that he gathers to eternal joys those who are perfect in the virtues of purity.

My beloved has gone down to his garden, to the bed of spices (Sg 6:2; Vulg. 6:1). It has already been noted who is the beloved's garden; for he himself said: **A garden enclosed is my sister, my bride** (Sg 4:12). Surely the garden is his church, and his garden is every elect soul. And when it has said, **My beloved has gone down to the garden**, properly does it go on to specify that it is **his**, that is, the one that he himself has made, that he himself has cultivated, that he himself has strewn with the perfumes of virtues, that he himself has watered with the fountain of his grace so that it may not run short, that he himself has enclosed with the wall of his protection so that it may not be desecrated by outsiders. This is what he says concerning it: *The kingdom of heaven is like a mustard seed that someone took and sowed in his garden, and it grew and became a great tree, and the birds of the air rested in its branches* (Lk 13:19). Surely the mustard seed is the word of the gospel, humble in appearance but fervent in power, which the God-man himself took from the Father and sowed in his church and gave it such increase that like a lofty tree it spread wide its branches of faith and virtue all over the earth, and in those branches the angelic spirits rejoice at the salvation of mortals, believing that their own rest as citizens of heaven will be augmented when those earth-born creatures are summoned to the realms above.

For the Lord willed to be arrested in a garden at the time of his passion (Jn 18:1), to be crucified in a garden, to be buried in a garden (Jn 19:41), to rise victorious over death in a garden, and Mary supposed him to be a gardener when she merited to be the first to see the glory of his resurrection (Jn 20:15), but all of this would have been to no purpose if in sowing his garden (namely, the church) with divine gifts he had not taken care to plant the virtue of patience in this life, contempt for death at the end of this life, the hope of blessed peace after the body's dissolution, and a longing for blessed immortality when the body is regained. And it is aptly said that he has gone down to his garden, but not that he has entered into it. For the Lord's place is heaven, since *he dwells on high and looks down on the lowly* (Ps 113:5–6; Vulg. 112:5–6), and the garden's place is among the lowly, in this vale of tears, but he has gone down to it from on high, and in his heart he has prepared a stairway by which it can come to the place of heavenly joy. For this reason it is rightly said above of this garden (that is, the church): **Who is she that comes up through the wilderness, like a column of smoke from aromatic spices**? (Sg 3:6). Therefore it is a wonderful display of heavenly kindness that the Lord is said to descend to the church, and the church is said to ascend to the Lord. For divine grace descends upon us from above and enables us to ascend above. This was mystically signified in Exodus when the Lord came down on Mount Sinai and Moses went up (Ex 19:20); surely Moses was ascending to receive an increase of virtue, and the Lord was descending to give it. Therefore when it has said: **My beloved has gone down to his garden**, it also goes on to specify how that same garden is made fecund with fruit when it immediately adds:

To the bed of spices (Sg 6:2; Vulg. 6:1). Surely the bed of spices is the mind of the faithful, which is instructed in the discipline of true faith as though it were constituted with equal sides all around and as though a skillful gardener had turned it frequently so as to remove all superfluous plants, doubtless because the gardener scrutinizes it carefully and considers it intently to make sure that it contains nothing profane, nothing unclean, nothing at all detrimental to heavenly salvation. He strives to make it worthy so that his beloved (namely, the beneficent sower of justice) should plant the spices of virtues in it and water it with his grace and continual assistance so that it never withers. This garden bed pleasingly expresses its heavenly desire at the beginning of the forty-first psalm (according to the Hebrew version only), saying: *As a garden bed prepared to be irrigated with water, so is my soul prepared for you, O God* (Ps 41:2; Vulg. *iuxta Hebr.*). And what the Lord does when he goes down there to his garden or to the bed of spices is shown when it is added:

To feed in the gardens, and to gather lilies (Sg 6:2; Vulg. 6:1). Now he feeds in the gardens because he delights in the pious deeds of the saints. He feeds in the gardens, doubtless because his members are those who produce the fruits of justice, and we should understand that the Lord was referring not only to bodily forms of benevolence but to spiritual ones as well when he told us what he is going to say at the last judgment: *As long as you did it to one of the least of these my brothers and sisters, you did it to me* (Mt 25:40). He gathers lilies when the just attain the perfect splendor of merits, and he leads them from this life to the heavenly kingdom. In the next two verses as well, [the bride] elaborates more fully on the incentive for boundless charity, when she adds:

I am my beloved's and my beloved is mine; he feeds among the lilies (Sg 6:3; Vulg. 6:2). "I am my beloved's, for I prepare a pleasant pasture in the beds of spices (that is, in the pure hearts of the faithful). And my beloved is mine, for he feeds among the holy desires of spotless souls. I offer this in return for his grace, so that he will fulfill the desires of his faithful, whom I have brought up. Now he has fulfilled them by plucking them from this garden of sacred delight and gathering them together in the secret places of the heavenly mansions, where in the eternal immortality of their bodies and their spirits they shine in his sight like lilies with a double nature (that is, part golden and part white), and it is as though in the unfading renown of their virtues they give forth the sweetest fragrance throughout all the inhabitants of the eternal homeland."

---

25. Hearing these things, the Lord praises the church's devotion and praises her works; nevertheless, he teaches her that it is not possible for him to be fully seen in this life, even though she has desired it so much.

Thus far, it has been the voice of holy church seeking her Lord, praising him, and desiring to see his face. However, the next voice is his, since he can never be absent from those who love him, but wherever two or three are gathered together in his name, there is he in the midst of them (Mt 18:20); in fact, if one of his own is separated from other mortals as a result of being shut up among lions (Dn 6:16–23), or held in the depth of the sea (Ps 69:1–2; Vulg. 68:2–3), or enclosed in the belly of a fish (Jon 2:1–10), there is he with that one. Here he assures his own who seek him that he has always been present to them while they have been talking of him among themselves, and that he has heard the things they have been saying (cf. Lk 24:13–35). He rewards their devotion to him with high praise when he says:

You are beautiful, my friend, sweet and comely as Jerusalem, terrible as an army drawn up in battle array (Sg 6:4; Vulg. 6:3). *Jerusalem* means "vision of peace," and this name frequently signifies the dwelling place of the heavenly homeland, which contains the highest peace.[7] The Bridegroom's friend is beautiful, sweet, and comely as Jerusalem, for the church (or any holy soul belonging to the church) imitates the condition of the heavenly city by the integrity of its innocent deeds, by the sweetness of the praises it renders to God, and by the pleasantness of its mutual affection. She is sweet and comely as Jerusalem in those things of which Isaiah speaks: *For as the new heavens and the new earth, which I shall make to stand before me, says the Lord; so shall your descendants and your name stand* (Is 66:22). She is also terrible as an army drawn up in battle array when by keeping her attention fixed in pure prayer she repels every assault the devil's army makes upon her, when by frequent preaching of the heavenly word she breaks down the armor of every erroneous doctrine, when by the continuous example of good works she also refutes the perverse character and life of those who only pretend to be faithful, and leads them back to the way of truth. The church is terrible as an army drawn up in battle array when any of her faithful members perseveres in the vocation to which they have been called, when rulers give their subjects a pattern of saving doctrine and excellent behavior, when the continent *cleanse themselves from every defilement of body and of spirit, making holiness perfect in the fear of God* (2 Cor 7:1), when married persons' enjoyment of this world does not lead them to neglect the frequent distribution of alms, so that they will procure a reward for themselves in the age to come. For the prophet teaches the church about the differences among these three sorts of faithful people when he declares that only three men are going to be delivered at the time of heavenly retribution: Noah, Daniel, and Job (Ez 14:14). And when they keep their respective stations inviolate, they doubtless present themselves as an army drawn up in battle array and thereby render the bride of Christ invulnerable against all her enemies. Similarly, every perfect soul continues to appear altogether terrible to her enemies, like an army drawn up in battle array, when she gives so much attention to the virtues that she leaves no gaps between them. But if, for instance, a soul were to practice continence in such a way that she forsook humility, or if she were to perform works of mercy without restraining her tongue from the fault of unnecessary talking, or if she were to be so devoted to frequent prayer that she failed to bestow loving affection on her neighbor, then she would appear less terrible to her enemies, because the battle array of her virtues would be drawn up in less than perfect fashion, part of it being set firmly enough in order, but part of it left incomplete.

But since it is one and the same church of Christ who partly rejoices already in heaven with her King and partly still does battle for him in this world, it is possible to understand this first thing he says (**You are beautiful, my friend, sweet and comely as Jerusalem**) as referring to that part of her that has already received the crown of justice, having fought her fight and finished her race (2 Tm 4:7–8), and to take what he says afterward (**terrible as an army drawn up in battle array**) as compatible with those still in the body who are firm in their faith and resist the adversary lying in wait for them like a roaring lion (1 Pt 5:8–9). Similarly, the church is beautiful, sweet, and comely as Jerusalem because she conducts herself inwardly in a way that is spiritual and worthy of God, and she is terrible as an army drawn up in battle array because she strives to spread her spiritual power throughout the earth among those who are fighting against the powers of this world. And surely an army of the ancient Romans or Greeks or of some other nation was drawn up in battle array because it conquered the world with its power, but it was not sweet and comely as Jerusalem, because it did not know how to hope for the joys of true peace or to follow in its ways. But the church is beautiful and sweet and comely as Jerusalem because she lives the heavenly life while on earth, and she is terrible as an army drawn up in battle array because she is engaged in drawing the barbarous souls and morals of diverse nations to her own way. Nevertheless, because she does not yet merit to see the face of her beloved, which she is seeking so eagerly, she subsequently hears:

Turn away your eyes from me, for they have made me flee away (Sg 6:5; Vulg. 6:4). It is as though he were to say openly, "I have given you the eyes of a dove, with which you can search out the mysteries of the scriptures, discern virtues from vices, and ascertain the paths of justice that will lead you to me, but be careful that you do not try to direct your eyes to see me as well, *for no one shall see my face and live* (Ex 33:20). For there will be a time when the bonds of the flesh will be dissolved and you will come to me, and then the promise I made to you will be fulfilled, since *those who love me will be loved by my Father, and I will love them and reveal myself to them* (Jn 14:21). But for now, as long as you are in the body and wander as pilgrims apart from eternal joys, turn the eyes of your mind away from the contemplation of my divine majesty and essence. **For they have made me flee away;** that is to say, those spiritual senses of yours by means of which you have desired to know me perfectly are not sufficient for you to comprehend me perfectly in this life, however high they try to climb. But they are only able to reach the point of understanding that the glory of the divine nature is of such sublimity that it can never be seen except by those who have been totally removed from this visible life and brought to that which is invisible." In the present time, therefore, we are commanded to turn our searching eyes away from knowing God's essence because they make him flee away from us. This does not mean that he withdraws very far away when he is being sought, for he has made a promise to us in saying, *Seek and you will find* (Mt 7:7), but rather that when he appears we should learn that the higher he is sought by the pure in heart, the more certainly is he comprehended as being incomprehensible. Similar to this is that saying of the psalmist: *A person comes to a heart that is high, and God will be exalted* (Ps 63:7–8, Vulg.), as though it were being said in other words, "Human frailty lifts up the eyes of the heart intent to see God, and they make him flee away because the senses, being trained and illuminated by that searching, realize that divinity's grandeur is more excellent than they could ever imagine." And in another psalm it is very truly said *of his greatness that it has no end* (Ps 145:3; Vulg. 144:3).

Now with this reply the Lord wishes to satisfy holy church's request in which she was earnestly asking the one she loves and longs for that she might see him plainly and not in obscurity, as the preceding portions of this song copiously declare. Therefore, he exhorts her to employ a discerning reckoning of times so that she will not seek on the road the reward that is reserved for her in the homeland, but will remember that for a while she must walk by faith until she is able to come to sight. John the Evangelist distinguishes these times in a very pleasing manner when he says: *Beloved, we are God's children now; what we will be has not yet been revealed, but we know that when it is revealed, we will be like him, for we will see him as he is* (1 Jn 3:2).

---

26. He says that the complete perfection of the catholic [church] has been displayed in many churches through the world, in many assemblies of false believers, in many choirs of innocents.

But lest by chance the church should be aggrieved that she is not yet able to enjoy full knowledge of her Creator, he enumerates the manifold pledges of the Spirit that he has paid to her in advance so that she may very patiently endure the delay of that one, highest, and single blessing that she has not received but is going to receive at the time of eternal recompense. For there follows: **Your hair is like a flock of goats that have appeared from Galaad; your teeth are like a flock of sheep that have come up from the washing** (Sg 6:5–6; Vulg. 6:4–5), and so forth. These little verses, along with those following, were found above and have been explained very fully according to our capacity. But it should not displease us to repeat ourselves in explaining what the author of the sacred song was not displeased to repeat in the act of writing, either so that in the course of our reading we may recall to mind the things previously said, or so that with the assistance of divine grace we may profitably add something new. Now the repetition of these things that have already been said, like countless others in the scriptures, is an indication that God's word is fixed and will truly be fulfilled, as the patriarch Joseph testified when he was interpreting the king's dream (Gn 41:32). Thus, the hairs of the bride suggest the manifold subtlety of her thoughts, while the teeth suggest the steadfast constancy of her words, since teeth cooperate with lips and tongue in the act of speaking, and hairs grow insensibly out of the skull and are not sorry when they are cut. For who is sorry to be wise and does not rather rejoice when the useless weight of frivolous thoughts is cut off? Hence, in a great mystery, we read that the Lawgiver would not lose his teeth even when he was full of days (Dt 34:7, Vulg.), and that no razor would ever pass over the head of Samuel because he would always be a Nazirite (that is, a consecrated person) for the Lord (1 Sm 1:11); for it was prefigured that *not one letter or one stroke might pass from the law until all is accom-*

plished (Mt 5:18), and that in the mind of the prophet there might be found no wavering of repentance or careless thought that would need to be cut off.

Now the same hairs of the bride are properly compared to a flock of goats. For the law commands that when any soul that sins through ignorance becomes aware of her guilt, she should offer to God the sacrifice of a female goat without blemish (Lv 4:27–28). And our hairs are comparable to a flock of goats whenever we offer prayers with tears of compunction as an oblation to the Lord in order to do penance for our wandering thoughts. Moreover, it is not inappropriate for us to understand that the flock of goats is set before him because it is customary to look for a sacrificial victim on the high places amid rocks or woods; for as long as the thoughts of the elect are constantly striving toward heavenly things above, doubtless they are also not delighting in the pleasures down below. Concerning these goats there is properly added:

That have appeared from Galaad (Sg 6:6; Vulg. 6:5). Surely it is said that Galaad is "the heap of witness."[8] And this name is rightly given to the spirit of the just when its virtues provide sure proof that it has renounced earthly desires. Indeed, the reason that Mount Galaad received its name was because Jacob and Laban erected a heap [of stones] upon it in witness to their friendship, or rather to their covenant not to harm one another after Laban had searched Jacob's lodgings for his idols but did not find them (Gn 31:25–54). For Laban signifies the world, Jacob signifies the spirit that is a supplanter[9] of vices, and Laban searches Jacob's lodgings for his idols but does not find them when the lovers of this world examine the hearts of the elect but discover nothing there that belongs to them. Jacob erects a heap [of stones] in witness that he has not touched Laban's possessions or his properties when the spirit devoted to God gathers to itself an abundance of virtues that are like living stones and says: *Forgetting what lies behind and straining forward to what lies ahead, I press on toward the goal for the prize of the heavenly call of God in Christ Jesus* (Phil 3:13–14). Laban too adds stones to the construction of this heap, when the world with its temptations provides the faithful with an opportunity to acquire virtues. Laban and Jacob make a covenant not to harm each other when the just bear witness and say: *The world has been crucified to me, and I to the world*

(Gal 6:14). Therefore the flock of goats, to which the hairs of the bride are compared, appears from this heap [of stones] when the faithful spirit produces a great multitude of thoughts that incline to things above. Out of this flock we offer to God a female goat without blemish for those sins we have committed through ignorance, when we acknowledge our sins and make retribution for them with a contrite and humble heart.

Now Galaad is the name not only of a mountain but also of a city built upon it. Hence it can rightly bear the figure of our Lord and Savior, and also of the church or of every holy soul found in him. Accordingly, when [a similar verse] above was set forth in an expanded form (**Your hair is like flocks of goats that come up from Mount Galaad**) (Sg 4:1), we understood it as referring to that incomparably high mountain who spoke of himself: *A city set on a mountain cannot be hid* (Mt 5:14). But here, where the word "mount" is not mentioned and it simply says, **that have appeared from Galaad**, nothing prevents us from understanding this saying as referring to that city which has been built upon him—that is, the church or the just soul. For the holy soul is also rightly called a "heap of witness" because it has been constructed on the height through the gathering together of various virtues, and the whole church is by right called by this name, since the apostle Peter said to her inhabitants: *Come to him, a living stone rejected indeed by mortals yet chosen and made honorable by God, and, like living stones, be built up* (1 Pt 2:4–5). As we have said above, this also corresponds with the Lord, to whom the whole company of the elect is joined in giving the witness of their pure conscience through profession of faith and upright deeds.

Your teeth are like a flock of sheep that have come up from the washing (Sg 6:6; Vulg. 6:5). We have said that the bride's teeth can be understood as referring to the words of holy church. They are properly said to be like a flock of sheep because nothing is seen in them except the brightness and innocence of virtues as long as they ask for the grace of their Creator in all their teaching, praying, and speaking of praise. These sheep are properly referred to as having come up from the washing because out of the mouth of the just is brought forth nothing that is sordid or unclean or that has not been purified in the font of knowledge in accordance with the exhortation of the Apostle who says: *Let no evil talk come out of your mouths, but only what is useful for building up faith, so that it may give grace to those who hear* (Eph 4:29). But on the other hand, the teeth of those who from an impure heart bring forth words that are abusive or hurtful, or even merely idle, are compared not to sheep coming up from the washing but rather to those who have come out of the mire. Now there is properly added:

All of them bear twins, and not one among them is barren (Sg 6:6; Vulg. 6:5). Surely all the sheep that compose the bride's teeth are multiplied in bearing twins because every word of the elect is fertile in bearing the fruit of a twofold love by which they love both God and neighbor. Their every word speaks of the eternal salvation of body and soul, protects their hearers *with the armor of justice on the right hand and on the left* (2 Cor 6:7), and yearns to treat the promise that is now and is to come; nothing proceeds from the mouth of the just that is not conducive to the fruit of eternal salvation. And the sheep to which it compares the bride's teeth are aptly said to bear twins, doubtless because through the things we speak we are able to benefit our neighbors and instruct them in the way of virtue, and through the wholesome thoughts that we keep to ourselves we benefit only ourselves by presenting ourselves on the altar of the heart as a living sacrifice to the Inner Judge. But what we do within does not build up our neighbors unless we bring it out in words. Hence a certain person who was trying to appease the Creator with such a sacrifice said: *In me, O God, are vows that I will pay, praises to you* (Ps 56:12; Vulg. 55:12).

If, as was said above, we understand that teeth represent preachers and hairs represent those who hear, surely this is most aptly suitable, not only because in the body it is teeth that govern speech and eating while hair provides a pleasing adornment for the head rather than supplying anything necessary for health, but also because teeth are positioned at the front of the face as though they are leading the way, but the hairs of the head cover its back part as though they are following. For it is obvious that the unlearned and those who are still relatively weak are meant to hear and obey the words of their elders, while teachers are not only supposed to fulfill the divine commandments but also to increase the flock of the Supreme Shepherd by their preaching.

Your cheeks are like the rind of a pomegranate beside your secrets (Sg 6:7; Vulg. 6:6). It was said above[10] that the church's modesty is prefigured by the appearance of her cheeks, and the mysteries[11] of the Lord's blood by a pomegranate. And the bride of Christ has cheeks like a pomegranate when the faithful soul does not blush with shame to confess the passion of her Redeemer in words or to imitate it in deeds, but lays aside every feeling of shame and disgrace that leads to death and delights to proclaim it openly, saying: *But may I never boast of anything except the cross of our Lord Jesus Christ* (Gal 6:14). And because he has compared the church's cheeks to the rind of the pomegranate, for that reason he astutely goes on to say, **beside your secrets**, evidently because the rind of the pomegranate not only shows itself to be red on the outside but hides within itself many seeds by which it bears fruit. For just so does a soul that is devoted to God and modestly wholesome in virtue always endeavor to protect itself with the life-giving cross, but under the sign of that same cross contains a great many kinds of virtues that are not at all apparent on the outside but renew the mind from within.

There are sixty queens and eighty concubines, and young maidens without number (Sg 6:8; Vulg. 6:7). Both queens and concubines approach the king's bed and give birth to the king's sons, but only one of them ennobles her head with a royal crown. Therefore both of them signify souls who draw near to the preaching of the truth and through the word of faith, and through the font of the saving washing, bear offspring for the eternal spiritual King, but with some difference, or rather no little difference, in their qualities of mind. For the queens are those minds that serve in consideration of the rule of heavenly doctrine, but the concubines are those that *proclaim Christ not sincerely* but only for the sake of carnal and worldly desires, such as those of whom the Apostle says: *Whether opportunely or truly, Christ is preached, and in this I rejoice; yes, and I will continue to rejoice* (Phil 1:17-18). The Lord himself also distinguishes these from one another when he says: *Therefore, whoever breaks one of the least of these commandments, and teaches others to do the same, will be called least in the kingdom of heaven; but whoever does them and teaches them will be called great in the kingdom of heaven* (Mt 5:19). Thus both of these approach the King's throne, but only one of them reigns together with him. For those souls who ruin their teaching by their works deprive themselves of the insignia of the eternal kingdom, and therefore they are rightly said to be eighty in number while the others are sixty; the number ten represents knowledge on account of the Decalogue of the divine law, and six represents the perfection of good works because God perfected the world [on the sixth day]. Since five multiplied by twelve makes sixty, the sixty queens can also surely be interpreted as meaning that those who govern all their bodily senses (namely, sight, hearing, taste, touch, and smell) in accordance with the rule of apostolic teaching are rightly designated by the number sixty, and that this number of queens, who in every function of their [bodily] members now follow the precepts of those apostles whose number is twelve, will in time to come obtain a share together with those same apostles in the joys of the eternal kingdom. Again, when eight is taken in a bad sense, it not undeservedly suggests the cares and entanglements of earthly and temporal things, doubtless because the course of time turns through four seasons and the world itself is divided into four zones, namely, east, west, north, and south. And so **there are sixty queens** because however many souls have received knowledge of the sacred law, if the perfection of good work follows and they serve here in the kingdom of faith, they will in future enter into heavenly marriage with the King. But [it says] **and eighty concubines** because those who appear to be pursuing the knowledge of the truth and the mystery of the word but expend it on the pleasures of base and transient things are certainly shut out from the entrance to the heavenly kingdom because their lamps of temporal desire have gone out when the Bridegroom comes (Mt 25:1–13).

And young maidens without number (Sg 6:8; Vulg. 6:7). We should understand that these young maidens are the souls who are not yet appointed to the preaching office because they have only recently been reborn in Christ. Since they are not yet of marriageable age (as it were) and thus not yet ready for a royal throne, they assist in the queens' ministry with constant vigilance because in humility they rejoice to obey the commandments of holy church. Of such as these we have read above: **Your name is oil poured out; therefore the young maidens have loved you** (Sg 1:2–3; Vulg. 1:1–2); that is, the souls who no longer grow old through sin but have already been renewed through grace. These are without number because the highest among the citizens of the heavenly homeland transcend the measure of our estimation. But surely it cannot be thought of our King of peace, namely Solomon, that he does not know the number of his faithful. For if *he numbers the multitude of the stars and calls them all by name* (Ps 147:4; Vulg. 146:4), how much more is he unable to be ignorant of the number of his elect whose names he wrote in heaven (Lk 10:20), a number he foreknew before the world began.

My dove, my perfect one, is only one (Sg 6:9; Vulg. 6:8). There are sixty queens because throughout the world there is an abundant number of faithful souls who have received knowledge of the word and impart it to others in order to increase the church's offspring for the sake of obtaining a heavenly kingdom. There are eighty concubines because there is also no lack of souls who devote themselves to teaching out of consideration for earthly things, and although they succumb to the charms of the flesh, they nonetheless bear spiritual offspring for God through their preaching. There are young maidens without number because there are to be found countless other Christian folk who, even though they are not yet ready to be advanced to the office of ruling and teaching, nevertheless willingly and faithfully demonstrate in faith and deed that they are devoted subjects of holy church, which is the bride of Christ. But the universal church is rightly exalted in all of these (that is, the church's true members and the false as well) because in these, her faithful members, she praises the name of the Lord from the beginning of the world unto its end, *from the rising of the sun to its setting, from the north and from the south* (Ps 113:3, 107:3; Vulg. 112:3, 106:3). In praise of her it is very pleasingly said:

My dove, my perfect one, is only one. She is one because she admits no schismatic division. She is one because she is not one before the law, another under the law, and still another under grace; nor is she one gathered from the circumcision and another from the uncircumcision, but just as there is *one Lord, one faith, one baptism, one God and Father of all* (Eph 4:5–6), so is there one catholic company of all the elect, in every place on earth and in every epoch of time subject to the same one God and Father. Luke teaches why she is called "catholic" when he says: *Now all the churches had peace* *throughout all Judea and Galilee and Samaria, and were built up, walking in the fear of the Lord, and were filled with the consolation of the Holy Spirit* (Acts 9:31). For what is described in Latin in this passage is what is known in Greek as "catholic." Thus it is plainly evident that from that time on the church is called "catholic" because throughout all parts of the world she is built up in one peace and in one fear of the Lord, and is filled with one and the same consolation of the Holy Spirit. On account of this unity in the Spirit, she is also rightly called a "dove," since the Spirit descended upon the Lord in the form of a dove (Lk 3:22) so that by that form he might show both his own innocence and that of the Lord upon whom he descended. Since the Lord has given his church a share of his own innocence and of the Spirit, he rightly calls her his "dove," and rightly describes her as "perfect," not only because she is made completely one out of the just from all the peoples, but also because she is made perfect by receiving all the divine virtues and gifts.

She is her mother's only one, the chosen of her that bore her (Sg 6:9; Vulg. 6:8). The mother that bore the present church is she of whom the Apostle said: Now *the Jerusalem above is free, and she is the mother of us all* (Gal 4:26). The reason she is the mother of us all, and is rightly so called, is that *every excellent endowment and every perfect gift is from above, coming down from the Father of lights* (Jas 1:17). Hence John also says in the Apocalypse: *And he showed me the holy city Jerusalem coming down out of heaven from God* (Rv 21:10). For the holy city Jerusalem surely came down out of heaven from God, since every good thing is known to do so. The present church expects everything from above, whether she has received it directly from the King of heaven or through the ministries of the citizens of heaven. Therefore she is her mother's only one, the chosen of her that bore her, doubtless because the only form of human life approved by that heavenly city is one that she finds to have been serving God in the unity of her own faith and love. But as for the Donatists or any others who separate themselves from catholic unity either by open profession or by wicked action, these she puts out of the ranks of the elect, separating them off to the left side at the judgment because they refuse to possess the perfection of dove-like innocence. The grace of the Holy Spirit, through whom the church herself has been reborn in God and knit together, can very aptly be understood as being designated by the term "mother of the church and the one who bore her," because in Hebrew the Spirit is called *ruha*, a word in the feminine gender.[12] Now the Lord himself teaches that this church is rightly called mother and birth-giver when he says: *No one can enter the kingdom of God without being reborn by water and the Spirit* (Jn 3:5), and in order to distinguish this spiritual birth of ours from the carnal one he added: *What is born of the flesh is flesh, and what is born of the Spirit is spirit* (Jn 3:6). The dove of Christ is this mother's only one, the perfect and chosen one of the one who bore her, doubtless because the grace of the Spirit now forsakes all the throngs of schismatics to suckle the church alone and keep her in the unity of catholic peace, and will in time to come raise her up to the joys of the heavenly homeland.

The daughters saw her and proclaimed her most blessed; the queens and concubines, and they praised her (Sg 6:9; Vulg. 6:8). Here he seems to speak of "daughters" with reference to those who above were called "young maidens," but here he has grouped them together in the order of "daughters, queens, and concubines," while there it was "queens, concubines, and young maidens." Therefore it greatly redounds to the praise of catholic unity that both the mother who bore her in grace and chose her forever and the daughters whom she bore and nurtured for God by the Spirit had good reason to praise her without ceasing as soon as they saw her; that is, as soon as they recognized the chastity of her life, and as soon as they heard about the gifts of the inheritance promised to her. But the queens and the concubines also extol her with well-deserved accolades. That is, whether they truly have a share in her kingdom or follow her in name but are earthbound in hope and in desire, all of these souls acknowledge that she is worthy of eternal praise because they understand that nothing true, constant, and good can be found outside her company.

---

27. Hearing the church being praised by the Lord, the synagogue is aroused to admire her also, especially because she is terrible before all her enemies in that unconquerable battle of powers that the Apostle teaches is coming at the end of the world.

But since before the end of the world Judea also must be brought to the grace of her Redeemer so that she too will praise the perfection of holy church along with the others, aptly is it added in the voice of an admiring synagogue: **Who is this who comes forth like the dawn arising**? (Sg 6:10; Vulg. 6:9). Turning to faith in Christ, the synagogue says these things because she is amazed that the church has been raised up so far by divine grace that no soldier of an earthly realm can surpass her, though she is herself most humble. **Who comes forth**, she says, because she is not content to be present only in one place or to appear only for a little while, but she has not ceased to spread her faith and her renown throughout the whole world and to contend for the crown of eternal life throughout all the ages of this world that is passing away. She **comes forth like the dawn arising** because in her the dawning of the true light is now being shown forth in the world after a long time in the darkness of ignorance, so that those who recognize her cry out and say that *the night is over, the day is near; let us then cast off the works of darkness and put on the armor of light* (Rom 13:12), and so forth.

Fair as the moon, bright as the sun, terrible as an army drawn up for battle (Sg 6:10; Vulg. 6:9). She is **fair as the moon** because she is so illuminated by the Sun of righteousness that when she rises up she fills the night of this world with the light of heavenly knowledge and life in accordance with the gospel. She is **bright as the sun** because she has received within herself the image of her Creator and Illuminator so that she may walk in all justice and holiness and truth and give thanks to him that *the light of your countenance has been signed upon us, O Lord* (Ps 4:6; Vulg. 4:7). Again, she is **fair as the moon** in the night of this present life when she imitates the moon's course as it waxes and wanes, as her own position changes over time: now brilliant in the world, now despised and oppressed; now full of virtuous splendor, now dishonored by the blemishes of many errors. She will be **bright like the sun** on the day of future blessedness, when her position will remain constant for eternity, and she will shine in the true vision of unchangeable light in fulfillment of the promise of him who says: *They will shine like the sun in the kingdom of their Father* (Mt 13:43). She is **terrible as an army drawn up for battle** because she could never be kept in obscurity by adversities but was always displaying within herself the beauty of the moon and the sun; of the moon, in the laborious light of her good deeds, but of the sun in her blessed hope for an eternal reward. And properly is she **terrible as an army drawn up for battle**, because the more perfectly she gathers virtues in order within herself, the more terrible does the church and every individual faithful soul appear before the powers of the air (Eph 2:2). For in certain good deeds—such as vigils, fasts, manual labor, meditation on the scriptures, preaching the word, and the modesty of silence—anyone who does not know how to keep things drawn up into the necessary order surely goes astray. For these things and others like them are practiced as often as they are beneficial and no more, so that it is sometimes advantageous to leave them off for a while. But the more excellent virtuous gifts are those such as faith, hope, and love (1 Cor 12:31, 13:13), without which no one can enter into life; accordingly, without consideration of time or place, they should never be absent from the hearts of the faithful even for a moment. Therefore, any soul who always equips herself with the more eminent virtues and diligently girds herself with the lesser ones as is appropriate for the place and hour, this soul goes forth terrible before all adversaries, like an army that is skillfully and powerfully drawn up for battle.

---

28. The church replies, declaring through her teachers what care they have taken for the sake of preparing her for battle—namely, the care for all the churches out of which she is composed as one and catholic.

When this throng of Jews follows after the small number of believers and marvels at the church's struggles with suitable admiration, she acknowledges the one praising her and immediately indicates the reason for her military array by responding in the voice of the teachers who are the leaders of her spiritual army: **I went down to the nut orchard to look at the fruits of the valley** (Sg 6:11; Vulg. 6:10). Surely the nut orchard is the present church in which we are unable to see into one another's consciences. Since in all nuts the kernels are covered with a harder shell so that they are generally spoken of in contrast to all soft fruits,[13] it is fitting to compare the condition of the just in this life to nuts that hold the sweetness of spiritual fruit inside so that no matter how many neighbors there are outside, they cannot see it. For this reason, mother church must always be careful to keep an army of teachers drawn up for battle as long as she must fight on behalf of those of whose minds and hearts she is unsure in order to defend them from the enemy.

Thus we can understand that *a nut or almond has a very bitter hull and is clothed with a very hard shell but, after the acrid and hard parts have been removed, inside there is found the sweetest fruit.*[14] In the same way, every reproof and every work of continence that exercises the church seems bitter at present, but eventually it yields the sweetest fruit in accordance with the Apostle's saying that *every discipline seems to be painful rather than pleasant at the time, but later it yields the most peaceful fruit of justice to those who have been exercised by it* (Heb 12:11). Now the fruits of the valley of which it speaks are the fruit of humility, such as that in the psalm: *The valleys will abound with grain* (Ps 65:13; Vulg. 64:14); for the humble will abound in the food of heavenly grace. The good works of the faithful in holy church are fruits of the valley because they are produced in the depths of the earth but when they have made progress in merits the laborers bring them forth to the heavenly kingdom. The psalmist also says of them: *In their heart they determined to ascend through the valley of tears to the place which you have determined for them* (Ps 84:5–6; Vulg. 83:6–7). The bride goes down to the nut orchard to see the fruits of the valley when the church's teachers turn their mind's attention away from the serene height of their accustomed contemplation of divine mysteries to inspect the church's condition so that they may adroitly ascertain how many of the faithful have already made progress in good works, how many still need the assistance of their teaching, and what labors they must expend to cultivate in them the fruits of life.

To see if the vineyards had flourished, and the pomegranates budded (Sg 6:11; Vulg. 6:10). She sees if the vineyards have flourished when she carefully examines the new hearts of those she teaches to see if they exhibit within themselves a devotion to the virtues with which they may be spiritually inebriated, in accordance with that saying of the psalmist: *They will go from virtue to virtue* (Ps 84:7; Vulg. 83:8). She sees if the pomegranates have budded when she diligently strives to find those who are eager to imitate the Lord's suffering by shedding their own blood, following the admonition of the apostle Peter who says: *Christ therefore having suffered in the flesh, arm yourselves with the same thought* (1 Pt 4:1).

---

29. But the synagogue says that she had not known these things, confessing that she had been suddenly disturbed from her stupor by the preaching of the gospel. Rejoicing over the beginnings of her salvation, the church bids her to return to the knowledge of her Redeemer.

In this way does the church proclaim her evangelical labors to an admiring synagogue who in compunction declares her salvation-giving repentance for having continued without this salvation for so long because of her blindness and ignorance. This is how she responds: **I knew not; my soul troubled me on account of the four-horse chariot of Aminadab** (Sg 6:12; Vulg. 6:11). "I knew not the gifts of spiritual grace with which you have been illuminated by the Lord to bring forth the fruits of faith among all nations; an inner anxiety of mind troubled me on account of the sudden introduction of the New Testament to complement the Old, when the books of the prophets and the law, which I knew to be divine and written by the Holy Spirit, were suddenly fulfilled by the preaching of the gospel to the whole world. To my amazement and wonder, this preaching quickly flew like a swift four-horse chariot not only through Judea and Samaria but to the lands of all nations (Acts 1:8). With good reason do I compare it not to all chariots without distinction but to a four-horse chariot, doubtless because it is commended by the authoritative narratives of four writers. Nevertheless, the minds and hands of those writers were directed to write by the one Spirit of God through Jesus Christ, in the same way that a single chariot is fitted out for the race with four horses joined together for speed but under the direction of one charioteer so that they may run in a straight course. To be sure, I had previously heard that the four authors wrote about Jesus with a common purpose, but alas, how late did I merit to understand and to know which Spirit guided them and what profit and truth their writings contain, or how much glory and salvation."

Now she calls the heralds of the New Testament "the four-horse chariots of Aminadab" because the name "Aminadab" signifies the Lord and Savior who like a driver upon a chariot fills the hearts of his preachers with the grace of the Spirit so that through them it might come to pass that the peoples would believe in him when the word of saving doctrine is recited to them. For Aminadab was a descendant of the patriarch Judah (Nm 1:7), and he represents the Lord and Savior both in his person and in name. In his person, because through him descended the genealogy of the Lord's incarnation from Abraham to David the king, and through David to Joseph and Mary, so that only for this reason did the prophets sometimes signify him by the names of Judah and David and Solomon and the other fathers *from whom was Christ according to the flesh* (Rom 9:5), as in the saying: *Judah is a lion's whelp; to the prey, my son, you have gone up; resting, you have crouched like a lion, and as a lioness—who shall rouse him*? (Gn 49:9). And again: *I will cleanse them, and they shall be my people, and I will be their God, and my servant David shall be over them* (Ez 37:23–24). And in this very book: *Come, O daughters of Sion, and look at King Solomon* (Sg 3:11). In his name, Aminadab (which means "acting voluntarily for my people"[15]) aptly designates the *Mediator between God and humankind* (1 Tm 2:5) who, although he was God before the ages, clothed himself in flesh. At the time he willed and in the manner he willed, the merciful Redeemer appeared among the people of the church, through voluntary kindness becoming a part of his own people, although by the power of his nature he was their Creator and Ruler. Now after the synagogue has confessed the prolonged lethargy of mind that was keeping her from understanding the mysteries of the Lord's incarnation, the church immediately consoles and exhorts her by replying:

Return, return, O Shulammite! Return, return, that we may look upon you (Sg 6:13; Vulg. 6:12). "Return to the knowledge of your Redeemer, away from whom you have been straying miserably for so long, and be imbued with his sacraments so that you will prove worthy to enter into heavenly life. Return to the peace of our sisterhood, which you have for so long considered as something to be scorned on account of religious discord. **Return, return, that we may look upon you**. Return in purity of faith, return in perfection of works to the love of the Lord as well, so that with joyful eyes and hearts we may contemplate the beauty of your chastity, which we have desired to see for so long. Joining with one another in the love of Christ, let us together build one house of faith upon him as our cornerstone." Now I do not remember having read the name "Shulammite" anywhere else, but it seems to be a name for some noble women. Whether derived from their own name or from that of a place, it was at that time a name noted for the many glories of its wisdom or beauty or virtue. But if, as some assert, this name of "Shulammite" means "despicable" or "captive," then it is appropriate for the synagogue.[16] For after she departed from her Maker's grace as a result of the crime of unbelief, she was held captive by the bonds of sin and remained unworthy of being regarded with divine pity. But the Shulammite is entreated to return so that through her obedient returning to the Lord she may merit to be freed from the chains of shameful captivity and made worthy in the sight of her Redeemer and Savior.

---

30. But the Redeemer himself, approving of her exhortation, testifies that there will be nothing in [the synagogue's] way of living other than zeal for virtues.

Now when the church has admonished the synagogue to return to the grace of her Redeemer, this Redeemer himself quickly assents to join his own words to her devout supplications and testifies that her exhortations will eventually attain their desired effect. For he says: **What will you see in the Shulammite but choruses of camps**? (Sg 6:13; Vulg. 7:1). It is as though he were to say openly, "You lament that the synagogue has been turned away for so long, and you beseech her to return to me, and it pleases you to see her face prepared for me. But know that the time is near when you will perceive in her nothing of her former faithlessness and turning away, but only works of virtue and spiritual combat." Therefore he says, **What will you see in the Shulammite but choruses of camps**?—that is, a militia of peace. For the voices of singers sound together in choruses, and the corps of soldiers fight in camps. What will you see in her, then, but choruses of the elect proclaiming their Maker's praises with one heart and soul? Likewise, there are choruses of camps because by serving in the Creator's army they repel and destroy the enemy's host.

---

31. Describing the praises of his beloved according to his custom, first of all in the joining of her thighs he designates the union in her of believers from two peoples who love one another.

He says these things and then with his accustomed sweetness turns to praise the church, who will rejoice that she has been anxious for the salvation of the synagogue, going on to say: **How beautiful are your steps in shoes, O prince's daughter** (Sg 7:1). Now it is appropriate that he should begin his praise of her with her steps and end with the gracefulness of her mouth. For so does he conclude: **And the scent of your mouth is like apples, your throat like the best wine** (Sg 7:8–9), and since he began above with the eyes (which are the superior members) this seems to make the commendation complete. This metonymy both serves to embellish the song and sets the mysteries that are being sung in their proper order. For since he perceived that she would not dwell at ease in peaceful serenity but would go forth to combat by preaching, rightly did he first admire the beauty of her steps, that is, the constancy of works through which she was showing a virtuous example to those whom she was trying to teach. It was doubtless concerning these steps that the psalmist prayed to the Lord, saying: *Perfect my steps in your paths* (Ps 17:5; Vulg. 16:5); that is, "Direct my actions in *the narrow way that leads to life*" (Mt 7:14). Now these steps are in shoes when our actions are protected by the examples of the just who have gone before us to the Lord, for shoes are made from the skins of dead animals,[17] and when we read about the just works with which the earlier saints were clothed we too walk along the path of virtue more confidently and smoothly by imitating them. Of such shoes does the Apostle say: *And feet shod in preparation for the gospel of peace* (Eph 6:15). For those who preach the true gospel of peace to others must first adorn and strengthen the steps of their works with the examples of the fathers who have gone before, so that in their life and in their teaching they will not show those who follow them any way other than that trod by the fathers, or rather by the Lord himself. As the apostolic command reminds us: *Be imitators of* *me, brothers and sisters, as I am of Christ* (1 Cor 11:1). For only thus does the teacher ascend to that sublimity and beauty of virtue which the prophet and the Apostle recall when they say: *How beautiful upon the mountains are the feet of those who preach good tidings, who preach the gospel of peace* (Is 53:7; Rom 10:15).

Now he calls her "the prince's daughter," which is surely she of whom it is written: *All the glory of the king's daughter is within* (Ps 45:13; Vulg. 44:14). Among other promises of heavenly gifts, he himself speaks to her through the prophet: *You will call me "Father," and you will not cease to follow after me* (Jer 3:19).

Now we should note that when Jerome, conscious of the Hebrew truth [that is, the Hebrew text of the Song of Songs], was writing against Jovinian concerning the prince's daughter in this passage, he called her the daughter of Aminadab; he also declares that in this verse it is possible to understand that Israel is being referred to as a virgin for God, for he says: *"Your steps are made beautiful in shoes, O daughter of Aminidab"; which is interpreted as saying of the people: "You offer yourself voluntarily." For virginity is a voluntary thing, and for that reason the church's steps are praised in the beauty of chastity.*[18] So it is evident that they go far astray who in the preceding verse interpret the four-horse chariots of Aminadab as a reference to the host of those persecuting the church or of unclean spirits or of evil persons,[19] because clearly it should rather be understood as referring to the Prince of princes himself and to his chosen people.

The joining of your thighs is like jewels that are fashioned by the hand of a craftsman (Sg 7:1). Scripture is accustomed to signify the generation of offspring by referring to "thighs." For it says that all the souls that came with Jacob into Egypt and those that came out "from his thigh" were seventy souls, not counting his sons' wives (Gn 46:27; Ex 1:1, 5). Hence the church's thighs are rightly taken to be the progeny and spiritual descendants that she acquires through the ministry of the word and the bath of regeneration. The joining of her thighs, then, is the union of the two peoples (namely, Jews and Gentiles) from which the one church universal is perfected in unity of faith and is made fruitful with spiritual offspring so that she increases unto the end of the age. This joining is compared to jewels because the catholic faith is manifested in the testimony of good works. Now these jewels are fashioned by the hand of a craftsman because the virtuous works with which the one church is built from two peoples are established upon the generosity of our ineffable Creator. For he is the craftsman of whom the Apostle says: *And he came and preached peace to you who were far off and peace to those who were near; for through him both of us have access in one Spirit to the Father* (Eph 2:17–18). Of his marvelous craftsmanship the psalmist also says: *The stone which the builders rejected has become the chief cornerstone; this is the Lord's doing, and it is marvelous in our eyes* (Ps 118:22–23; Vulg. 117:23). In his praise of Abraham, the Apostle makes mention of this craftsman when he says: *For he looked forward to the city that has foundations, whose architect and builder is God* (Heb 11:10). Rightly then is the joining of the bride's thighs praised after her steps in shoes, because the harmonious union of believing peoples is effected through the ministry of preaching. And after these things our attention is aptly turned to the joining of the thighs, wherein it is promised that at the end the company of both peoples united in Christ will be gathered together to faith, along with the Jews. There follows:

Your navel is a rounded bowl that never lacks cups (Sg 7:2). The navel, which is the weakest member of our body, rightly represents the infirmity of our mortal nature, and our navel becomes a rounded bowl that never lacks cups when consciously mindful of our mortality and infirmity we strive to give our neighbors a drink from the cup of the saving word so that we who do mercy may be rewarded with the blessing of mercy from heaven. Indeed, there is nothing to prevent us from also understanding it as the common cup of kindness of which the Judge himself will say: *I was thirsty and you gave me drink* (Mt 25:35). For a bowl is a larger cup having two handles, of which the poet says:

And when the main banquet is over and the food has been removed,
they set out great bowls and crown them with wine.[20]

And it is properly said that this bowl is rounded (for a vessel that is made so that it is rounded will fill up more quickly than other receptacles) in order to express the swiftness of kindness that ought to be shown to those in need of an earthly cup or a heavenly one, or even both at once, in accordance with that saying of Solomon: *Do not say to your neighbor, "Go, and come again, and tomorrow I will give to you," when you are able to give immediately* (Prv 3:28). But we should also repeat what we have mentioned above,[21] which is that turning things round [on a wheel] is less prone to error than other crafts, doubtless because within itself it produces its own rule, through which it guides its work to a perfectly rounded shape, and for that reason it rightly suggests the true simplicity of a generous mind that performs an act of charity with a pure intention. For those who give a thirsty person a drink only so that the One who gives a just reward will bestow an abundance of earthly drink on them as well, or who extend the cup of the word to those who have gone astray only so that the Lord will supply them with a profusion of greater knowledge by which they may appear marvelous before others, these are shown to have navels that are not bowls rounded by the Lord but are rather compared to those made with other tools, since they are seeking to make their works of mercy visible not so that their frailty may be sustained by a true and unfailing reward from the Lord, but for the sake of a reward that is merely temporal. The bride's navel can also be understood as having been called a rounded bowl that never lacks cups because the more that the church (or any holy soul) remembers her frailty and is mindful that the immortality and incorruption for which she hopes are still far away in the future, the more diligently does she refresh herself continually from the cups of God's word and warm herself with his love, saying with the psalmist: *And your cup which inebriates me, how excellent it is!* (Ps 23:5; Vulg. 22:5).

Your belly is like a heap of wheat surrounded with lilies (Sg 7:2). The belly, like the navel, represents our mortal nature, for it is most certainly the greatest indication of our weakness since we will die unless it renews our body with nourishment daily, until there comes to pass that which we have been promised: *Food is for the body and the body for food, but God will destroy both the one and the other* (1 Cor 6:13). Therefore our body is like a heap of wheat when, mindful of our frailty, we equip ourselves with the fruits of good works by which we are continually nourished in this present life. Now it appropriately refers to a heap of wheat, and not simply to an abundance of wheat, in order to represent the increase of virtues mounting up on high. For since it is common knowledge that a heap is produced when something that is wider below rises up to a point above, this figure rightly corresponds to our good actions, the higher ones of which are indeed found to be performed by fewer people. For you see that there are many more who from their possessions give alms to the poor than there are those who give away all that they possess, many more good married folk than celibates, many more who abstain from carnal pleasures than who lay down their lives for the truth's sake.

And this heap of wheat is appropriately said to be surrounded with lilies so that we may do all our good works in order to see the beauty of an eternal brightness and so that there will be no way for hostile enemies to enter the field of our heart because we completely encircle all our works with regard for a heavenly reward. This heap of wheat can also be understood as referring to those works of charity we do for Christ's poor, concerning which he himself says: *I was hungry and you gave me food* (Mt 25:35). And after the bowl with an abundance of cups, the bride's members are appropriately compared to a heap of wheat in order to signify that she gives both drink and bread to the poor. Surely this can be taken as referring equally to both spiritual and corporeal nourishment; that is, to those things with which we renew the hungry person's body, and to those with which we instruct the mind of the neighbor who has gone astray. For the same spiritual instruction is recognized as being like a cup in some sayings, and as like the bread of life in others; it is like a cup in those that are open, but like bread in mysteries. It holds forth a cup in those things that can be easily understood as soon as they are heard and do not require further explanation, such as that saying: *You shall not kill; you shall not steal; you shall not bear false witness; and you shall love your neighbor as yourself* (Dt 5:17, 19; Mt 19:18–19). It provides bread when it gives its hearers sayings that are more difficult to understand, so that they must be explained before they come into the inner reaches of our mind, just as food must be chewed before it comes into our bellies. The entire sequence of sayings in this song is of this sort, as is that saying in the law: *Remember that you keep holy the Sabbath day* (Ex 20:8), where we are mystically admonished that we should keep holy the light of spiritual grace in which alone our true rest is found; that is, we should keep it as unblemished as we receive it on the day of our redemption, in a heart that is holy and pure.

Therefore these sayings and others of the sort, of which we attain understanding through laborious explanation, are rightly compared to a heap of wheat that is made useful for our nourishment through no small labor involved in its being ground, sifted, baked, and chewed. They are rightly compared to something that is flatter than the bowl that never lacks cups, because the scriptures abound with the open commandments and promises of God, which are like drinks that can be drunk without delay or labor as soon as they are heard, and once understood can be preserved as though in the belly of our memory to sustain our growth in salvation. In the bride's belly there is most aptly figured the immaculate womb of the divine font from which we are reborn as a new creation (2 Cor 5:17). It is like a heap of wheat surrounded with lilies because it teaches all those whom it consecrates through new birth in Christ that they should pursue good works only in consideration of heavenly glory. It is like a heap of wheat because it cleanses those whom it washes from the chaff of all their sins and through a second birth conforms them to the one who says concerning himself: *Unless a grain of wheat falls into the earth and dies, it remains alone; but if it dies, it bears much fruit* (Jn 12:24; Vulg. 12:24–25). It is surrounded with lilies because those whom it frees from the entanglements of sin with which they were born in the flesh, these it also adorns with gifts and strengthens with the light of heaven.

Your two breasts are like two young hinds of a goat that are twins (Sg 7:3). We have said a great deal about this verse above,[22] but now it should be briefly noted that he rightly commends the bride's breast after her belly, doubtless because after holy church has given birth to her little ones from the sacred womb of saving water, she gives them the milk of softer doctrine (1 Cor 3:2) until little by little she trains them to receive the bread of higher wisdom. Therefore the church's breasts are those who instruct her little ones (that is, those who have recently been reborn in faith). Well are they said to be two in number, doubtless because those whom the saving font washes and prepares for the heavenly mystery are gathered from two peoples, namely, Jews and Gentiles. Well are they compared to two young hinds of a goat, because true teachers take everything they preach out of the scriptures of both testaments. Well are the young hinds said to be twins, because those testaments were published by one and the same Author, namely, the one of whom the Preacher says: *The sayings of the wise are like goads and like nails firmly fixed, which are given through the counsel of the teachers by one shepherd* (Eccl 12:11).[23] Therefore the bride's two breasts are like two young hinds of a goat that are twins because the teachers of neophytes do not preach to them anything that is their own, nor do they adulterate *God's word, but they speak as from God, before God, in Christ* (2 Cor 2:17).

This one shepherd is he who makes one sheepfold (Jn 10:16) out of two flocks of sheep, the one for whom the bride was crying out above with burning desire: **Show me, you whom my soul loves, where you pasture [your flock], where you lie down at midday** (Sg 1:7; Vulg. 1:6). He is the one teacher of teachers who commands those who are his disciples but our teachers, saying: *Go therefore and teach all nations, baptizing them in the name of the Father and of the Son and of the Holy Spirit, and teaching them to obey everything that I have commanded you* (Mt 28:19–20). The name of "goat" is also justly ascribed to him since it is a clean animal noted for its vision and its speed, with a cloven hoof and chewing its cud and, like all clean quadrupeds, armed with horns. For [animals] of this sort are rightly associated with the saints who have cloven hoofs in discerning good and evil and, once they have separated the good things from the evil, speak them sweetly as though chewing their cud. They have learned to direct the eyes of their heart to things far away; that is, to contemplate heavenly blessings while on earth. They eagerly desire to enter the path of virtues with all due speed. They rejoice that through the grace of their Creator they have been made clean in mind and body. Equipped by God against the strength of this world, they are accustomed to say with faithful assurance: *Through you we will toss our enemies upon the horn* (Ps 44:5; Vulg. 43:6). If all this is so, how much more fitting is it that the nature of this animal should signify him who both possesses these same virtuous gifts within himself and distributes them to others *according to the measure of his giving* (Eph 4:7).

Your neck is like an ivory tower (Sg 7:4). Since, as we have asserted above, voice and speech come forth through the neck and through it also enters the food by which all the members of the body are nourished, rightly does the neck represent the form of the teachers who both strengthen the entire body of the church with a voice of exhortation and renew it with the food of life. This neck is like an ivory tower because like ivory the teachers serve to adorn the city of God (that is, holy church) and display to all who see them the vigor and beauty of a life in which they seem already to have died to this world, and like a tall and impregnable tower they defend the city of God against invasion from all enemies. For they acknowledge that they are set like a tower in the rampart of the holy city since they say: *The weapons of our warfare are not carnal, but mighty unto God to pull down fortifications, destroying counsels and every height that exalts itself against the knowledge of God* (2 Cor 10:4–5). When Paul describes his life and that of his fellow workers, saying: *For through the law I have died to the law, so that I may live to God; with Christ I have been nailed to the cross* (Gal 2:19), he signifies that they possess in themselves the properties of ivory, which is indeed a dead bone but noted for its extraordinary beauty.

Your eyes are like pools in Heshbon, which are at the gate of the daughter of the multitude (Sg 7:4). The same holy preachers who were compared to the bride's neck on account of the nourishment from their word are also represented by eyes on account of their contemplation of the mysteries they have learned in secret so that they can declare them openly, and so that through these things that they have received in secret meditation they may administer manifest nourishment to holy church by teaching. Now these eyes are rightly compared to pools built at the gate of the city of Heshbon, which city it also calls "daughter of the multitude" on account of the abundance of its inhabitants. For just as these pools were accustomed to supply a continuous and plentiful supply of water for the crowds of citizens who came to them, so do the preachers never cease to supply their hearers with streams of doctrine; surely they are always so filled with these streams within themselves that they are pools abounding with channels of living water. Now corresponding to these pools is that famous sheep pool in Jerusalem in which the water was stirred up at certain times when an angel descended and only the first sick person to descend would be cured (Jn 5:2–4), doubtless because there is *one God, one faith, one* *baptism* (Eph 4:5) that washes the one faithful people when the Holy Spirit descends upon the font of life, and it excludes the anointing of a second rebirth. This pool is properly said to be for sheep (that is, for the flocks) to indicate according to the letter that the priests were accustomed to wash the sacrificial victims in it, and to express typologically that those who are being led to the holy altar and being offered in sacrifice to the Lord should first be washed in the water of rebirth.

Heshbon is aptly set as a type of the church, either on account of its name, which is interpreted as "belt of mourning,"[24] or because it had once belonged to Sihon, king of the Amorites, and after he was killed it came into the possession of the children of Israel (Nm 21:21–26). For it is widely known that the church was once subjected to the power of the devil, who is the king of all enemies, but after he had been driven out and renounced, she became the city of her Redeemer. She who was formerly called "foreigner" has now received the name of "church," for she has girded herself with the most useful belt of mourning on account of the wanton and transient joys of this world—with a belt, in order to restrain the loins of her mind from every uncleanness, and with a belt of mourning so that by being rendered utterly remote and alien from temporal joys she may attend to the more reliable joys that she hopes to receive in heaven. Now this city (that is, the church), which is also called "daughter of the multitude" on account of the numerous peoples who come to faith, has at her gate pools that are compared to the eyes of the bride because no one can enter her without first being sprinkled with the water of saving doctrine, cleansed in the bath of the water of rebirth, and consecrated by a life-giving drink from the font. This was figured quite openly and beautifully in the tabernacle and in Solomon's temple, at the entrance of which there was placed a basin or a bronze sea in which the priests would wash their hands and feet before they entered (Ex 30:18–19; 1 Kgs 7:23; 1 Chr 18:8); surely this was for the sake of a mystery, because the Lord provides for us a bath of heavenly doctrine and a font of rebirth in which we are initiated so that we can enter both the fellowship of the present church and the house of the eternal dwelling which is in heaven.

Your nose is like a tower of Lebanon that looks toward Damascus (Sg 7:4). Since odors and stenches are distinguished through the nose,[25] the stewards of God's word, who above were for various reasons designated as the church's breasts, neck, and eyes, are now also designated as a nose on account of their most salubrious discretion, which the fathers esteem as the mother of virtues,[26] doubtless because it is as though they exercise the olfactory function more fully than others in discerning which actions or words burn with the good odor of Christ, and which breathe the deadly stench of heresy. For a teacher, or any one of the faithful, frequently has need of careful discretion lest by chance vices should hide under the guise of virtues or wear something wolfish under sheep's clothing (Mt 7:15), and lest cunning should deceive by masquerading as prudence, or stinginess as frugality, or lust for revenge as justice, or harshness as strength, or foolish obstinacy as constancy. Hence the teachers and all the elect who have received this grace from the Lord, so that they are able to separate the odors of virtues from the stench of vices, are rightly said to be like towers of Lebanon that look toward Damascus because they hold the highest place in holy church and always keep watch with their mind's careful eye against the assaults of the ancient enemy.

Truly, Lebanon (as we have already said repeatedly) is a mountain that signifies the Lord and Savior and his church, and it is obviously clearer than light that it is toward Damascus, which figuratively indicates the city of the devil (that is, the reprobate multitude of angels and human beings). For this chief city of all Syria, with its most impious and powerful kings who rightly bore the type of the devil, frequently inflicted the people of God with wars and captivities that plainly figure the temptations and assaults with which the devil is constantly assailing the church. But since Damascus is also said to be a "drink of blood" or "cup of blood,"[27] it appropriately signifies those who delight in the pleasures of flesh and blood, among which is also reckoned the shedding of blood that is inflicted upon the innocent; it also corresponds to the most evil demons who strive to slaughter us spiritually and to deprive us of the life within that we have in Christ. Against both of these does the psalmist pray to the Lord, saying: *Deliver me from blood, O God, O God of my salvation* (Ps 51:14; Vulg. 50:16). For all those who diligently take precautions to see that they and those who belong to them remain resolutely steady in Christ so that they will not be overcome by the sorts of wars that are waged openly by humans or secretly by the devil, these can rightly be called a nose such as that of the bride of Christ. They are like a tower built on Mount Lebanon that looks toward Damascus because by their expertise in discernment and in constantly watching for life above they ensure that the church will never be troubled by the sudden and unforeseen incursions of the wicked.

On the Song of Songs
Book 5

Your head is like Carmel, and the hairs of your head are like the king's purple bound in strands (Sg 7:5). In the bride's head is rightly understood the mind of the faithful soul, because just as the members are ruled by the head, so are thoughts ordered by the mind. Hence also these same innumerable thoughts that proceed from the human mind at every hour and moment are aptly figured by hairs. Now the astute reader will remember that what is said of one elect soul ought to be understood of the whole church, because even though the multitude of believers differ in merits, nevertheless they have a single heart and soul (Acts 4:42) inasmuch as they all yearn for the heavenly homeland with one and the same faith, hope, and love. Now scripture relates how Elijah on Mount Carmel prayed on bended knee and after a long drought obtained rain from the Lord. Hence the bride's head is like Carmel because the hearts of the elect are raised up through repentance,[1] and they make in themselves a way up to the Lord through daily progress in virtues. Surely Elijah, who prays to the Father and calls down rain from heaven as though upon these dry fields, is said to be "God the Lord"[2] because it is he who invisibly incites these [hearts] to pray to God and through their prayers and merits quite often bestows his own gifts upon a world in danger. The name "Carmel," which is interpreted as "knowledge of circumcision,"[3] is appropriate for the head of the bride (that is, the mind of the church), who is well aware that she ought not to glory in the fleshly circumcision but in the one that is spiritual, concerning which the Apostle disputes so much with the Galatians (Gal 3:1–5, 5:1–21, 6:7–8) and about which the prophet teaches, saying: *Be circumcised to the Lord, and remove the foreskins of your hearts* (Jer 4:4). The Jews were refusing to have this knowledge when they prided themselves on account of the circumcision that was only external and were thereby unable to have a head like Carmel because they had set their mind upon a lower and fleshly glory. Hence they are justly reproved by the voice of the blessed protomartyr Stephen when he says: *You stiff-necked and uncircumcised in heart and ears, you always resist the Holy Spirit* (Acts 7:51).

It says: **And the hairs of your head are like the king's purple bound in strands**. As we have said, the hairs of the bride's head are the thoughts of the faithful soul, and the king's purple signifies the imitation of the Lord's passion, to which the hair of the bride's head is rightly compared because every thought of the elect is protected by faith in the holy cross, and their whole heart is intent upon being ready to suffer for the Lord so that they might merit to be raised with him. Now this same purple is said to be bound in strands, which can be taken as meaning either that the pieces of wool[4] are at first kept separate when they are dyed and then woven into strands, or that the wool which has already been divided into parts that are individually bound in strands is colored with the blood emitted by purple fish. For when they are cut with a knife the purple fish (that is, the sea crustaceans that are also called mollusks) shed purple-colored tears, which are collected to produce purple dye.[5] Mystically, both of these yield one and the same meaning. Surely the strands that absorb the king's purple are the heart of Christ's faithful, and the wool, which is put forth bound in strands to receive the purple color so that after it is dyed it may be used to adorn the king, is the softest and most pleasing humility of the faithful conscience that through sufferings and works of justice makes its way into the raiment of the eternal King. For it says: *As many of you as have been baptized into Christ have put on Christ* (Gal 3:27). Now this wool bound in strands is dyed with a purple color because the virtue of humility, which is fixed and fastened (as it were) in the hearts of the elect, is animated by the continual memory of the Lord's cross for the endurance of worldly tribulations, through which it is able to attain a share in the Lord's kingdom. Now we have said that the purple can be understood as bound with strands in such a way that once the pieces of wool have been sufficiently dyed with purple fish they are kept separated in little pieces before being braided into strings. This pertains to the figure of a higher virtue because it expresses the humility of those who have already suffered so many tribulations for the Lord that it is well established that they cannot be overcome by the pressure of any adversities.

For they say that once something has been dyed purple it will never be faded by the sun or by washing in water, nor will it lose the coloring that has been received. Therefore the hairs of the bride's head are like the king's purple bound in strands when the thoughts of a heart devoted to God either prepare themselves or are already prepared to die for Christ so that they might merit to reign with Christ. They offer this purple in strands to adorn the High King when, being given an occasion for suffering, they bravely show what they have borne in their heart for the sake of their Redeemer's glory, being prepared to endure all the world's misfortunes and, if necessary, death itself. This is well figured in the Acts of the Apostles by Lydia, the dealer in purple cloth who feared God. She was the first person to believe and be baptized with her household when Paul was preaching in Macedonia, and she received him into her own lodging, both at first when he was preaching the word of faith to her, and also after he had endured scourgings, imprisonment, and chains at the hands of unbelievers (Acts 16:14–15, 40). Surely in her craft, in her believing, and in her obedience she represented the church of the Gentiles, which was imbued with the confession of the Lord's passion, which would pour out her own blood for its sake, and which would receive the teaching of the apostles into her inmost heart when it was driven out by unbelievers.

How beautiful you are, and how comely, dearest, in delights (Sg 7:6). It is said above in praise of the bride: **You are beautiful, my friend, sweet and comely as Jerusalem, terrible as an army drawn up in battle array** (Sg 6:4; Vulg. 6:3). In that place, then, along with beauty and comeliness she is said to be terrible as one drawn up in battle array; here she is described as beautiful and comely in delights. But it is quite contrary to human custom for one and the same person both to spend life in delights and to be terrible as an army drawn up in battle array, doubtless because delights soften the mind so that it is unable to concentrate on military matters. But when the delights are spiritual (that is, when the soul's mouth is filled with desire for eternal sweetness), then the soul becomes terrible to her spiritual enemies and shatters all their spears like an army drawn up in battle array. In fact, the more intensely she perceives the satisfying flavor within, the more terrible does she appear to those who have completely squandered the glory of heavenly sweetness for which they were created in exchange for the bitterness of arrogant tyranny. And when the holy soul's Lover himself had said, **How beautiful you are, and how comely** (that is, how perfect both in faith and in work), it is well that he immediately added, **Dearest, in delights;** for it is suitable that the one dearest to the Lord should be the soul determined to devote herself to heavenly delights. Doubtless this is because the more fully the mind tastes the food of heavenly life, the more it burns with love of that food, and the more ardently it loves things above, the more perfectly is it loved by him who is the Author and Giver of heavenly blessings. Thus the holy soul is dearest in delights to the Lord because as long as she ardently hungers for the joys of inner refreshment, the love of her Creator increases in her. And since, even in the struggle of the present life, this sort of soul has no little foretaste of the joys of her future reward, rightly is it added:

Your stature is like that of a palm tree, and your breasts are like grape-clusters (Sg 7:7). Surely the church's stature is the uprightness of her good work, by which she disdains to bend down to all earthly concupiscence and raises herself up to win the things of heaven. The Apostle admonishes about this, saying: *Keep watch and stand up in the faith, act courageously* (1 Cor 16:13). The Lord himself also speaks about this: *I am the Lord who brought you out from the servitude with which the Egyptians were oppressing you, that you might go upright* (Lv 26:13). Now the victor's hand is adorned with a palm, but among the ancients all those who were victorious in the contest were also crowned with a palm of gold. Therefore the bride's stature is likened to a palm when the whole attention of the faithful is raised up to the love of heavenly things and, even while standing in the fray, meditates on that palm with which the victor is presented when the contest is complete. Likewise, since the palm appears rough at the bottom but at the top displays its beauty and the sweetness of its fruit, rightly is it compared to the stature of the church or of any faithful soul that bears rough labors for the Lord on earth but hopes to receive a most gracious reward from the Lord in heaven. The palm is rough near the ground because the elect *suffer persecution for the sake of justice* (Mt 5:10), and it is beautiful and sweet at the top because they rejoice in afflictions and exult because they know that their *reward is great in heaven* (Mt 5:12). Likewise, since the palm is *clothed with long-lasting fronds and does not shed its leaves,*[6] who does not see that it contains a type of the stature of the faith that, amid the changing condition of this passing age, always retains the same words of a right confession like leaves that will never fall, and keeps the same perfection of works that it began from the start, as though it were an ornament of palm leaves kept undefiled in her elect unto the end of the age?

And your breasts, it says, **are like grape-clusters** (Sg 7:7). As has often been said, the church's teachers are breasts when they administer the milk of elementary instruction to Christ's little ones. But the same breasts are compared to grape-clusters when these teachers who have committed the first mysteries of his incarnation to these [little ones] also reveal the secrets of the divinity with which he is equal to the Father. Formerly they said: *We have decided to know nothing among you except Christ Jesus, and him crucified* (1 Cor 2:2), but afterward they speak more boldly to those who are able to comprehend: *Theirs are the fathers, and from them is Christ according to the flesh, who is over all things, God blessed for ever* (Rom 9:5). Or perhaps the church's breasts are compared to grape-clusters when the teachers of truth at one and the same time both open the great mysteries or commandments of the scriptures to their elder hearers and give them to the little ones in a sense that they are able to receive as the food of life. To these [little ones] they say: *If you wish to enter into life, keep the commandments: you shall not murder; you shall not commit adultery; you shall not steal; you shall not speak false witness; honor your father and your mother; and you shall love your neighbor as yourself* (Mt 19:17–19). But to those [elders] they say: *If you wish to be perfect, go and sell all that you have and give to the poor* (Mt 19:21), and other things of that sort. But these breasts are also compared to grape-clusters because the Apostle says: *For if we go out of our mind, it is for God; if we are temperate, it is for you* (2 Cor 5:13). Surely they exercise the function of breasts when they temper their speech to the weak according to what they are able to hear, but they bear grape-clusters when they go out of their mind to things above and are inebriated by the abundance of God's house (Ps 36:8; Vulg. 35:9), namely, that house which was not made by hand but is eternal in the heavens (2 Cor 5:1). But since the saints have surely received every good thing they have through the dispensation of heavenly grace, there is rightly added:

I have said, I will go up in the palm tree and I will lay hold of its fruit, and your breasts will be like grape-clusters of the vine (Sg 7:8). Surely the only reason that the church's breasts are comparable to grape-clusters is that the Lord has deigned to come up to her and give her his grace. For when teachers preach things both lowly and sublime to the little ones and to the perfect as well, and when they condescend to become temperate for the unlearned and become sublimely inebriated through contemplation of celestial things, this is not by their own merit but through a celestial gift. Above it was said of the Lord, **My beloved has gone down to his garden** (Sg 6:1), and now he himself says, **I will go up in the palm tree**. Now it is the same church or perfect soul that is the Lord's garden who is also the palm tree. But the difference is between the Lord's going up or going down to her. Surely he goes down to her when he sends down upon her his celestial grace, with which she is made celestial herself and transported to heaven, but he goes up in her when he reveals the knowledge of his majesty to the faithful more and more, when he inspires the love of the celestial homeland in those who are making progress, moving as though by certain stages toward realms above. After he has first said to them: *When you have done all that I have commanded you, say, "We are worthless servants, for we have done only what we ought to have done"* (Lk 17:10), he gives them better things when he goes on to say: *No longer will I call you servants, for a servant does not know what his lord is doing; but I have called you friends* (Jn 15:15), and again: *Tell my brothers* (Mt 28:10). Thus the Lord goes down to his garden when he bestows celestial gifts upon the faithful, and he goes up in the palm tree when he graciously imparts increases in virtues to those making progress among his elect for as long as he is leading them to perfection. Concerning these virtues there is aptly added here:

I will lay hold of its fruit (Sg 7:8). Surely he lays hold of the virtues of the faithful soul so that by the most wholesome touch of his compunction he may make them yield a more abundant blessing forever. The fruits of the palm tree can also be taken as all the elect produced for the Lord by the church, which is his palm tree. Doubtless, he lays hold of these fruits when he strengthens them in faith and love, and so that they may never fall, he shields them with his own protection unto perfect maturity of life in accordance with that [saying] of the psalmist: *And you have given me that protection of your salvation, and your right hand has supported me* (Ps 18:35; Vulg. 17:36).

And your breasts will be like grape-clusters from Cyprus (Sg 7:8; cf. Sg 1:14; Vulg. 1:13). This is also to be understood as referring to those who do not neglect to announce the little things that they know to their neighbors in a kind and simple manner, even while they are inebriated with the gift of better wisdom. Unless the Lord goes up in the palm tree and lays hold of its fruit, unless he grants us increase in his grace, unless he defends our hearts with his right hand, we are unable to have any good things, whether large or small. Now the most victorious tree of the cross can also be aptly designated by the name of the palm tree and the bride's stature rightly compared to it, because it is through the passion of her Redeemer that holy church is able to raise herself up to stand so upright, stable, and unmovable. Also rightly compared to this [cross] are those saints who came before the times of the Lord's incarnation and signified the mysteries of his passion, whether by prophesying or by suffering, as well as the saints of our time, all of whom celebrate the triumph of the sacred passion by their believing and confessing, and many of them by their dying as well.

Now what the Bridegroom says—**I have said, I will go up in the palm tree, and I will lay hold of its fruit**—is consistent with that age in which Solomon sang these things, when through the voices of numerous prophets the Lord promised that he was going to come in the flesh to redeem the human race, when he predicted that of his own free will he was going to go up on the tree, dying in order to destroy the power of death so that he might return to life as the victor. Now the fruits of the palm tree that he said he was going to lay hold of are the subsequent events of glory that followed his ascent upon the cross, that is, the brightness of his resurrection and ascension to heaven, the coming of the Holy Spirit, and the salvation of a believing world. Aptly compatible with this meaning is that which follows:

And your breasts will be like grape-clusters of the vine (Sg 7:8), doubtless because after his passion and resurrection were accomplished, those first teachers of the church (that is, the apostles) had a far greater knowledge of saving doctrine than they had possessed up to that time, when appearing after the resurrection *he opened their mind to understand the scripture* (Lk 24:45), or when he sent the Spirit from above to give them knowledge of every tongue, at the time that the mockers falsely said that *they were filled with new wine* (Acts 2:13). But they actually were made to be like grape-clusters of the vine because they were refreshed with the grace of spiritual gifts in fulfillment of that true saying in which he said that new wine is put into new wineskins, and both are preserved (Mt 9:17). Now aptly congruent with both meanings is what follows:

And the scent of your mouth is like apples, your throat like the best wine (Sg 7:8–9). The "scent of the mouth" refers to the report of fine speech, and the "throat" to the role of a voice devoted to God. Both of these are worthy of being praised in the catholic church, and also in every elect soul, because both the voice that instructs those who are present and the report of speech that comes to those who are absent, whether through writings or through those who have heard, are shown to be full of virtue and grace. Now it is possible to distinguish why the scent of the bride's mouth is compared to apples, and her throat to the best wine, because apples contain their full flavor when they are new, but the value of a wine increases with age; thus the church's speaking voice and its report are compared to the form of both of these because it is acknowledged to be wonderful from its beginning to its completion. Likewise, since the excellence and the warmth of the best wine are greater than that of apples, rightly is it said: **And the scent of your mouth is like apples, your throat like the best wine**. As [wine] surpasses the beauty of apples, so does the speech of God's holy church in person excel the report of it that can be disseminated by the word of those who have heard.

---

32. Seizing upon the word from his mouth in this declaration of praise, she adds to the praise and beseeches him to come so that with his help she may be able to undertake pious labors, whether of working or of preaching.

Now at this point in the praise spoken about the bride, when he came to say that her throat was like the best wine, she seized upon the word from the Bridegroom's mouth and, moved with great love, she yearned for it to be more fully accomplished; for she understood that by the term "best wine" he was designating the word of the gospel, in which alone there is eternal salvation for those who believe, and so she says: **It is worthy for my beloved to drink, and for his lips and his teeth to chew** (Sg 7:9). She is saying, "The best wine, which he has compared to my throat, is worthy for my beloved to drink because the word of the gospel that he deigned to put in my mouth is so sublime that it should not be proclaimed in the world by anyone other than my beloved Bridegroom and Redeemer himself." When he appeared in the flesh, he was the first to open a way to heaven for the human race through the mystery of rebirth. He was the first to proclaim the sacrament of his passion, resurrection, and ascension, by which the world might be saved, and then he left it to be proclaimed by his faithful ones. He drank the cup of salvation and then held it out for the church to drink. Nor should it seem absurd that she speaks of the wine as being **for his lips and his teeth to chew**, although chewing usually applies to food rather than to drink. For speaking figuratively, she calls the holy teachers the beloved's lips and teeth; as was shown above, they chew the good wine that he himself has drunk when in frequent meditation they rejoice to study the word of grace that he taught and to share it with one another.

Some people understand the church's reply to the Lord's word as an addition, as though when he had said in praise of her, **Your throat** (that is, the sweetness of your confession) **is like the best wine**, she immediately assented to his words by adding: **It is worthy for my beloved to drink, and for his lips and his teeth to chew**, as though she were to say openly, "I have for a very long time desired that my beloved should thoroughly examine my mind to discern the affection and sincerity that I have for him, for I am confident that even if in his investigation he examines it as closely as he is accustomed to examine the food or drink that he has studiously endeavored to taste or chew, he will indeed attest that it is worthy of his praise." For the same reason, the church's first pastor [Peter] responded to the Lord who was questioning him: *You know that I* *love you;* and again: *You know everything; you know that I love you* (Jn 21:15–17). Then, still burning with great love for him, she goes on to say to the beloved:

I am for my beloved, and his turning is toward me (Sg 7:10). "I expend all my service and devotion as a gift for my beloved, and not for any other, and his turning is toward me, so that as long as I am in this mortal life I shall not cease from laboring, nor shall I carry my lamps without oil (Mt 25:8) (that is, my good works without charity) so that he will always be present to help, and at the end lead me to undying joys with him in the celestial marriage chamber." When she says, **and his turning is toward me**, that can be understood as being spoken specifically in the guise of the synagogue, that is, of that people who preceded the times of the incarnation. Further above, when she had heard him vowing: **I say, I will go up in the palm tree, and I will lay hold of its fruits** (that is, "I will go up on the wood of the cross upon which I will die, and I will take the fruits of resurrection and offer them to those who believe so that they may be nourished unto eternal life"), she rightly rejoices to declare: **I am for my beloved, and his turning is toward me**, which is to say: "He who has always been ready to help me with his invisible presence deigns to appear to me in my own nature and condition." Now what follows aptly applies to the lovers from both times:

Come, my beloved, let us go out into the field, let us linger in the villages (Sg 7:11), and so forth. For a great many of the earlier saints desired for the Lord to come for the salvation of the human race. Hence they also prayed, saying: *Stir up your power and come to save us* (Ps 80:2; Vulg. 79:3). They desired that he should go out into the field; that is, that he who was invisible among the fathers should appear visible in the world, in accordance with the [saying] of Habakkuk, who in the prophetic manner sang of things to come as though they had already taken place: *You came forth for the salvation of your people, to save your anointed ones* (Hb 3:13). They were also wishing to go forth with him into the field so that they might proclaim that the grace of the gospel, which they were preaching as something they beheld from afar and hailed as yet to come, is present in the world. They were yearning to linger with him in the villages; that is, to bring the word of faith to the pagans also. For who does not know that in Greek the name "pagans" is taken from [those who live in] villages, since they are a long way from the abode of the heavenly city, or even far from the knowledge of it? Moreover, you consider that Isaiah, Jeremiah, Joel, and the rest of the prophets, who prophesied with such foresight[7] of Christ who was to come in the flesh, suffered as many adversities and accomplished as many things in their capacity as his heralds as if they had lived with him in the flesh.

Not a few of the things that follow are also very properly applied to the faithful prayers of the ancient saints. But the church of our time, burning with like affection, rightly proclaims: **Come, my beloved, let us go out into the field**. "Although in rising to heaven you have set the humanity you assumed for my welfare at the right hand of the Father, I ask that you would deign to come to me very often through the presence of divine grace. You order me to cultivate the field in which you have sown good seed (that is, you command me to preach the gospel you have given to the whole world), but since apart from you I can do nothing (Jn 15:5), I beseech you to go out into the field with me (that is, to be my co-worker and helper in all the places where you want me to preach the word)." We read that when he comes on the day of judgment there will be two working in the field: *One will be taken, and the other left* (Lk 17:36; Vulg. 17:35). Now the one taken has been cultivating the field of the heart (whether that person's own or that of a neighbor) with the Lord as co-worker, but the one who claims to have produced fruit (whether of teaching or of good action) unaccompanied is rightly left by him from whom that person neglected to seek assistance. **Let us linger in the villages**. "Let us engage in teaching the hearts of outsiders also. Let us not only visit them in passing, but let us linger in them for a while, until we change them from being residences for pagans, and homes for outsiders and foreigners, into our own possessions."

In the morning, let us go up to the vineyards; let us see if the vineyards have flowered (Sg 7:12). "Let us linger in the villages in such a way that we may also go up to cultivate the vineyards; let us make a home among those who have already been converted to the faith in such a way that by preaching the gospel we may also undertake to gain others in which we can abide." And when she was about to say, **Let us go up to the vineyards**, it was well for her to preface it with **in the morning**; for she means that the morning is the rising of the true light through which the world has been snatched away from the power of darkness. Therefore she says, **In the morning, let us go up to the vineyards**, and it is as though she were to say openly, "Since the night of ancient unfaithfulness has departed, and since the gleaming light of the gospel has already begun to appear, let us go up to the vineyards, I pray; that is, let us work to establish churches for God throughout the world."

Let us see if the vineyards have flowered, if the flowers have borne fruit, if the pomegranates have flowered (Sg 7:12). The vineyards flower when the early church receives the rudiments of devout faith and confession, and the flowers bear fruit when the saints' faith and confession is made ready to perform works of justice lest their faith apart from works be found useless or dead (Jas 2:17–18, 20). The pomegranates, since they appear to be the color of blood, aptly express figuratively the passion of the Lord Savior or of his faithful. Now in each of these things the bride rightly seeks the presence of her beloved, saying: **Let us go out into the field, let us linger in the villages, let us go up to the vineyards, let us see if the vineyards have flowered**, and so forth, because the church is by no means sufficiently capable to advance by going out to work well, or to linger by persisting in the exercise of good work, or even to rise up to the intention of doing well, or to discern how far the souls of her hearers might be progressing, unless she is accompanied by the grace of him who promised when he was about to ascend to heaven: *And behold, I am with you all days, unto the consummation of the age* (Mt 28:20).

If you wish to take these things as having been spoken by the character of the ancient persons of old, it is not incongruent to understand that when she says, **In the morning, let us go up to the vineyards**, the term "in the morning" designates the time of the Lord's incarnation. For many prophets and just persons were desiring to see the times that the apostles saw (Mt 13:27), and they yearned to remain in the flesh until the new light of his coming, if they possibly could, in order that they might be able both to listen to the words and to hold on to the promises that he would teach in the flesh when he was present in the flesh to talk to those among his own people who would believe. The rest can be taken in the same sense as above.

There I will give you my breasts (Sg 7:12). That is to say, "In the place where we have come to see if the vineyards and the pomegranates are flowering and bearing fruit." Now it is established that the church's teachers are breasts for her little ones. She doubtless gives these breasts to the Lord when in obedience to him she employs both the deeds and the words of her preachers. Just as nurses give careful attention to providing milk for the little ones, those [preachers] strive to act in such a way that by seeing and hearing them, those who are still immature in Christ will be enabled to make progress and to attain to spiritual vigor so that they will be worthy of what is said to them in the voice of blessed John the apostle: *I have written to you young people, because you are strong, and the word of God remains in you, and you have overcome the evil one: do not love the world or the things that are in the world* (1 Jn 2:14–15). Now when the church had prayed to the Lord, saying, **Come, my beloved, let us go out into thc field**, and the other things that follow, she rightly concluded with **I will give you my breasts**, as though she were to say openly, "The reason that I am praying to you so much is so that you will enter with me into the spiritual labor through which I will always be able to acquire new peoples for you and will know how to discern the condition of those who have already been acquired, and how much progress they are making in faith, for as the tutor of my little ones I am striving very diligently to deliver them to you in such a way that neither my example nor my word will induce them to follow anything except what you yourself have commanded." Knowing that he had attained to these breasts, there was one who said: *We became little ones in your midst, like a nurse caring for her children, so desirous are we of you* (1 Thes 2:7–8). The bride gives breasts of this sort to her beloved, and not to some other, when she is continually intent on obeying the command she hears from him: *Set apart for me Paul and Barnabas for the work to which I have called them* (Acts 13:2).

The mandrakes give forth fragrance in our gates (Sg 7:13). The gates of Christ and the church are the same teachers who were also described by the term of "breasts." As we have often said, they are breasts because they act with abundant industry to give milk to her little ones and to those yet unable to speak, so that perfect praise may be brought forth for the Lord from their mouth also. Concerning them the psalmist says: *The Lord loves the gates of Sion more than all the tabernacles of Jacob* (Ps 87:2; Vulg. 86:2); hence in the Apocalypse, John also says of that same city: *It has a great high wall with twelve gates* (Rv 21:12). Therefore, since these chosen ones are the teachers of the early church (that is, the twelve apostles), mandrakes give forth fragrance in gates of this sort when the apostles and the apostles' successors spread the palm branch of spiritual virtues far and wide around themselves. Rightly, then, does the church pray for the Lord to come and bring assistance to heavenly preaching in the place where she knows that those preachers are ablaze with exceptional virtues.

But anyone who diligently inquires about the other properties of the mandrake or whether it is used for medicines will surely find that it is well suited to signify the virtues of the faithful. For it is an aromatic herb that has *a root shaped similarly* to a human body and *sweet-smelling fruit about the size of a Matianus apple, whence the Latins also call it the "apple of the earth."*[8] Now it has a power such that it is *often used to bring sleep to those who are afflicted with the ailment of insomnia.*[9] Of course, the worst insomnia is suffered by those who seek to divest their souls of the cares and desires of this world but are still held back by the practice of bad habits and are thus unable to obtain the rest they seek. However, those who endeavor to remedy their infirmity by the conscientious exercise of spiritual studies, so that they gradually develop their ability to make war against vices, will attain to that peace of mind of which the bride speaks in previous parts of this song: **I sleep and my heart keeps watch** (Sg 5:2); that is, "I rest from the cares of temporal things, and my heart keeps watch in the contemplation of eternal blessings."

Likewise, if their bodies are going to be operated on *as part of their treatment, the bark* of this [herb] *is mixed with wine and given to them to drink so that they will fall asleep and not feel any pain.*[10] It is easy to see how the explanation of this property signifies what is done in the case of spiritual remedies. Surely a soul grows gravely ill when she is overcome by the great weight of vices, and she is brought to the physicians as a patient (as it were) when the holy teachers exhort her to resist carnal desires. But since she experiences severe pain in giving up that which she has been holding on to with such great love, it seems as though she is being operated upon by the one who draws her away from the allure of old habits. But lest that sort of surgery should perhaps seem intolerable to the sick soul, she will be given a healing potion, after which she will effectively go into a serene sleep and feel no pain. Then she will recall to mind the eternal punishment of Gehenna's fire, which will perpetually torment the souls that neglect their own health, and she will remember the glory of the heavenly homeland, in which the souls of the just will be raised to reign with Christ forever. When a soul has been sick for a long time, surely this is the potion of saving doctrine that makes her so asleep to this world (as it were)—or rather dead to it—that she readily suffers the removal of all the pleasures to which she was previously clinging; rather, she even rejoices in it.

The mandrake is also said to relieve those who suffer from nausea in such a way that they are unable to retain food or do not enjoy taking it. Now the soul's food is the word of truth, and those who are unable either to receive it by hearing or to keep it in the belly of their memory once it has been taken in by the hearing are certainly gripped with a most harmful and dangerous illness, doubtless because their life is necessarily without hope if they are loath to keep the bread of life that they have received, or even to take it in.[11] The numerous examples of the saints and the presence of a virtuous model are accustomed to supply a remedy for this illness, as long as the nauseated and disgusted person sees and hears the works of good people, recalls the glory of a heavenly reward, and then seeks to imitate the temporal deeds and labors of the good by which one merits to become a co-heir of their eternal felicity. Therefore, everyone of this sort is led to the hope of salvation and life as though by the fruit of a mandrake. All of the teachers exhibit such grace of the Spirit and such exercise of piety that anyone who sees or hears them immediately has a change of heart and begins to follow their way of life. Rightly, then, does it hold the form of a mandrake, since it causes the food of life to stay in the hearts of those who are feeling nauseated.

And pleasingly does the bride promise the Bridegroom riches along with life-giving delights—not only the fruits of vineyards and apples for his consideration, but also the fragrances and healing juices of mandrakes; not only things that can be eaten and drunk, but also those that she boasts of having because they have the capacity to make food and drink agreeable and sweet to those who are feeling nauseated. For the church brings the food of the heavenly word and the cups of life as gifts in the sight of her Maker; she brings capable ministers who by their preaching carry these things to those who are hungering and thirsting and, moreover, even render them sweet to those who are feeling nauseated by tasting them beforehand (that is, by first doing those things themselves); she brings countless numbers of the elect like companies of vines; she brings the band of martyrs as pomegranates in the precious splendor of an unconquerable confession; she brings the spiritual gifts with which she enkindles the hearts of the indolent to behold and to imitate the examples of good people.

---

33. Beginning from her youthful origin, the church wishes for the Lord to become incarnate so that with the help of his human support (as it were, through the sustenance of his left hand), she may merit to ascend to the contemplation of divine glory (as it were, to the embrace of his right hand).

All fruits new and old, my beloved, I have kept for you (Sg 7.13.) The fruits new and old are the commandments or promises of the New Testament and of the Old. The church has kept all of them for her beloved because she knew that he alone gives both sets of commandments and renders those who keep them worthy of a reward, and she knew that he alone both promulgated the commandments and proffered the promises—the lesser ones to his servants through angels of old, and the greater ones to us through himself. In this verse the church is boldly rebutting the Photinians, who denied that the Lord and Savior had existed before Mary,[12] and she is also refuting the madness of the Manichaeans, who taught that there was one God of the law and another of the gospel.[13]

Likewise, the fruits new and old are the just of the New Testament and the Old, none of whom was able to enter the door of the heavenly kingdom before the incarnation, passion, resurrection, and ascension of the Lord and Savior, no matter how distinguished for extraordinary holiness. The church of that time (which is now called the "synagogue" for the sake of distinction) said: **All fruits new and old, my beloved, I have kept for you;** as though she were to say openly: "I know most certainly that no one can be saved except through your grace, and no one among mortals can now become perfectly blessed until you become mortal and open the way to the heaven of true blessedness; for all the just that I have seen, I have kept in certain faith for your sacred advent, through which I have learned that they will attain to perfect felicity." Like unto her, the church of the New Testament also states her opinion in the voice of her first pastor [Peter] as he contends against those who had another understanding: *Why are you putting God to the test by placing on the necks of the disciples a yoke that neither our ancestors nor we have been able to bear? But we believe that we will be saved through the grace of the Lord Jesus, just as they will* (Acts 15:10–11). Now the following verse proves that this exposition of this verse is true when there is added:

Who will give you to me as my brother sucking my mother's breasts? (Sg 8:1). Frequently and everywhere, and especially in this passage, this song testifies that it resounds with nothing carnal or according to the letter, but wishes that the whole of it be understood spiritually and typologically. For who among women would suddenly desire that her lover and beloved, whom she has already been desperately in love with as an adult, should not be a young man as he has been, but should be born anew into an infantile state as her brother, and be nursed as a little one at her own mother's breasts? Therefore, the voice is that of the just persons of old, who were believing in the Lord and Savior who was consubstantial in divinity with the Father and the Holy Spirit, worshiping him with the obligatory rites, and longing to see him in human form, consubstantial with humanity, so that they might see fulfilled in him the things that they knew as having been predicted about him in prophecy. They were desiring to hear that most fitting utterance of their Creator, which he pronounced while extending his hands toward his disciples, saying: *Behold my mother and my brothers* (Mk 3:34). They were longing to hear that delectable announcement which the same disciples heard after the triumph of the resurrection: *Go tell my brothers to go to Galilee; there they will see me* (Mt 28:10), as the beloved himself attests when he says to his disciples elsewhere: *Many prophets and just people have been longing to see what you see, but have not seen it, and to hear what you hear, but have not heard it* (Mt 13:17).

When she says, **sucking my mother's breasts**, it cannot be understood as referring specifically to that glorious Mother of God of whom it was truly said: *Blessed is the womb that bore you, and the breasts that you sucked* (Lk 11:27), and of whom he himself says in the psalm: *From my mother's womb, you are my God* (Ps 22:10; Vulg. 21:11), which is to say openly, "You who were my Father before the worlds, you are also my God since I began to be human." For neither Solomon nor any other just person of that age could speak of blessed Mary as a mother to him, since she was going to be born into the world so long after that time.[14] But the one that the synagogue calls her mother is the substance of human nature, from which she was born and from which she was desiring that the Redeemer of all should also be born and nourished. Still burning with great desire for his birth, she added:

And I will find you outside and kiss you, and now let no one despise me (Sg 8:1). Surely the beloved was inside because *in the beginning was the Word, and the Word was with God, and the Word was God* (Jn 1:1), but so that he could also be found outside, *the Word became flesh and dwelt among us* (Jn 1:14). Surely the patriarchs saw God, and the prophets saw God, but inside (that is, in the contemplation of a spiritual mind, not in the view of a carnal eye) they saw him only in an image, only in the form of an angelic substance, but they were by no means able to see his very nature, which revealed itself in its preferred manner, through angels. Accordingly, the Lawgiver himself, who merited to hear, *I will show you all my goodness*, heard again: *You cannot see my face, for no human shall see me and live* (Ex 33:19–20). But happy are those who have merited to converse among themselves: *We have found the Messiah, who is called Christ* (Jn 1:41), and again: *We have found him about whom Moses in the law and also the prophets wrote, Jesus son of Joseph from Nazareth* (Jn 1:45); for to such as these also aptly applies that which says: **And I will find you outside and kiss you**. The synagogue indeed found and kissed the beloved in those who merited to see him face to face in the reality of the flesh that he assumed, and to speak with him mouth to mouth. For surely this is the kiss (that is, the most loving gift of his mouth and the exchange of mutual endearment) that the synagogue was seeking above all in this song so that she begins: **Let him kiss me with the kiss of his mouth** (Sg 1:1). Now it is well that she goes on to wish:

And now let no one despise me (Sg 8:1). Surely the church was despised by the people outside as small and worthless because she was for a long time enclosed within the narrow confines of Judea. But when the Lord came in the flesh she began to be spread throughout all nations, and soon she was made terrible in the world, as though she were about to fill the entire earth and overthrow the worship of all the gods. Surely she proved to be not despised but rather as terrible as an army drawn up in battle array (Sg 6:4; Vulg. 6:3), especially because, in spite of the fact that war was openly inflicted upon her throughout the entire earth, she became yet more victorious whether she was living or dying in that war, and thus terrible to the whole world. The church was also despised by unclean spirits, since they were boasting that they had ensnared the human race and pulled it down from the heavenly homeland into this place of exile and manifold afflictions, and that no human could ever be completely free from their tyranny. But after *the Mediator between God and humankind, the human Christ Jesus* (1 Tm 2:5) came into the world and, being tempted, conquered the very enemy by whose temptation the first human had once been conquered, he also *went about doing good and healing all those who were oppressed by the devil* (Acts 10:38). By dying, he at last destroyed *the one who held the power of death* (Heb 2:14), and bringing back with him from hell the whole multitude of the just who had gone before, he led them to the joys of that kingdom which the first human had lost and set the sign of his triumph on the foreheads of the faithful (Rv 14:1). Now [the unclean spirits] no longer despise the life of good people, because they see that they have been conquered by a human being, and they lament that the human race has been transported to the kingdom that they lost by being proud. It is also permissible to believe that this refers to the holy angels who were less despising of the life of the elect after they perceived that their God and Lord loved the human race so much that he deigned to become human himself also and to live and die among humans. For this is the reason that before his incarnation they patiently endured being worshiped by humans, but in the Apocalypse the angel stops John, who was starting to worship him, saying: *See that you do not do this! I am the fellow servant of you and your comrades who hold the testimony of Jesus. Worship God!* (Rv 19:10). Hence that ancient multitude of the elect was sighing for the coming of the same Lord Jesus, saying: **Who will give you to me as my brother sucking my mother's breasts? And I will find you outside and kiss you, and now let no one despise me** (Sg 8:1). Here there is also aptly added:

I will seize you and lead you into the house of my mother (Sg 8:2). Now the synagogue says these things in the same way that Paul says: *We who are alive, who are left until the coming of the Lord, will not precede those who have fallen asleep* (1 Thes 4:15). Although he certainly knows that he cannot continue in the flesh until the day of judgment, nevertheless, because they share in one and the same fellowship, he includes himself in the number of those who would be found alive in the flesh at the coming of the Judge. Therefore here also the ancient people of God speaks in the persona of that part of her that was going to see him when he appeared in the flesh. "I will seize you and lead you into the house of my mother; with ready and faithful devotion I will receive you when you come, and with eager longing I will fulfill your admonitions and await your promises. When you return after having accomplished the divine purpose for being in the flesh, I will lead you in before joyful eyes and announce you to all with a joyful voice." For this is the house of her mother—namely, the happiness of the celestial homeland that human nature was created to inhabit. If no one had sinned, the whole human race would have moved from the delights of the paradise in which the first human was placed directly into the eternal possession of that homeland, without death intervening. Therefore the church promises that she will lead the Lord into this house—not having the power to accomplish this by her own strength, but desiring in her prayers that it may be accomplished, and proclaiming through her heralds that it would be accomplished or has been accomplished, in the same way that the psalmist who could not exalt him to heaven nevertheless said: *I will exalt you, O Lord, because you have sustained me* (Ps 30:1; Vulg. 29:2), which is to say openly: "Because you have deigned to sustain my fragile nature, rightly does my mind take unwearied delight in declaring the tidings of your power, which you have made glorious in me."

There you will teach me, and I will give you a cup of spiced wine (Sg 8:2). "There you will teach me, in the very substance of flesh in which I will find you outside and kiss you; there you will give me the precepts of your gospel that the prophets and the law and the psalms have promised; there you will teach me to hope for greater gifts than I have read in the law and the prophets." Or perhaps it should be understood more profoundly: "There you will teach me, in that house of my mother into which I rejoice to lead you before the eyes of the multitude, and into which I also desire to lead you with words of praise." For there he has taught and continues to teach that part of the church which he has taken thither to himself, and there he will teach the whole church since after the universal judgment has been accomplished there will not be any saints of his except all of those in heaven with him. What he teaches there he explains in the gospel when, in that sweetest and most extensive discourse he had with them on the final [night] before his passion, he says among other things: *I have said these things to you in proverbs. The hour is coming when I will no longer speak to you in proverbs, but I will tell you plainly of the Father* (Jn 16:25), that is, I will show the Father to you plainly.

And I will give you a cup of spiced wine and the new wine of my pomegranates (Sg 8:2). The church gives the Lord a cup of wine when, having received his benefits, she returns the abundant thanks of fervent love, and the same wine is not unmixed but made with a mixture of noble juices, as it were, when that love of his blessings is also proved by the testimony of her works; for he teaches us to possess not only the works that prove our love for the Creator, but no less those that prove our neighborly love, if we take care to offer him the proper and acceptable cup of our devotion. He himself openly distinguishes these things when, admonishing the disciples not to perform their justice before humans so that they may be seen by them, in completion of the same verse he immediately adds three kinds of good actions—namely, almsgiving, prayer, and fasting (Mt 6:1–18), clearly signifying that our justice should consist of these three. To almsgiving pertain all the things we do out of mercy to provide for the neighbor's necessity; to prayer, all that we do with pious devotion so that our Creator will be favorably disposed toward us; to fasting, the entire restraint of mind by which we take care to abstain from the vices and contagions of the world.

And since holy church not only offers her beloved the purity of her life but also lifts up the precious chalice of death in many of her members on account of her love for him, when she has said, **And I will give you a cup of spiced wine**, she added: **and the new wine of my pomegranates**. Surely these are the pomegranates [*mala granata*] that are also called *mala punica—granata* on account of the profusion of their seeds [*granorum*], and *punica* because they are abundant in Africa and especially around Carthage;[15] their red color serves to indicate that they contain the figure of the blessed martyrs. And properly does she identify the drink from pomegranates as "new wine" [*mustum*] and not "unmixed wine" [*merum*] or "strong wine" [*siceram*] in order to signify the fervor of inextinguishable love in the heart of the triumphal army [of martyrs]. For *new wine (that is, wine drawn straight from the vat)*[16] is accustomed to be more fervid, and thus it rightly corresponds to the most ardent virtue of those who do not doubt that they will pass over to the vision of the Creator, even through sword and flames. For since *a drink of this sort is said not only to cure an upset stomach and a sour belly but also to benefit the other organs*,[17] who does not see that the more the fervor of charity abounds, the more fully it covers—or even extinguishes—a multitude of sins? (Jas 5:20; 1 Pt 4:8). Therefore, let the ancient congregation of the just say that she desires to see the coming of her Maker in the flesh; let her say, **There you will teach me, and I will give you a drink of spiced wine and the new wine of my pomegranates**, as if she were to declare openly: "There (that is, at the time and place in which I will find you outside and be worthy to address you) you will give me those commandments and gifts that befit the Son of God when he appears to humans in human form, and I will give you the thing that truly should be devoted to God, which is the obedience of a pure heart." For to the church laboring amid the adversities of the world, his coming doubtless bestows celestial rest—for the meantime, in hope; in the future, in reality.

His left arm under my head, and his right arm will embrace me (Sg 8:3). Surely by "his left arm" she designates the mysteries of his incarnation and the gifts of his presence, but by the "right arm" there are figured those rewards that the elect will receive in the future, which include not only a vision of his divine majesty but also the splendor of the glorified humanity of one and the same *Mediator between God and humankind* (1 Tm 2:5). Hence the bride properly desires for his left arm to be set under her head but for his right arm to embrace her, so that now she may rest from the world's confusion through his assistance with temporal things, and then she may enjoy the manifest vision of him forever. And surely no storm will ever interfere with the saints' eternal rest. Hence it is rightly said: **And his right hand will embrace me**, doubtless because in the heavenly kingdom the presence of his divine majesty covers them around on every side lest the happiness worthy of God should be invaded by any memory of misery, or constricted by any apprehension that it will come to an end. Hence in the Apocalypse, John also says: *And God will wipe away every tear from their eyes, and death will be no more; mourning and crying and sorrow will be no more, for the first things have passed away* (Rv 21:4); and again: *And there will be no more night; and they will not need the light of the lamp or the light of the sun, because the Lord God will enlighten them, and they will reign forever and ever* (Rv 22:5). But the rest that is granted to the faithful at the present time can never be perfect, because the ancient enemy, death, has not yet been destroyed (1 Cor 15:26). Thus it happens that the happy repose of many good people (that most welcome sleep, as it were, which causes their mind to be insensible to this world while intent upon things divine) is disturbed by the assaults of the wicked, who are ignorant of this most happy sleep and thus accustomed rather to stay awake out of love for the world that is passing away.

---

34. Rejoicing in her desires, he adjures the believers from among the Jews not to disturb the faith of the Gentiles. Complying with his commands, they marvel with an admiring mind at her sudden conversion.

Would that these things pertained only to those who openly fight against the peace of the church, and not also to those she holds within herself who impede her spiritual pursuits by their carnal ways! But since she also produces many people of this sort, the Lord admonishes them that they should not presume to disturb those souls among the church's faithful who are devoted to prayer or reading or other pious activities. For as soon as he had heard her heart's desire, he immediately added:

I adjure you, O daughters of Jerusalem: do not arouse and awaken the beloved until she wishes (Sg 8:4). For souls such as these are also rightly called "daughters of Jerusalem," since they have been united to the body of holy church through the bath of regeneration, and since they are moving toward the heavenly kingdom, even though they are building upon the foundation of right faith *not with gold, silver, and precious stones* but *with wood, hay, and straw* (1 Cor 3:12). Therefore he says, **Do not arouse the beloved** with the tumult of carnal disturbances **and awaken** her from the repose of calm devotion in which she delights to stand in the sight of her Creator, **until she wishes;** that is, until having duly fulfilled the obligations of her divine service and having been reminded of things that are necessary, she consents to return to the common concern of human frailty. And because it followed that after Judea had streamed to faith in the Lord's incarnation, the multitude of Gentiles also hastened to share in its grace, Judea marvels at their unexpected conversion and quickly exclaims:

Who is she that comes up from the wilderness flowing with delights and leaning upon my beloved? (Sg 8:5). The church of the Gentiles comes up from the wilderness because she who has for a very long time been left behind by her Creator now came to his grace by taking the steps of faith and good works in fulfillment of what Isaiah the prophet says: *The wilderness and the impassable land shall be glad, and the desert shall rejoice and blossom like the lily* (Is 35:1). She was doubtless flowing with those delights of which the Bridegroom speaks above: **How beautiful you are, and how comely, dearest, in delights** (Sg 7:6)—that is, in desires for the heavenly life—and she was **leaning upon my beloved**, duly leaning upon him without whose aid she was unable not only to come up to the heights but even to rise, for we are not able to make progress in virtues, or even the very beginnings in faith, unless the Lord grants it. Therefore, as the Book of the Acts of the Apostles quite openly attests (Acts 10:45), Judea marveled greatly at the grace of the Gentiles' recent conversion, for she believed that it belonged only to her and to those who were admitted into her form of worship through the sacrament of circumcision. Hence after she had said, marveling: **Who is she that comes up from the wilderness flowing with delights**? she now concludes with what there is that is so marvelous: **and leaning upon my beloved**. She says, **my beloved;** that is, the one whom I imagined to love only me and to be unknown by other nations.

---

35. He also reminds her of his love for the church that he redeemed through the wood of the cross, and he commands her always to bear his memory upon her heart and in her work.

Responding to her, he who *is our peace, who has made both one and came to preach peace* to us who were *far off and peace to those who were near* (Eph 2:14, 17), admonishes her to remember the grace through which she was snatched away from the gravest evils and turned to the way of truth, and to rejoice in the salvation of others also, since the Author of salvation and life himself is *generous to all who call upon him* (Rom 10:12). He says: **Under the apple tree I raised you up; there your mother was corrupted; there she who bore you was violated** (Sg 8:5). The apple tree most aptly depicts the wood of the holy cross upon which he deigned to hang for the salvation of all, in praise of which the church said above: **As an apple tree, among the trees of the woods, so is my beloved among sons** (Sg 2:3). Thus the Lord raised up the synagogue under the apple tree when through faith in his passion he called her back from eternal death. Under this apple tree his mother and she who bore him (namely, the elder and older portion of his people) was corrupted and violated, doubtless because, being seduced by the persuasiveness of their leaders, they chose Barabbas instead of the Lord, crying out with foolish audacity: *His blood be on us and on our children* (Mt 27:25). For she too was under the tree of the cross—not being humbly delivered by him through faith, but obstinately calling down his retribution upon herself. Separating them from fellowship with her, the Lord exhorts the people who have consented to believe that they should keep the memory of the grace they shared with her fixed in their heart, but also join to it works worthy of the faith received, for there follows:

Set me as a seal upon your heart, as a seal upon your arm (Sg 8:6). "Set me upon your heart by meditation, and set me upon your arm by working, so that inside there may be *the charity from a pure heart and a good conscience and an unfeigned faith* (1 Tm 1:5), and also so that the same devotion of heart that the Inner Judge sees within may also be shown to observers on the outside through the performance of good work, to the glory of the Father who is in heaven" (Mt 5:16). Now it is well that he says: **Set me as a seal**. For we are often accustomed to put some band around a finger or arm as a sign that will remind us of something that we want to remember frequently. Thus the Lord also wishes us to keep his commandments in this manner, so that we are always being reminded by the presence of a seal, in accordance with what he himself also commands when he says concerning the law that he has given: *And it shall be as a sign on your hand and as something hanging before your eyes, as a remembrance* (Ex 13:16). Now it happens that if we continually bear his memory in our breast, then he who has bestowed this grace upon us will remember us forever like a seal before him and keep us happy in his heavenly kingdom, in accordance with what he promises to the chosen leader of his people, saying: *I will take you, O Zerubbabel my servant, son of Shealtiel, and set you as a seal, because I have chosen you, says the Lord* (Hg 2:23; Vulg. 2:24). On the contrary, rejecting and casting off the one who was turned to apostasy after having come to faith, he says: *If Coniah son of King Jehoiakim of Judah were the ring on my right hand, from there I would tear him off* (Jer 22:24).

Or perhaps we should understand this more profoundly, since the setting of a seal usually indicates that there are secrets, and precious things, and things that must not be desecrated, as it is written concerning the Lord: *And he shuts up the stars as though under a seal* (Job 9:7), evidently so that they may not be opened except by the permission and order of the one who sealed them. For on this account did Abraham *receive the sign of circumcision as a seal of the justice of faith which he had while he was uncircumcised* (Rom 4:11). Surely the circumcision that he received in the flesh signified that the faith he had already received even prior to circumcision was sufficient for the cleansing of both heart and body; we too have this faith in a manner apart from the circumcision of the flesh, in that we too are justified in accordance with that [saying] of the prophet and of the Apostle: *But the just person lives by faith* (Hb 2:4; Rom 1:17). And so our Lord Jesus Christ is set as a seal upon our heart, as a seal upon our arm, so that we will realize that all the things he did or said in the flesh are secrets and heavenly things. For since he is the virtue of God and the wisdom of God (1 Cor 1:24), we set him as a seal upon our heart when we study the things he said as though they are truly the words of divine wisdom, and we set him as a seal upon our arm when we hasten to hear about the things he did, and to follow them to the best of our ability, as though they are examples of true virtue. Likewise, we set the Lord as a seal upon our heart and arm when we keep the commandments at the present time in order to receive that reward which we are not yet able to see.

For love is strong as death, jealousy as hard as hell (Sg 8:6). This love or jealousy can rightly be understood both in our Lord and Redeemer and in his elect. For the love with which he loved us was so strong that through it he came to die for us. Hence he says: *No one has greater love than this, to lay down one's life for one's friends* (Jn 15:13). The jealousy with which he was zealous for us was hard as hell because the temptations of opposing enemies could not draw him away from care for our salvation, just as the tortures of the wretched cannot appease hell or alter the severity of its judgment. This comparison seems harsh indeed, but the harsher the comparison being given, the more intensely does it denote the passion of the Lord's zeal toward us, concerning which he himself says to the Father when he is turning the faithless ones out of the temple: *Zeal for your house has consumed me* (Jn 2:17). Now the greater the jealousy that he shows, the more severe is the damnation that follows for us if we spurn it. But the love of his faithful ones is also strong as death because they cannot be parted from it by the pain of their own death. Hence they boldly say: *Who will separate us from the love of Christ? Will tribulation, or distress, or persecution, or famine, or nakedness, or peril, or sword*? (Rom 8:35). Their zeal, which is pure and devoted to God, is compared to hell, because just as it never lets go of those whom it has once taken, so will the constancy of their fervent zeal never grow cold at any time. For this is the zeal with which Phineas struck down the fornicators in the desert (Nm 25:1–9); this is the zeal with which Elijah was burning when, after he had held the rain up in heaven and then recalled it after three years, after he had slain the prophets of Baal and turned the people's heart to the Lord, he said: *With zeal have I been zealous for the Lord of hosts, because the children of Israel have forsaken the Lord's covenant, thrown down your altars, and killed your prophets with the sword* (1 Kgs 19:10; 3 Kgs 19:10, Vulg.); this is the zeal with which Peter was exercised when he brought to death the neophytes who were deceiving God (Acts 5:1–10); this was the zeal concerning which Paul says to the Corinthians: *I am jealous for you with the jealousy of God, for I have espoused you to one husband, to present you as a chaste virgin to Christ. But I am afraid that as the serpent seduced Eve by its cunning, so your minds will be corrupted and fall from the simplicity which is in Christ Jesus* (2 Cor 11:2–3).

Now the great magnitude of perfect love or zeal was fittingly introduced here at the place where Judea was marveling at the recent conversion of the Gentiles and the Lord was admonishing her that she should bring to mind the gifts of kindness that he provided, for after the corruption of the one who bore her and her mother, she was raised up by the tree of the cross to the grace of the first resurrection. Therefore, this verse can be suitably adapted to those above: "Remember, O church gathered from the Jews, that you have attained to life through the wood of my passion, and never forget that a great magnitude of love and jealousy led me to death for your sake. Do not be amazed that I have accepted the multitude of Gentiles who turned to faith in me, for you see how they burn with so much love and so much zeal to do my will that it appears easier to persuade death not to take any more souls out of the world, or hell not to claim those who have been taken, than to persuade these at any time to depart from faith in me. Do not think that you can please me with the bare profession of words alone; rather, if you want to come to life you must set the memory of my will as a seal upon your heart, and set it upon your arm: fill your mind with so much love (both for the Divine and for the neighbor), be so zealous lest the total number of the citizens of heaven be completed without the gathering in of your people, that your love and your jealousy cannot be changed or diminished by circumstantial conditions, whether adverse or favorable."

Some take that which is said here, **jealousy hard as hell**, as referring to the jealousy of envy that the synagogue often had toward the church of the Gentiles, of which we also read in the Acts of the Apostles: *Now on the following Sabbath almost the whole city gathered to hear the word of the Lord, but when the Jews saw the crowds, they were filled with zeal; and they contradicted what was being said by Paul* (Acts 13:44–45). This jealousy is evidently hard as hell, doubtless because it consumes the soul that it catches with the disease of ungodliness. For this reason it is written: *Zeal lays hold of an ignorant people, and now fire devours your adversaries* (Is 26:11, Old Latin). If it is understood in this way, the Lord is rightly admonishing the synagogue not to hold this jealousy toward the church when she sees her flowing with celestial delights when she comes up from the wilderness of vices, but to cleave to his love with an unchangeable mind, lest by chance through envying others she may lose the good things that she might otherwise have had. Having said this, he continues by amassing many things about the power of love, saying:

Its lamps are lamps of fire and flames (Sg 8:6). The lamps of love are the hearts of the elect that subject themselves to all persons out of love for their Maker, and love their neighbors as themselves. These lamps are truly lamps of fire and flames—of fire, in the charity with which they burn on the inside, and of flames, in the working of justice with which they also shine before others far and wide. Did they not show themselves to be lamps of fire, those who said: *Was not our heart burning within us when he was speaking on the road and opening the scriptures to us*? (Lk 24:32). And does the Lord not wish us to be lamps of flames, those to whom he says: *Let your light shine before others, so that they may see your good works* (Mt 5:16)? These are the lamps that the virgins have—those who will enter the eternal kingdom with the Bridegroom when he comes to the marriage chamber (Mt 25:10). But the lamps of the foolish are extinguished at that time, doubtless because the works with which they are seen to shine before others will grow dark when the Inner Judge comes and makes manifest the counsels of their hearts (1 Cor 4:5). But these who enter into the marriage feast with him are those who have set his love and the fear of the

Lord upon their heart and arm, that is, who have subjected all their thoughts and actions to his precepts.

Many waters cannot extinguish charity, nor rivers drown it (Sg 8:7). What it calls "many waters" and "rivers" are the assaults of temptations that do not cease to assail the souls of the faithful, whether visibly or invisibly. For they endeavor to conquer them through the open adversaries of the faith, and through false believers, and through the secret attacks of the ancient enemy, but hearts that have been rooted and founded in love (Eph 3:17) certainly know how to avoid yielding to temptations. For Truth's promise stands firm in saying: *When you pass through the waters, I will be with you; and through the rivers, they shall not overwhelm you* (Is 43:2); and in the gospel he says of the house that has been built upon a rock: *When the flood came, the river beat against that house but could not shake it, for it was founded upon a rock* (Lk 6:48). Now for a house to be founded upon a rock is for the lamps of the saints' hearts to be filled with the fire and flames of sincere devotion. And because the love of eternal goods abounds in every soul as soon as all possession of perishing things becomes worthless, rightly is it added:

If one were to give all the wealth of one's house for love, one would despise it as nothing (Sg 8:7). This verse does not need to be explained in words, since its truth was confirmed by the example of [the Lord] himself among the first apostles, and afterward by that of an innumerable throng of believers when for the love of truth they were seen to give up everything they possessed in this world and seemed to themselves to have lost nothing, if only they may receive true goods in heaven. In the gospel, the Lord openly signified this with two consecutive parables, saying: *The kingdom of heaven is like treasure hidden in a field, which a man found and hid, and in his joy he goes and sells all that he has and buys that field; again, the kingdom of heaven is like a merchant searching for fine pearls; on finding one pearl of great price he went and sold all that he had and bought it* (Mt 13:44–46). Hence the distinguished preacher said in a most distinguished way: *On account of the excellent knowledge of Jesus Christ my Lord, on account of whom I have suffered the loss of all things and count them as dung, in order that I may gain Christ and be found in him* (Phil 3:8–9).

If this is read as **he would despise that person**, as some codices have it, it produces a very different sense, namely, what the Apostle commends when he says: *If I distribute all my goods to feed the poor; and if I hand over my body to be burned, but do not have charity, it profits me nothing* (1 Cor 13:3). Therefore, if one gives all the wealth of one's house to the poor for love (that is, as a substitute for loving), it is as though one gives nothing, and so is despised by the Judge who perceives that one's heart is empty of love. Even though this sense seems to be quite contrary to the one above, nevertheless the power of love, which is greater than the necessaries of life, declares no less in the one than in the other that we should always carry sincere love around like a seal upon our work.

---

36. He also asks the synagogue what should be done for the early church from among the Gentiles, since she does not yet possess those who are ready to be ordained as teachers, and he goes on to say that if any among them are distinguished in life or in speech, they should be instructed in the divine writings and then they can be promoted to that position. But those who are simpler in nature should have laid upon them the examples of the saints, by which they may be more fully strengthened in faith.

Our sister is small, and she has no breasts (Sg 8:8). The Lord speaks these things to the synagogue, who is marveling at the faith or the acceptance of the church of the Gentiles, with great dispensation of charity indeed identifying her as their sister (that is, both his own and that of the synagogue), so that the same synagogue may both recall that she herself was made the sister of her Creator through grace, and rejoice more and more for the one who has been joined together with her in the grace of sisterly fellowship. Now the sister of the Lord and Savior is his whole church gathered together from both peoples, and also every holy soul—not only because he assumed her very nature when he became human, but also on account of the gift of grace by which he gave those who believe in him power to become children of God (Jn 1:12), so that he who was by nature the only Son of God became by grace *the firstborn within a large family* (Rom 8:29). Hence there is that sweetest word he speaks to Mary: *But go to my brothers and* *tell them that I am ascending to my Father and your Father, and to my God and your God* (Jn 20:17).

Therefore when he says, **Our sister is little, and she has no breasts**, he is referring to the early days of the church born from the Gentiles, when she was little in the number of believing persons and still remained less capable of preaching the word of God.[18] Read the Book of the Acts of the Apostles, which stretches from the nineteenth year of Tiberius Caesar to the fourth year of Nero,[19] and you will find that many throngs of Gentiles believed in the apostles' preaching, yet nowhere during that whole time will you learn that they themselves preached, throughout nearly thirty-two years. Surely the church of the Gentiles was little and not yet capable of birthing children for Christ or of nurturing them through teaching, for which reason the Lord admonishes the synagogue that she should employ sisterly charity under the salutary guidance of him in whom she delights to supply his little one also with the assistance that will enable her to grow up. To which he also adds, as though reflecting in a brotherly fashion upon her welfare:

What shall we do for our sister on the day when she is spoken to? (Sg 8:8). The Lord speaks to the church, and he speaks to every elect soul, when he admonishes her concerning eternal salvation, whether through the secret illumination of his Spirit or through the public voice of the preachers. In this speaking, heavenly Kindness examines the measure of our abilities and bestows gifts upon each one in proportion to our human capacity. Therefore he says, **What shall we do for our sister, on the day that she is spoken to**? as though he were to say openly, "The church of the Gentiles is indeed little in number and not yet capable of assuming the ministry of the word; therefore, O synagogue, what do you think we ought to do for the care of this sister of ours at the time in which I will begin to speak to her through my apostles and the successors of the apostles? While she is yet little, should we entrust the mysteries of celestial secrets to her as though to little ones? Or should we now be making her larger through increases so that by growing well she can become capable of more perfect virtues?" Since she is silent and would rather listen to what he himself wishes, he immediately discloses what ought to be done, adding in the following manner:

If she is a wall, let us build upon her bulwarks of silver; if she is a door, let us seal it with boards of cedar (Sg 8:9). Now in sacred scripture the Lord himself is very often designated by the name of "wall" or "door." Surely he is rightly called a "wall," because he fortifies his church on every side lest she be ravaged by enemies, and rightly a "door," because we do not enter either the fellowship of this church or the fortress of the eternal kingdom except through him. For surely he says of himself: *I am the door of the sheepfold; whoever enters through me will be saved* (Jn 10:9), and again: *No one comes to the Father except through me* (Jn 14:6). Of him the prophet speaks, foretelling the church's future gifts: *A wall and a bulwark shall be set in her* (Is 26:1); the wall is the Lord himself appearing in the flesh, and the bulwark is the prophets' revelation, which supports the structure of the church to no small degree by predicting from the beginning of the world that he was going to become incarnate. But in truth, the one who has deigned to make the church his sister by appearing in the flesh is the same one who has also given her a share in his own title, so that she may be called both "wall" and "door." She is a wall in those endowed by the Spirit with greater learning and virtue, who are capable of fortifying and defending the minds of the faithful from the attacks of those who are in error by resisting the armies of wickedness, and she is a door in those who, even though they are not well enough established to repel the sophistries of heretics or pagans, are nevertheless so imbued with the simplicity of the catholic faith that by preaching they show the entrance of the kingdom to those who are willing, and through the mystery of the second rebirth lead them into the courts of heavenly life. In the same way, he does not hesitate to confer upon the more perfect members of his bride the names of other virtues that undoubtedly apply particularly to himself; for example: *You are the light of the world* (Mt 5:14), and again: *See, I am sending you out like sheep in the midst of wolves* (Mt 10:16), although he himself is *the true light which enlightens every person that comes into the world* (Jn 1:9), and he himself is the immaculate and pure Lamb that takes away the sins of the world (Jn 1:29).

Therefore he says, **If she is a wall, let us build upon her bulwarks of silver**, as if he were to say openly, "Even though the church of the Gentiles has the capacity in some of her members to oppose the teachings of those who have gone astray, possessing individuals who are keen for speaking either because they are skilled as a result of natural talent or because they are versed in philosophic training, I by no means wish that we should raise the ministry of speaking upon them, but rather that we should assist them by giving them the pages of the holy scriptures, by means of which they can more stoutly and more easily protect the weak and unlearned from the assaults of deceptive teaching or corrupting example." For the bulwarks of silver are the pinnacles of the divine words, concerning which it was said above, **Your neck is like the tower of David, which is built with bulwarks** (Sg 4:4), and of which it says in the psalm, *The words of the Lord are pure words, silver from the earth, tried by fire* (Ps 12:6; Vulg. 11:7).

If she is a door, let us seal it with boards of cedar (Sg 8:9). "If there are in her those who know how to imbue little ones with the word of simple doctrine and to lead them into the innermost depths of holy living, let us lay upon them the unfading examples of the more excellent just persons, through which they can fulfill that noble office more efficaciously and more perfectly." Indeed, it has often been said that cedars designate the virtues of the elect, for the shape of the boards expresses the wideness of their hearts, in which they receive the memory of the celestial words of which the prophet says: *I have run the way of your commandments, when you enlarged my heart* (Ps 119:32; Vulg. 118:32). The Apostle was teaching that he himself was furnished with these boards, and desiring that his hearers should be furnished with them, when he says: *Our mouth is open to you, O Corinthians; our heart is expanded. You are not being restricted in us, but you are restricted in your own inmost parts. I speak as to children—be yourselves expanded also* (2 Cor 6:11–13). For this reason it also admonishes the lover of wisdom, saying: *Write it on the boards of your heart* (Prv 7:3).

---

37. She replies that it is by his gift that she has been raised up and made fit in her more perfect members for the position of teacher. In order to show that the nations of the Gentiles belong to her, he adds that the church is called to hold many peoples in the peace of her Creator.

Now when the church heard these counsels or promises of her Redeemer in regard to herself, she did not then expect assent or response from the synagogue to whom he was speaking, so she responded to him in a devout voice: **I am a wall and my breasts are like towers, since I am made in his presence as one who finds peace** (Sg 8:10). "Surely I am rightly called a 'wall' because I have been composed of living stones (1 Pt 2:5) and joined together with the glue of charity; I have been placed upon a sure foundation and cannot be cast down by any blow of any heretical battering ram. For *God's firm foundation stands, bearing this seal: 'The Lord knows those who are his'* (2 Tm 2:19). But there are also those in me who have been granted a greater grace so that through the extraordinary height of their virtues they surpass the common life of the faithful as much as towers do walls, who like breasts nourish the little ones and those still weak in the faith with the milk of simpler exhortation, and who like towers repel all the spears of those who have gone astray with their superior powers of speaking. Surely I would [not[20]] have been able to possess all of these things, except that I received them through his generosity **since I am made in his presence as one who finds peace;** that is, since he deigned to present me with the gift of his peace through *the message of reconciliation* (2 Cor 5:19). For even in my industriousness, I would not have been able to come into the presence of him from whom I had departed so long before, or to have regained the peace that I had lost, unless I very joyfully accepted the offering of grace from him. Now since he has bestowed upon me this gift by which I immediately grew through increases in virtue, I confess that I can rightly be compared to a wall and that I have breasts that resemble towers because I constantly drive hostile armies away from injuring that city and always strive to rear new peoples for him. Since I am unable to do this except through the gift of peace conferred by him, it pleases me to relate yet more things concerning the power of his peace."

There was a vineyard for the Peaceable One in that which has peoples (Sg 8:11). Now he is speaking to the church, or to the synagogue that she perceived to be envying her or (as I might say more delicately) marveling greatly at her conversion to the Lord, or perhaps to her attendants, whom this song is accustomed to call "daughters of Jerusalem." Now the one he names as "the Peaceable

One" is her own Bridegroom and beloved, the *Father of the world to come, the Prince of peace* (Is 9:6), of whom Solomon presents a figure both by the peaceable condition of his reign and by his very name. In this same peace of his there was a vineyard, because through his grace the catholic church was constructed for him throughout the world. Mention of this is indeed made in very many places in the scriptures, but most openly in the gospel parable in which it is said: *The kingdom of heaven is like a landowner who went out early in the morning to hire laborers for his vineyard*, and so on (Mt 20:1), wherein it is plainly expressed through the laborers of the first, third, sixth, ninth, and eleventh hours that one and the same church of Christ is cultivated by the indefatigable labor of spiritual teachers throughout the whole time of this age, which is comprehended as being signified by a single day. Again, **there was a vineyard for the Peaceable One in that;** that is, in that peace concerning which she had previously said that she would be made in his presence as one who finds peace; for all who neglect to have peace do not belong to Christ's church, however much they may seem to confess Christ and obey his commandments. For *his place is in peace* (Ps 76:2; Vulg. 75:3); and the Apostle says: *Pursue peace with everyone, and the holiness without which no one will see God* (Heb 12:14).

That the fellowship of this peace is something for us to pursue, he himself also sets forth in the appearance and form of a most beautiful vine that (as I say in the words of blessed Ambrose[21]) *in imitation of our life, first thrusts down a living root, and then, since it is of a nature to be easily bent and frail, it touches whatever it takes hold of with its tendrils as if with some sort of arms, and with them it raises itself up and stands aloft. Similar to this is the church's folk who are planted with some root of faith, as it were, and restrained by the offshoot of humility*. But *lest they should be bent over by the winds of the world and brought down in the storm, they clasp some neighbors with those tendrils and chains as if with embraces of love, and in union with them they find rest*. This vine is obviously dug around when we are set free *from the rock pile of earthly cares; for nothing oppresses the mind more than anxiety over this world and lust for money or power*. Now *the vine is encircled with stones, tied back, and held erect* when by the example of the saints *our affection is held aloft so that it does not lie humble and despicable, but each one's mind lifts itself up to higher things, so that it is bold to say: "Now our con-*

versation is in heaven" (Phil 3:20). Now this vine has peoples because holy church has been gathered together not from the single nation of Judea but from the peoples of all nations. Therefore he especially added this with reference to the church of the Gentiles in order to teach that she could belong to this vine and that Judea ought not to boast of the uniqueness of the divine knowledge given to her, which is why the psalm says: *Praise the Lord, all you nations* (Ps 117:1; Vulg. 116:1); and Moses himself declares: *Rejoice, O nations, with his people* (Dt 32:43, Vulg.; cf. Rom 15:10). Since the Lord takes great care for this vine so that it might be kept undefiled, and since it is a matter of great necessity that people should become participants in it, rightly was there added:

He handed it over to custodians; a virile person brings for its fruit a thousand pieces of silver (Sg 8:11). Surely the custodians of the church are the prophets; her custodians are the apostles; her custodians are the successors of the prophets and apostles in the various ages of the world who have been assigned to govern her by heavenly command; her custodians are the host of the celestial militia who exercise care for the condition of the church in every age of this perishing world lest she be disturbed by an incursion of malicious people or spirits. Now a virile person brings for its fruit a thousand pieces of silver because someone who is perfect abandons all the things that are in the world in order to gain the kingdom of heaven; for surely the fruit of the labors that are done for the Lord at the present time is the receiving of eternal rest with the Lord and of the kingdom of which he himself says: *I have appointed you that you should go and bear fruit, and that your fruit should remain* (Jn 15:16); that is, "that you should work and receive a reward, and that your reward should never come to an end." Now scripture is accustomed to call someone of perfect virtue a "virile person"; for the virile person takes that name from virtue, and assuredly the virile person (that is, someone distinguished on account of virtue) brings for the fruit of this vine a thousand pieces of silver whenever someone relinquishes all temporal possessions in order to merit obtaining eternal goods. The term "pieces of silver" designates every kind of money that ought to be relinquished, and "a thousand" (which is a number that is perfect and complete) customarily designates an entirety; therefore, by the thousand pieces of silver that the virile person is said to bring for the fruit of this vine there is intimated the entirety of things that all the perfect relinquish for the Lord. Even when these things are small in value, they are judged great and plenteous indeed in the estimation of the one who considers not the amount of money given but the conscience of the giver. Now this is the same idea that was also set forth above in other words: **If one were to give all the wealth of one's house for love, one would despise it as nothing** (Sg 8:7). If the thousand pieces of silver here stand for all the wealth of one's house, which is being relinquished, then the love that embraces us forever in the celestial homeland, even when other gifts have ceased (1 Cor 13:8), is that fruit of the vineyard that will then satisfy the blessed, who now hunger and thirst for justice (Mt 5:6) as they labor in that same vineyard.

---

38. Being well-disposed toward them, the Lord declares that he has concern for the whole church. He commands those who have learned well that they should also undertake the ministry of preaching.

Then follows the voice of the Peaceable One himself, in which he teaches how much care he has for his vineyard (that is, for the church), what he stores up in eternity for those who relinquish their own possessions, and what kind of special reward he determines to give to the custodians of his vineyard (that is, to the teachers). He says: **My vineyard is before me; a thousand peacemakers for you, and two hundred for those who guard its fruit** (Sg 8:12). "Truly," he says, "you have been shown that I have handed my vineyard over to custodians who cultivate it both by their words and by their examples, but you must know that I have entrusted its care to those custodians in such a way that I myself am no less constantly attentive to what is done in it. I see with what purpose and with what industriousness someone labors in it, and therefore I perceive how many attacks it endures from adversaries, how much flagrant strife." And what more could there be? "*Lo, I am* with that [vineyard] *always, to the end of the world* (Mt 28:20). But when this occurs, then will I repay them all with the rewards that are due, depending on whether they are laboring in my vineyard, or on behalf of my vineyard, or against my vineyard." For those who, for the sake of its fruit (that is, for the hope of a heavenly inheritance), have distributed all the possessions that they have in the world, or have been able to acquire, and have given them to the poor, will obtain the sure result of their hope—or rather, I should say that in heaven they will receive greater gifts than they knew how to hope for, namely, those things that no *eye has seen, nor ear heard, neither has it come into the human heart, things God has prepared for those who love him* (1 Cor 2:9). But those who were custodians of his own vineyard through preaching or through shining brightly with more sublime deeds will be given a reward twice as great as the rest of the just. Surely for this reason is it said to Daniel through the angel: *Those who are learned shall shine like the brightness of the firmament, and those who instruct many for justice, like the stars for eternity forever* (Dn 12:3). And this is what [is being said] here also to those who despise transitory goods in order to receive those that are eternal, who because of the steadfastness of their unanimous hope are considered under the name of a single virile person.

A thousand peacemakers for you, he says, and immediately he explains about the greater reward reserved for those who guard the state of the church with greater industriousness, adding: **and two hundred for those who guard its fruit**. Since both of them are perfect numbers, surely both a thousand and a hundred are rightly understood to stand for the perfection and plenitude of the eternal recompense; but two hundred (that is, a hundred doubled) designates the greater rewards of the perfect teachers, which the Apostle says are to have a beginning even in this life: *Let the elders who rule well be considered worthy of a double honor, especially those who labor in the word and in teaching* (1 Tm 5:17). Thus he says, **A thousand peacemakers for you**: "For you the thousand silver pieces that you brought for the sake of receiving the fruit of my vineyard remain peaceful (that is, preserved complete in their number) in my presence, and you must by no means be afraid that through the forgetfulness or ignorance of the just Judge you will lose any of these good works you have done; for I am coming to gather all human works and thoughts together when I render to all nations and tongues and to each one individually according to what has been done in the body" (2 Cor 5:10). Likewise, since "peacemakers" are so called because they are accustomed to make peace, just as those who guard the courts of peace are "peaceful," the peacemakers for the saints are the pieces of silver that they give for the sake of truth, for with them they open the way to the vision of eternal peace that is customarily expressed by the name of the heavenly city and mother of us all, the New Jerusalem (Gal 4:26), and they have preferred to distribute Christ's inheritance to the poor rather than to keep it for themselves. **And two hundred for those who guard its fruit;** this is to be understood as referring to peacemaking pieces of silver, so that the full sense is: "A thousand peacemaking pieces of silver for you, and two hundred peacemaking pieces of silver for those who guard its fruit." For those who undertake a twofold labor at present, by living soberly and justly and devoutly so that the church's fruits do not fail, and by defending them with their preaching so that they are not ravaged by enemies, will in future doubtless obtain twofold gifts. Hence the same Giver of gifts immediately exhorts his church, or any soul dedicated to good actions, that she should also pursue the preaching of the word of truth as far as she is able, saying:

You who live in the gardens, the friends listen; make me hear your voice (Sg 8:13), as though he were to say openly: "Since our conversation, which has continued for a long time, must now come to an end, this is what I especially ask of you; this is what I demand to hear. Absolutely nothing could be sweeter to me than for you to live in the gardens (that is, for you to make your dwelling in the cultivation of spiritual fruits). Do not construct in them a hut for yourself, as if you were intending to depart after a short time from a work hastily done, but establish yourself there and await my coming with an unwavering mind. For you know that I am very often wont to come down to my garden and to the bed of spices, so that I may feed in the gardens and gather lilies (Sg 6:2; Vulg. 6:1); that is, so that I may observe, judge, and reward the efforts of good labors. Accordingly, as a further service I require of you that you should make me hear your voice by preaching to all you can about the commandments of my law and the promises of my recompense. Indeed, as often as you do these things, I am always listening and mindful of what you do, as I am always wont to be attentive to your prayers; but our friends are listening also—both the angels whom I have given you as helpers in the daily struggles against evil spirits, and those spirits of just persons whom I have chosen from among your company to see even now that vision of my glory to which you will eventually be gathered together forever. For both of them are your friends; both of them observe your deeds and your words and rejoice greatly when they perceive that you act courageously for the sake of receiving the blessedness that they themselves enjoy. Whenever some of your faithful ones enter therein, they exult and hasten to take them into their arms."

---

39. Obedient to his commands, the church prays that he will very often make himself present in the hearts of the faithful in order to assist them in their spiritual endeavors.

Assenting to these words, the church immediately replies:[22] **Flee, my beloved, and be like a wild goat or a young deer upon the mountains of spices** (Sg 8:14). This saying can rightly be taken as referring both to the triumph of the Lord's ascension and to those things that take place daily in holy church. For the beloved flees after he has conversed with his bride and sister, since he returned to heaven after having completed the plan for our redemption.[23] Now he is like a wild goat or a young deer upon the mountains of spices because through the grace of compunction he frequently appears in the hearts of his faithful, which are mountains of spices because, having despised desires for things below, they are occupied with love for heavenly things, and, having been purged of the stench of vices, they give off the aroma of spiritual virtues, saying with the Apostle: *Now our conversation is in heaven* (Phil 3:20), and *We are the good aroma of Christ* (2 Cor 2:15). And it is surely appropriate at the end of this sacred song that mention should be made of his ascension and the ensuing grace, doubtless because a little earlier the bride was longing for the joys of his incarnation, saying: **Who will give you to me as my brother sucking my mother's breasts**? (Sg 8:1), and he himself called attention to the fruit of his passion, saying: **Under the apple tree I raised you up** (Sg 8:5), and again: **For love is strong as death** (Sg 8:6). Therefore she says, **Flee, my beloved, and be like a wild goat or a young deer upon the mountains of spices**, as though she were to say openly, "After you appeared in the flesh and deigned to bestow upon me the commandments and the gifts of heavenly life that I had always desired, you have now accomplished the work of the divine plan and are returning to the bosom of the Father in heaven; nevertheless, I pray from the bottom of my heart that you will not withdraw the light of your frequent visitation from me. But just as a wild goat or a young deer, although they are untamed animals not readily accustomed to dwell among humans, are nevertheless wont to be seen upon the mountains, now I beseech you to remember to deal with me in such a way that even if in the body you remain in heaven and do not again enter into human habitations, you will nevertheless bring me the constant help of the divine presence. For only in this way can I carry out that greatest commandment, which you have given me as a last farewell, so that I may always live in the gardens of virtues and always make you hear the voice of my confession and of my preaching."

Now, as we have said, it would not be inappropriate to understand this verse as also referring to the daily condition of holy church. Surely the beloved dwelling in the gardens flees from the bride to whom he has been speaking when for a while he withdraws that grace that he has been accustomed to provide to the mind intent upon good actions or virtues, or even allows her to be tested by the storms of temptations so that she is truly compelled to say, *How long, O Lord, will you forget me forever? How long will you turn your face from me*? (Ps 13:1; Vulg. 12:1), and the rest, until the end of the psalm. He is like a wild goat or a young deer appearing upon mountains of spices when, at a time that he himself determines to be opportune, he again raises the light of his presence upon her, or takes away the besetting dangers of temptations, or restores the accustomed gifts of virtues he seemed to have withdrawn, such as, for example—to say nothing of the greatest gifts of all—the healing of the sick, the resuscitation of the dead, the casting out of demons, the certain knowledge of things secret, the bright contemplation of celestial joys, and other things of this sort that cannot be always present even in the most distinguished members of the church. For it is a mark of our littleness that we are by no means able to persevere in the sweetness of prayer always in one and the same manner, or to shed tears either out of consciousness of our guilt or out of desire for the heavenly homeland, or to console the sorrowing neighbor, or to withstand the trials that assail us. In the same way, those of us who know much are sometimes unable to accomplish these good things, while, on the other hand, those of us who have studied very little sometimes possess them in abundance. What reason could there be for this, except that at one time the beloved flees from our mind and at another time he comes again, in both cases acting with divine foresight so that when grace is conferred we may grow in the increase of virtues, and when it is taken away we may learn to keep the virtue of humility? He withdraws the desired effect of virtue for a time so that afterward it may be held more firmly when it is restored, and he restores that which has been withdrawn so that the soul will be stirred by its frequent renewal to strive more ardently for heavenly things.

Therefore, when she says, **Flee, my beloved**, she is not speaking this as an expression of desire, for who wishes that the one she loves should flee from her presence? But she is rather delighting in the memory of his inclination; that is, his habit of leaving her in the middle of the conversation to move away and turn aside, in such a way that even the memory of her own creation can be found only by a long and thorough search, since she cannot see him continually in this time and place of exile. But when she added, **Be like a wild goat or a young deer upon the mountains of spices**, she was following up with an expression of great desire and a prayer, knowing that the greatest happiness available to her in this present life would be for her at least to be consoled by his frequent visitation, since she is not capable of a continual vision. Doubtless this happiness is granted only to those who through contempt for earthly joys and desire for heavenly ones have merited to be called "mountains of spiritual spices."

Part Two

HOMILIES ON THE GOSPELS

Homily 1.19: After Epiphany
(Luke 2:42–52)

The reading from the holy gospel that has been recited is clear to us, dearly beloved brothers, so that there is no need for us to speak by way of expounding what is in it. It describes our Redeemer's infancy and childhood, by which he deigned to become a partaker of our humanity, and it recalls the eternity of the divine majesty by which he remained and always does remain equal to the Father. In this way, as the humility of his incarnation is recalled to our memory, we too may take care to train ourselves in true humility as a remedy for the wounds of all our sins, always considering with a devout mind that it behooves us, who are dirt and ashes, to humble ourselves as much for the sake of divine love as for the sake of our salvation, since the highest Power did not refuse to humble himself so much for us that he came down to assume the weakness of our frailty. Likewise, since we have heard, believed, and confessed the divinity of the Lord and Savior, by which he always continues to be consubstantial and co-eternal with the Father and Holy Spirit, let us hope that through those sacraments of his humanity with which we have been imbued, we will be able to attain to the contemplation of the glory of his divinity, which contemplation he himself promises to his faithful servants when with faithful kindness he says: *They who have my commandments and keep them are those who love me. And those who love me are loved by my Father, and I will love them and reveal my own self to them* (Jn 14:21). "My own self," he says, "I will reveal"; that is, "Not myself such as everyone can perceive, such as even the infidels can see and crucify, but the King of the ages, such as only the pure eyes of the saints can see in his beauty (Is 33:17); such is my self that I will show as a reward paid out in return for the love of those who love me."

Therefore, as we have said, let us hope that through the sacraments of his humanity we may be able to ascend to see the form of his divinity, if we keep those sacraments as we have received them, undiminished with due honor of justice and holiness and truth, if we follow the examples of his human way of life, if we humbly follow the words of the teaching that he ministered to us through a human being. For how can one who refuses to follow the footsteps of his humility be so foolhardy as to have hope of entering far enough to behold the joys of his splendor?

Therefore, it is doubtless a sign of the Lord's human humility that he comes to Jerusalem with his parents every year at Passover. Surely it is characteristic of human beings to come together to offer vows of spiritual sacrifices to God and to procure their Creator's favor toward them with copious prayers and tears. Therefore the Lord, being born as a human being among human beings, did that which as God he had divinely ordered through angels that human beings should do. He himself observed the law that he gave, so that he might show those of us who are simply human beings that in every respect we should observe whatever God commands. Let us follow the path of his human way of life, if we love to behold the glory of his divinity, if we want to dwell in his eternal home in heaven for all the days of our life, if it pleases us to see the Lord's favor and find shelter in his holy temple (Ps 27:4; Vulg. 26:4). And lest we should be forever battered by the wind of misfortunes, let us remember the necessity of frequenting the house of this present church with the offerings of pure prayers. The fact that when he himself was twelve years old he sat in the temple in the midst of the teachers, listening and asking them questions (Lk 2:46), is a sign of his human humility, but it is also an excellent example of humility for us to learn. Indeed, the Power of God and the Wisdom of God (1 Cor 1:24) and the eternal Divinity says: *I, Wisdom, dwell in counsel, and I am present among learned thoughts. Counsel and equity are mine; prudence is mine, strength is mine. Through me kings reign and makers of laws discern things that are just. Blessed is the person who listens to me, who keeps watch daily at my gates and waits at the posts of my doorway* (Prv 8:12, 14–15, 34). Putting on [the form of] a human being, [Wisdom] herself deigned to come listening to human beings, doubtless so that she might ask people who were greatly endowed with the highest intelligence about the form necessary for learning, lest if any should shrink from becoming disciples of truth they would have cause to become teachers of error. And the one who was going to undertake the office of teaching as a youth did well to listen to the elders and ask them questions while he was still a little boy, evidently so that through this prudent plan he might curb the audacity of those who, although they are not only uneducated but also immature, wish to rush forth into teaching rather than submitting to learning. Let us follow the path of his humanity, if we delight in the dwelling place of the divine vision, always mindful of that commandment: *Listen, my child, to your father's discipline, and do not forsake your mother's law, so that grace may be added to your head, and a gold chain to your neck* (Prv 1:8–9). Through listening to the father's discipline and through the observance of the mother's law, grace is surely added to our head and a gold chain to our neck, because the more attentively one listens to the divine commandments, and the more diligently one strives to observe the things that one learns in the unity of mother church, the more worthily may one now ascend to the honor of preaching, and the more sublimely may one in future ascend to the blessedness of reigning with Christ forever. But lest anyone should aver that it was on account of the necessity imposed by ignorance that the Lord and Savior appeared before the masters, listened to them, and asked them questions, let us see what follows:

Now all who heard him were amazed at his prudence and at his answers, and seeing him they were astonished (Lk 2:47–48). For he was himself true human being and true God; in order to show that he was a human being, he was humbly listening to human masters, and in order to prove that he was God, he was sublimely answering them when they spoke to him. To his mother who was searching for him and saying, **Son, why have you done so to us? Look, your father and I have been searching for you grieving**, he responded, **Why were you searching for me? Did you not know that I must be about my Father's things**? (Lk 2:48–49). This was a sign of his divine majesty, of which he says elsewhere, *All that the Father has is mine* (Jn 16:15). And thus he quite rightly testifies that the temple belongs no less to him than to the Father. Indeed, when he is found in the temple he says, **That**

I must be about my Father's things, doubtless because just as they have one majesty and glory, so also do they have one throne and house. It is evident that not only the material house built for worshiping him in time but also the intellectual house constructed for praising him in eternity are common to the Father and to the Son alike, and of course to the Holy Spirit as well. Accordingly, the same Son who to those who love him promises concerning himself and the Father that *we will come to them and make our dwelling with them* (Jn 14:23), says concerning the Spirit, *And I will ask the Father, and he will give you another Advocate to abide with you forever, the Spirit of truth, because he will abide with you, and he will be in you* (Jn 14:16–17). Since the nature of this holy Trinity is one and indivisiblc, evidently the dwelling place of their divinity in the hearts of the elect cannot be disparate. Thus that the Lord while sitting in the temple says, **I must be about my Father's things**, is a declaration that his power and glory are co-eternal with those of God the Father. But returning to Nazareth he was subject to his parents (Lk 2:51), which is a sign of his true humanity and at the same time an example of humility. For surely he was subject to human beings in that nature in which he was less than the Father. Hence he himself says: *I am going to the Father, because the Father is greater than I* (Jn 14:28). In this [nature] he was also made less, *a little less than the angels* (Ps 8:5; Vulg. 8:6; Heb 2:9). But in that [nature] in which he and the Father are one (Jn 10:30), and in which he does not go to the Father at a particular time but is always in him, *all things were made through him* (Jn 1:3) *and he is before all things* (Col 1:17). The plan adopted out of his great kindness is much to be marveled at, for when he saw that his parents did not yet comprehend the mystery of his divine majesty, he showed them the subjection of his human humility so that through it he might train them up little by little to the recognition of his divinity. For when he had said, **Why were you searching for me? Did you not know that I must be about my Father's things**? the evangelist fittingly intimates: **And they did not understand the word that he spoke to them** (Lk 2:50).

He went down with them and came to Nazareth and was subject to them (Lk 2:51). Thus he spoke the secrets of his divine power to the parents of his human frailty, namely, to the mother of his true flesh and to the most pure guardian of her chastity. (For throughout that time when the light of the gospel was not yet generally known, nearly all those who were able to know them reckoned [Joseph] to be her husband by way of carnal union and also referred to him as the father of the Lord and Savior by reason of his administration of the affairs of the flesh.[1]) As I was saying, he said to them, **That I must be about my Father's things**. Since they could not ascend to the pinnacle of such a mystery by understanding, nor was there any way for them to discern that he was truly abiding in those things that were his Father's other than by learning to comprehend them, he went down with them to the lower regions of their way of life and began to abide among the things that were theirs, and in accordance with the divine plan he was subject to them until, through the efficacious instruction of his humility, they would realize how much he was to be preferred above all creatures. With regard to these things, let us, I beseech you, consider how our pride behaves. When we sense as we are speaking that some of the simpler brothers are unable to understand those secrets of the scriptures that we ourselves have not known eternally but have only learned at a particular time with the Lord's help, perhaps we are inclined to extol ourselves immediately. Despising them, we boast of our erudition as though it were something unique and very grand, as though there were not also a great many much more learned than we are. And because we do not want to be despised by the more learned, we ourselves take delight in despising those who are less learned than we, or even in laughing at them, and we do not care to remember that the doorway into the kingdom lies open not to those who perceive the mysteries of the faith or the commandments of their Maker only by meditating, but rather to those who by their working put into practice the things that they have been able to learn. Also, in addition, *Anyone who knows how to do good and does not do it is guilty of sin* (Jas 4:17). And as the Lord himself testifies, *From everyone to whom much has been given, much will be required* (Lk 7:48). Therefore, so that knowledge may not puff us up, but charity rather build us up instead (1 Cor 8:1), let us follow the example of the Son of God when he appeared in human form. With benevolent humility, he subjected himself to those whom he perceived to be not yet capable of following him to the learning of things sublime, instructing their souls through his example to make them worthy of heavenly grace and capable of receiving a heavenly secret.

And his mother, it says, **kept all these words, bearing them in her heart** (Lk 2:51). The Virgin Mother diligently held in her heart everything that she had come to know about the Lord, whether from the Lord's sayings or from his deeds, and she assiduously committed them all to memory so that, when the time should come for preaching about the Lord or for writing about his incarnation, she would be sufficiently able to tell inquirers about everything just as it had happened. Let us also, my brothers, imitate the devout mother of the Lord, and by keeping all the words and deeds of the Lord and Savior fixed in our heart through meditation on them day and night, let us drive away the troublesome attacks of useless and noxious thoughts. Through frequent discussion of them, let us take care to restrain both ourselves and our neighbors from unnecessary talk and from conversations sweetened with the evil of slander, and to arouse ourselves for the frequent celebration of divine praise. For if, dearly beloved brothers, we desire to dwell in the Lord's house in the blessedness of the world to come, and to praise him forever, we must assiduously show beforehand in this world what it is that we seek in the future, namely by frequently entering the doors of the church and not only by singing the praises of the Lord there but also by showing forth *in every place of his dominion* (Ps 103:22; Vulg. 102:22), with words and also with deeds, those things that contribute to the praise and glory of our Maker.

And Jesus, it says, **advanced in wisdom and in age and in grace before God and human beings** (Lk 2:52). This indicates the nature of his true humanity, in which he willed to advance for a time even though in his divinity he is the same and his years have no end (Ps 102:27; Vulg. 101:28). In accordance with his human nature he indeed advanced in wisdom, not by becoming wiser over time—since he remained full of the Spirit of wisdom from the first hour of his conception (Is 11:2; Lk 1:35)—but by demonstrating to others, gradually over time, that same wisdom with which he was filled. In accordance with his human nature he advanced in age, since in the customary sequence of human growth he passed from infancy to childhood and from childhood to youth. In accordance with his human nature he advanced in grace, not by receiving through the passage of time that which he did not possess, but by revealing the gift of grace that he possessed. And after it had been said that **Jesus advanced in wisdom and in age and in grace**, there was properly added **before God and human beings**, for the more that he, as he was advancing in age, disclosed to human beings the gifts of wisdom and grace that were in him, the more did he take care always to call them forth to the praise of God the Father, carrying out himself what he commanded others to do: *Let your light shine before human beings, so that they may see your good works and glorify your Father who is in heaven* (Mt 5:16). And therefore it is said not only that he advanced in grace and wisdom before human beings, inasmuch as they were able to recognize his wisdom and grace, but also before God, inasmuch as they ascribed the wisdom and grace they recognized in [Jesus] to the praise and glory of him, for whose kindnesses and favors be praise and thanksgiving for all ages of ages. Amen.

Homily 1.22: In Lent
(Mt 15:21–28)

In the reading from the holy gospel that has just been read to us, dearly beloved brothers, we have heard about a woman's great faith, patience, constancy, and humility.[2] Her devout mind is all the more to be admired since, inasmuch as she was a Gentile, she was completely separated from the teaching of the divine eloquences, but even so she was not bereft of those virtues which the same eloquences proclaim. For surely she possesses great perfection of faith when, imploring the kindness of the Savior, she says:

Have mercy on me, Lord, Son of David (Mt 15:22). For when she calls him both "Lord" and "Son of David," it is assuredly clear that she believes him to be both truly human and truly God. Although she was entreating on behalf of her daughter, she did not bring her along with her, nor did she beseech the Lord to come to her; thus it is very plainly evident that she believed that he could bestow health by a word and that she did not require his bodily presence. But since after many tears she at last fell prostrate and adored him, saying, **Lord, help me** (Mt 15:25), she shows that she is by no means uncertain of the divine majesty of the one whose power she says is to be adored as God's. She has the virtue of patience in no small amount, for when the Lord did not answer a word to her first petition she by no means ceased from her prayers, but with even greater earnestness she implores the aid of his kindness, as she had begun. Now the Lord defers answering her not because he despises her prayers—for he is the merciful medical doctor of the miserable,[3] and of him it is very truly written, *The Lord has heard the desire of the poor* (Ps 10:17; Vulg. 9:38)—but so that he might demonstrate the woman's perseverance as something for us to imitate always, for the more she seemed to be disdained by the

Lord, the more ardently did she persist in the prayers that she had begun. He defers answering so that he might show the minds of his disciples that they also should be merciful. As human beings, they blushed with shame at the clamor of the woman as she publicly pursued them; but he himself knew the temperateness of his mercy, since he *disposed all things in measure and number and weight* (Wis 11:21). He deferred answering lest an occasion for making false accusations should be given to the Jews because he was giving preference in teaching or healing to the Gentiles over them,[4] and they should on that account refuse to adopt faith in him. And this is what he says:

I have not been sent except to the lost sheep of the house of Israel (Mt 15:24). Since the one who was teaching the Jews by himself alone also called the Gentiles to the grace of faith through his disciples, he says of them elsewhere: *And I have other sheep that are not of this fold, and I must bring them, and they will hear my voice, and there will be one flock and one shepherd* (Jn 10:16). This is why, when he was going to heal the one Gentile girl by himself in person, he did not carry this out until the mother's incomparable faith had been proven to everyone. Now the same mother also possesses the outstanding characteristic of constancy and humility. Even when the Lord compared her to dogs, she did not desist from the earnestness of her beseeching or turn her mind away from hoping for a favor of kindness. Willingly embracing the insult she had received, not only did she not deny that she was like the dogs, but she even added that she should be compared to puppies, and with a clever argument she indeed confirmed the Lord's statement. Nevertheless, she did not rest from the audacity of her petition. Surely she confirms the Lord's statement in which he says, **It is not good to take the children's bread and give it to dogs** (Mt 15:26), for she replies, **Yes, Lord** (Mt 15:27)—that is, "Truly, as you maintain, so it is that it is not good to take the salvation specified from heaven for the people of Israel and give it to the Gentiles." But when she says, **For even the puppies eat of the crumbs that fall from their masters' table** (Mt 15:27), she very cleverly shows how much humility and what sort of constancy she bears in her inmost heart. Indeed, she may be unworthy of being refreshed with the entire banquet of the Lord's teaching that the Jews enjoyed, but however small the grace imparted to her by the Lord might be, she believed that it could suffice for her salvation. For this reason, she rightly merited to hear from the kind Savior who deferred her prayers for a while, not out of proud disdain but out of provident dispensation:

O woman, great is your faith; let it be done for you as you wish (Mt 15:28). She certainly had faith great enough, since although she knew neither the ancient miracles, commandments, or promises of the prophets nor the recent ones of the Lord himself, and moreover was insulted by the Lord so many times, she persevered in her prayers and did not cease to knock by entreating him whom she had learned to be the Savior only through the report that was being spread among the crowd. On account of this, she also obtains the great outcome of her entreaty when the Lord says, **"Let it be done for you as you wish," and her daughter was healed at that very hour** (Mt 15:28). Now this woman, a Gentile indeed by birth but constant and trusting in heart, rightly signifies the faith and devotion of the church gathered together from the nations, which the holy preachers who were driven out of Judea imbued with the word and the mysteries of heavenly grace. For let us read again the preceding lection from the holy gospel, and we will find that when scribes and Pharisees coming from Jerusalem were attacking the Lord and his disciples with very severe agitation on account of their unbelief, he soon afterward left them chastised with the invective they deserved (Mt 15:1–9), **and going on from there he withdrew to the regions of Tyre and Sidon** (Mt 15:21). Here it is clearly prefigured that after his passion and resurrection the Lord in his preachers was going to leave the unbelieving hearts of the Jews and withdraw to the regions of foreign nations. Surely Tyre and Sidon, which were cities of the Gentiles, indicate the fortresses of Gentile doctrine and life in which fools put their confidence. Hence the woman who is beseeching with trust in the Lord is properly said to have come out from that territory, because unless she had abandoned the vain habitations of her former way of life, the church never would have come to Christ; unless she had anathematized the dogmas of her ancient error, she would by no means have known to receive the new grace of faith.

The daughter possessed by a demon, on whose account she entreats, is any soul in the church who is given over to the deceptions of evil spirits rather than to her Maker's precepts. It is necessary for the church to be a solicitous mother importuning the Lord on her behalf so that when she cannot cure her by admonishing, entreating, and chiding her from without, he may do so by inspiring her from within, and may arouse her to turn away from the shadows of error to the knowledge of the true light. Even if the Lord defers responding to the first tears of the church when she is entreating (that is, defers granting to those who have gone astray the health of mind they desire), she must not desist from asking, seeking, and knocking (Mt 7:7), nor should she be overwhelmed by despair about having her request granted, but rather she should persevere with even greater earnestness, she should frequently resort to the Savior with a cry even more obstinate, and amid her prayers she should strive even more to obtain the help of his saints until they too supplicate the Lord from heaven for the church to be heard. And so it happens that if she will not turn her mind away from its declared intention, she will by no means be deprived of the fruit of her petition, but whether it be on account of her own fragility or on account of others, the one who intervenes will obtain the desired effect.

For if one of us has a conscience polluted by the filth of avarice, pride, vainglory, indignation, irascibility, or envy and the other vices, that person assuredly has a daughter sorely troubled by a demon. Let that person run to the Lord as a suppliant for her healing, for she is doubtless suffering from a thought begotten from the heart of the devil and driven mad by his craft. With frequent or even continual lamentations and prayers, that person should demand her cleansing from the kind Maker. If perchance one has defiled the good things one has done with the pestilence of perjury, theft, blasphemy, slander, quarreling, or even uncleanness of the body and other things of this sort, then one has a daughter disturbed by the furies of an unclean spirit, since the action produced by laboring well has now been spoiled by foolishly serving the deceits of the devil. Therefore, as soon as such a person becomes aware of sin, it is necessary to have recourse to prayers and tears, and to seek the frequent intercessions and help of the saints who, entreating the Lord for the salvation of that person's soul, may say, "We beseech you, Lord, *merciful and gracious, patient and abounding in mercy* (Ex 34:6; Ps 85:15; Vulg. 86:15), forgive her because she is crying after us; forgive her sin and grant her grace because, bowed down with inmost feeling, she is seeking our help." It is necessary for one to be submissive with due humility, not yet considering oneself worthy of the company of the sheep of Israel (that is, of the clean animals), but rather thinking oneself to be comparable to a dog, and unworthy of heavenly gifts. Nevertheless, without despairing, one must not rest from earnestness in praying, but with a mind free from doubt one should be confident of the goodness of the supreme Giver, since the one who was able to make a confessor out of a robber (Lk 23:39–43), an apostle out of a persecutor (Acts 9:1–30), an evangelist out of a publican (Mt 9:9), and children of Abraham out of stones (Mt 3:9) is also able to convert the most impudent dog into an Israelite sheep to whom, on account of the chastity with which it is endowed, he will surely also give the pasture of eternal life—that is, he may deign to make a sinner who has turned from the evil way into a just person whom he may lead to the heavenly kingdom on account of good action. And when the Lord sees how great is the ardor of our faith and how persistent is our perseverance in praying, he will be merciful to us at last. And may he also grant to us that it may be done as we wish, namely, that with the tumults of our unhealthy thoughts driven away and the bonds of our sins released, both pure serenity of mind and perfection of good work may be restored to us.

Meanwhile, we should note that this persistence in praying only deserves to be fruitful if what we pray with our mouth we also meditate on in our mind, and if the cry of our lips is not split off in another direction from the attention of our thoughts. For there are those who, when they enter the church, prolong their psalmody or prayer with many words but because the attention of their heart is directed elsewhere, they do not reflect upon what they are saying. They are indeed praying with their mouth, but they are depriving their mind of every fruit of prayer because it is wandering outside; they think that their prayer will be heard by God, although those who utter it are not listening to it themselves. There is no one who cannot perceive that this is taking place at the instigation of the ancient enemy. For knowing the usefulness of praying and begrudging human beings the grace of obtaining what they request, he sends various trivial thoughts into those who are praying, and sometimes even phantasms of shameful and noxious things with which he impedes their prayer, to such a degree that sometimes while we are prostrating ourselves in prayer we have to endure so many waves of thoughts of so many kinds running this way and that, such as we have not known ourselves to endure while lying flat on our backs in bed. For this reason it is necessary, dearly beloved brothers, that we take care to overcome the malice of the devil when we perceive its presence, by clearing our mind, as far as we are able, of the mists of every sort, which the enemy delights in scattering, and by summoning the perpetual protection of the kind Defender who is able to grant to those who are beseeching, however unworthy they may be, the grace both of praying purely and of obtaining what they request.

Now the purity of prayer is of great benefit if at every place or time we abstain from illicit actions, if we always restrain our sense of hearing as well as our tongue from idle conversations, if we accustom ourselves to walk in the law of the Lord and to search out his testimonies with our whole heart (Ps 119:1–2; Vulg. 118:1–2). For whatsoever we are wont to do, speak, or hear very often, these things will necessarily return to our mind very often, as though to their usual and proper seat, and just as pigs are accustomed to frequent marshy bogs and doves to frequent clear streams, so do impure thoughts disturb an unclean mind, while spiritual thoughts sanctify one that is chaste. Truly, if we persist in praying and remain constant after the example of the Canaanite woman, then the grace of our Maker will come to correct everything in us that is in error, to sanctify everything unclean, and to calm everything that is turbulent. Surely *he is faithful and just to forgive our sins and cleanse us from all iniquity* (1 Jn 1:9), if with the attentive voice of the mind we cry to him who lives and reigns with the Father in the unity of the Holy Spirit, God throughout all ages of ages. Amen.

HOMILY 2.25: ON THE DEDICATION OF A CHURCH (Lk 6:43–48)

Since by divine favor, dearly beloved brothers, we are celebrating the solemnities of the dedication of a church, we should be in accord with the solemnity that we keep. Just as we have spent the night, according to custom, in joyful vigils within this church's walls, which are so carefully adorned and illuminated with so many lamps, with an increased number of lessons and the music of additional psalms, so also should we always decorate the inmost recesses of our hearts with the indispensable adornments of good works, always let the flame of divine as well as neighborly charity increase with us, always let the remembrance of heavenly precepts and the holy sweetness of evangelical praise resound in the sanctuary of our breast. For these are the fruits of the good tree, these are the treasures of the good heart, these are the foundations of the wise master builder that today's reading from the holy gospel commends to us so that we may have not only the form of godliness, but rather its power (2 Tm 3:5). The mystical history of the Old Testament also diligently suggests this to us when Moses constructed a tabernacle for the Lord, or Solomon a temple, as a type of holy church.[5] For both houses are reported to have been firmly founded—the tabernacle because its walls were put together from boards set upon silver bases (Ex 26:15–23), and the temple because it stood upon a foundation of squared stones (1 Kgs 5:17). The wood from which the tabernacle was made, and with which the temple was adorned within and covered above so that it was gleaming, was also imperishable (Ex 26:15; 1 Kgs 5:8; 6:15). The finest gold was also brought forth from a goodly treasure; the walls of the tabernacle were covered with it inside and out (Ex 26:29, 37), and not only were the walls of the temple covered as well, but also the ceiling panels, roof beams, doorposts, and the floors (1 Kgs 6:21–22; 2 Chr 3:4–10). But nearly all the vessels and utensils of both houses were also of gold; nor was it permissible for these to be made out of any but the purest gold (Ex 25:10–38; 37:1–28; 1 Kgs 7:48–50; 2 Chr 4:7–21). The fruits of the trees that were to be offered in the house of the Lord were commanded to be most pure and choice, that is, [the fruits] of the vine, the olive, frankincense, myrrh or stacte, and others of this sort (Ex 30:23–24, 34). Spiritually understood, all these things denote the true sincerity of our faith and work. For, as we have said, both houses surely show beforehand the figure of the universal church. Nor should anyone think it incongruous that two houses of the Lord were built in a mystery, when no faithful person would doubt that the church is the one house of Christ. Two houses were fashioned in order to signify the two peoples (namely, Jews and Gentiles) who would come to the same faith. Hence it was appropriate that the Hebrew people alone fashioned the tabernacle in the desert, but the proselytes (that is, as many from the nations as could then be found among the people of Israel) completed the structure of the temple with devout faith. But the most powerful king of Tyre, as contracted by Solomon, very happily assisted him by supplying workers and wood (1 Kgs 5:1–10), doubtless because prior to the Lord's incarnation God was known only in Judea (Ps 76:1; Vulg. 75:2). But afterward, in the flesh in which he was born and suffered, raised from the dead, and exalted as God above the heavens (Ps 57:5; Vulg. 56:6), he immediately shone over all the earth through the glory of his name, and the entire world joyfully hurried to the erection of his house, having received from him the promise of heavenly gifts. Therefore, let us hear what our Maker and Redeemer says in the reading from the holy gospel that was just recited to us about the construction of that house of his, which we are.

No good tree bears bad fruit, nor does a bad tree bear good fruit (Lk 6:43). Thus the Wise King is seeking good trees and their good fruit for the construction and ministry of his temple. Indeed, the same one elsewhere teaches what the end of a bad tree is, saying: *Every tree that does not bear good fruit will be cut down and thrown into the fire* (Mt 3:10). Surely he is referring to human beings as trees, and to their works as fruit. Do you want to know which are the bad trees and which are the bad fruits? The Apostle teaches this, saying: *Now the works of the flesh are manifest: they are fornication, impurity, licentiousness, the service of idols, sorceries, enmities, strife, jealousy, anger, quarrels, dissensions, factions, envy, murder, drunkenness, carousing, and things like these* (Gal 5:19–21). Do you want to hear whether trees that bear fruits of this sort belong in the heavenly temple of the eternal King? The Apostle continues, saying: *I am warning you, as I have warned you before, that those who do such things will not reach the kingdom of God* (Gal 5:21). Subsequently he also lists the fruits of a good tree when he says: *But the fruit of the Spirit is charity, joy, peace, patience, goodness, kindness, faith, gentleness, continence* (Gal 5:22–23). Also admonishing about these things in another place, he says: *Walk as children of light; now the fruit of light is in all goodness and justice and truth* (Eph 5:8–9). Without a doubt, these fruits, with the trees from which they proceed, truly belong both here in the house of faith and there in the dwelling place of celestial blessedness. Accordingly, let us listen to a good tree rejoicing about the increase of good fruits: *But I, like a fruitful olive tree in the house of God, have hoped in the mercy of* my *God forever, and for age after age* (Ps 52:8; Vulg. 51:10). Surely the fruit of the olive tree is the luminous work of mercy, and thus one who shines in the present house of God with the grace of mercy rightly hopes for God's mercy in the temple of eternity. Rightly confident of belonging in the temple of the great King, such a one says elsewhere: *And his mercy shall follow me all the days of my life, so that I may live in the house of the Lord for length of days* (Ps 23:6; Vulg. 22:6). But on the other hand, let us see what kinds of fruit a bad tree bears, and let us avoid bearing such ourselves. The prophet Jeremiah says: *Cursed is the person who trusts in human beings and makes flesh an arm [of strength], whose heart departs from the Lord; for that one will be like a tamarisk in the desert* (Jer 17:5–6). Surely the tamarisk is an unfruitful and lowly tree, exceedingly bitter in taste, and in short unworthy of all human cultivation, and for that reason growing in deserts.[6] Rightly compared to it is the one who, departing from divine fear and love, hopes for a kingdom and riches from human beings. How far exiled from the beauty of God's house we must judge this person to be the prophet makes plain by adding: *And this one shall not see good when it comes, but shall live in the desert in dryness, in a salt and uninhabited land* (Jer 17:6). Therefore, my brothers, let none of those living evilly in secret flatter themselves because of the crowd's favorable opinion as though they were good, for even if they are producing the beautiful foliage of words or the fragrant blossom of a fine reputation, no good tree bears bad fruit. And let none of those who do the good of which they are able with an upright heart despair of their own salvation, because no bad tree bears good fruit.

Each tree is known by its own fruit (Lk 6:44). This knowledge must be taken as referring only to open vices and virtues such as those we have recounted above from the Apostle's statement. For surely there are some things of which our neighbors are ignorant of the spirit in which they are being done; hence they can be interpreted in either way. But doubtful things are more justly interpreted as good by those who love the good, so that the [saying] of the Apostle may be fulfilled: *Do not pronounce judgment before the time* (1 Cor 4:5).

For people do not gather figs from thorns, nor do they gather grapes from a bramble-bush (Lk 6:44). Thorns and bramble-bushes, trees full of prickles, designate the hearts of those who are marred by the stings of licentiousness, envy, and concupiscence, or who perhaps become disagreeable and, as it were, intractable to their neighbors through the sharpness of their irascibility, slander, hatred, pride, and bitterness. But figs signify the sweet recollection of the heavenly kingdom, and the grape the ardor of love of the Lord. Therefore, **people do not gather figs from thorns, nor do they gather grapes from a bramble-bush** because all those who are still sullied with the prickles of vices can by no means be worthy to serve as examples or to administer the teaching of virtues to their neighbors.

The good person out of the good treasure of the heart produces good, and the bad person out of the bad produces bad (Lk 6:45). The treasure of the heart is the intention of thought, by which the Inner Judge assesses the result of one's work. Hence it often happens that some people perform lesser good works for a greater reward of heavenly grace, which is because of the intention of the heart by which they have a desire to accomplish greater good works if they could do so. Others, who display greater works of virtue, are allotted lesser rewards by the Lord as a result of the indifference of a lukewarm heart. Accordingly, the work of the widow who donated two coins to the temple was preferred to the countless gifts of the rich by the Inner Searcher of hearts (Mk 12:42–44).

For it is out of the abundance of the heart that the mouth speaks (Lk 6:45). Human judgment often misleads, because the neighbor's heart does not know how to weigh [a deed] except on the basis of speech and action, but the Lord ponders our deeds and words on the basis of their root in the heart. Thus the mouth speaks to him out of the abundance of the heart when it is not ignorant of the intention by which its words are uttered. Subsequently, [the Lord] also adds to this by clearly showing that good speech without the attestation of works is of no benefit at all:[7]

And why do you call me, "Lord, Lord," he says, **and not do what I say**? (Lk 6:46). Surely to call him "Lord" seems to be the gift of a good treasure and the fruit of a good tree. For everyone who calls upon the name of the Lord will be saved (Jl 2:32; Acts 2:21; Rom 10:13). But if anyone who calls upon the name of the Lord resists the Lord's commands by living wrongly, it is assuredly evident that the good thing that the tongue has uttered has not been brought forth from the good treasure of the heart, and that the fruit of such a confession was not produced from the root of a fig tree but from that of a thorn—that is, from a conscience bristling with vices, and not one filled with the sweetness of love of the Lord. But the Lord designates what this true distinction between good and bad fruits might be by adding under another figure:

Everyone who comes to me and hears my words and does them, I will show you what that person is like. That one is like a man building a house (Lk 6:47–48). Now this man building a house is *the Mediator between God and humankind, the human Christ Jesus* (1 Tm 2:5), who deigned to build and consecrate for himself a beloved and holy house (namely, the church) in which he would abide forever.

He dug deep and laid the foundation upon rock (Lk 6:48), because he took pains to root out utterly whatever earthly intentions he found in the heart of his faithful so that when the rubble of old habits and superfluous thoughts had been cast out, he could have in them a stable and unshaken dwelling place. He himself is the rock upon which he laid the foundation of a house of this sort. For just as in the building of a house nothing is placed before the rock on which the foundation is set, so does holy church have her rock, namely Christ, buried in the depths of her heart. She does not put anything above her faith and love of him, since he did not hesitate even to suffer death for her sake. Doubtless it was because he clung so firmly to this rock that the prince of the church received his name from it when he heard: *For you are Peter, and upon this rock I will build my church* (Mt 16:18).

And when a flood arose, the river beat against that house and could not shake it, for it had been founded upon the rock (Lk 6:48). The explanation is clearly that the church is often struck by afflictions but is not cast down. But if any believers yield when overcome by evils, they certainly did not belong to this house, for if they had made their stand founded upon the rock of faith instead of upon the sand of faithlessness or inconstancy, surely they never could have been shaken. Now we should note that this flood of trials assails the church in three ways. For one is either tempted by one's own concupiscence, being drawn and enticed by it (Jas 1:14), or wearied by the wickedness of false believers, or assaulted by the more obvious snares of outsiders. Elsewhere the Lord calls these trials "the gates of hell," and rightly so, doubtless because if they are victorious, they drag us down to eternal destruction. *And upon this rock*, he says, *I will build my church, and the gates of hell will not prevail against her* (Mt 16:18). Therefore, although the devil's gates strike against the church of Christ, nevertheless they do not cast her down; although the flood of wickedness encroaches upon her, it does not undermine the house of faith. For she is able to say truthfully to her helper: *When my heart was in anguish, you raised me up on a rock* (Ps 61:2; Vulg. 60:3). She is not vanquished by strangers because she conquers the rage of persecuting unbelievers by suffering for the crown of martyrdom; she is not corrupted by false believers because she both refutes the dogmas of heretics by believing rightly and avoids the depraved example of certain catholics by living soberly and justly and godly (Ti 2:12); she is not blinded by the smoke of her own lust because she is inwardly ablaze only with the ardor of the Lord's charity. Now the elect, each in that one's own way, are likened to this man (that is, to our Redeemer who joined the church universal to himself with an unconquerable strength of mind) when they each take care to perform individually in their own hearts what he accomplishes generally in the whole church. For by digging deep, as it were, they carefully examine their conscience lest anything sordid lie hidden in it; they diligently seek out all hiding places of useless thoughts from the foundation of the heart and draw them out by means of meticulous discernment so that they may prepare in themselves a firm and serene resting place for that most steadfast rock, which is Christ. And thus it happens that through his presence they continue unconquerable to the end amid the adversities of an alarming age, as well as the prosperities of an alluring one.

With the Lord's help, dearly beloved brothers, we have quickly run through these things by way of an explanation of the gospel reading, but it seems appropriate to the solemnity that we are celebrating to recall a few things concerning the building of the temple, and to explore how suitably its decoration accords with the signification of the church. Therefore: scripture relates that Solomon ordered *that they should bring great stones, costly stones to the foundation of the temple, and square them* (1 Kgs 5:17). Now the great and costly stones that are laid on the foundation and bear the entire weight of the temple, which is placed upon them, suggest the distinguished teachers of holy church: "grand" in the excellence of their merits; "costly" in the splendor of the signs that those who heard the word from the Lord himself produced by their preaching for the fabric of the growing church. For in the scriptures, whenever "foundations" are spoken of in the plural number, they signify either holy preachers or the immovable thoughts of the just. Hence there is that [saying] of the psalmist: *Its foundations are on the holy mountains* (Ps 87:1; Vulg. 86:1). But when "foundation" is put in the singular number, it usually indicates the Author of all good things himself, of whom the Apostle says: *For no one can lay any other foundation except that which has been laid, which is Christ Jesus* (1 Cor 3:11); and concerning whom he says again to those who believe: *But you are citizens with the saints and members of the household of God, built upon the foundation of the apostles and prophets* (Eph 2:19–20). On this foundation, therefore, were set great and costly stones who bear the whole temple, because through him they were instructed for the spreading of the church throughout the whole world—first the patriarchs and prophets, and afterward the apostles. The more closely they clung to their love for him, the more stoutly did they support those who came after them in the heavenly building. The king ordered them to square these stones so that he might signify that the church's teachers ought to be composed in character and unmoved in mind. For just as something squared will stand upright however it is turned, so also the life of the perfect, which is carefully drawn up on the plumb line of truth, is not able to be cast down from its stability by any pressures of temptations.[8]

Now the temple was constructed out of Parian marble, which is a white stone,[9] so that it might express the radiance of the church's chastity, concerning which the Lord says in the song of love: *As a lily among thorns, so is my friend among daughters* (Sg 2:2). It was sixty cubits in length, twenty cubits in width, and thirty cubits in height (1 Kgs 6:2). Therefore the temple's length designates the faith of holy church, through which she bears with long-suffering amid her good works the adversities she receives from the wicked; its width, the charity with which she spreads out inwardly through the kindness of her heart;[10] its height, the hope with which she awaits the rewards of heavenly life on account of the good deeds that she performs through charity. And the length is properly sixty cubits, for the perfection of good works is customarily designated by the number sixty, because the Lord completed the adornment of the world in six days (Gn 2:1–11), and also because there are six ages of this world in which holy church presses on with her pious actions for the sake of eternal rest. The width is properly twenty cubits because of the twofold commandment of charity by which the church is extended in tribulation when someone who is perfect is proved to love the Maker with all one's heart, all one's mind, and all one's strength, and one's neighbor as one's self (Mk 12:30–31). It is properly thirty cubits in height because every hope of the elect prepares them as much as it is able, by training and purifying them, for the vision of the holy Trinity. Therefore, six pertains to the long-suffering of faith, three to the loftiness of hope, and two to the breadth of love; by these three characteristics of the virtues, the whole state of holy church is known to be perfected. That all of these are multiplied by ten, which is a perfect number, figuratively denotes the multifarious increase of her perfection. Of course, we should note that the thirty cubits in height did not pertain to the highest point on the temple's roof, but to the ceiling panels; from there another thirty cubits in height rose up to the ceiling panels of the middle story. Then above that there was a third story that was sixty cubits in height, and so the entire height of the house was extended to one hundred twenty cubits (2 Chr 3:4). Therefore the first [part of the] house rose thirty cubits in height because the present church is being lifted up with her complete attention toward the sight of the beauty of the holy Trinity. The [part of the] house above that likewise rose to thirty cubits high, because the souls of the perfect, freed from their bodies, are now enjoying the vision of this same blessed and indivisible Trinity until the day of universal judgment. The highest [part of the] house is twice thirty cubits high because, when all the elect are raised from the dead, they will rejoice in the eternal immortality of the spirit and also of the body, in contemplation of their Maker, who is one God in three persons.

Now there was in the temple a middle wall made of boards of cedar twenty cubits high; it divided the oracle (that is, the holy of holies) from the first part of the temple. The oracle was twenty cubits long, twenty cubits wide, and twenty cubits high (1 Kgs 6:20). Thus in the temple itself there were forty cubits in front of the doors of the oracle (1 Kgs 6:17), in which there were tables and golden candelabra, and also a golden altar near the door of the oracle (Ex 25:23–31; 30:1–6), so that when incense was burned upon it the cloud of smoke would rise up and cover the oracle, where there was the ark of the covenant (Lv 16:13), *and above it the cherubim of glory overshadowing the mercy seat* (Heb 9:5). Therefore the first part of the house designates the condition of the present church, the inner part the entrance into heavenly life. Hence the table and the candelabra were placed in the first part, doubtless because in this life we have need of the light of the holy scriptures and the refreshment of the heavenly sacraments, but in the future we do not need such aids in that place where, according to the word of the psalmist, whoever appears with justice will be satisfied when the glory of the Lord is manifested (Ps 17:15; Vulg. 16:15). In this life the hearts of the just, like the golden altar of incense, shine brightly through the purity of their holiness; they are filled with the fragrant spices of spiritual desires; they burn with the fire of continual love; and as if set near the entrance to heaven, they send forth the sweetest smoke of their prayer within the holy of holies on high, *where Christ is, sitting at the right hand of God* (Col 3:1). The ark of the covenant, which was within the veil (Ex 30:6), and *in which* there was *a golden urn containing manna, and Aaron's rod that budded, and the tablets of the covenant* (Heb 9:4), quite aptly designates [Christ], for surely the ark itself designates the nature of his humanity; the urn of manna designates the fullness of his divinity; Aaron's rod designates the inviolable power of his priesthood; and the tablets of the covenant designate that it is he who gave the law and he who will also give a blessing to those who do the law (Ps 83:8).[11]

Now the [part of the] temple in front of the doors of the oracle was properly forty cubits long, because while we are still in this life it is necessary for us to be chastened by fasts and self-control so that we may be worthy to attain to the satisfaction of inner sweetness. For everyone who has wished to understand rightly the forty-day fast of Moses (Ex 34:28) or Elijah (1 Kgs 19:8) or the Lord himself (Mt 4:2) understands that the chastening of this present life is signified by this number. The oracle itself, in which the ark was covered by the cherubim of glory, was properly twenty cubits in length, width, and height, for this number (as we have said) suggests the perfection of twofold love, since whatever is done for the Lord's sake in this pilgrimage is made completely perfect in that dwelling place of the Father's eternal home, where his magnificence is raised aloft upon the continual praise of blessed spirits in the only true fullness of love. *There was also a porch in front of the temple, twenty cubits in length, in accordance with the measure of the width of the temple* (1 Kgs 6:3). It had a door opposite the door of the temple, and was ten cubits wide, facing the east. Evidently, this porch designates that people of the holy church who preceded the times of the Lord's incarnation yet through faith in his incarnation did not remain empty. For there to be a door of the porch opposite the door of the temple, toward the rising of the sun, is for the faith of the people before Christ to be the same as that of the people coming after, and for the hearts of all the faithful to be illumined by the same light of the grace of the rising Sun. Hence it is appropriately reported that two bronze pillars of outstanding and marvelous work were set up on this same porch around the door of the temple, and that capitals as though with lily-work were placed upon them (1 Kgs 7:15–22). For pillars stand before the door of the temple because preceding the coming of our Redeemer who says, *I am the door; anyone who enters through me will be saved* (Jn 10:9), there were eminent teachers, concerning whom the Apostle says, *James and Cephas and John, who were considered to be pillars* (Gal 2:9), who gave testimony to his coming. Now one of these stood at the right of the door and the other at the left because they foretold the future incarnation of their Redeemer to the people of Israel, who were then inflamed with divine faith and charity, and no less did they proclaim to the Gentiles, who were still, as it were, positioned to the north, numb with the cold of unbelief, that an entranceway would be opened for the same Redeemer. That thc capitals of the pillars were made by an artisan as though with lily-work signifies that the sum total of their preaching resounded with the splendor of everlasting blessedness, and promised that his glory would be seen by their hearers. He who existed as God before the ages became a human being at the end of the ages so that like the flower of the lily he might have a golden color on the inside and white on the outside. For what is the blush of gold amid whiteness except the brilliance of divinity in a human being? First he displayed this human being bright with virtues, and after death he clothed him in the snow-white splendor of incorruptibility.

On the joyous occasion of our present festival, dearly beloved, it has been pleasing for me to explain to your fraternity these few points out of the many concerning the making of the temple, so that what you have heard about the marvelous artistry of the Lord's earthly house might delight you, and also so that this same [artistry] spiritually understood might raise our minds up to more ardent love of the heavenly dwelling place. Therefore, my brothers, with our whole heart let us love the beauty of the eternal house (Ps 26:8; Vulg. 25:8) that we have from God in heaven (2 Cor 5:1), and let us take care to think attentively about the place of the tabernacle of his glory (Ps 26:8; Vulg. 25:8) and to admonish one another. Above all, let us ask one thing from him, and let us seek this with unwearied intention: that we may be worthy to dwell in his house all the days of our life (Ps 27:4; Vulg. 26:4), that is, to be happy in everlasting life and light. He does not scorn or despise the prayer of the poor (Ps 22:24; Vulg. 21:25) when we pray for what he himself loves, but mercifully listening he will grant us to see his good things in the land of the living (Ps 27:13; Vulg. 26:13), Jesus Christ our Lord, who lives and reigns with the Father in the unity of the Holy Spirit, God throughout all ages of ages. Amen.

Part Three

ECCLESIASTICAL HISTORY OF THE ENGLISH PEOPLE
(SELECTIONS)

2.9 Of the reign of King Edwin, and how Paulinus, coming to preach the gospel to him, first initiated his daughter and others into the mysteries of the Christian faith.

At this time[1] the people of the Northumbrians, that is, the nation of the English living on the north side of the river Humber, together with their king, Edwin, also received the word of faith through the preaching of Paulinus, already mentioned. As an omen that he was to receive the faith and the heavenly kingdom, the power of this king's earthly rule increased, so that he held under his dominion all the territories of Britain that were kingdoms inhabited by either the Britons or the English, a thing that none of the English before him had done. He even subjugated the islands of Anglesey and Man to English rule, as we have said above. The first of these, which is to the south, is the larger in size, and the more fruitful in produce of crops and more fertile, containing 960 hides according to English reckoning, while the other has more than 300.[2]

Now the occasion of this nation's acceptance of the faith was that this king became related to the kings of Kent by taking in marriage King Æthelberht's daughter Æthelburh, who was also called Tate. When he first sent ambassadors to her brother Eadbald, who was then ruling over the Kentish kingdom, to ask for her in marriage, the reply was that it was not permissible for a Christian maiden to be given in marriage to a pagan, lest the faith and sacraments of the heavenly King should be profaned by her association with a king who was wholly ignorant of the worship of the true God. When the messengers brought Edwin this reply, he promised that he would place no obstacles of any kind in the way of the Christian faith that the maiden practiced, but he would allow her and all those who came with her, men and women, priests or servants, to observe the faith and worship of their religion after the Christian manner. Nor did he deny that he might accept the same religion himself also, if upon examination by wise persons it could be found holier and more worthy of God.

Thereupon the maiden was betrothed and sent to Edwin, and in accordance with the agreement Paulinus, a man beloved of God, was ordained bishop to accompany her and strengthen her and her attendants by daily exhortation and celebration of the heavenly sacraments, in order that they might not be polluted by the company of pagans.

Paulinus was ordained bishop by Archbishop Justus on July 21 in the year 625 from the Lord's incarnation,[3] and so came to King Edwin with the maiden as though he were an attendant for their union in the flesh. But his mind was actually completely set on calling the nation to which he was sent to knowledge of the truth so that, in accordance with the words of the Apostle, he might present it to Christ as a chaste virgin espoused to one husband (2 Cor 11:2). When he arrived in the kingdom, he labored, not only with the Lord's help, to keep those who came with him from forsaking the faith, but also to convert some of the pagans, if he could, to the grace of faith through his preaching. But as the Apostle says, although he labored in the word for a long time, "the god of this world blinded the minds of the unbelievers, lest the light of the glorious gospel of Christ should shine upon them" (2 Cor 4:4).

The following year there came into the kingdom a certain assassin named Eomer, who had been sent by Cwichelm, king of the West Saxons, hoping to deprive King Edwin of his kingdom together with his life. He had a two-edged dagger dipped in poison, so that if the sword wound would not suffice to kill the king, the deadly poison would finish the job. He came to the king on the first day of Easter at the royal residence, which was then beside the river Derwent, and entered under the pretext of bringing a message from his master. While artfully delivering his pretended embassy, he suddenly sprang up, drew the dagger from under his garment, and made a violent attack upon the king. When Lilla, the king's minister[4] and greatest friend, saw this, since he did not have a shield at hand to protect the king from death, he quickly interposed his own body to receive the blow; but even so, the enemy thrust the sword with such force that it killed the retainer and wounded the king as well through his dead body. [The assassin] was immediately attacked with swords on all sides, but in the tumult he also killed with his heinous dagger yet another retainer, whose name was Forthhere.

On that same holy night of Easter Sunday, the queen had borne the king a daughter, named Eanflæd. As the king, in the presence of Bishop Paulinus, gave thanks to his gods for the birth of his daughter, the bishop, on the other hand, began to give thanks to the Lord Christ, and to tell the king that by his own prayers to Christ he had obtained that the queen should give birth safely and without much pain. The king was delighted with his words, and promised that if Christ would grant him life and victory in fighting against the king who had sent the assassin who wounded him, he would renounce his idols and serve Christ. As a pledge that he would fulfill his promise, he committed his daughter to Bishop Paulinus to be consecrated to Christ. On the holy day of Pentecost, she was the first of the Northumbrian nation to be baptized, along with eleven others of her household.

When the king had been healed of the wound previously inflicted upon him, he gathered his army and marched against the nation of the West Saxons, and in the ensuing campaign he either slew or forced into surrender all those whom he discovered to have plotted his death. So he returned to his homeland as a victor, but he was unwilling to receive the sacraments of the Christian faith immediately and unadvisedly, even though he no longer served idols, ever since he had promised that he would serve Christ. But first he wanted, as time allowed, diligently to learn an account of the faith from that venerable man Paulinus, and to confer with those of his nobles whom he knew to be the wisest, as to what they thought ought to be done in these matters. But since he was by nature a very prudent man, he would often sit alone for a long period in silence, but in his inmost heart he was talking things over with himself, pondering what he ought to do and which religion to follow.

* * * * * * * *

2.13 Of the council he held with his chief men about receiving the faith of Christ, and how his high priest profaned his own altars.

When the king had heard these things,[5] he answered that he was indeed both willing and bound to accept the faith that Paulinus taught. He said, however, that he would yet confer about this with his principal friends and councilors so that, if they also would agree with him, all of them might be consecrated together by Christ in the font of life. Paulinus agreed, and he did as he had said. For holding a council with the wise ones, he inquired of each one in turn what he thought of this hitherto unheard-of doctrine and this new way of worshiping divinity that was being proclaimed.

Coifi, the chief among his own priests, immediately answered him: "Consider, O King, what sort of thing this is that is now being proclaimed to us; for I quite frankly declare to you what I have learned as fact, which is that the religion we have maintained up to now has absolutely no virtue or usefulness. For none of your people has been more earnestly devoted to the worship of our gods than I, but nevertheless there are many who receive greater favors and greater honors from you than I, and are more prosperous in all the things they set out to accomplish or to acquire. Now if the gods were able to do anything, they would rather have helped me, who has taken care to serve them more zealously. Therefore it follows that if upon examination you perceive that these novelties now being proclaimed to us are better and more powerful, let us hasten to accept them without any delay."

Another of the king's nobles gave assent to his advice and wise words and immediately went on to say: "This is how the present life of human beings on earth seems to me, O King, in comparison to that time which is unknown to us. It is as though you were sitting at dinner with your ealdormen and thegns[6] in wintertime, with a good fire burning in the midst to warm the hall, but outside the storms of winter rain or snow are raging, when a sparrow flies swiftly through the room. As soon as it comes in through one door, it quickly goes out through another. Just for the time it is inside, it is safe from the wintry tempest, but after the briefest period of calm has passed in a moment, it soon slips out of your sight, coming out of winter and returning into winter again. So this life of human beings appears for a short while; but of what comes after, or what went before, we know nothing at all. Therefore, if this new teaching has brought anything more certain, it seems right that we should follow it." The other elders and king's councilors followed up in a similar manner, being divinely prompted to do so.

Now Coifi added that he would like to listen more carefully to what Paulinus himself had to say about the God whom he was proclaiming. When this had been done at the king's bidding, Coifi, having heard the words of Paulinus, exclaimed: "For a long time now I have realized that there is nothing in that which we worship;

for the more diligently I sought after truth in that cult, the less I found it. But now I openly declare that such truth shines forth in this proclamation as can bestow on us the gifts of life, salvation, and eternal happiness. Therefore I advise, O King, that we should speedily consign to desecration and flame the temples and altars that we have hallowed without reaping any benefit." What more is there to say? The king gave blessed Paulinus permission to preach the gospel publicly, renounced idolatry, and professed his acceptance of the faith of Christ. And when he asked the high priest of their religion who should be the first to profane the altars and shrines of the idols, together with the enclosures with which they were surrounded, he replied: "I will. For now that God has given me wisdom, who is more fitting than I to provide an example for all by destroying those things that I worshiped through folly?" And at once, casting aside empty superstition, he asked the king to furnish him with arms and a stallion horse, and mounting it he set out to destroy the idols. For previously it had not been lawful for a high priest of that religion to bear arms or to ride, except upon a mare. So, girded with a sword, he took a spear in his hand, and mounting the king's stallion, he proceeded to the idols. When the common people saw this, they thought that he had gone mad. He did not hesitate, but as soon as he drew near the shrine, he profaned it by casting the spear he was holding into it;[7] and rejoicing greatly in the knowledge of the worship of the true God, he ordered his companions to destroy and set fire to the shrine, together with all its enclosures. Now the place where the idols once stood is still shown [to visitors], not far from York, to the east, beyond the river Derwent, and today it is called Goodmanham, where the high priest himself, by the inspiration of the true God, defiled and destroyed the altars that he himself had hallowed.

2.14 How Edwin and his people became believers, and where Paulinus baptized them.

So King Edwin, with all the nobles of his race and a great many of the common people, received the faith and the washing of holy regeneration in the eleventh year of his reign as king, which is the year of the Lord's incarnation 627, and about 180 years after the coming of the English to Britain. He was baptized at York on the holy day of Easter, on the twelfth of April, in the church of Peter the Apostle, which he had hastily built there of wood while he was being catechized and instructed in preparation for receiving baptism. In this same city he also established the episcopal see of his teacher and bishop, Paulinus. But as soon as the baptism occurred, he took care, under the guidance of Paulinus, to build in the same place a larger and nobler basilica of stone, in the middle of which that same oratory that he had made earlier was to be enclosed. Once the foundations were laid, he began to build the square basilica around the former oratory. But before the walls were brought up to their full height, the king's impious murder and death left the work to be completed by his successor, Oswald. For six years after that time (that is, until the end of that king's reign), Paulinus preached the word of God in that land with his consent and favor; and as many as were foreordained to eternal life believed and were baptized (Acts 13:48), among whom were Osfrith and Eadfrith, sons of King Edwin, who were both born to him while he was in exile, of Cwenburh, daughter of Ceorl, king of the Mercians.

At a later time, other children of his by Queen Æthelburh were also baptized, Æthelhun and a daughter Æthelthryth and another son, Uscfrea; the first two of these were snatched from this life while still clothed in white [baptismal robes] and are buried in the church at York. Yffi, son of Osfrith, was also baptized, and many other nobles and those of the royal family. So great is said to have been the fervor of faith and the desire for the washing of salvation among the people of Northumbria then, that one time when Paulinus came with the king and queen to the royal residence that is called Yeavering, he stayed there with them for thirty-six days, fully occupied in the task of catechizing and baptizing. During all those days, from morning till evening, he did nothing else but instruct the people who flocked together there from all the villages and neighborhoods in Christ's saving word, and when they had been instructed he bathed them with the washing of forgiveness in the river Glen, which was nearby. This residence was abandoned in the time of the later kings, and another was built instead of it, at the place that is called Mælmin.

These things took place in the kingdom of Bernicia; but also in the kingdom of Deira, where he used to stay very often with the king, he baptized in the river Swale that flows by the town of

Catterick. For during the early infancy of the church in that place, neither oratories nor baptisteries were as yet able to be built. Nevertheless, in Campodonum, where at that time there was also a royal residence, he built a basilica that afterward was burned, together with that whole residence, by the pagans who killed King Edwin; in its place, later kings built a residence for themselves in the region known as Loidis. But the altar, which was of stone, escaped the fire, and it is still preserved in the monastery of the most reverend abbot and presbyter Thrythwulf, which is in the forest of Elmet.

* * * * * * * *

3.1 How King Edwin's immediate successors betray their people's faith and the kingdom, and how the most Christian king Oswald restores both.

After Edwin had been killed in battle, the kingdom of the Deiri, from which province he derived his family of origin and the beginnings of his kingdom, passed to a son of his uncle Ælfric whose name was Osric, who had been initiated into the mysteries by the preaching of Paulinus. But the kingdom of the Bernicians—for the nation of the Northumbrians had in former times been divided into these two provinces—passed to a son of Æthelfrith named Eanfrith, who derived the origin of his race and claim to kingship from that province. For all the time that Edwin reigned, the sons of King Æthelfrith who had reigned before him, together with many young nobles, were living in exile among the Irish or the Picts, where they were catechized according to the teaching of the Irish[8] and re-created by the grace of baptism. Upon the death of their enemy the king, they were permitted to return to their homeland, and the eldest of them, Eanfrith, as we have said, received the kingdom of the Bernicians. Both of these kings, as soon as they obtained the insignia of an earthly kingdom, renounced and betrayed the mysteries of the heavenly kingdom into which they had been initiated, and delivered themselves up to be defiled and destroyed by the filth of their former idolatry.

Not long afterward, Cædwalla, king of the Britons, killed them both—a godless act of violence, but a just vengeance. First, in the following summer Osric was rashly besieging him in a fortified town, when he suddenly burst forth with all his forces, caught Osric unprepared, and destroyed him with all his army. After this, he occupied the provinces of the Northumbrians for a whole year, not like a victorious king but like a raging tyrant, despoiling and tearing them apart with terrible slaughter until at length he condemned Eanfrith to a similar fate when he unadvisedly came to him with only twelve chosen soldiers in order to ask for peace. To this day, that year remains accursed and hateful to all good folk, not only on account of the apostasy of the English kings, by which they divested themselves of the mysteries of the faith, but also because of the savage tyranny of the British king. Hence all those who compute the dates of kings have agreed to abolish the memory of those perfidious kings and to assign that year to the reign of the following king, Oswald, a man beloved of God.[9] After his brother Eanfrith was killed, he attacked with an army small in number but fortified with faith in Christ, and the abominable leader of the Britons was killed, together with those vast forces that he had boasted nothing could resist, at a place that in the English tongue is called Deniseburn, that is, the brook of Denis.

3.2 How, among innumerable miracles of healing worked by the wood of the cross that that same king Oswald set up when he was about to fight against the barbarians, a certain man was cured of the affliction of a sore arm.

The place is shown to this day and held in great veneration where Oswald, when he was about to enter into this battle, set up the sign of the holy cross and on bended knee prayed that God would hasten to give heavenly assistance to his worshipers in their great need. It is further reported that when the cross had been hurriedly made and the hole prepared in which it should be erected, he seized it himself with fervent faith, placed it in the hole, and held it upright with both hands until the soldiers heaped dirt around it so that it stood firm. When this was done, he raised his voice and cried out to the whole army: "Let us all kneel and together pray to Almighty God, living and true, that in his mercy he will defend us from the proud and fierce enemy; for he knows that we have undertaken a just war on behalf of the salvation of our nation." They all did as he had commanded, and advancing against the enemy just at the break of dawn, they obtained the victory that their faith deserved. Innumerable miracles of healing are known to have been performed in the place of his prayer, doubtless as a token and memorial of the king's faith. For even to this day many are accustomed to cut off splinters from the wood of this holy cross, which they put into water, and when sick people or beasts drink of it or are sprinkled with it, they are soon restored to health.

This place is called in the English tongue Heavenfield, which in Latin can be translated as *Caelestis Campus*, a name that it certainly received in former times as a portent of things to come, doubtless signifying that a heavenly trophy would be set up there, a heavenly victory begun, and heavenly miracles celebrated there until this day. This place is close to that wall to the north with which the Romans once girded the whole of Britain from sea to sea to hold off the attacks of the barbarians, as we have said above. The brothers of the church of Hexham, which lies not far away, have long made it their custom to come there every year on the day before that on which King Oswald was killed to keep vigil for the health of his soul, to celebrate with many psalms of praise, and in the morning to offer for him the sacrifice of the holy oblation. And since that good custom has spread, they have recently built a church there, making the place still more sacred and worthy to be honored by all. And rightly so, for we know that no emblem of the Christian faith, no church, and no altar was erected in the whole nation of the Bernicians before that new leader of the army, prompted by his devotion to the faith, set up the holy cross as a standard before he was going to fight against his most monstrous enemy.

It is not out of place to relate one of the many powerful miracles that have taken place at this cross. One of the brothers of the same church of Hexham named Bothelm, who is still living, a few years ago was walking carelessly on the ice at night when he suddenly fell and broke his arm. He suffered such severe discomfort from the fracture that he was unable to raise his arm to his mouth because of the pain. Hearing one morning that one of the brothers intended to go up to the place of the holy cross, he asked him to bring some part of that revered wood back to him, saying he believed that by this means the Lord might grant him to be healed. The brother did as he was asked, and returning at evening while the brothers were sitting at table, he gave him some of the old moss that covered the surface of the wood. Since he was sitting at table and had nowhere to put the proffered gift, he placed it in his bosom. When he went to bed, he forgot to take it out and allowed it to remain in his bosom. When he awoke in the middle of the night, he felt something cold lying next to his side, and putting his hand down to find out what it was, he discovered that his arm and hand were as sound as if he had never had any such affliction.

3.3 How the same king Oswald asked for a bishop from the Irish nation and received Aidan, and granted him an episcopal see on the island of Lindisfarne.

As soon as he became king, Oswald longed for the whole nation under his rule to be imbued with the grace of the Christian faith, of which he had acquired such great proof in conquering the barbarians. So he sent to the elders of the Irish, among whom he and his companions had received the sacrament of baptism, asking them to send him a bishop by whose teaching and ministry the nation of the English over which he ruled might learn the benefits of faith in the Lord and receive the sacraments. His request was granted without delay, and he received Bishop Aidan,[10] a man of outstanding gentleness, devotion, and moderation, who had a zeal for God, though not entirely according to knowledge (Rom 10:2). For he was accustomed to observe Easter Sunday after the manner of his nation, which, as we have often mentioned, was between the fourteenth and twentieth days of the moon.[11] For at that time the northern province of the Irish and the whole nation of the Picts were still celebrating Easter Sunday according to this method, thinking that in this observance they were following the writings of the holy and praiseworthy father Anatolius.[12] Whether this is true, every knowledgeable person can easily discern. But the Irish nations who dwelt in the southern part of Ireland had long since learned to observe Easter according to canonical custom, through the admonition of the bishop of the Apostolic See [in Rome].

When the bishop arrived, the king gave him a place for his episcopal see on the island of Lindisfarne, according to his own request. As the tide flows and ebbs, this place is twice a day surrounded by the waves of the sea like an island, and twice, when the shore is left dry, it is rejoined to the land. Humbly and willingly listening to his admonitions in all matters, the king diligently applied himself to build up and extend the church of Christ in his kingdom. When the bishop, who was not completely fluent in the English language, preached the gospel there, it was most delightful to see the king acting as interpreter of the heavenly word for his ealdormen and thegns, for he had fully learned the Irish language during the long period of his exile. From that time on, many from the country of the Irish began to arrive day by day to preach the word of faith with great devotion in Britain and those English kingdoms over which Oswald reigned, and those who possessed priestly orders administered the grace of baptism to those who believed. Churches were built in various places; the people gladly flocked together to hear the word; estates and lands were given from the king's bounty to establish monasteries; English children, along with their elders, were instructed by Irish teachers in studies and in the observance of the discipline of a rule.

For most of those who came to preach were monks. Bishop Aidan was himself a monk sent from the island called Hii [Iona], whose monastery was for a long time chief among nearly all the monasteries of the northern Irish, and all those of the Picts, having authority of direction over their people. The island itself belongs to Britain and is separated from it by a narrow strait, but the Picts who inhabit those parts of Britain gave it to the Irish monks, because they had received the faith of Christ through their preaching.

3.4 When the nation of the Picts received the faith of Christ.

In the year of the Lord's incarnation 565, when Justin the Younger[13] took over control of the Roman Empire after Justinian, there came from Ireland to Britain a presbyter and abbot named Columba,[14] distinguished as a monk by his habit and his life, to preach the word of God to the kingdoms of the northern Picts,[15] which are separated from the southern regions by steep and rugged mountains. For the southern Picts who dwell on this side of those mountains had long before, as is reported, given up the error of idolatry and accepted the true faith through the word preached to them by Bishop Ninian,[16] a most reverend and holy man of the British nation, who had been regularly instructed in the true faith and mysteries at Rome. His episcopal see, named after St. Martin[17] and notable for the church in which his body rests along with those of many other saints, is now held by the English nation. This place, which belongs to the kingdom of the Bernicians, is commonly called *Candida Casa* ["white house" = Whithorn], because he built a church of stone there, in a manner unusual among the Britons.

Columba came to Britain in the ninth year of the reign of Bridius, the son of Meilochon, a most powerful king of the Picts, and he converted that nation to the faith of Christ by his word and example; as a result, he received from them the island [of Iona] in order to establish a monastery there. For it is not very large, being only about five hides, according to English reckoning. His successors hold it to this day, and he himself was buried there at the age of seventy-seven, about thirty-two years after he came to Britain to preach. Before he came to Britain, he had established a famous monastery in Ireland, which in the Irish language is called *Dearmach* [Durrow]—that is, "field of oaks"—from the great number of oaks there. From both of these monasteries, very many other monasteries were founded by his disciples both in Britain and in Ireland;[18] but the island monastery in which his body lies holds preeminence over them all.

This island always has for its ruler an abbot who is a presbyter, to whose authority the whole kingdom, even including the bishops, has to be subject.[19] This unusual arrangement is according to the example of their first teacher, who was not a bishop but a presbyter and monk; some writings about his life and sayings are reported to have been preserved by his disciples.[20] But whatever he was himself, we know this for certain about him, that he left successors distinguished for their great continence, love of God, and practice of the [monastic] rule. It is true that they followed dubious cycles for determining the time of the great festival, since they were so far away from the rest of the world that there was no one to bring them the synodical decrees concerning the observance of Easter. But they diligently observed such works of piety and chastity as they could learn from the writings of the prophets, evangelists, and apostles. This manner of observing Easter persisted among them for a long time, for the space of 150 years, up until the year of the Lord's incarnation 715.

At that time the most reverend and most holy father and priest Egbert,[21] of the English nation, came to them. He had long lived in Ireland in exile for Christ's sake and was both most learned in the scriptures and renowned for longstanding perfection of life. He corrected them and brought them over to the true and canonical Easter Day. Not that they had ever celebrated it with the Jews on the fourteenth day of the moon, as some supposed, but on Sunday, though not in the proper week.[22] For as Christians they knew that the Lord's resurrection, which took place on the first day after the Sabbath, should always be celebrated on the first day after the Sabbath; but, rude barbarians as they were, they had never learned when this first day after the Sabbath, which is now called the Lord's Day, should come. But because they were not lacking in the fervent grace of charity, they were worthy to obtain full knowledge in this matter also, in accordance with the promise of the Apostle when he says, "And if you think differently about anything, this too God will reveal to you" (Phil 3:15).[23] But we will speak more fully about this later on in its proper place.

3.5 Of the life of Bishop Aidan.

It was from this island and from the community of these monks that Aidan was sent to instruct the English kingdom in Christ after he had received the rank of bishop while the abbot and presbyter Ségéne presided over that monastery. Among other instructions for living, he left his clergy a most wholesome example of abstinence and continence; it was the highest recommendation of his teaching to all that he taught nothing other than that which he and his followers were living. For he neither sought nor loved anything of this world, but rejoiced to distribute immediately among the poor everything that he was given by kings or rich people of the world. Whether in town or country he used to travel everywhere on foot, never on horseback unless compelled by urgent necessity, so that as he walked along, wherever he met people, whether rich or poor, he might turn aside to them at once and, if they were unbelievers, invite them to accept the mystery of the faith, or, if they were believers, strengthen them in the faith and encourage them by words and actions to pursue almsgiving and good works.

His life was so different from the slothfulness of our time, that all those who accompanied him, whether tonsured [monks] or laity, were required to meditate, that is, to occupy themselves in reading the scriptures or in learning psalms. This was the daily task for him and all those with him, wherever they went. And if by chance it happened, as it rarely did, that he was summoned to dine with the king, he went with one or two clerics, and when he had eaten just a little, he quickly hastened to be gone with them, either to read or to pray. At that time many religious men and women adopted the custom of prolonging their fast on Wednesdays and Fridays until the ninth hour[24] throughout the year except during the fifty days of Easter. If wealthy people did wrong, he never kept quiet out of respect or fear but would correct them with a stern rebuke. He would never give money to powerful people of the world, but only food if he happened to entertain them; on the contrary, whenever rich people bestowed gifts of money upon him, he either distributed it for the needs of the poor, as we have said, or paid it out for the ransoming of those who had been unjustly sold [into slavery].[25] In fact, many of those whom he ransomed by paying their price he afterward made his disciples and, after having educated and trained them, advanced them to the rank of priesthood.

They say that when King Oswald had asked the kingdom of the Irish for a bishop to administer the word of faith to him and his nation, there was first sent another man of a more austere disposition. After preaching to the English nation for some time with no success, for the people would not willingly listen to him, he returned to his homeland. At a council of the elders he reported that he had not been able to make any progress in teaching the people to whom he had been sent, because they were unruly human beings, and of a stubborn and barbarous disposition. It is related that they began to have a great discussion in the council about what ought to be done, for they wanted to afford that nation the salvation for which they were asked, but they were sorry that the preacher whom they sent had not been accepted. Then Aidan, who was present at the council, said to the priest in question, "It seems to me, brother, that you have been unreasonably harsh toward your unlearned hearers, and did not first offer them the milk of simpler teaching, in accordance with the apostolic discipline (1 Cor 3:2), until little by little, as they were nourished with the word of God, they should be capable of receiving more perfect things, and of carrying out the loftier precepts of God." Having heard this, all present turned their faces and eyes toward him and began diligently discussing what he had said, and they determined that he was worthy to be made a bishop and that he should be sent to instruct the unbelieving and unlearned, since he had been proven to be particularly endowed with the grace of *discretion, which is the mother of virtues.*[26] So they ordained him and sent him to preach. As time went on, he proved himself remarkable not only for discretion, but for the other virtues as well.

3.6 Of the wonderful devotion and piety of King Oswald.

Instructed by the teaching of such a bishop, King Oswald, together with the nation of the English over which he ruled, not only learned to hope for heavenly kingdoms unknown to his progenitors, but also was granted from the one God, who made heaven and earth, greater earthly kingdoms than any of his ancestors. For at length he held under his dominion all the nations and kingdoms of Britain, which are divided into four languages, that is, British, Pictish, the Irish, and the English.

Although he was raised to such a height of royal authority, he was always wonderfully humble, kind, and generous to the poor and to strangers. Indeed, it is reported that on a certain occasion, on the holy day of Easter, when he had sat down to dinner with the bishop, a silver dish filled with rich foods was set on the table before him. They were just raising their hands to bless the bread when the servant he had assigned to relieve the needy suddenly came in to inform the king that a great crowd of poor persons coming from all parts were sitting in the street begging some alms from the king. He immediately ordered the banquet that had been set before him to be carried to the poor, and the dish to be broken up and divided among them. The bishop, who was sitting beside him, was delighted at the sight of this act of piety, and taking hold of his right hand, he said, "May this hand never decay." Things transpired in accordance with the prayer contained in his blessing, for when Oswald was killed in battle, his hand and arm were cut off from the rest of his body, and they remain uncorrupted until the present time. In fact, they are preserved in a silver casket in St. Peter's Church in the royal city [Bamburgh], which is named after a former queen named Bebbe, where they are venerated with fitting respect by all.

Through the industriousness of this king, the kingdoms of Deira and Bernicia, which until then had been in conflict with one another, were peacefully united and joined together as one people. Now he was the nephew of King Edwin by his sister Acha, and it was fitting that so great a predecessor should have from his own blood relations so worthy an heir of both his religion and his kingdom.

* * * * * * * * *

4.20 (22) How the fetters of a certain captive were loosed when masses were sung on his behalf.

In this battle in which King Ælfwine was killed, a remarkable thing is known to have happened, which I think should by no means be passed over in silence, since telling it will be conducive to the salvation of many. During the battle, one young man named Imma, one of the king's thegns, was struck down among others; he lay as though dead all that day and the following night among the bodies of the slain. At length he recovered consciousness, sat up, and bound up his wounds as best he could; then, having rested a while, he stood up and started off in search of some friends who could take care of him. But as he was doing so, he was found and captured by men of the enemy forces and taken to their lord, who was a nobleman of King Æthelred's. When asked who he was, he was afraid to admit that he was a soldier and answered instead that he was a poor married peasant, declaring that he had come to the army with others of his kind to bring food to the soldiers. So the nobleman took him in and cared for his wounds, and when he began to recover, he commanded for him to be bound at night to prevent his escaping. But it was impossible for him to be bound, for as soon as those who bound him had gone, his fetters were loosed.

Now he had a brother whose name was Tunna, a presbyter and abbot of a monastery in the city that is still called Tunnacæstir after him. When he heard that his brother had been killed in battle, he went to see whether he could find his body, and finding another like him in every respect, he thought that it was his. So he carried it back to his monastery, buried it with honor, and took care to offer frequent masses for the absolution of his soul. It was due to the celebration of these masses that, as I have said, no one was able to bind him, but he was immediately set free. Meanwhile, the nobleman who held him captive began to marvel and to ask why he could not be bound, and whether perhaps he had with him any written charms for loosing, such as those told about in stories, on account of which he could not be bound. But he answered that he knew nothing of such arts. "However," he said, "I have a brother who is a presbyter in my country, and I am sure that he believes me killed and is offering frequent masses on my behalf, so that if I were now in the other life, my soul would be loosed from its pains by his intercessions." When he had been held captive by the nobleman for some time, those who were watching him closely realized from his appearance, manner, and speech that he was not a poor commoner, as he had said, but from the nobility. Then the nobleman sent for him privately and asked him earnestly where he was from, promising that no harm would come to him if he would plainly disclose his identity to him. When he did so, revealing that he was one of the king's thegns, the nobleman responded, "I knew by every one of your answers that you were no peasant, and now you deserve to die, because all my brothers and kindred were killed in that battle, but I will not kill you because I do not want to break my promise to you."

As soon as Imma had recovered, the nobleman sold him to a Frisian in London, but he could not be bound either by the Frisian or while he was being taken to him. After his enemies had put one kind of fetter after another upon him and his master saw that no fetters could hold him, he gave him leave to ransom himself, if he could. Now it was at the third hour,[27] when masses are usually offered, that the fetters were most frequently loosed. Having sworn with an oath that he would either return or send his master the money for his ransom, he went to King Hlothhere of Kent, who was the son of Queen Æthelthryth's sister, because he had formerly been one of that queen's thegns. From him he asked for and received the money for his ransom and sent it to his master as he had promised.

After this he returned to his own country, where he met his brother and gave him a full account of all his troubles and the solace that came to him in those troubles, and from what he was told he realized that for the most part his fetters had been loosed at the times when masses were being celebrated on his behalf. Besides this, he understood that other comforts and advantages that had come to him while in danger had been bestowed on him from heaven through the intercession of his brother and the offering of the saving sacrifice. Many who heard about this from Imma were stirred up in their faith and pious devotion to pray, or to give alms, or to offer God the sacrifice of the holy oblation for the deliverance of their kinsfolk who had departed from the world, for they understood that the saving sacrifice availed for the everlasting redemption of both body and soul.

This story was told to me by some of those who heard it from the very man to whom it happened; therefore, since I had such clear verification, I thought that it should undoubtedly be inserted into our *Ecclesiastical History*.

4.21 (23) Of the life and death of Abbess Hild.[28]

In the following year, that is, the year of the Lord's incarnation 680, the most religious servant of Christ, Hild, abbess of the monastery that is called Streanaæshalch [Whitby], as we have mentioned above, after having performed many heavenly works on earth, passed away from this earthly life to receive the rewards of the heavenly life on the seventeenth of November. She lived for sixty-six years, divided into two equal parts, for she spent the first thirty-three years living most nobly in the secular habit and dedicated the same number of years even more nobly to the Lord in the monastic life. She was of noble birth, being the daughter of King Edwin's nephew Hereric. With King Edwin she received the faith and the sacraments of Christ through the preaching of Paulinus of blessed memory, the first bishop of the Northumbrians, and she preserved this faith undefiled until she merited to attain to the vision of Christ.

When she had decided to give up the secular habit and serve him alone, she withdrew to the kingdom of the East Angles, as she was a relation of their king; for she desired, if possible, to go over to Gaul, forsaking her homeland and all that she had, and to live as an exile for the Lord's sake in the monastery of Chelles, so that she might more easily attain an everlasting homeland in heaven. For her sister Hereswith, mother of Ealdwulf, king of the East Angles, was at that time living in that same monastery under the disciplines of a [monastic] rule, awaiting her eternal crown. Inspired by her example, Hild remained in that kingdom for an entire year with the intention of going abroad as an exile, but she was recalled home by

Bishop Aidan to receive a hide of land on the north side of the river Wear, where for another year she lived the monastic life with a few companions.

After this she was made abbess in the monastery called Heruteu [Hartlepool], which had been founded not long before by Heiu, a devout servant of Christ who is said to have been the first woman in the kingdom of the Northumbrians to take vows and be clothed as a nun, having been consecrated by Bishop Aidan. But soon after she founded that monastery, she retired to the city of Calcaria, which the English call Kælcacæstir [Tadcaster?], and there she made her dwelling. Now Hild, the servant of Christ, was appointed to rule this monastery, and at once she began to set it in order according to a rule of life in every respect like that she had been taught by learned men; for Bishop Aidan and other devout persons who knew her were accustomed to visit her frequently, love her steadfastly, and instruct her diligently because of her innate wisdom and love of God's service.

When she had presided over this monastery for some years, wholly intent upon establishing a rule of life, it happened that she undertook either to build or to set in order another monastery at a place called Streanæshalch, a task imposed upon her that she carried out with great energy. She established the same disciplines of a rule of life as in the former monastery,[29] and taught there the strict observance of justice, devotion, chastity, and the other virtues, but especially of peace and charity. As a result, after the example of the early church, no one there was rich, no one was in need, for everything was held in common by all, and nothing was considered to be anyone's private property (Acts 2:44–45; 4:32–34).[30] So great was her prudence that not only ordinary people, but kings and princes as well, sought and obtained her advice in their difficulties. She required those subject to her to devote so much time to the reading of the divine scriptures, and to exercise themselves so much in works of justice, that it was easy to find many there fit for entering ecclesiastical orders, that is, for the service of the altar.

In fact, we have afterward seen five bishops out of this monastery, and all of them men of singular merit and holiness; their names are Bosa, Ætla, Oftfor, John, and Wilfrid. As we have said above, the first was consecrated as bishop of York; of the second it may be briefly noted that he was ordained as bishop of Dorchester; of the last two it will be said hereafter that the first was ordained bishop of the church of Hexham, and the second of York. Concerning Oftfor, let us now say that after he had devoted himself to the reading and observance of the scriptures in both of Abbess Hild's monasteries, being desirous of still greater perfection, he went to Kent to find Archbishop Theodore of blessed memory. After he had spent some further time in sacred studies there, he decided to go to Rome as well, which at that time was considered an act of great virtue. On his return to Britain he went to the kingdom of the Hwicce over which King Osric then ruled and remained there for a long time, preaching the word of faith and providing a living example for all who saw and heard him. At that time the bishop of that kingdom, Bosel by name, was laid low with such bodily infirmity that he could not fulfill his episcopal office himself; for this reason Oftfor was by universal consent chosen bishop in his place and ordained at King Æthelred's command by Bishop Wilfrid of blessed memory, who was then acting as bishop of the Middle Angles, because Archbishop Theodore was now dead, and no one else had been ordained bishop in his place. A little earlier, before that man of God Bosel, a most energetic and learned man of excellent ability by the name of Tatfrith, also from the monastery of Abbess Hild, had been chosen as bishop, but he had been carried off by a premature death before he could be ordained.

This handmaiden of Christ and abbess Hild, whom all who knew her called "Mother" because of her notable piety and grace, was not only an example of life for those in her own monastery, but she also provided an opportunity for salvation and amendment for many living far away who heard the happy story of her industry and virtue. For this was bound to happen in order to fulfill the dream that her mother, Breguswith, had during her infancy. While her husband Hereric was living in exile under the British king Cerdic, where he also died of poison, she dreamed that he was suddenly taken away, and although she was searching for him with all diligence, no trace of him appeared anywhere. But after she had searched for him very thoroughly, suddenly she found a most precious necklace under her garment, and as she was looking at it very closely, it seemed to shine with such a brilliant light that it filled the whole country of Britain with its gracious splendor. This dream was truly fulfilled in her daughter, whose life furnished examples of the works of light not only to herself but to many who desired to live well.

After she had presided over this monastery for many years, it pleased the merciful Provider of our salvation to try her holy soul with a long sickness of the flesh, so that, according to the Apostle's example, her strength might be made perfect in weakness (2 Cor 12:9). Racked with fever, she began to be tormented with its violent heat, and she suffered from this illness continually for six years. During all this time she never failed either to give thanks to her Maker or to instruct the flock committed to her charge, both publicly and privately. Taught beforehand by her own example, she advised them all to serve the Lord obediently when in bodily health and always to give thanks to the Lord faithfully when in adversity or bodily sickness. In the seventh year of her own sickness, the pain passed into her internal organs and she approached her last day. About cockcrow she received the viaticum of the most holy communion and, summoning the handmaidens of Christ who were in that monastery, she admonished them to maintain the gospel peace among themselves, and indeed with everyone. In the midst of her words of exhortation, she joyfully saw death, or rather, if I many speak in the words of the Lord, she "passed from death to life" (Jn 5:24).

That same night the almighty Lord saw fit to make her death known by a vision shown in another monastery some distance away, which she had built that same year, and which is called Hackness. In this monastery there was a certain nun by the name of Begu, who had dedicated her virginity to the Lord and for more than thirty years served him in the monastic life. As she was resting in the sisters' dormitory, she suddenly heard in the air the well-known sound of the bell with which they used to be awakened for prayers or called together when one of them had been summoned out of the world. Opening her eyes, as it seemed to her, she saw the roof of the house open and a light pour in from above and fill the whole place. As she was looking intently at that light, she saw the soul of the servant of God being borne up to heaven in the midst of that light, accompanied and guided by angels. Roused from sleep, she saw the other sisters lying around her and realized that what she had seen had been shown to her either in a dream or in a vision. Rising at once in great alarm, she ran to the virgin named Frigyth, who was then presiding over the monastery in place of the abbess, and with many lamentations, tears, and sighs announced that Abbess Hild, the mother of them all, had departed from the world and that she had seen her in a great light being led by angels as she ascended to the abode of eternal light and to the company of the citizens of heaven. When Frigyth heard this, she roused all the sisters and, having called them into the church, admonished them to devote themselves to prayers and psalms on behalf of their mother's soul. They did this diligently for the remainder of the night, and at early dawn brothers from the place where she had died came to announce her death. The sisters answered that they already knew it, and when they in turn explained how and when they had learned it, they discovered that her passing had been shown to them in a vision at the very hour at which the brothers said that she had departed from the world. By a beautiful harmony of events, it was divinely arranged that while some of them were watching her departure from this life, others were at the same time learning of her entrance into the everlasting life of souls. Now these two monasteries are about thirteen miles apart.

People also say that, on that same night and in the same monastery in which that servant of God died, her death was seen in a vision by one of the virgins devoted to God who had loved her with great affection. She saw Hild's soul go up to heaven in the company of angels, and she declared this openly to those servants of Christ who were with her at the very hour that it happened. She aroused them to pray for her soul, even before the rest of her community knew of her death. This series of events became known to the community as soon as it was morning. For this sister was at that time with some other handmaidens of Christ in the remotest part of the monastery, where the women who had recently entered [monastic] life were in a period of probation until they were instructed according to the rule and admitted into the fellowship of the community.

4.22 (24) How there was in her monastery a brother on whom was bestowed the divine gift of song.[31]

In the monastery of this abbess[32] there was a certain brother who was especially marked by divine grace because he used to compose appropriately religious and godly songs, so that whatever he learned from the divine writings through interpreters, he quickly turned into extremely delightful and moving poetry in English, which was his own language. By his songs the minds of many were often enkindled to despise the world and desire the heavenly life. To be sure, others in the English nation after him attempted to compose religious poems, but none could compare with him. For he did not learn the art of song from human beings, nor by human instruction (Gal 1:1), but he received the gift of song for free through God's help. For this reason he never could compose any frivolous or useless poems, but only those that pertained to religion were suitable for his religious tongue. While living in the secular habit until he was well advanced in years, he had never learned anything about poetry. For this reason sometimes at a feast, when it was decided for the sake of merriment that all of them should sing in turn, as he saw the harp coming toward him he would get up in the middle of the meal, go out, and return to his home.

On one such occasion when he did so, he left the feasting hall and went out to the stable, where he was to take care of the beasts of burden that night. In due time he stretched his limbs out there and went to sleep. He dreamed that someone stood beside him, greeting him and calling him by name: "Cædmon," he said, "sing me a song." But he answered, "I do not know how to sing; that is why I left the feast to come out here, because I could not sing." Again the one speaking to him said, "Nevertheless, you must sing for me." "What should I sing?" said Cædmon. And he said, "Sing about the beginning of created things." Then Cædmon immediately began to sing verses in praise of God that he had never heard before, of which this is the sense:[33] "Now we must praise the Fashioner of the heavenly kingdom, the power of the Creator and his counsel, the deeds of the Father of glory. How he, since he is the eternal God, became the Author of all wonders, who first created heaven as a roof for the children of human beings, and then the almighty Guardian of the human race created the earth." This is the sense, but not the precise order, of the words that he sang as he slept; for it is not possible to translate verses, however excellently composed, word for word from one language into another without some loss of their beauty and dignity. When he awoke from sleep, he remembered all that he had sung while he slept, and soon added more verses in the same style of song worthy of God.

In the morning he went to the reeve who was his superior and told him about the gift he had received. Then he was taken to the abbess [Hild], who ordered him to tell his dream in the presence of many learned men and recite his song so that all of them might reach a considered judgment about what he was saying, what kind of thing it was and where it came from. They all agreed that heavenly grace had been given him by the Lord. Then they expounded to him a passage of sacred history or doctrine, bidding him to translate it into rhythmical verse, if he could. Having undertaken the task, he went away, and when he returned the next morning he gave the passage back to them as they had ordered, composed in most excellent verse. Then the abbess, welcoming the grace of God in the man, instructed him to forsake the secular habit and take monastic vows. Then she received him into the monastery along with the rest of her people, admitted him into the company of brothers, and ordered that he should be taught the sequence of the sacred history. So he remembered all that he could learn by listening, and by ruminating like some clean animal chewing the cud (Lv 11:3; Dt 14:6), he turned it into the most sweet-sounding verse, so that his delightful recitation of it made his teachers in turn become his hearers. He sang about the creation of the world, the origin of the human race, and the whole history of Genesis; about the departure of Israel from Egypt and the entry into the promised land; about many other stories in sacred scripture; about the Lord's incarnation, passion, resurrection, and ascension into heaven; about the coming of the Holy Spirit and the teaching of the apostles. He also made many songs about the terror of future judgment, the horrors of the pains of hell, and the joy of the heavenly kingdom, besides a great many others about the divine blessings and judgments, by which he sought to turn all people away from delight in wickedness and excite them to the love and performance of good works. For he was a very religious man who humbly submitted himself to the disciplines of the rule, but inflamed with a zeal of great fervor against those who wished to do otherwise. For this reason his life concluded with a beautiful ending.

When the time of his departure drew near, he was afflicted for fourteen days by the onset of bodily infirmity, yet so moderately that he was able both to speak and to walk for the whole time. Now close by there was a house to which they used to take those who were infirm or who seemed to be near death. As evening fell on the night on which he was to leave the world, he asked his attendant to prepare a place for him to rest in this building. The attendant wondered why he would ask this, since he did not yet appear as though he were about to die; nevertheless, he did as he had asked. So Cædmon was taken there, and he was cheerfully talking and joking together with those who were already there. When it was past midnight, he asked if they had the eucharist in the house. They answered, "Why do you need the eucharist? For you are not likely to die yet, since you are talking as cheerfully with us as if you were well." "Nevertheless," he said again, "bring me the eucharist." Taking it into his hands, he asked if they all were kindly disposed toward him, and without any complaint arising from quarrel or rancor. They answered that they all were kindly disposed toward him, and free from all anger. Then they in turn asked him if he was kindly disposed toward them. He answered without delay, "Little children, I am kindly disposed toward all the servants of God." So, fortifying himself with the heavenly viaticum, he prepared for his entrance into the other life, and asked whether it was near the time when the brothers should be roused to sing their nocturnal praises to the Lord. They answered, "It is not long." And he said, "Good, let us wait until then." Signing himself with the sign of the holy cross, he laid his head down on the pillow and slept for a little while, and so ended his life in silence. Thus it happened that, as he had served the Lord with a simple and pure mind and with quiet devotion, so he also departed into his presence, leaving the world by a quiet death; and his tongue, which had composed so many wholesome words in praise of the Creator, also uttered its last words in his praise as he signed himself and commended his spirit into his hands; and from what we have related here, he seems to have had foreknowledge of his death.

4.23 (25) Of the vision that appeared to a certain man of God before the monastery at Coldingham was destroyed by fire.

At this time, the monastery of virgins called Coldingham,[34] which we have previously mentioned, was burned down through carelessness. However, all who knew of it could easily observe that it happened because of the wickedness of those who dwelled in it, and especially of those who were supposed to be their elders. But divine Goodness did not fail to give them a warning of their punishment, so that they might have been corrected, and by fasting, tears, and prayers, avert the anger of the just Judge from themselves, as did the Ninevites (Jonah 3:1–10).

There was in that monastery a man of the Irish race named Adamnán,[35] who was leading a life so devoted to God in continence and prayer that he never took any food or drink except on Sunday and Thursday, and often spent whole nights keeping watch in prayer. He had first adopted the severity of this stricter life out of necessity in order to correct his wicked tendencies, but as time went on he turned necessity into custom.

In his youth he had committed some crime on account of which, when he came to his senses, he was completely horrified and feared that he would be punished for it by the strict Judge. So he went to a priest who he hoped could show him the way of salvation, confessed his sin, and asked him for advice as to how he could flee from the wrath to come (Mt 3:7; Lk 3:7). When he had heard his offense, the priest said: "A severe wound requires an even greater remedy. Therefore, devote yourself to fasting, psalms, and prayers as far as you are able, so that when you come before the face of the Lord in confession (Ps 95:2; Vulg. 94:2) you may deserve to find him merciful." But as he was greatly troubled by a guilty conscience, and longed to be freed as quickly as possible from the inward bonds of the sins that burdened him, he said: "I am still young in age, and strong in body; I shall easily bear whatever you may compel me to do, if only I may be saved in the day of the Lord (1 Cor 5:5), even if you command me to pass the whole night standing in prayer, or to spend the entire week fasting." The priest said: "It is too much that you should endure the whole week without bodily nourishment; it is enough to keep a fast for two or three days. Do this until I return to you after a short time, when I will show you more fully what you should do, and how long you should continue this penance." With these words, having described to him the measure of his penance, the priest went away, and for some urgent reason he suddenly withdrew to Ireland, which was his native land, so that he never returned to him as he had agreed to do. But the man remembered his injunction, as well as his own promise, and he gave himself up completely to tears of penitence, holy vigils, and continence. So, as I have said, he ate only on Thursday and Sunday, and remained fasting the other days of the week. When he heard that his priest had withdrawn to Ireland and died there, ever afterward he observed that manner of continence in accordance with his agreement; what he had once begun out of fear of God because he felt remorse for his sins, he now continued unweariedly out of divine love because he delighted in its rewards.

When he had practiced this diligently for a long time, it happened one day that he had gone out some distance from that monastery, accompanied by one of the brothers, and they were returning at the end of the journey. When they drew near to the monastery and beheld its buildings rising up loftily, the man of God burst into tears, and his face betrayed the sadness of his heart. Seeing this, his companion asked the reason, and he said: "The time is nigh when fire will consume all these buildings that you see, both public and private, and turn them to ashes." Having heard this, as soon as they entered the monastery the companion went to tell the mother of the community, whose name was Æbbe. Naturally disturbed by such a prophecy, she called the man to her and carefully inquired of him concerning this matter, and how he knew of it. He said: "One night recently I was occupied in vigils and psalms when I suddenly saw someone standing beside me whose face I did not recognize. I was startled at his presence, but he told me not to fear and spoke to me in a kindly voice, saying: 'You do well in choosing to spend this nighttime of rest in vigils and prayers, instead of indulging in sleep.' And I said: 'I know that I have great need of devoting myself to salutary vigils, and of praying earnestly to the Lord for the sake of my transgressions.' He went on to say: 'You speak truly, for you and many others need to atone for their sins by good works and, when they cease from laboring about temporal affairs, to labor then the more eagerly for the sake of a desire for eternal blessings; but there are very few who do this. For I have just visited every part of this monastery in turn, examining everyone's room and bed, and I have not found anyone except yourself concerned with the welfare of his or her own soul. But all of them, men and women alike, either loll about in sluggish sleep, or are awake in order to sin. Even the cells, which were built for praying and for reading, have now been turned into rooms for feasting, drinking, gossip, and other amusements. Whenever they have leisure, even the virgins dedicated to God disdain to have proper respect for their profession and spend their time weaving fine clothes with which they either adorn themselves as if they were brides, to the peril of their position, or attract the friendship of strange men. For this reason a heavy punishment from heaven is rightly being prepared for this place and its inhabitants in the form of ferocious fire." The abbess said: "And why were you unwilling to reveal this information to me earlier?" He replied: "I was afraid on account of respect for you, lest you should be too greatly disturbed; nevertheless, you may have this consolation, that this calamity will not happen in your days" (1 Kgs 11:12; 21:29). When this vision became known, those who lived in the place were somewhat fearful for a few days and began to leave off their misdeeds and restrain themselves. But after the death of their abbess they returned to their former filthy ways and committed even greater wickedness. And when they said, "Peace and safety" (1 Thes 5:3), they were immediately punished with the penalty of the vengeance that had been foretold.

It was my most reverend fellow presbyter Eadgisl, who was then living in that monastery, who told me that all these things happened in this way. Afterward, when most of the inhabitants had left the place on account of its desolation, he lived for a long time in our monastery, and died here. We have thought it desirable to include these things in our history so that we might warn the reader about the works of the Lord, how terrible he is in his dealings with the children of mortals (Ps 66:5; Vulg. 65:5), lest we should at any time indulge in the amusements of the flesh and have so little fear of God's judgment that his wrath should suddenly come upon us and he should justly and ferociously afflict us with temporal losses, or else judge us even more strictly and bear us away to everlasting perdition.

* * * * * * * * *

4.25 (27) How Cuthbert the man of God was made bishop, and how he lived and taught while he was still in monastic life.

In the same year that he departed this life, King Ecgfrith caused the holy and venerable man Cuthbert[36] to be ordained bishop of Lindisfarne, as we have said. He had for many years lived a solitary life, in great continence of body and mind, on a very small island called Farne, which lies in the ocean about nine miles away from that same church. From his earliest boyhood he had always burned with zeal for the religious life, but it was when he became a young man that he assumed both the name and the habit of a monk. He first entered the monastery of Melrose, which is on the banks of the river Tweed and was then ruled by Abbot Eata, the gentlest and simplest of men, who later became bishop of the church of Hexham, or rather of Lindisfarne, as we have previously noted. The prior there at that time was Boisil, a priest of great virtues and a prophetic spirit. Cuthbert humbly submitted himself to Boisil's instruction and received from him both a knowledge of the scriptures and an example of good works.

After Boisil departed to the Lord, Cuthbert was made prior of that same monastery and trained many in life according to the rule, both by his authority as a teacher and by the example of his own conduct. Not only did he furnish the monastery itself with admonitions as well as examples of life according to the rule, but he also endeavored to convert the neighboring folk far and wide from a life of foolish customs to a love for heavenly joys. For many profaned the faith they possessed by wicked deeds, and at a time of pestilence some were even abandoning the sacraments of faith into which they had been initiated and resorting to the false remedies of idolatry, as though they could ward off a plague sent from God the Creator by means of incantations or amulets or any other secrets of the devilish art. So he frequently went forth from the monastery to correct both of these kinds of errors, sometimes on horseback, but more often on foot, entering the neighboring villages and preaching the way of truth to those who had gone astray, just as Boisil had been accustomed to do in his time. Now at that time it was the custom of the English people that when a cleric or a presbyter came to a village, all of them would gather together at his command to hear the word; gladly would they hear the things that were being said, and even more gladly would they strive to practice the things they were able to hear and understand. But Cuthbert was so skillful in speaking, so ardent in persuading them to accept what he was saying, and had such a light on his angelic face, that none of those present would presume to conceal from him the hidden recesses of their hearts, but they all openly confessed what they had done (doubtless because they realized that there was no way to hide these things from him) and they wiped away the sins they had confessed by fruits worthy of repentance (Mt 3:8; Lk 3:8), as he commanded them to do. Now he was accustomed especially to travel to those places and preach in those villages that were located far away on steep and rugged mountains, which others dreaded to visit and whose poverty and rusticity kept other teachers off at a distance. Gladly giving himself over to this pious task, he skillfully applied himself to teaching with so much industry that he often left the monastery and would not return home for a whole week, sometimes two or three, and occasionally even an entire month; but lingering among the mountain people, he would call the country folk to heavenly things by the word of preaching and also by deeds of virtue.

So when the venerable servant of the Lord had passed many years in the monastery at Melrose and was renowned for the signs of his great virtues, the most reverend Abbot Eata transferred him to the island of Lindisfarne so that there too he might instruct the brothers in the observance of the discipline of the rule through his authority as prior, and show them how to keep it through his personal example. For at that time the same most reverend father Eata ruled that place as abbot also. Indeed, from ancient times the bishop there used to live with his clergy, and the abbot with his monks, who were themselves also under the bishop's care as members of his household. Doubtless this was because Aidan, who was the first bishop of this place and himself a monk, came there with his monks to establish the monastic life. Even earlier, the blessed father Augustine[37] is known to have done the same thing in Kent, for (as we have already related) in writing to him the most reverend father Gregory says: "But you, my brother, having been trained under the rules of a monastery, should not live apart from your clergy in the English church, which at God's initiative has recently been brought to faith. You must establish there the manner of life that our fathers followed at the beginnings of the early church: no one among them claimed anything as a private possession, but they held all things in common" (Acts 2:44–45; 4:32).

4.26 (28) How while living as a hermit he produced a spring from dry soil by praying, and how he obtained a crop from the work of his hands by sowing seed out of season.

As we have said, Cuthbert, growing in the merit of his religious zeal, later attained to the secret silence of a life of solitude and contemplation. But since some years ago we wrote at sufficient length about his life and virtues, both in heroic verse and in prose,[38] it may be enough at present to mention that when he was about to go to the island he made a declaration to the brothers, saying: "If divine grace permits me to be able to live in that place by the work of my hands, I will gladly remain there; but if not, I will, God willing, return to you very soon." Now the place was completely destitute of water, grains, and trees, and being frequented by evil spirits it was ill suited for human habitation; but as the man of God wished it became habitable in all respects, because at his coming the evil spirits departed. Having driven out the enemies, with the brothers' helping hand he built there a small dwelling surrounded with a rampart, within which were the necessary buildings, namely, an oratory and a common dwelling place. Then he ordered the brothers to dig a well in the floor of that dwelling place, although the ground was so hard and rocky that there seemed to be no hope whatever of a spring. When they did so, by the faith and prayers of the servant of God it was found the next day to be full of water, and to this day it provides an ample supply of its heavenly bounty to all who come to that place. He also asked for farming implements and wheat to be brought to him, but although he prepared the ground and sowed at the proper season, not even a single ear, nor so much as a blade, had sprouted from it by summertime. So when the brothers were making one of their customary visits, he ordered them to bring some barley, in case either the nature of the soil or the will of the heavenly Giver required that a crop of that kind should grow there rather than wheat. Although the barley was brought to him long after the time for sowing, when there was no hope of its producing anything, he sowed it in the same field and an abundant crop of wheat quickly sprang up, providing the man of God the desired means of supporting himself by his own labor.

Thus he served God in solitude there for many years, and the rampart that surrounded his dwelling was so high that from it he could see nothing but heaven, which he longed to enter. Then it happened that a great synod was gathered together in the presence of King Ecgfrith near the river Aln at a place called Adtuifyrdi [Twyford] (which means "at the two fords"), over which Archbishop Theodore[39] of blessed memory presided, and by the unanimous consent of all Cuthbert was elected to the episcopacy of the church of Lindisfarne. But although many messengers and letters were sent to him, he could by no means be drawn out of his monastery. Finally, the king himself sailed to the island together with the most holy bishop Trumwine and many other religious and powerful men. Many of the brothers from the island of Lindisfarne assembled for the same purpose as well, and they all knelt down, adjured him by the Lord, and begged him with tears until at last they drew him, also in tears, from his beloved retreat and dragged him to the synod. When he arrived there, after a great deal of resistance, he was overcome by their unanimous desire and compelled to submit his neck to accept the office of episcopacy. He was chiefly prevailed upon by the words of the Lord's servant Boisil, who with prophetic insight had disclosed all that was to happen to him and had also predicted that he would become a bishop. However, it was decided that his ordination would not take place immediately, but after the winter, which was imminent. It was performed at York, at the feast of Easter, in the presence of King Ecgfrith; there were seven bishops in attendance at the consecration, with Theodore of blessed memory holding primacy among them. Cuthbert was first elected to the episcopacy of the church of Hexham in the place of Turnberht, who had been deposed from the episcopacy; but since he much preferred to be placed over the church of Lindisfarne, in which he had lived, it was arranged that Eata should return to the see of the church of Hexham, to which he had first been ordained, and that Cuthbert should take up the government of the church of Lindisfarne.

Having taken up the episcopal dignity, he adorned it with works of virtue in imitation of the blessed apostles. He protected the people committed to his charge with constant prayers and summoned them to heavenly things by most wholesome admonitions. And, what is the greatest help in teachers, he first showed in his own behavior whatever he was teaching them to do. Before all else, he was burning with the fire of divine love, modest with the virtue of patience, diligently attentive in prayerful devotion, friendly to all who came to him for comfort. He regarded it as equivalent to prayer if he bestowed the help of his exhortation on the weaker brothers, knowing that the one who said, "You shall love the Lord your God" also said, "Love your neighbor" (Mt 22:37, 39). He was remarkable for the strictness of his abstinence, and through the grace of contrition he was also intent upon heavenly things. Finally, when he offered God the sacrifice of the Saving Victim, he commended his prayers to the Lord not by raising up his voice but by pouring forth tears from the depths of his heart.

4.27 (29) How this bishop predicted to the hermit Herebert that his own death was coming near.

After he had spent two years in the episcopate, he returned to his island monastery, having been warned by a divine oracle that the day of his death was drawing near, or rather the day of his entrance into that life that alone can be called life. With his customary simplicity, he made this known to several people at the time, but in obscure language so that they only understood it clearly later on; but to others he revealed it openly.

There was a presbyter of venerable life by the name of Herebert who had long been linked to the man of God by the bond of spiritual friendship. He lived a solitary life on an island in the great lake from which spring the origins of the river Derwent, and he used to visit Cuthbert every year and listen to his counsels concerning eternal salvation. When he heard that Cuthbert had come to the city of Lugubalia [Carlisle], he went there according to custom, wishing to be inspired more and more to heavenly desires by his wholesome exhortations. While they were refreshing one another with intoxicating draughts of heavenly life, the bishop said, among other things: "Brother Herebert, remember to ask me now whatever you need to know and to say whatever you need to say, for after we part from one another we shall never again see one another in this world with the eyes of the flesh. For I am certain that the time of my death is at hand, and *the laying aside of my tabernacle is soon to come*" (2 Pt 1:14). Hearing these words, Herebert fell down at his feet and with sighs and tears said: "I beseech you by the Lord not to desert me, but to remember your most faithful companion and ask his heavenly kindness that, as we have served him together on earth, we may depart together to see his grace in heaven. For you know that I have always tried to live according to your spoken directions, and whatever faults I have committed through ignorance or frailty, I have equally taken care to amend at once according to the judgment of your will." The bishop applied himself to prayer and soon, having learned in the spirit that he had obtained what he was asking from the Lord, he said: "Rise, my brother, and do not weep, but rejoice gladly because heavenly Mercy has granted us what we have asked."

The subsequent issue of events proved the truth of this prophetic promise, for after they had parted they never again saw one another in the flesh, and on the same day (that is, on the twentieth of March) their spirits left their bodies and were immediately joined together in the beatific vision, and together they were borne by the ministry of angels to the heavenly kingdom. But Herebert was first consumed by a long illness that was, as we may believe, from the dispensation of the Lord's mercy, so that if he had any less merit than blessed Cuthbert, it might be made up by the chastening pain of a long sickness, in order that being made equal in grace to his intercessor, as he departed the body at one and the same time with him, he would also merit to be received into one and the same abode of eternal bliss.

The most reverend father died on the island of Farne, earnestly asking the brothers that he might be buried in the place where he had soldiered for the Lord for no small amount of time. But at length he yielded to their entreaties and gave his assent to being carried back to the island of Lindisfarne and buried in the church there. This being done accordingly, the venerable Bishop Wilfrid held the episcopate in that church for one year, until someone was chosen to be ordained as bishop in place of Cuthbert.

Afterward, Eadberht was ordained, a man as widely known for his knowledge of the divine scriptures as for his observance of the heavenly commands, and especially for almsgiving, so that in accordance with the law he gave to the poor the tenth part not only of his beasts but also of all his grains and fruits, and of his clothes as well.

4.28 (30) How his body was found free from corruption after it had been buried for eleven years, and not long afterward his successor in the episcopate departed this life.

In order to show more widely in how much glory the man of God Cuthbert lived after his death, his sublime life having been attested by frequent signs and miracles, when he had been buried for eleven years Divine Providence put it into the minds of the brothers to take up his bones—which they were expecting to find dried, as is usual with the dead, with the rest of his body already decayed and reduced to dust—and to place them in a new coffin in the same place, but above the floor, so that they might receive the veneration due to them. When they reported their plan to Eadberht their bishop, he consented to it and ordered them to carry it out on the anniversary of his burial. They did so, and when they opened the grave they found the body as whole and intact as though he were still alive, with the joints of the limbs flexible, so that he seemed more like a sleeping person than one who was dead. Moreover, all the vestments in which he had been clothed appeared to be not only undefiled but also as new as ever, and wonderfully bright. The brothers were struck with great fear when they saw this, so that they hastened to tell the bishop what they had found. At the time he happened to be living alone in a place somewhat remote from the church and surrounded on every side by the waves of the sea at flood tide. There he was always accustomed to spend the season of Lent and the forty days before the Nativity of the Lord in deep devotion, with abstinence, prayers, and tears. There also his venerable predecessor Cuthbert had soldiered in secret for the Lord for a while, before he went to Farne Island.

They brought him some of the garments that had encompassed the holy body. When he had gratefully accepted these gifts and gladly listened to the account of the miracles, he kissed the garments with great affection, as though they still enwrapped the father's body. Then he said, "Wrap the body with fresh garments in place of those you have brought, and replace it so in the coffin you have prepared. I know most certainly that the place that has been consecrated by the grace of so heavenly a miracle will not long remain empty, and how blessed is the one to whom the Lord, the Author and Giver of all blessedness, shall deign to give the privilege of resting in it." When the bishop had finished saying these things and more to the same effect in a trembling voice, with many tears and great emotion, the brothers did as he had commanded: they wrapped the body in fresh clothing, laid it in a new coffin, and placed it on the floor of the sanctuary.

Not long afterward, Bishop Eadberht, beloved of God, was devastated by a severe illness that grew worse by the day as the pain of the sickness increased. In a short time, that is on the sixth of May, he too departed to the Lord. They laid his body in the tomb of the blessed father Cuthbert, and over it they put the coffin in which they had placed the father's incorrupt limbs. The miracles of healing that sometimes occur in that place bear testimony to the merits of them both. Some of these we have previously recorded in our book about his life, but we have considered it fitting in this history to add some others that we have recently chanced to hear.

4.29 (31) How a certain man was healed of paralysis at his tomb.

There was in the same monastery a brother named Baduthegn, who had been serving as guest master for some time, and who is still alive. All the brothers and all the guests who visited there testified that he was a man of great piety and devotion, who served in the office laid upon him only for the sake of a heavenly reward. One day, after going down to the sea to wash the cloths and blankets that he used in the guesthouse, he was returning home when in the middle of his journey he was seized by a sudden pain so that he fell to the ground, lying prostrate for some time, and getting up again only with difficulty. When he got up, he realized that one-half of his body was afflicted with paralysis from head to foot, and with great effort he made it home by leaning on a staff. The ailment gradually increased and when night came it became even more serious, so that the next day he could hardly rise or walk on his own. Afflicted with this infirmity, he conceived the most excellent plan of going to the church as best he could to visit the tomb of the most reverend father Cuthbert, and on bended knee humbly to beg heavenly Goodness that he might either be delivered from this illness, if that were to his good, or if by the grace of Divine Providence he must be chastened by this affliction for a while longer, that he might bear the pain patiently and calmly. Then he acted according to his plan, and, supporting his feeble limbs with a staff, he entered the church and prostrated himself before the body of the man of God, devoutly praying that the Lord would be gracious toward him through Cuthbert's assistance. In the midst of his prayers he fell into a deep sleep, and as afterward he used to relate, he seemed to feel a great and broad hand touch the part of his head where the pain lay, and with that touch the entire part of his body that was afflicted by the illness was gradually freed from pain and he was healed all the way down to his feet. When this happened, he soon awoke, arose completely healed, and giving thanks to God for his renewed health he told the brothers what had happened to him. To the joy of all, he returned to the office that he had been accustomed to perform so diligently, as though chastened all the more by the reproving scourge.

Moreover, even the garments that had covered Cuthbert's body, dedicated to God as it was, both while he was still living and after he was dead, were not devoid of the grace of healing, as anyone who reads the book of his life and miracles will find.

* * * * * * * *

5.12 How a certain man in the kingdom of the Northumbrians rose from the dead and told of many things that he had seen, both those to be dreaded and those to be desired.[40]

About this time a memorable miracle, like those of ancient times, occurred in Britain. For, in order to arouse the living from spiritual death, a certain man already dead rose again to bodily life and told of many noteworthy things that he had seen, some of which I have thought it fitting to relate briefly here. There was the head of a family living a religious life together with his household in the region of the Northumbrians that is called Incuneningum [Cunningham]. He was taken with a bodily illness that grew worse by the day until he came to his end and died in the early hours of the night. But at dawn he came to life again and suddenly sat up so that all those who were sitting weeping around the body were stricken with tremendous fear and ran away; only his wife, who loved him more dearly, remained, though trembling and fearful. He comforted her, saying, "Do not be afraid, for I have truly risen from death, which held me, and I have been permitted to live among human beings again; nevertheless, from now on I must not live as I was accustomed to before, but in a very different way of life." At once he got up and went to the village oratory and continued steadfastly in prayer until daybreak. Then he divided all the property he possessed into three parts, one of which he gave to his wife, another to his sons, and the third he retained for himself and immediately distributed to the poor. Not long afterward, he freed himself from worldly cares and entered the monastery at Melrose, which is almost completely surrounded by a bend in the river Tweed. Having received the tonsure, he went into a solitary dwelling place provided by the abbot. There he remained until the day of his death in such contrition of mind and body that, even if he had kept silence, his life would have declared that he had seen many things to be dreaded or desired that were hidden from others.

He described what he had seen in this way: "The one who guided me had a shining countenance and bright robes. We proceeded in silence in what seemed to me to be toward the rising of the sun at the summer solstice.[41] As we walked we came to a very wide and deep valley of infinite length. It lay on our left, and one side was quite terrible with burning flames, while the other side was no less unbearable with raging hail and freezing snow blowing and driving in all directions. Both sides were full of human souls that seemed to be hurled from one side to the other in turn, as though by the fury of the tempest. For when the wretches could no longer bear the force of the immense heat, they leapt into the midst of the deadly cold, and when they could not find any respite there, they jumped back to be burned in the midst of the unquenchable flames. Since a countless multitude of misshapen spirits was being tormented far and wide in this unhappy vicissitude, as far as I could see without any interval of rest, I began to think that perhaps this was hell, of whose unbearable torments I had often heard tell. But my guide who went before me answered my thought, saying: 'Do not think this; for this is not hell as you suppose.'

"But when he had gradually led me farther on, terrified by so dreadful a sight, I suddenly saw that the places before us began to grow dim, and darkness covered everything. As we entered it, the darkness soon became so dense that I saw nothing else, except the form and the garment of the one leading me. As we went on *through the shades in the solitary night*,[42] suddenly there appeared before us numerous masses of monstrous flames, rising as though from a great pit and falling into it again. When my guide had brought me to this place, he suddenly disappeared and left me alone in the midst of the darkness and this horrible sight. But as the masses of fire sometimes rose up above, and sometimes fell to the depths of the chasm without ceasing, I saw that as all the tips of the flames rose up they were filled with human spirits that, like cinders rising up with smoke, were now thrown to the heights, and now sunk back to the depths as the fumes of the flames drew back. Furthermore, an indescribable stench bursting forth with these fumes filled all those gloomy places. When I had stood there a long time terrified, uncertain what to do, where to turn, or what end awaited me, I suddenly heard behind me the noise of a most hideous and wretched lamentation, and at the same time a shrill laughter as though a rude mob was taunting its captured enemies. As that noise grew clearer and came right up to me, I noticed a crowd of evil spirits dragging five human souls wailing and shrieking into the midst of the darkness while they themselves exulted greatly and laughed. Among the humans I could make out one tonsured like a cleric, a layman, and a woman. The evil spirits dragged them down into the midst of the burning chasm, and it happened that as they descended deeper I was unable to distinguish clearly between the humans' lamentation and the devils' laughter, but I still had a confused noise in my ears. Meanwhile, some of the gloomy spirits rose up out of that flaming abyss and rushed to surround me, tormenting me with their flaming eyes and the foul fire that issued from their mouths and nostrils. They threatened to seize me with the fiery tongs they held in their hands, but although they frightened me, they did not dare to touch me. Enclosed on all sides by enemies and blind darkness, I was casting my eyes this way and that to see if help would come from any direction to save me, when there appeared behind me, on the road by which I had come, something like the brightness of a star shining in the darkness, which gradually grew and hastened rapidly toward me. When it drew near, all the hostile spirits who were seeking to snatch me with their tongs scattered and fled.

"The one whose approach put them to flight was the same one who was guiding me before. Turning directly to a path on the right, he began to lead me toward the rising of the winter sun.[43] Without delay he brought me out of the darkness into an atmosphere of clear light, and as he led me on in open light I saw before us a very great wall that seemed to be infinitely long and high in every direction. I began to wonder why we were approaching the wall, since I did not see any gate, window, or stairs on it anywhere. But when we reached the wall we were immediately on top of it, by what means I do not know. And behold, there was a very broad and pleasant field, full of such a fragrance of blooming flowers that the sweetness of its marvelous scent quickly dispelled all the stench of the gloomy furnace that had permeated me. So great was the light that flooded the whole place that it seemed to be more brilliant than the brightness of daylight or the sun's rays at noon. In this field there were innumerable bands of people in white robes, and many happy companies sitting together. As he led me through the midst of these crowds of happy inhabitants, I began to think that perhaps this was the kingdom of heaven, which I had heard preached about so often. But he answered my thought, saying: 'No, this is not the kingdom of heaven, as you suppose.'

"When we had passed through these abodes of the blessed spirits and gone further on, I saw ahead of us a much lovelier light than before, and in it I heard the sweetest sound of people singing. Moreover, so wonderful was the fragrance of the scent that flowed out from the place that the other scent, which I had considered so superior when I savored it earlier, now seemed to me quite ordinary. Even the wondrous light of the flowery field seemed utterly thin and slight in comparison with this light that now appeared. As I was hoping that we were going to enter that delightful place, my guide suddenly stood still and then, retracing his steps, quickly led me back by the way we had come.

"When we returned to those joyful abodes of the white-robed spirits, he said to me: 'Do you know what all these things are that you have seen?' I answered, 'No.' Then he said: 'The valley that you saw, with its horrible burning flames and freezing cold, is the place where the souls being tried and punished are those who delay to confess and amend the wicked things they have done until they have recourse to repentance at the very point of death, and so depart from the body. But because they did perform confession and repentance, even at death, all of them will attain to the kingdom of heaven on the Day of Judgment. Moreover, the prayers of the living, their alms and fastings and especially the celebration of masses, help many of them so that they are set free even before the Day of Judgment. But the flaming and foul pit that you saw is the very mouth of hell; whoever once falls into it will never be set free from it for all eternity. This flowery place, where you see this fair youthful band so joyful and bright, is where the souls being received are those who depart from the body in good works but are not so perfect that they merit to be immediately brought into the kingdom of heaven; nevertheless, all of them on the Day of Judgment will enter into the vision of Christ and the joys of the heavenly kingdom. For any who are perfect in every word and deed and thought attain to the heavenly kingdom as soon as they leave the body; this kingdom is near that place where you heard the sound of sweet singing, with the pleasant fragrance and brilliant light. You must now return to the body and live among human beings again; but if you will strive to examine your actions more carefully and keep your ways and your words in uprightness and simplicity, after death you too will receive a dwelling place among the joyful companies of blessed spirits that you see. For when I left you for a while, I did so in order to find out what should become of you.' When he had spoken these things to me, I returned to the body with great loathing, for I was delighted with the sweetness and beauty of that place which I had seen, and with the company of those whom I saw in it. However, I did not dare to question my guide, and meanwhile, I know not how, I suddenly found myself alive among human beings."

This man of God would not relate these and other things he had seen indiscriminately to any whose lives were slothful or careless, but only to those who would be terrified by the fear of torments or delighted with the hope of eternal joys and thus make use of his words to advance in godliness. Accordingly, in the vicinity of his cell there lived a monk whose name was Hæmgisl, an eminent presbyter whose good works were equal to his rank. He is still alive, leading a solitary life in Ireland, supporting his latter years on coarse bread and cold water. He often used to visit this man and by repeated questioning hear from him what sort of things he saw when he was out of the body; it is from his account that these few things we have briefly recounted came to our knowledge. He also related his visions to King Aldfrith, a man most learned in all respects, who listened to him so willingly and attentively that, at the king's request, he was admitted to the monastery previously mentioned and crowned with the monastic tonsure. Whenever the king visited those parts, he often went to hear him. At that time the ruler of that monastery was the abbot and presbyter Æthelwold of pious and sober life, who now holds the episcopal office at Lindisfarne with deeds worthy of his rank.

The man was given a more secret dwelling place in that monastery where he could more freely devote himself to the service of his Maker with continual prayers. And since that place was situated on the bank of a river, he often used to go into it on account of his great desire to chastise his body, frequently plunging himself under the flow of the waters and remaining there motionless while continuing to say psalms or prayers for as long as he was able to endure it, while the river's water came up to his loins and sometimes to his neck. When he came out from there to the shore, he never took off his wet and cold garments until they grew warm and dry from the heat of his body. When in wintertime the half-broken pieces of ice were floating around him, which he had broken in order to have a place to stand and plunge himself into the river, those who saw him would say, "It is wonderful, Brother Dryhthelm"—for that was his name—"that you are able to bear such bitter cold." He answered simply, for he was a man of simple character and modest disposition, "I have seen it colder." And when they said, "It is wonderful that you are willing to endure such austere self-restraint," he used to answer, "I have seen it more austere." And so until the day of his being called away, in his unwearied desire for the blessings of heaven, he subdued his aging body with daily fasts and brought many to salvation by his words and manner of life.

NOTES

INTRODUCTION

1. Earlier versions of some material in this introduction appeared in Arthur G. Holder, "Bede and the Tradition of Patristic Exegesis," *Anglican Theological Review* 72 (1990): 399–411; and Holder, "The Venerable Bede on the Mysteries of Our Salvation," *American Benedictine Review* 42 (1991): 140–62.

2. *Ecclesiastical History* 5.24, trans. in *Bede's Ecclesiastical History*, ed. Bertram Colgrave and R. A. B. Mynors (Oxford: Oxford University Press, 1969; reprinted with corrections, 1991), 567.

3. The stories of the Roman and Irish missions to Northumbria are told by Bede in *Ecclesiastical History* 2.9–14, pp. 281–87, and 3.1–6, pp. 287–96.

4. See Caitlin Corning, *The Celtic and Roman Traditions: Conflict and Consensus in the Early Medieval Church* (New York: Palgrave Macmillan, 2006).

5. *Ecclesiastical History* 3.25. On the Synod of Whitby, see Henry Mayr-Harting, *The Coming of Christianity to Anglo-Saxon England*, 3rd ed. (University Park: Pennsylvania State University Press, 1991), 103–13; Arthur G. Holder, "Whitby and All That: The Search for Anglican Origins," *Anglican Theological Review* 85 (2003): 231–52; and Benedicta Ward, *A True Easter: The Synod of Whitby 664 AD* (Oxford: SLG Press, 2007).

6. Gerald Bonner, "Ireland and Rome: The Double Inheritance of Christian Northumbria," in *Saints, Scholars, and Heroes: Studies in Medieval Culture in Honour of Charles W. Jones*, ed. Margot H. King and Wesley M. Stevens (Collegeville, MN: Hill Monastic Manuscript Library, Saint John's Abbey and University, 1979), vol. 1: *The Anglo-Saxon Heritage*, 101.

7. Patrick Wormald, "The Venerable Bede and the Church of the English," in *The English Religious Tradition and the Genius of*

Anglicanism, ed. Geoffrey Rowell (Nashville, TN: Abingdon Press, 1992), 13–32; Nicholas Brooks, "Bede and the English," Jarrow Lecture, 1999. The exception to Bede's unifying vision was his rebuke of the British for refusing to evangelize their Anglo-Saxon conquerors.

8. Bede, *History of the Abbots* 11, ed. Charles Plummer, in *Venerabilis Baedae opera historica* (Oxford: Clarendon Press, 1896), 1: 375. See Henry M. R. E. Mayr-Harting, "The Venerable Bede, the Rule of St. Benedict, and Social Class," Jarrow Lecture, 1976; Patrick Wormald, "Bede and Benedict Biscop," in *Famulus Christi: Essays in Commemoration of the Thirteenth Centenary of the Birth of the Venerable Bede*, ed. Gerald Bonner (London: SPCK, 1976), 141–46; A. G. P. Van der Walt, "Reflections of the Benedictine Rule in Bede's Homiliary," *Journal of Ecclesiastical History* 37 (1986): 367–76; Scott DeGregorio, "Bede, the Monk, as Exegete: Evidence from the Commentary on Ezra-Nehemiah," *Revue Bénédictine* 115 (2005): 343–69.

9. On prayer and worship in early medieval English monasteries, see Sarah Foot, *Monastic Life in Anglo-Saxon England, c. 600–900* (Cambridge: Cambridge University Press, 2006), 186–210.

10. Jean Leclercq, *The Love of Learning and the Desire for God*, trans. Catherine Misrahi, 3rd ed. (New York: Fordham University Press, 1982), 11–24. The relevance for Bede's writings is noted in Gerald Bonner, "Bede and Medieval Civilization," *Anglo-Saxon England* 2 (1973): 78.

11. M. L. W. Laistner, "The Library of the Venerable Bede," in *Bede: His Life, Times, and Writings*, ed. A. Hamilton Thompson (Oxford: Clarendon Press, 1935), 237–66; Michael Lapidge, *The Anglo-Saxon Library* (Oxford: Oxford University Press, 2006), 34–37, 191–228.

12. Bede, *Commentary on Luke*, prologue (CCSL 120: 7).

13. Alan Thacker, "Bede's Ideal of Reform," in *Ideal and Reality in Frankish and Anglo-Saxon Society: Studies Presented to J. M. Wallace-Hadrill*, ed. Patrick Wormald with Donald Bullough and Roger Collins (Oxford: Basil Blackwell, 1983), 130.

14. Foot, *Monastic Life in Anglo-Saxon England*, 286.

15. *Bede the Venerable: Homilies on the Gospels* 1.7 (CCSL 122: 49), trans. Lawrence T. Martin and David Hurst (Kalamazoo, MI: Cistercian Publications, 1991), 1: 69.

16. Bede, *Letter to Egbert*, ed. Charles Plummer in *Venerabilis Baedae opera historica* (Oxford: Clarendon Press, 1896), 1: 405–23; trans. Judith McClure and Roger Collins, *Bede: The Ecclesiastical History*

of the English People; The Greater Chronicle; Bede's Letter to Egbert (Oxford: Oxford University Press, 1994), 343–57.

17. Boniface, Letter 76, in *Briefe des Bonifatius; Willibalds Leben des Bonifatius nebst einigen zeitgenossischen Dokumenten*, ed. Reinhold Rau (Darmstadt: Wissenschaftliche Buchgesellschaft, 1968), 234; translated as Letter 60 in *The Letters of Saint Boniface*, trans. Ephraim Emerton (New York: Columbia University Press, 2000), 112.

18. "Cuthbert's Letter on the Death of Bede," trans. in Judith McClure and Roger Collins, *Bede: The Ecclesiastical History of the English People; The Greater Chronicle; Bede's Letter to Egbert* (Oxford: Oxford University Press, 1994), 300–303. This Cuthbert is not the same man as the St. Cuthbert about whom Bede wrote in his two lives of the saint and in the *Ecclesiastical History*.

19. Alcuin, *The Bishops, Kings, and Saints of York*, ed. and trans. Peter Godman (Oxford: Clarendon Press, 1982), 103–4.

20. *Sacrorum conciliorum noua et amplissima collectio*, ed. Giovanni Domenico Mansi, 31 vols. (Venice: Antonio Zatta, 1759–98), 14: 726.

21. Bede, *Commentary on Luke*, prologue (CCSL 120: 7). In both that commentary and the one on Mark, Bede used a system of marginal notation to identify his borrowings from these four patristic authors. For a variety of perspectives on Bede's use of the phrase "following the footsteps of the fathers," see the essays in Scott DeGregorio, ed., *Innovation and Tradition in the Writings of the Venerable Bede* (Morgantown: West Virginia University Press, 2006).

22. Paul Meyvaert, "Bede and Gregory the Great," Jarrow Lecture, 1964; and Scott DeGregorio, "The Venerable Bede and Gregory the Great: Exegetical Connections, Spiritual Departures," *Early Medieval Europe* 18 (2010): 43–60.

23. Michael Lapidge, "Bede the Poet," Jarrow Lecture, 1993.

24. Bede, *Ecclesiastical History*, prologue, trans. Colgrave and Mynors, 2.

25. Bede, *Ecclesiastical History* 5.23, trans. Colgrave and Mynors, 561.

26. See Scott DeGregorio, "Bede's *In Ezram et Neemiam* and the Reform of the Northumbrian Church," *Speculum* 79 (2004), 1–25; and John Blair, *The Church in Anglo-Saxon Society* (Oxford: Oxford University Press, 2005), 101–11.

27. Mayr-Harting, *Coming of Christianity to Anglo-Saxon England*, 219. See also Alan Thacker, "Bede and the Ordering of Understanding," in *Innovation and Tradition in the Writings of the Venerable Bede*, ed. Scott DeGregorio (Morgantown: West Virginia University Press, 2006), 37–63.

28. The most comprehensive study of Bede's spirituality to date is Sister M. Thomas Aquinas Carroll, *The Venerable Bede: His Spiritual Teachings* (Washington DC: Catholic University of America Press, 1946). Among recent works on Bede, the one that gives most attention to spirituality is Benedicta Ward, *The Venerable Bede* (Wilton, CT: Morehouse Publishing, 1990; reprinted Kalamazoo, MI: Cistercian Publications, 1998).

29. Bede, *On the Song of Songs* 3 (CCSL 119B: 260), pp. 125–26.

30. Bede, *On the Song of Songs* 5 (CCSL 119B: 337), p. 223.

31. Mary Prentice Lillie Barrows, "Bede's *Allegorical Exposition of the Canticle of Canticles*: A Study in Early Medieval Allegorical Exegesis" (PhD dissertation, University of California at Berkeley, 1962), 148–61.

32. Bede, *History of the Abbots* 9 (Plummer, 1: 373).

33. Bede, *On the Song of Songs* 3 (CCSL 119B: 251), p. 114.

34. Bede, *On the Song of Songs* 1 (CCSL 119B: 214–15), pp. 67–69.

35. Gregory the Great, *Letter to Leander* 4 (CCSL 143: 177–78).

36. A good introduction is Barbara C. Raw, *Trinity and Incarnation in Anglo-Saxon Art and Thought* (Cambridge: Cambridge University Press, 1997).

37. Bede, *Homilies on the Gospels* 1.19 (CCSL 134). The phrase "sacraments of his humanity," one of Bede's favorite terms, was derived from Gregory the Great, *Morals on Job* 34.14 (CCSL 143B: 1750).

38. Bede, *On the Song of Songs* 4 (CCSL 119B: 292), p. 166.

39. See Arthur G. Holder, "The Feminine Christ in Bede's Biblical Commentaries," in *Bède le Vénérable entre tradition et postérité*, ed. Stéphane Lebecq, Michel Perrin, and Olivier Szerwiniack (Lille: 3-CEGES, 2005), 109–18.

40. Bede, *On the Song of Songs* (CCSL 119B: 191–2), pp. 39–40. The other biblical passages Bede references are Revelation 1:12–13, Isaiah 66:9, Isaiah 66:13, and Matthew 23:37.

41. See Ritamary Bradley, "Patristic Background of the Motherhood Similitude in Julian of Norwich," *Christian Scholar's Review* 8 (1978): 101–13.

42. Bede, *On the Song of Songs* 3 (CCSL 119B: 258), p. 123.

43. For later developments, see Caroline Walker Bynum, *Jesus as Mother: Studies in the Spirituality of the High Middle Ages* (Berkeley and Los Angeles: University of California Press, 1982); and Barbara Newman, *God and the Goddesses: Vision, Poetry, and Belief in the Middle Ages* (Philadelphia: University of Pennsylvania Press, 2003).

44. Bede, *Homilies on the Gospels* 2.13 (CCSL 122: 269).

45. Bede, *Homilies on the Gospels* 1.22 (CCSL 122: 158), p. 263.

46. Bede, *On Proverbs* 3 (CCSL 119B: 149–63). This part of the commentary circulated as a treatise *De muliere forti* in some manuscripts.

47. There is also a seventh age, contemporaneous with the first six, during which the souls of the faithful departed enjoy a sabbath rest, and an eighth and final age that will begin on the Day of Judgment and last eternally. See Peter Hunter Blair, *The World of Bede*, rev. ed. (Cambridge: Cambridge University Press, 1990), 265–68; and Jan Davidse, "The Sense of History in the Works of the Venerable Bede," *Studi Medievali* 23 (1982): 656–71.

48. See Andrew P. Scheil, *The Footsteps of Israel: Understanding Jews in Anglo-Saxon England* (Ann Arbor: University of Michigan Press, 2004).

49. See W. Trent Foley and Nicholas J. Higham, "Bede on the Britons," *Early Medieval Europe* 17 (2009): 154–85.

50. Bede, *On the Song of Songs* 4 (CCSL 119B: 317), p. 197.

51. Bede, *Homilies on the Gospels* 2.25 (CCSL 122: 369), p. 267; cf. *On the Tabernacle* 2 (CCSL 119A: 43).

52. Bede, *On the Song of Songs* 5 (CCSL 119B: 348), p. 236.

53. Scott DeGregorio, "*Nostrorum socordiam temporum*: The Reforming Impulse of Bede's Later Exegesis," *Early Medieval Europe* 11 (2002): 107–22.

54. Bede, *Homilies on the Gospels* 2.25 (CCSL 122: 373), p. 271.

55. Bynum, *Jesus as Mother*, 148.

56. Bede, *On the Song of Songs* 3 (CCSL 119B: 258), p. 123.

57. *Ecclesiastical History* 4.26 (28), p. 313. The encomium of Cuthbert at the end of this chapter is a catalog of these clerical and monastic virtues.

58. Bede, *On the Tabernacle* 2 (CCSL 119A: 89); cf. Gregory the Great, *Homilies on Ezekiel* 2.3.3 (CCSL 142: 238).

59. Jennifer O'Reilly, "Bede on Seeing the God of Gods in Zion," in *Text, Image, Interpretation: Studies in Anglo-Saxon Literature and Its Insular Context in Honour of Éamonn Ó Carragáin*, ed. Alastair Minnis and Jane Roberts (Turnhout: Brepols Publishers, 2007), 3–29.

60. Bede, *On the Song of Songs* 2 (CCSL 119B: 236–37), p. 96.

61. Bede, *On the Song of Songs* 4 (CCSL 119B: 302), pp. 178–79.

62. Bede, *On the Song of Songs* 5 (CCSL 119B: 329), p. 212.

63. Bede, *On the Song of Songs* 3 (CCSL 119B: 261), p. 127.

64. Bede, *On the Song of Songs* 4 (CCSL 119B: 302), p. 178.

65. Bede, *On the Song of Songs* 4 (CCSL 119B: 297), p. 172.

66. Bede, *Ecclesiastical History* 4.23 (25), p. 307.

67. Bede, *On the Song of Songs* 2 (CCSL 119B: 229), p. 86. See Scott DeGregorio, "The Venerable Bede on Prayer and Contemplation," *Traditio* 54 (1999): 1–39.

68. Bede, *On the Song of Songs* 3 (CCSL 119B: 280), p. 151.

69. Bede, *On the Song of Songs* 3 (CCSL 119B: 274–75), p. 144.

70. Bede, *On the Song of Songs* 1 (CCSL 119B: 218), p. 73.

71. See DeGregorio, "The Venerable Bede on Prayer and Contemplation," 29–32.

72. Bede, *On the Song of Songs* 1 (CCSL 119B: 218), pp. 72–73.

73. *Bede the Venerable: Homilies on the Gospels* 1.9 (CCSL 122: 64), trans. Martin and Hurst, 1:91; *Commentary on the Canticle of Habakkuk* (CCSL 119B: 400), trans. Seán Connolly, in *Bede: "On Tobit" and "On the Canticle of Habakkuk"* (Dublin: Four Courts Press, 1997), 85–86.

74. Bede, *On the Song of Songs* 4 (CCSL 119B: 298–99), p. 174.

75. Bede, *On the Song of Songs* 4 (CCSL 119B: 303), p. 180.

76. Bede, *On the Song of Songs* 4 (CCSL 119B: 303–4), p. 180.

77. *Collectio psalteriii Bedae* (CCSL 122: 452–70), trans. Gerald M. Browne, *The Abbreviated Psalter of the Venerable Bede* (Grand Rapids, MI: William B. Eerdmans, 2002). See also Benedicta Ward, "Bede and the Psalter," Jarrow Lecture, 1991.

78. Bede, *Homilies on the Gospels* 1.22 (CCSL 122: 160), p. 264.

79. DeGregorio, "The Venerable Bede on Prayer and Contemplation," 24.

80. Augustine, Letter 130.9.18 (CSEL 44: 60).

81. Bede, *On the Song of Songs* 3 (CCSL 119B: 261), p. 128. See DeGregorio, "The Venerable Bede on Prayer and Contemplation," 20, for the suggestion that this may have been derived from Cassiodorus, *Exposition of the Psalms* 85.3 (CCSL 98: 782) or Augustine, *On the Psalms* 148.2 (CCSL 40: 2166).

82. Bede, *Ecclesiastical History* 4.26 (28), p. 313.

83. Alcuin, *Letter* 284 in MGH, Epistolarum IV, *Epistolae Karolini Aevi*, ed. Ernst Dümmler, 2: 443.

84. See David Rollason, *Saints and Relics in Anglo-Saxon England* (Oxford: Basil Blackwell, 1989).

85. Bede, *Ecclesiastical History* 3.2, pp. 288–90.

86. Bede, *Ecclesiastical History* 4.20 (22), pp. 296–97.

87. Bede's approach to miracles followed that of Gregory the Great, but for Bede modern-day miracles served primarily to prove

that a person was truly a saint, whereas for Gregory the form of the miracle served as an object lesson for moral instruction. See William D. McCready, *Miracles and the Venerable Bede* (Toronto: Pontifical Institute of Mediaeval Studies, 1994), esp. 124–53.

88. Bede, *Commentary on Mark* 4 (CCSL 120: 645). See McCready, *Miracles and the Venerable Bede*, 83–85.

89. Bede, *Commentary on Mark* 2 (CCSL 120: 534).

90. Bede, *On the Song of Songs* 5 (CCSL 119B: 336), p. 221.

91. See also Bede, *Homilies on the Gospels* 1.2 (CCSL 122: 12–13), where there is a similar division of states in the afterlife (although hell is not mentioned explicitly). In this homily, but not in the vision of Dryhthelm, Bede used the terms "paradise" and "purgatory" for the two intermediate states.

92. On the medieval tradition of Song commentaries, see Ann W. Astell, *The Song of Songs in the Middle Ages* (Ithaca, NY: Cornell University Press, 1990); and E. Ann Matter, *The Voice of My Beloved: The Song of Songs in Western Medieval Christianity* (Philadelphia: University of Pennsylvania Press, 1990).

93. See Arthur G. Holder, "Christ as Incarnate Wisdom in Bede's Commentary on the Song of Songs," in DeGregorio, *Innovation and Tradition in the Writings of the Venerable Bede*, 169–88.

94. Bede, *On the Song of Songs* 3 (CCSL 119B: 275), p. 144.

95. In his comment on 1 Samuel 25:43 (CCSL 119: 241–42), Bede cites two verses from the Song that speak of Christ as the church's brother. First he interprets Song 4:9 ("You have wounded my heart, my sister, my bride") as the Lord's affirmation that he shares one and the same human nature with his sister the church. Then he explains Song 8:1 ("Who will give you to me as my brother sucking my mother's breasts, so that I may find you outside and kiss you?") as being spoken by the church in the persona of the faithful people of old (that is, the synagogue) who were eagerly awaiting the incarnation of Christ. Both verses are interpreted similarly in the Song commentary, but at somewhat greater length.

96. See Arthur Holder, "The Anti-Pelagian Character of Bede's Commentary on the Song of Songs," in *Biblical Studies in the Early Middle Ages*, ed. Claudio Leonardi and Giovanni Orlandi (Florence: SISMEL, Edizioni del Galluzzo, 2005), 91–103.

97. See Arthur G. Holder, "The Patristic Sources of Bede's Commentary on the Song of Songs," *Studia Patristica* 34 (2001), 370–75.

98. For differing opinions on the question of Bede's having preached these homilies in church, see the preface by Benedicta Ward (affirmative) and the introduction by Lawrence T. Martin (negative) in Martin and Hurst, *Bede the Venerable: Homilies on the Gospels*.

99. See Lawrence T. Martin, "The Two Worlds in Bede's Homilies: The Biblical Event and the Listeners' Experience," in *De Ore Domini: Preacher and Word in the Middle Ages*, ed. Thomas L. Amos, Eugene A. Green, and Beverly Mayne Kienzle (Kalamazoo, MI: Medieval Institute Publications, 1989), 27–40.

ON THE SONG OF SONGS, Book 1

1. Apponius, *On the Song of Songs* 1.7 (CCSL 19: 5–6), prefaces his exposition of the first verse of the Song with a long digression on the various names given to the church in scripture, beginning with the comment: "Everyone knows that in Greek the word *Ecclesia* means 'congregation of the people,' which in Hebrew is called the 'synagogue.'" Bede ignores all the other names for the church listed by Apponius and subtly corrects the etymological information because he knows that *Ecclesia* and synagogue are derived from different Greek verbs. Apponius had treated the words as synonyms, but Bede distinguishes between them on the basis of their Greek etymologies and then uses the distinction to make a theological point about the New Covenant's superiority to the Old.

2. *typicus liber*, i.e., a book filled with allegorical types and symbols.

3. In Bede's *Commentary on the Apocalypse* (CCSL 121A: 245) he interpreted the "paps" (*mamillas*) of Revelation 1:13 as "the two testaments with which he feeds the body of the saints in union with himself." In Jerome's *Commentary on Isaiah* (CCSL 73A: 780) the image of the mother hen in Matthew 23:37 is cited as one of several biblical passages that, like Isaiah 66:13, depict God in maternal terms.

4. "this gift that" = *hoc donum quod*; Vulg.: *hunc quem* = "this thing (masc.) that." In his *Retraction on the Acts of the Apostles* (CCSL 121: 115) Bede notes that "this gift" is the original reading of the Greek text of Acts.

5. Gregory the Great, *Morals on Job* 24.4 (CCSL 143B: 1194).

6. Bede would have known the association of the Saracens (i.e., Muslim Arabs) with Ishmael from Isidore, *Chronica* 34 (CCSL 112: 31).

7. Jerome, *Interpretation of Hebrew Names* (CCSL 72: 63, 138).

8. The Latin is *fratribus*, literally, "brothers," translated here as "members." Note that the translations throughout this volume render such masculine terms in gender-inclusive language whenever Bede's Latin appears to be referring to both men and women.

9. Bede is here refuting Apponius, *On the Song of Songs* 1.45 (CCSL 19: 31).

10. In the introduction to *The Venerable Bede: Commentary on the Acts of the Apostles* (Kalamazoo, MI: Cistercian Publications, 1989), xix, Lawrence T. Martin notes that Bede is "at least in the majority of cases, not translating himself from the Greek text, but simply giving the parallel translation of *e*," which is the standard abbreviation for Bodleian Library MS Laudianus Graecus 35, a manuscript containing the Greek text of Acts with an Old Latin version alongside. Here, however, Bede does cite the Greek word.

11. On Bede's frequent references to heretics, see Arthur Holder, "Finding Snakes in the Grass: Bede as Heresiologist," in *Listen, O Isles, unto Me: Studies in Medieval Word and Image in Honour of Jennifer O'Reilly*, ed. Elizabeth Mullins and Diarmuid Scully (Cork: Cork University Press, 2011), 104–14.

12. Cf. Bede, *Homilies on the Gospels* 1.18 (CCSL 122: 130); Jerome, *Against Jovinian* 1.30 (PL 23: 252b); Pliny, *Natural History* 10.52.104 (LCL 3: 358).

13. Isidore, *Etymologies* 19.31.14 (Lindsay, vol. 2).

14. I.e., a pre-Vulgate Old Latin version.

15. According to his pupil and hagiographer Cuthbert, Bede on his deathbed echoed this same verse in his prayer: "My soul longs to see Christ my King in his beauty." *Epistle on the Death of Bede*, in *Bede's Ecclesiastical History*, ed. Bertram Colgrave and R. A. B. Mynors (Oxford: Oxford University Press, 1969; reprinted with corrections, 1991), 584.

16. This information and the material that follows come from Pliny, *Natural History* 12.26.42 (LCL 4: 30); cf. Bede, *Commentary on Mark* 4 (CCSL 120: 606).

17. Apponius, *Commentary on the Song of Songs* 3.17 (CCSL 19: 69).

18. Cf. Bede, *Commentary on the First Book of Samuel* 4 (CCSL 119: 223).

19. Pliny, *Natural History* 12.54.112–8 (LCL 4: 80–82).

20. Jerome, *Book of Places* (PL 23: 894 b–c).

21. Pliny, *Natural History* 12.54.118 (LCL 4: 82).

22. Jerome, *Interpretation of Hebrew Names* (CCSL 72: 93).

23. Cf. the Nicene Creed.

24. Isidore, *Etymologies* 17.7.33–4 (Lindsay, vol. 2).

25. Virgil, *Georgics* 3.414–5 (LCL 1: 204). On Bede's knowledge of Virgil, see Neil Wright, "Bede and Virgil," *Romanobarbarica* 6 (1981–82): 361–79, reprinted in *History and Literature in Late Antiquity and the Early Medieval West: Studies in Intertextuality* (Aldershot, UK: Ashgate Variorum, 1995).

26. Isidore, *Etymologies* 17.7.33 (Lindsay, vol. 2); cf. Pliny, *Natural History* 24.11.17 (LCL 7: 16).

27. Gregory the Great, *Morals on Job* 1.1 (CCSL 143: 25).

28. The Vulgate text does not have the word *rex* ("the king") here, but Bede has added it in order to make this verse conform to Song 1:4 (Vulg. 1:3) above.

29. Gregory the Great, *Homilies on the Gospels* 2.25.2 (CCSL 141: 207).

30. Gregory the Great, *Homilies on Ezekiel* 2.3.9 (CCSL 142: 242–3).

31. Gregory the Great, *Homilies on the Gospels* 2.21.2 (CCSL 141: 174); *Homilies on Ezekiel* 2.5.12 (CCSL 142: 285).

32. Isidore, *Etymologies* 12.1.15–17 (Lindsay, vol. 2).

33. Ovid, *Metamorphoses* 7.61. Bede may have picked this phrase up from his reading of a grammatical text.

34. The title given to Psalm 23 in the Vulgate is *Psalmus Dauid prima sabbati* ("A psalm of David, on the first day after the Sabbath"), i.e., on Sunday.

35. Apponius, *Commentary on the Song of Songs* 4.34 (CCSL 19: 104).

36. Jerome, *Against Jovinian* 1.30 (PL 23: 252b).

ON THE SONG OF SONGS, Book 2

1. Ambrose, *Hexameron* 3.12.50 (CSEL 32.1: 92).

2. *potandi*; some mss. read *putandi*, "for pruning."

3. Isidore, *Etymologies* 12.2.29 (Lindsay, vol. 2).

4. Pliny, *Natural History* 21.74.126 (LCL 6: 252).

5. Jerome, *Against Jovinian* 1.30 (PL 23: 252a–b).

6. Jerome, *Interpretation of Hebrew Names* (CCSL 72: 66, 81, 119).

7. See Arthur G. Holder, "Using Philosophers to Think With: The Venerable Bede on Christian Life and Practice," in *The Subjective*

Eye: Essays in Culture, Religion, and Gender in Honor of Margaret R. Miles, ed. Richard Valantasis et al. (Eugene, OR: Pickwick Publications, 2006), 48–58.

8. Gregory the Great, *Homilies on Ezekiel* 2.10.22–3 (CCSL 142: 396–97).

9. Jerome, *Interpretation of Hebrew Names* (CCSL 72: 138).

10. Jerome, *Interpretation of Hebrew Names* (CCSL 72: 108).

11. Jerome, *Interpretation of Hebrew Names* (CCSL 72: 75).

12. Gregory the Great, *Book of Pastoral Rule* 3.32 (SC 382: 492).

13. Bede is refuting Apponius, *On the Song of Songs* 5.33 (CCSL 19: 130).

14. Gregory the Great, *Homilies on Ezekiel* 2.3.13–14 (CCSL 142: 246).

15. Isidore, *Etymologies* 12.6.50; 19.28.2–4 (Lindsay, vol. 2).

16. Jerome, *Interpretation of Hebrew Names* (CCSL 72: 108; 121).

17. Gregory the Great, *Morals on Job* 9.11 (CCSL 143: 469).

18. Jerome, *Interpretation of Hebrew Names* (CCSL 72: 67).

19. Gregory the Great, *Morals on Job* 11.33 (CCSL 143A: 610–11).

20. Gregory the Great, *Morals on Job* 9.11 (CCSL 143: 469).

21. Augustine, *On Christian Doctrine* 2.6.7 (CCSL 32: 35–36).

22. Augustine, *On Christian Doctrine* 2.6.7 (CCSL 32: 36).

23. See Bede's comment on the bride's cheeks in Song 1:10 (Vulg. 1:9), p. 53.

24. See George Hardin Brown, "Patristic Pomegranates, from Ambrose and Apponius to Bede," in *Latin Learning and English Lore: Studies in Anglo-Saxon Literature for Michael Lapidge*, ed. Katherine O'Brien O'Keeffe and Andy Orchard, 2 vols. (Toronto: University of Toronto Press, 2005), 1:132–49; idem, "Bede and the Cross," in *Cross and Culture in Anglo-Saxon England: Studies in Honor of George Hardin Brown*, ed. Karen Louise Jolly, Catherine E. Karkov, and Sarah Larratt Keefer (Morgantown: West Virginia University Press, 2007), 19–35.

25. See Bede's comment on the bride's neck in Song 1:10–11 (Vulg. 1:9–10), p. 53.

26. Jerome, *Interpretation of Hebrew Names* (CCSL 72: 103).

27. Gregory the Great, *Homilies on Ezekiel* 2.3.23 (CCSL 142: 255).

THE VENERABLE BEDE

ON THE SONG OF SONGS, Book 3

1. Jerome, *Interpretation of Hebrew Names* (CCSL 72: 108).

2. Bede also explains night as the earth's shadow (with reference to Sg 2:16–17) in *The Reckoning of Time* 7 (CCSL 123B: 296–97).

3. Gregory the Great, *Morals on Job* 23.20 (CCSL 143B: 1173).

4. Jerome, *Commentary on Ezekiel* 5 (CCSL 75: 222).

5. Gregory the Great, *Morals on Job* 17.22 (CCSL 143A: 882–83).

6. Gregory the Great, *Morals on Job* 19.1 (CCSL 143A: 956).

7. See Bede's comment on the eyes of the bride in Song 1:15 (Vulg. 1:14), p. 60.

8. See Bede's comment on the hair of the bride in Song 4:1, p. 106.

9. See Bede's comments on the bride's neck in Song 1:10 (Vulg. 1:9), p. 53, and in Song 4:4, p. 111.

10. Christ is a nursing mother converting the food of divine wisdom into milk in Augustine, *Homilies on the Gospel of John* 98.6 (CCSL 36: 579).

11. Gregory the Great, *Homilies on the Gospels* 2.24.5 (CCSL 141: 201); note, however, that Gregory interprets honey in wax as Christ's divinity in his humanity, whereas Bede refers to the spiritual sense contained in the letter of scripture.

12. Cf. Bede, *On the Tabernacle* 1 (CCSL 119A: 25); John Cassian, *Conferences* 14.8 (SC 54: 189–92).

13. In *On Schemes and Tropes* 2.2 (CCSL 123A: 164–69), Bede's example of "allegory in deeds" is that of Abraham's two wives, Hagar and Sarah, who were actual historical personages that St. Paul took as types of the two covenants (Gal 4:21–31). As an example of "allegory in words," Bede cites the purely verbal (i.e., non-historical) imagery of Isaiah 11:1: "And there shall come forth a rod out of the root of Jesse, and a flower shall rise up out of his root."

14. Isidore, *Etymologies* 17.8.2 (Lindsay, vol. 2); Pliny, *Natural History* 12.31.55—12.32.58 (LCL 4: 38–40).

15. The information in the rest of this paragraph comes from Pliny, *Natural History* 12.30.51 and 12.32.58–60 (LCL 4: 36–38; 40–42).

16. Pliny, *Natural History* 12.51.109 (LCL 4: 78); cf. 13.2.5 (LCL 4: 100).

17. Apponius, *Commentary on the Song of Songs* 7.41 (CCSL 19: 172).

18. Isidore, *Etymologies* 17.8.12 (Lindsay, vol. 2); cf. Pliny, *Natural History* 12.43.95–97 (LCL 4: 68–70).

19. The botanical information here and in the remainder of this paragraph is derived from Isidore, *Etymologies* 17.8.10 (Lindsay, vol. 2).

20. Isidore, *Etymologies* 17.8.4 (Lindsay, vol. 2); cf. Pliny, *Natural History* 12.34.67 (LCL 4: 48).

21. Isidore, *Etymologies* 17.8.9 (Lindsay, vol. 2).

22. Jerome, *Commentary on Ezekiel* 5 and 8 (CCSL 75: 222, 360).

23. Gregory the Great, *Morals on Job* 31.27 (CCSL 143B: 1588).

24. Gregory the Great, *Homilies on Ezekiel* 1.2.9 (CCSL 142: 22).

25. Gregory the Great, *Homilies on the Gospels* 2.25.2 (CCSL 141: 206).

26. Cf. the Nicene Creed.

27. Some mss. read "she is asked…"

28. *magistra ueritas;* that is, Christ as Holy Wisdom.

29. Apponius, *Commentary on the Song of Songs* 8.37 (CCSL 19: 196).

30. These passages from Julian of Eclanum's treatise *On Love* have been preserved only through Bede's quotation of them here.

31. Pliny, *Natural History* 12.62.134 (LCL 4: 92).

32. Apponius, *Commentary on the Song of Songs* 8.41 (CCSL 19: 197–98). Bede uses the imagery of doves on the waters in *Commentary on Luke* 1 (CCSL 120: 64) and again (with reference to Sg 5:12) in *Homilies on the Gospels* 1.12 (CCSL 122: 86).

ON THE SONG OF SONGS, Book 4

1. For Bede's knowledge of lathes, see Paul Meyvaert, "Bede the Scholar," in *Famulus Christi: Essays in Commemoration of the Thirteenth Centenary of the Birth of the Venerable Bede*, ed. Gerald Bonner (London: SPCK, 1976), 47.

2. Isidore, *Etymologies* 16.9.3 (Lindsay, vol. 2).

3. Virgil, *Eclogues* 3.63 (LCL 1: 42).

4. I.e., a pre-Vulgate Old Latin version.

5. Pliny, *Natural History* 8.5.12 (LCL 3: 10).

6. Jerome, *Interpretation of Hebrew Names* (CCSL 72: 147–48).

7. Gregory the Great, *Homilies on Ezekiel* 1.8.6 (CCSL 142: 105).

8. Jerome, *Interpretation of Hebrew Names* (CCSL 72: 67).

9. Jerome, *Interpretation of Hebrew Names* (CCSL 72: 67); cf. Gn 27:36.

10. See Bede's comments on Song 1:10 (Vulg. 1:9), p. 53, and Song 4:3, p. 110.

11. CCSL: *ministerium*, "ministers," emended to *mysterium*. Alexander Souter, *A Glossary of Later Latin to 600 AD* (Oxford: Clarendon Press, 1949), 253, s.v. *ministerium*, notes that these two words are often confused in manuscripts.

12. Jerome, *Commentary on Isaiah* 3 and 11 (CCSL 73: 111, 459).

13. Isidore, *Etymologies* 18.7.22 (Lindsay, vol. 2).

14. Jerome, *On the Prophet Jeremiah* 1.12 (CCSL 74: 8).

15. Jerome, *Interpretation of Hebrew Names* (CCSL 72: 74).

16. Cf. Apponius, *On the Song of Songs* 9.50 (CCSL 19: 234).

17. Gregory the Great, *Homilies on the Gospels* 1.7.3 and 2.22.9 (CCSL 141: 50, 190).

18. Jerome, *Against Jovinian* 1.31 (PL 23: 254b–c).

19. Apponius, *Commentary on the Song of Songs* 9.46 (CCSL 19: 232–33).

20. Virgil, *Aeneid* 1.723–4 (LCL 1: 312), perhaps by way of Isidore, *Etymologies* 20.1.3 (Lindsay, vol. 2).

21. See Bede's comment above on Song 5:14, p. 00: *his hands are rounded gold.*

22. See Bede's comments on Song 4:5, pp. 114–15.

23. Jerome, *Commentary on Ecclesiastes* 12.11 (CCSL 72: 358).

24. Jerome, *Interpretation of Hebrew Names* (CCSL 72: 81).

25. For what follows, see Gregory the Great, *Homilies on Ezekiel* 1.11.7 (CCSL 142: 172); *Morals on Job* 31.44 (CCSL 143B: 1609); *Book of Pastoral Rule* 1.11 and 3.32 (SC 381: 166; SC 382: 494).

26. Discretion is "the mother of virtues" in *Rule of Benedict* 64.19.

27. Jerome, *Interpretation of Hebrew Names* (CCSL 72: 64; 145).

ON THE SONG OF SONGS, Book 5

1. *per conuersationem*: alternate translations would be "through their manner of life" or "through conversion."

2. Jerome, *Interpretation of Hebrew Names* (CCSL 72: 111).

3. Jerome, *Interpretation of Hebrew Names* (CCSL 72: 110).

4. "pieces of wool," *uellera* (nominative plural), following the reading of PL rather than the grammatically difficult *uellere* (ablative singular) of the CCSL edition.

5. Isidore, *Etymologies* 12.6.50 and 19.28.4 (Lindsay, vol. 2).

6. Isidore, *Etymologies* 17.7.1 (Lindsay, vol. 2).

7. *dispensatione.*

8. Isidore, *Etymologies* 17.9.30 (Lindsay, vol. 2).

9. Ambrose, *Hexameron* (CSEL 32.1: 85).

10. Isidore, *Etymologies* 17.9.30 (Lindsay, vol. 2).

11. Gregory the Great, *Homilies on the Gospels* 1.15.2 (CCSL 141: 105).

12. The followers of Photinus (bishop of Sirmium, d. 376) were condemned at the Council of Constantinople in 381 and also by Emperor Theodosius II in 428 for allegedly denying the preexistence of Christ before the incarnation.

13. The Manichaeans were followers of the Persian teacher Mani (216–76). Their dualistic teaching claimed that particles of light created by God are imprisoned in the world of matter, which is identified as the creation of demonic powers.

14. Here Bede is apparently correcting Julian of Eclanum. In the prologue to this commentary (CCSL 119B: 172–73), Bede had taken issue with Julian's interpretation of Song 8:2 in which the speaker (the synagogue for Bede, but apparently Christ himself for Julian) says, "I will seize you and lead you into my mother's house." Identifying the mother as the Blessed Virgin, Julian had argued that Christ's entry into Mary's body (that is to say, her "house") showed that there was nothing sinful about human birth, since the Lord was completely encircled in flesh and at the same time free from sin. Such an interpretation, so useful to Julian's Pelagian program of affirming the natural goodness of human procreation, was dependent upon the identification of the Virgin as the "mother" of both 8:1 and 8:2. By denying such an interpretation here, Bede was effectively countering Julian's reading of the following verse as well.

15. Pliny, *Natural History* 13.34.112 (LCL 4: 164).

16. Isidore, *Etymologies* 20.3.4 (Lindsay, vol. 2).

17. Jerome, *Commentary on Zechariah the Prophet* 3 (CCSL 76A: 870).

18. Gregory the Great, *Morals on Job* 19.12 (CCSL 143A: 970).

19. I.e., AD 33–58.

20. The negative element does not appear in the majority of early manuscripts, but it is required by the context.

21. Ambrose, *Hexameron* (CSEL 32.1: 92–94); cf. Is 5:1–2; Mt 21:33; Mk 12:1.

22. The CCSL text reads *ecclesiam respondit* ("he responds to the church"), but Bede's interpretation of the following verse clearly implies that it is spoken by the church to Christ.

23. Gregory the Great, *Morals on Job* 17.27 (CCSL 143A: 874).

HOMILIES ON THE GOSPELS

1. In *Commentary on Luke* 1 (CCSL 120: 67), Bede borrows from Jerome's *Against Helvidius* (PL 23: 187C) to note that when Luke referred to Joseph as the "father" of Jesus, he was simply following *uera lex historiae* ("a true law of history") by reporting vulgar opinion whether or not it was factually true. In the preface to the *Ecclesiastical History*, Bede uses the same term to describe his practice as a historian writing for the edification of posterity.

2. Jerome, *Commentary on Matthew* 15.25 (CCSL 77: 133).

3. The alliteration in Bede's Latin is *misericors medicus miserorum*.

4. Jerome, *Commentary on Matthew* 15.23–24 (CCSL 77: 133).

5. The Old Testament houses of God were a favorite theme for Bede. In addition to this homily and another (2.24) on the dedication of a church, see *On the Tabernacle*, trans. Arthur G. Holder (Liverpool: Liverpool University Press, 1994); *On the Temple*, trans. Seán Connolly (Liverpool: Liverpool University Press, 1995); and *On Ezra and Nehemiah*, trans. Scott DeGregorio (Liverpool: Liverpool University Press, 2006).

6. Isidore, *Etymologies* 17.7.49 (Lindsay, vol. 2).

7. Jerome, *Commentary on Matthew* 7.21 (CCSL 77: 45).

8. Gregory the Great, *Homilies on Ezekiel* 2 (CCSL 142: 359).

9. Josephus, *Antiquities of the Jews* 8.3.2 (LCL 5: 604).

10. *per uiscera pietatis*, literally, "through the internal organs of kindness." There is a subtle biblical allusion here, which is explicit in Bede's explication of Exodus 26:16 in *On the Tabernacle* 2 (CCSL 119A: 60, trans. Holder, 66–67): "Accordingly, let us consider that one of the boards of the tabernacle might suggest how the apostle Paul expanded himself in two ways. Concerning [his] inward parts (that is, the wide-

ness of [his] heart), he says: *Our mouth is open to you, O Corinthians; our heart is expanded. You are not being restricted in us, but you are restricted in your own internal parts* [uisceribus]. *I speak as to children—be yourselves expanded also* (2 Cor 6:11–3)."

11. Bede's allusion is to the so-called Roman psalter based on the Greek text of the Septuagint, in which Psalm 83:8 begins: "For the law-giver shall give a blessing." These words do not appear in the Vulgate (Gallican) psalter that Jerome translated from the Greek he found in Origen's *Hexapla* or in modern versions that translate directly from the Hebrew.

ECCLESIASTICAL HISTORY OF THE ENGLISH PEOPLE

1. Presumably 625, since Bede says further on in this chapter that Paulinus was consecrated bishop in that year. But these events may have been as early as 618/9. See J. M. Wallace-Hadrill, *Bede's Ecclesiastical History of the English People: A Historical Commentary* (Oxford: Clarendon Press, 1988), 65.

2. The hide was the customary Anglo-Saxon unit of land area, indicating the amount of land necessary to sustain one household.

3. The system of dating events from Christ's incarnation (understood as the beginning of the world's Sixth Age) had been used by the Scythian monk Dionysius Exiguus in the sixth century, but Bede's *Ecclesiastical History* was the first major historical work to employ that chronological system consistently.

4. As the king's thegn (Anglo-Saxon term for a freeman granted land by the king in return for military service), Lilla was pledged to give his life for the king.

5. The reference is to the events of the previous chapter, in which Paulinus reminded Edwin of a vision he had received while in exile and his promise to follow the direction of a mysterious visitor (apparently Paulinus) who assured him that he would be delivered from his troubles and made king of Northumbria.

6. Bede uses the Latin terms *ducibus ac ministris* ("leaders and ministers") but the reference is clearly to the noble members of the king's council known in Anglo-Saxon terminology as ealdormen and thegns.

7. Coifi's act of profaning the temple may reflect the pagan Germanic ritual in which followers of Woden would cast a spear over their enemies in order to dedicate their destruction in honor of the god.

8. Bede uses the Latin word *Scotti* to refer to the Irish people, both those in Ireland and those living in what is now Scotland.

9. Oswald, king of Northumbria (634–42), was revered by Bede as a saint and by later generations as a martyr. See Clare Stancliffe and Eric Cambridge, eds., *Oswald: Northumbrian King to European Saint* (Stamford, UK: Paul Watkins, 1995).

10. Aidan was bishop of Lindisfarne ca. 634–51.

11. For an explanation of the complicated calendrical issues involved in the controversy over the date of Easter that divided Christians in early medieval England and Ireland, see Faith Wallis's introduction to her translation of Bede's *The Reckoning of Time* (Liverpool: Liverpool University Press, 1999), xxxiv–lxiii.

12. Anatolius (died ca. 282) was bishop of Laodicea on the coast of Syria.

13. Justin II, nephew of Justinian I, reigned as Byzantine emperor 565–78.

14. For Columba (died ca. 597, known in Irish as Colum Cille), see the introduction in Richard Sharpe, ed. and trans., *Adomnán of Iona: Life of St. Columba* (London: Penguin Classics, 1995); Brian Lacey, *Colum Cille and the Columban Tradition* (Dublin: Four Courts Press, 1997); and Dauvit Broun and Thomas Owen Clancy, eds., *Spes Scotorum, Hope of Scots: Saint Columba, Iona and Scotland* (Edinburgh: T&T Clark, 1999).

15. The Picts were the indigenous pre-literate people of northern Scotland who had never been conquered by the Romans.

16. For Ninian (early fifth-century bishop of Whithorn in southern Scotland, who was also known as Nynia), see John MacQueen and Winifred MacQueen, *St. Nynia*, 2nd ed. (Edinburgh: John Donald Publishers, 2005).

17. For Martin (died 397), the former soldier who became a monk and later bishop of Tours, see Clare Stancliffe, *St. Martin and His Hagiographer: History and Miracle in Sulpicius Severus* (Oxford: Clarendon Press, 1983).

18. See Máire Herbert, *Iona, Kells and Derry: The History and Hagiography of the Monastic Familia of Columba* (Oxford: Clarendon Press, 1988).

19. Rule by abbots (rather than bishops) used to be considered a distinctive feature of Celtic Christianity, but it appears rather to have been peculiar to the Columban monastic family. See Richard Sharpe, "Churches and Communities in Early Medieval Ireland," in *Pastoral Care before the Parish*, ed. John Blair and Richard Sharpe, 81–109 (Leicester: Leicester University Press, 1992).

20. Bede seems not to have known the life of Columba written by the Irish saint's successor, Adamnán, though he produced an abridgement of Adamnán's work *On the Holy Places* and included extracts in the *Ecclesiastical History* 5.15–17, where he notes that Adamnán had visited Northumbria.

21. This Egbert (not the same as the later bishop of York to whom Bede wrote in 734) lived on Iona from 716 to 729. Bede praises his virtuous life and orthodox teaching again in *Ecclesiastical History* 3.27.

22. Bede knew the Irish on Iona had been wrongly accused of following the practice of the late second-century Quartodeciman heretics because they observed Easter on the fourteenth day of the Jewish month of Nisan regardless of the day of the week on which it occurred. See Dáibhí O'Crónín, "'New Heresy for Old': Pelagianism in Ireland and the Papal Letter of 640," *Speculum* 60 (1985): 505–16.

23. Bede makes the same point about persisting in faith and good works so that one's errors will eventually be corrected in his explanation of Romans 14:5 in *On Eight Questions* 5 (PL 93: 458A–B), where he also cites Philippians 3:15.

24. Fasting on Wednesday (the day of Christ's betrayal) and Friday (the day of his crucifixion) was common Christian practice from the earliest times, probably in contradistinction from the Jewish practice of fasting on Monday and Thursday. The ninth hour after sunrise would be about 3:00 p.m.

25. For the background, see David Anthony Edgell Pelteret, *Slavery in Early Mediaeval England: From the Reign of Alfred until the Twelfth Century* (Woodbridge, UK: Boydell Press, 1995).

26. *Rule of Benedict* 64:19.

27. I.e., at nine o'clock in the morning.

28. For appreciative interpretations of Hild's contributions to Anglo-Saxon religious and literary culture, see Christine Fell, "Hild, Abbess of Streanæshalch," in *Hagiography and Medieval Literature: A Symposium*, ed. Hans Bekker-Nielsen (Odense, Denmark: Odense University Press, 1981), 76–99; Peter Hunter Blair, "Whitby as a Centre of Learning in the Seventh Century," in *Learning and Literature*

in Anglo-Saxon England: Studies Presented to Peter Clemoes on the Occasion of his Sixty-Fifth Birthday, ed. Michael Lapidge and Helmut Gneuss (Cambridge: Cambridge University Press, 1985), 3–32; and Patrick Wormald, "Hilda, Saint and Scholar (614–680)," in *The Times of Bede: Studies in Early English Christian Society and Its Historian*, ed. Stephen Baxter (Malden, MA: Blackwell Publishing, 2006), 267–76. For critical readings that see Bede's masculine monastic ideal as leading him to obscure Hild's active role in teaching and political life, see Stephanie Hollis, *Anglo-Saxon Women and the Church: Sharing a Common Fate* (Woodbridge, UK: Boydell Press, 1992), 243–70; and Clare Lees and Gillian Overing, "Patristic Maternity: Bede, Hild, and Cultural Production," in *Double Agents: Women and Clerical Culture in Anglo-Saxon England* (Philadelphia: University of Pennsylvania Press, 2001), 15–39.

29. Whitby (and presumably Hartlepool, since Whitby was modeled after it) was a double monastery, that is, monks and nuns lived in separate houses under the rule of a single abbess. See Sarah Foot, *Veiled Women*, vol. 1, *The Disappearance of Nuns from Anglo-Saxon England* (Aldershot: Ashgate, 2000), 49–56.

30. See Glenn Olsen, "Bede as Historian: The Evidence from His Observations on the Life of the First Christian Community in Jerusalem," *Journal of Ecclesiastical History* 33 (1982): 519–30.

31. This is the famous story of Cædmon, the first English poet. See Allen J. Frantzen and John Hines, eds., *Cædmon's Hymn and Material Culture in the World of Bede* (Morgantown: West Virginia University Press, 2007).

32. I.e., Whitby.

33. Bede records Cædmon's hymn only in Latin, but the Old English is preserved in several Latin and Old English manuscripts of the *Ecclesiastical History*.

34. As becomes clear further on in this chapter, Coldingham was in fact a double monastery containing both monks and nuns.

35. This is not Adamnán the abbot of Iona who wrote a life of Columba.

36. See Gerald Bonner, David Rollason, and Clare Stancliffe, eds., *St. Cuthbert: His Cult and Community to AD 1200* (Woodbridge, UK: Boydell Press, 1989).

37. Augustine of Canterbury was sent as a missionary to England by Gregory the Great, arriving in 597. His work in Kent is chronicled

by Bede in *Ecclesiastical History* 1.23—2.3. See Richard Gameson, ed., *St. Augustine and the Conversion of England* (Stroud, UK: Sutton, 1999).

38. Bede's two lives of Cuthbert were based on an anonymous prose life by a monk of Lindisfarne. The metrical life (c. 706–7), which sacrifices historical detail in favor of symbolic allusion, puts emphasis on the saint's miracles. The prose life (c. 721) was written at the request of Bishop Eadfrith and the monks at Lindisfarne; portions were incorporated directly into the *Ecclesiastical History*.

39. Theodore of Tarsus, a Greek monk living in Rome, was consecrated archbishop of Canterbury in 668 and died in 690. In *Ecclesiastical History* 4.2, Bede describes him as "the first of the archbishops whom the whole church of the English consented to obey." See Michael Lapidge, ed., *Archbishop Theodore: Commemorative Studies on His Life and Influence* (Cambridge: Cambridge University Press, 1995).

40. On the four-part otherworld in Dryhthelm's vision, see Ananya Jahanara Kabir, *Paradise, Death, and Doomsday in Anglo-Saxon Literature* (Cambridge, UK: Cambridge University Press, 2001), 77–110. On the influence of Gregory the Great's *Dialogues*, see William D. McCready, *Miracles and the Venerable Bede* (Toronto: Pontifical Institute of Mediaeval Studies, 1994), 179–87.

41. I.e., northeast.

42. Virgil, *Aeneid* 6.268 (LCL 1: 550).

43. I.e., southeast.

Selected Bibliography

GENERAL STUDIES

Brown, George Hardin. *A Companion to Bede*. Woodbridge, UK: Boydell Press, 2009.

Carroll, Sister M. Thomas Aquinas. *The Venerable Bede: His Spiritual Teachings*. Washington, DC: Catholic University of America Press, 1946.

DeGregorio, Scott, ed. *The Cambridge Companion to Bede*. Cambridge, UK: Cambridge University Press, 2010.

———, ed. *Innovation and Tradition in the Writings of the Venerable Bede*. Morgantown: West Virginia University Press, 2006.

Hunter Blair, Peter. *The World of Bede*. Rev. ed. Cambridge, UK: Cambridge University Press, 1990.

Ward, Benedicta. *The Venerable Bede*. Wilton, CT: Morehouse Publishing, 1990; reprinted Kalamazoo, MI: Cistercian Publications, 1998.

ON THE SONG OF SONGS

Barrows, Mary Prentice Lillie. "Bede's *Allegorical Exposition of the Canticle of Canticles*: A Study in Early Medieval Allegorical Exegesis." PhD dissertation, University of California at Berkeley, 1962.

Holder, Arthur G. "Christ as Incarnate Wisdom in Bede's Commentary on the Song of Songs." In *Innovation and Tradition in the Writings of the Venerable Bede*, edited by Scott DeGregorio, 169–88. Morgantown: West Virginia University Press, 2006.

———. "The Anti-Pelagian Character of Bede's Commentary on the Song of Songs." In *Biblical Studies in the Early Middle Ages*, edited by Claudio Leonardi and Giovanni Orlandi, 91–103. Florence: SISMEL, Edizioni del Galluzzo, 2005.

———. "The Patristic Sources of Bede's Commentary on the Song of Songs." *Studia Patristica* 34 (2001): 370–75.

HOMILIES ON THE GOSPELS

Martin, Lawrence T. "The Two Worlds in Bede's Homilies: The Biblical Event and the Listeners' Experience." In *De Ore Domini: Preacher and Word in the Middle Ages*, edited by Thomas L. Amos, Eugene A. Green, and Beverly Mayne Kienzle, 27–40. Kalamazoo, MI: Medieval Institute Publications, 1989.

Martin, Lawrence T., and David Hurst, trans. *Bede the Venerable: Homilies on the Gospels*. 2 vols. Kalamazoo, MI: Cistercian Publications, 1991.

ECCLESIASTICAL HISTORY OF THE ENGLISH PEOPLE

Colgrave, Bertram, and R. A. B. Mynors, eds. *Bede's Ecclesiastical History*. Oxford: Oxford University Press, 1969; reprinted with corrections, 1991.

Higham, N. J. *(Re-)Reading Bede*. London: Routledge, 2006.

McClure, Judith, and Roger Collins, eds. *Bede: The Ecclesiastical History of the English People; The Greater Chronicle; Bede's Letter to Egbert*. Oxford: Oxford University Press, 1994.

Plummer, Charles, ed. *Venerabilis Baedae opera historica*. Oxford: Clarendon Press, 1896.

Sherley-Price, Leo. *Bede: A History of the English Church and People with Bede's Letter to Egbert and Cuthbert's Letter on the Death of Bede*. Rev. ed. Revised by R. E. Latham. Edited by D. H. Farmer. Harmondsworth: Penguin Books, 1990.

Wallace-Hadrill, J. M. *Bede's Ecclesiastical History of the English People: A Historical Commentary*. Oxford: Clarendon Press, 1988.

Wright, J. Robert. *A Companion to Bede: A Reader's Commentary on "The Ecclesiastical History of the English People."* Grand Rapids, MI: William B. Eerdmans Publishing Company, 2008.

OTHER SECONDARY WORKS CITED

Astell, Ann W. *The Song of Songs in the Middle Ages*. Ithaca, NY: Cornell University Press, 1990.

Blair, John. *The Church in Anglo-Saxon Society*. Oxford: Oxford University Press, 2005.

Bonner, Gerald. "Ireland and Rome: The Double Inheritance of Christian Northumbria." In *Saints, Scholars, and Heroes: Studies in Medieval Culture in Honour of Charles W. Jones*, vol. 1, *The Anglo-Saxon Heritage*, edited by Margot H. King and Wesley M. Stevens, 101–16. Collegeville, MN: Hill Monastic Manuscript Library, Saint John's Abbey and University, 1979.

———. "Bede and Medieval Civilization." *Anglo-Saxon England* 2 (1973): 71–90.

Bonner, Gerald, David Rollason, and Clare Stancliffe, eds. *St. Cuthbert: His Cult and Community to AD 1200*. Woodbridge, UK: Boydell Press, 1989.

Bradley, Ritamary. "Patristic Background of the Motherhood Similitude in Julian of Norwich." *Christian Scholar's Review* 8 (1978): 101–13.

Brooks, Nicholas. "Bede and the English." Jarrow Lecture, 1999.

Broun, Dauvit, and Thomas Owen Clancy, eds. *Spes Scotorum, Hope of Scots: Saint Columba, Iona and Scotland*. Edinburgh: T&T Clark, 1999.

Brown, George Hardin. "Bede and the Cross." In *Cross and Culture in Anglo-Saxon England: Studies in Honor of George Hardin Brown*, edited by Karen Louise Jolly, Catherine E. Karkov, and Sarah Larratt Keefer, 19–35. Morgantown: West Virginia University Press, 2007.

———. "Patristic Pomegranates, from Ambrose and Apponius to Bede." In *Latin Learning and English Lore: Studies in Anglo-Saxon Literature for Michael Lapidge*, edited by Katherine

O'Brien O'Keeffe and Andy Orchard, vol. 1: 132–49. Toronto: University of Toronto Press, 2005.

Bynum, Caroline Walker. *Jesus as Mother: Studies in the Spirituality of the High Middle Ages*. Berkeley and Los Angeles: University of California Press, 1982.

Corning, Caitlin. *The Celtic and Roman Traditions: Conflict and Consensus in the Early Medieval Church*. New York: Palgrave Macmillan, 2006.

Davidse, Jan. "The Sense of History in the Works of the Venerable Bede." *Studi Medievali* 23 (1982): 647–95.

DeGregorio, Scott. "Bede, the Monk, as Exegete: Evidence from the Commentary on Ezra-Nehemiah." *Revue Bénédictine* 115 (2005): 343–69.

———."Bede's *In Ezram et Neemiam* and the Reform of the Northumbrian Church." *Speculum* 79 (2004): 1–25.

———. "*Nostrorum socordiam temporum*: The Reforming Impulse of Bede's Later Exegesis." *Early Medieval Europe* 11 (2002): 107–22.

———. "The Venerable Bede and Gregory the Great: Exegetical Connections, Spiritual Departures." *Early Medieval Europe* 18 (2010): 43–60.

———. "The Venerable Bede on Prayer and Contemplation." *Traditio* 54 (1999): 1–39.

Fell, Christine. "Hild, Abbess of Streanæshalch." In *Hagiography and Medieval Literature: A Symposium*, edited by Hans Bekker-Nielsen, 76–99. Odense, Denmark: Odense University Press, 1981.

Foley, W. Trent, and Nicholas J. Higham. "Bede on the Britons." *Early Medieval Europe* 17 (2009): 154–85.

Foot, Sarah. *Monastic Life in Anglo-Saxon England, c. 600–900*. Cambridge, UK: Cambridge University Press, 2006.

———. *Veiled Women*. Vol. 1, *The Disappearance of Nuns from Anglo-Saxon England*. Aldershot: Ashgate, 2000.

Frantzen, Allen J., and John Hines, eds. *Cædmon's Hymn and Material Culture in the World of Bede*. Morgantown: West Virginia University Press, 2007.

Gameson, Richard, ed. *St. Augustine and the Conversion of England*. Stroud, UK: Sutton, 1999.

Herbert, Máire. *Iona, Kells, and Derry: The History and Hagiography of the Monastic Familia of Columba*. Oxford: Clarendon Press, 1988.

Holder, Arthur G. "Bede and the Tradition of Patristic Exegesis," *Anglican Theological Review* 72 (1990): 399–411.

———. "The Feminine Christ in Bede's Biblical Commentaries." In *Bède le Vénérable entre tradition et postérité*, edited by Stéphane Lebecq, Michel Perrin, and Olivier Szerwiniack, 109–18. Lille: 3-CEGES, 2005.

———. "Finding Snakes in the Grass: Bede as Heresiologist." In *Listen, O Isles, unto Me: Studies in Medieval Word and Image in Honour of Jennifer O'Reilly*, edited by Elizabeth Mullins and Diarmuid Scully, 105–14. Cork: Cork University Press, 2011.

———. "Using Philosophers to Think With: The Venerable Bede on Christian Life and Practice." In *The Subjective Eye: Essays in Culture, Religion, and Gender in Honor of Margaret R. Miles*, edited by Richard Valantasis in collaboration with Deborah J. Haynes, James D. Smith III, and Janet F. Carlson, 48–58. Eugene, OR: Pickwick Publications, 2006.

———. "The Venerable Bede on the Mysteries of Our Salvation." *American Benedictine Review* 42 (1991): 140–62.

———. "Whitby and All That: The Search for Anglican Origins." *Anglican Theological Review* 85 (2003): 231–52.

Hollis, Stephanie. *Anglo-Saxon Women and the Church: Sharing a Common Fate*. Woodbridge, UK: Boydell Press, 1992.

Hunter Blair, Peter. "Whitby as a Centre of Learning in the Seventh Century." In *Learning and Literature in Anglo-Saxon England: Studies Presented to Peter Clemoes on the Occasion of his Sixty-Fifth Birthday*, edited by Michael Lapidge and Helmut Gneuss, 3–32. Cambridge, UK: Cambridge University Press, 1985.

Kabir, Ananya Jahanara. *Paradise, Death, and Doomsday in Anglo-Saxon Literature*. Cambridge, UK: Cambridge University Press, 2001.

Lacey, Brian. *Colum Cille and the Columban Tradition*. Dublin: Four Courts Press, 1997.

Laistner, M. L. W. "The Library of the Venerable Bede." In *Bede: His Life, Times, and Writings*, edited by A. Hamilton Thompson, 237–66. Oxford: Clarendon Press, 1935.

Lapidge, Michael, ed. *Archbishop Theodore: Commemorative Studies on His Life and Influence*. Cambridge: Cambridge University Press, 1995.

———. "Bede the Poet." Jarrow Lecture, 1993.

———. *The Anglo-Saxon Library*. Oxford: Oxford University Press, 2006.

Leclercq, Jean. *The Love of Learning and the Desire for God*. 3rd ed. Translated by Catherine Misrahi. New York: Fordham University Press, 1982.

Lees, Clare, and Gillian Overing. *Double Agents: Women and Clerical Culture in Anglo-Saxon England*. Philadelphia: University of Pennsylvania Press, 2001.

MacQueen, John, and Winifred MacQueen. *St. Nynia*. 2nd ed. Edinburgh: John Donald Publishers, 2005.

Matter, E. Ann. *The Voice of My Beloved: The Song of Songs in Western Medieval Christianity*. Philadelphia: University of Pennsylvania Press, 1990.

Mayr-Harting, Henry. *The Coming of Christianity to Anglo-Saxon England*. 3rd ed. University Park: Pennsylvania State University Press, 1991.

———. "The Venerable Bede, the Rule of St. Benedict, and Social Class." Jarrow Lecture, 1976.

McCready, William D. *Miracles and the Venerable Bede*. Toronto: Pontifical Institute of Mediaeval Studies, 1994.

Meyvaert, Paul. "Bede and Gregory the Great." Jarrow Lecture, 1964.

———. "Bede the Scholar." In *Famulus Christi: Essays in Commemoration of the Thirteenth Centenary of the Birth of the Venerable Bede*, edited by Gerald Bonner, 40–69. London: SPCK, 1976.

Newman, Barbara. *God and the Goddesses: Vision, Poetry, and Belief in the Middle Ages*. Philadelphia: University of Pennsylvania Press, 2003.

O'Crónín, Dáibhí. "'New Heresy for Old': Pelagianism in Ireland and the Papal Letter of 640." *Speculum* 60 (1985): 505–16.

Olsen, Glenn. "Bede as Historian: The Evidence from His Observations on the Life of the First Christian Community in Jerusalem." *Journal of Ecclesiastical History* 33 (1982): 519–30.

O'Reilly, Jennifer. "Bede on Seeing the God of Gods in Zion." In *Text, Image, Interpretation: Studies in Anglo-Saxon Literature and Its Insular Context in Honour of Éamonn Ó Carragáin*, edited by Alastair Minnis and Jane Roberts, 3–29. Turnhout: Brepols Publishers, 2007.

Pelteret, David Anthony Edgell. *Slavery in Early Mediaeval England: From the Reign of Alfred until the Twelfth Century*. Woodbridge, UK: Boydell Press, 1995.

Raw, Barbara C. *Trinity and Incarnation in Anglo-Saxon Art and Thought*. Cambridge, UK: Cambridge University Press, 1997.

Rollason, David. *Saints and Relics in Anglo-Saxon England*. Oxford: Basil Blackwell, 1989.

Scheil, Andrew P. *The Footsteps of Israel: Understanding Jews in Anglo-Saxon England*. Ann Arbor: University of Michigan Press, 2004.

Sharpe, Richard. "Churches and Communities in Early Medieval Ireland." In *Pastoral Care before the Parish*, edited by John Blair and Richard Sharpe, 81–109. Leicester: Leicester University Press, 1992.

———, ed. and trans. *Adomnán of Iona: Life of St. Columba*. London: Penguin Classics, 1995.

Stancliffe, Clare, and Eric Cambridge, eds. *Oswald: Northumbrian King to European Saint*. Stamford, UK: Paul Watkins, 1995.

———. *St. Martin and His Hagiographer: History and Miracle in Sulpicius Severus*. Oxford: Clarendon Press, 1983.

Thacker, Alan. "Bede and the Ordering of Understanding." In *Innovation and Tradition in the Writings of the Venerable Bede*, edited by Scott DeGregorio, 37–63. Morgantown: West Virginia University Press, 2006.

———. "Bede's Ideal of Reform." In *Ideal and Reality in Frankish and Anglo-Saxon Society: Studies Presented to J. M. Wallace-Hadrill*, edited by Patrick Wormald with Donald Bullough and Roger Collins, 130–53. Oxford: Basil Blackwell, 1983.

Van der Walt, A. G. P. "Reflections of the Benedictine Rule in Bede's Homiliary." *Journal of Ecclesiastical History* 37 (1986): 367–76.

Ward, Benedicta. "Bede and the Psalter." Jarrow Lecture, 1991.

———. *A True Easter: The Synod of Whitby 664 AD*. Oxford: SLG Press, 2007.

Wormald, Patrick. "Bede and Benedict Biscop." In *Famulus Christi: Essays in Commemoration of the Thirteenth Centenary of the Birth of the Venerable Bede*, edited by Gerald Bonner, 141–46. London: SPCK, 1976.

———. "Hilda, Saint and Scholar (614–680)." In Patrick Wormald, *The Times of Bede: Studies in Early English Christian Society and Its Historian*, edited by Stephen Baxter, 267–76. Malden, MA: Blackwell Publishing, 2006.

———."The Venerable Bede and the Church of the English." In *The English Religious Tradition and the Genius of Anglicanism*, edited by Geoffrey Rowell, 13–32. Nashville, TN: Abingdon Press, 1992.

Wright, Neil. "Bede and Virgil." *Romanobarbarica* 6 (1981–82): 361–79; reprinted in *History and Literature in Late Antiquity and the Early Medieval West: Studies in Intertextuality*. Aldershot, UK: Ashgate Variorum, 1995.

INDEX

Other Volumes in This Series

Abraham Isaac Kook • THE LIGHTS OF PENITENCE, LIGHTS OF HOLINESS, THE MORAL PRINCIPLES, ESSAYS, LETTERS, AND POEMS
Abraham Miguel Cardozo • SELECTED WRITINGS
Abū al-Ḥasan al-Shushtarī • SONGS OF LOVE AND DEVOTION
Albert and Thomas • SELECTED WRITINGS
Alphonsus de Liguori • SELECTED WRITINGS
Anchoritic Spirituality •ANCRENE WISSE AND ASSOCIATED WORKS
Angela of Foligno • COMPLETE WORKS
Angelic Spirituality • MEDIEVAL PERSPECTIVES ON THE WAYS OF ANGELS
Angelus Silesius • THE CHERUBINIC WANDERER
Anglo-Saxon Spirituality • SELECTED WRITINGS
Apocalyptic Spirituality • TREATISES AND LETTERS OF LACTANTIUS, ADSO OF MONTIER-EN-DER, JOACHIM OF FIORE, THE FRANCISCAN SPIRITUALS, SAVONAROLA
Athanasius • THE LIFE OF ANTONY, AND THE LETTER TO MARCELLINUS
Augustine of Hippo • SELECTED WRITINGS
Bernard of Clairvaux • SELECTED WORKS
Bérulle and the French School • SELECTED WRITINGS
Birgitta of Sweden • LIFE AND SELECTED REVELATIONS
Bonaventure • THE SOUL'S JOURNEY INTO GOD, THE TREE OF LIFE, THE LIFE OF ST. FRANCIS
Cambridge Platonist Spirituality •
Carthusian Spirituality • THE WRITINGS OF HUGH OF BALMA AND GUIGO DE PONTE
Catherine of Genoa • PURGATION AND PURGATORY, THE SPIRITUAL DIALOGUE
Catherine of Siena • THE DIALOGUE
Celtic Spirituality •
Classic Midrash, The • TANNAITIC COMMENTARIES ON THE BIBLE
Cloud of Unknowing, The •
Devotio Moderna • BASIC WRITINGS
Dominican Penitent Women •
Early Anabaptist Spirituality • SELECTED WRITINGS
Early Dominicans • SELECTED WRITINGS
Early Islamic Mysticism • SUFI, QUR'AN, MI'RAJ, POETIC AND THEOLOGICAL WRITINGS
Early Kabbalah, The •
Early Protestant Spirituality •
Elijah Benamozegh • ISRAEL AND HUMANITY
Elisabeth Leseur • SELECTED WRITINGS

Other Volumes in This Series

Elisabeth of Schönau • THE COMPLETE WORKS
Emanuel Swedenborg • THE UNIVERSAL HUMAN AND SOUL-BODY INTERACTION
Ephrem the Syrian • HYMNS
Fakhruddin 'Iraqi • DIVINE FLASHES
Farid ad-Din 'Attār's Memorial of God's Friends • LIVES AND SAYINGS OF SUFIS
Fénelon • SELECTED WRITINGS
Francis and Clare • THE COMPLETE WORKS
Francis de Sales, Jane de Chantal • LETTERS OF SPIRITUAL DIRECTION
Francisco de Osuna • THE THIRD SPIRITUAL ALPHABET
George Herbert • THE COUNTRY PARSON, THE TEMPLE
Gertrude of Helfta • THE HERALD OF DIVINE LOVE
Gregory of Nyssa • THE LIFE OF MOSES
Gregory Palamas • THE TRIADS
Hadewijch • THE COMPLETE WORKS
Henry Suso • THE EXEMPLAR, WITH TWO GERMAN SERMONS
Hildegard of Bingen • SCIVIAS
Ibn 'Abbād of Ronda • LETTERS ON THE ṢŪFĪ PATH
Ibn Al'-Arabī • THE BEZELS OF WISDOM
Ibn 'Ata' Illah • THE BOOK OF WISDOM AND KWAJA ABDULLAH ANSARI: INTIMATE CONVERSATIONS
Ignatius of Loyola • SPIRITUAL EXERCISES AND SELECTED WORKS
Isaiah Horowitz • THE GENERATIONS OF ADAM
Jacob Boehme • THE WAY TO CHRIST
Jacopone da Todi • THE LAUDS
Jean Gerson • EARLY WORKS
Jeremy Taylor • SELECTED WORKS
Jewish Mystical Autobiographies • BOOK OF VISIONS AND BOOK OF SECRETS
Johann Arndt • TRUE CHRISTIANITY
Johannes Tauler • SERMONS
John Baptist de La Salle • THE SPIRITUALITY OF CHRISTIAN EDUCATION
John Calvin • WRITINGS ON PASTORAL PIETY
John Cassian • CONFERENCES
John and Charles Wesley • SELECTED WRITINGS AND HYMNS
John Climacus • THE LADDER OF DIVINE ASCENT
John Comenius • THE LABYRINTH OF THE WORLD AND THE PARADISE OF THE HEART
John of Avila • AUDI, FILIA—LISTEN, O DAUGHTER
John of the Cross • SELECTED WRITINGS

Other Volumes in This Series

John Donne • SELECTIONS FROM DIVINE POEMS, SERMONS, DEVOTIONS AND PRAYERS
John Henry Newman • SELECTED SERMONS
John Ruusbroec • THE SPIRITUAL ESPOUSALS AND OTHER WORKS
Julian of Norwich • SHOWINGS
Knowledge of God in Classical Sufism • FOUNDATIONS OF ISLAMIC MYSTICAL THEOLOGY
Late Medieval Mysticism of the Low Countries •
Luis de León • THE NAMES OF CHRIST
Luther's Spirituality •
Margaret Ebner • MAJOR WORKS
Marguerite Porete • THE MIRROR OF SIMPLE SOULS
Maria Maddalena de' Pazzi • SELECTED REVELATIONS
Martin Luther • THEOLOGIA GERMANICA
Maximus Confessor • SELECTED WRITINGS
Mechthild of Magdeburg • THE FLOWING LIGHT OF THE GODHEAD
Meister Eckhart • THE ESSENTIAL SERMONS, COMMENTARIES, TREATISES AND DEFENSE
Meister Eckhart • TEACHER AND PREACHER
Menahem Nahum of Chernobyl • UPRIGHT PRACTICES, THE LIGHT OF THE EYES
Miguel de Molinos • THE SPIRITUAL GUIDE
Nahman of Bratslav • THE TALES
Native Mesoamerican Spirituality • ANCIENT MYTHS, DISCOURSES, STORIES, DOCTRINES, HYMNS, POEMS FROM THE AZTEC, YUCATEC, QUICHE-MAYA AND OTHER SACRED TRADITIONS
Native North American Spirituality of the Eastern Woodlands • SACRED MYTHS, DREAMS, VISIONS, SPEECHES, HEALING FORMULAS, RITUALS AND CEREMONIALS
Nicholas of Cusa • SELECTED SPIRITUAL WRITINGS
Nicodemos of the Holy Mountain • A HANDBOOK OF SPIRITUAL COUNSEL
Nil Sorsky • THE COMPLETE WRITINGS
Nizam ad-din Awliya • MORALS FOR THE HEART
Norbert and Early Norbertine Spirituality •
Origen • AN EXHORTATION TO MARTYRDOM, PRAYER AND SELECTED WORKS
Philo of Alexandria • THE CONTEMPLATIVE LIFE, THE GIANTS, AND SELECTIONS
Pietists • SELECTED WRITINGS
Pilgrim's Tale, The •

Other Volumes in This Series

Pseudo-Dionysius • THE COMPLETE WORKS
Pseudo-Macarius • THE FIFTY SPIRITUAL HOMILIES AND THE GREAT LETTER
Pursuit of Wisdom, The • AND OTHER WORKS BY THE AUTHOR OF THE CLOUD OF UNKNOWING
Quaker Spirituality • SELECTED WRITINGS
Rabbinic Stories •
Richard Rolle • THE ENGLISH WRITINGS
Richard of St. Victor • THE TWELVE PATRIARCHS, THE MYSTICAL ARK, BOOK THREE OF THE TRINITY
Robert Bellarmine • SPIRITUAL WRITINGS
Safed Spirituality • RULES OF MYSTICAL PIETY, THE BEGINNING OF WISDOM
Shakers, The • TWO CENTURIES OF SPIRITUAL REFLECTION
Sharafuddin Maneri • THE HUNDRED LETTERS
Sor Juana Inés de la Cruz • SELECTED WRITINGS
Spirituality of the German Awakening, The •
Symeon the New Theologian • THE DISCOURSES
Talmud, The • SELECTED WRITINGS
Teresa of Avila • THE INTERIOR CASTLE
Theatine Spirituality • SELECTED WRITINGS
'Umar Ibn al-Fāriḍ • SUFI VERSE, SAINTLY LIFE
Valentin Weigel • SELECTED SPIRITUAL WRITINGS
Vincent de Paul and Louise de Marillac • RULES, CONFERENCES, AND WRITINGS
Walter Hilton • THE SCALE OF PERFECTION
William Law • A SERIOUS CALL TO A DEVOUT AND HOLY LIFE, THE SPIRIT OF LOVE
Zohar • THE BOOK OF ENLIGHTENMENT

The Classics of Western Spirituality is a ground-breaking collection of the original writings of more than 100 universally acknowledged teachers within the Catholic, Protestant, Eastern Orthodox, Jewish, Islamic, and Native American Indian traditions.